UNFINISHED BUSINESS

MAISIE WARD

UNFINISHED BUSINESS

SHEED AND WARD
NEW YORK

Library of Congress Catalog Card Number: 64-19907

This book is set in 11 pt. Monotype Ehrhardt

Manufactured in the United States of America

CONTENTS

PART 3

THIRD QUARTER-CENTURY

1939–1964

FOREWORD

EACH private world is small in relation to the whole, but mine seems so vast I have hardly explored it in three quarter-centuries of which, curiously enough, the first ended in 1914, the second in 1939, the opening years of World Wars 1 and 2. The book is published in the year which completes the third quarter, 1964. Wandering in one's own past is very different from writing a biography. I have known fascinating people, and I want to make them known, to describe movements through which I came to know some of them, to try to cast an occasional gleam of light on a period of almost unparalleled interest and variety.

But no two people look with equal interest at the same things, and this makes a difficulty for the writer which the painter is spared. Pascal says that if Cleopatra's nose had been shorter the face of the earth would be different; but to the painter only the difference in Cleopatra's face would matter. For the writer as for the painter, proportion is everything. But the demands of their publics are not the same. No lover of art would say, "I am not interested in noses, just do eyes." But many a reader may say, "I am not interested in Priest-Workmen or in Canadian co-operatives—just do writers you have known, or Modernism in the Church——" Yet all these things and a dozen others make the face of my earth. They all belong, but in what proportion?

This voyage of discovery into a lifetime almost wrote itself. But the rewrite has been agony. The criticisms of my pre-publication readers have set up in me a Cleopatra's-Nose Complex. Because the book wrote itself, and because it is much concerned with movements, there is a strong element of chanciness on one side particularly: who is there, who is not, and how much of each. "More about the family," says one, "especially the fun and games." "Less," says another, "it's not that kind of book." I wish I knew what kind of book it was! With vast affection for all who remain and all who are gone ahead among what childhood's prayer entitled "my kind friends and relations", I have not the special talent that creates a family chronicle.

My family is central in my life and I have made no effort to keep it out. But the book does, as it goes on, look outward into the world, more than inward into one private home. The keynote of this home has been an immense hilarity which I cannot capture for exhibition, though it is still around me: I am grateful for the gift of my husband's and my children's laughter.

PART 1

FIRST QUARTER-CENTURY

1889–1914

I

EASTBOURNE

CHILDHOOD in literature seen through the magnifying glass of memory usually appears as hell or else as a lost paradise. My own was neither. I was a happy child, but life is better now than then.

I came to know my birthplace so well later that I feel I must have known it always in its astonishing variety. The Isle of Wight is forty miles by seventeen and in that narrow compass are sharp white and brilliant sandstone cliffs, bare green spines of down and heather-clad expanses with deep clefts, called chines, covered with shrubs and trees running down between the hills, always with the sea as a constantly changing background. My love for the sea may have begun in infancy; the sound of it, the sight of it, especially through trees. But how deep and shady the lanes were by which the poet Tennyson made his way to congratulate my mother on her first baby.

"We've both been ill," he said in his deep chanting voice, "you've got something to show for it; I haven't." And then, with a brief disparaging glance at me, "She's exactly like Henry VIII."

My father's family had long lived in the Island, owning most of the town of Cowes and a good deal of land at the Freshwater end, including Alum Bay and the curious serrated cliffs known as The Needles (recently climbed for the first time). His grandfather owned Lord's Cricket Ground, being known in cricketing circles as "the great Mr. William Ward". He also convened the group which established the Surrey Cricket Club at the Oval. My father's father, William George, better known as Ideal Ward from his book *The Ideal of a Christian Church*, was the first of the Oxford Movement converts to Rome.

A word must be said of this brilliant and eccentric man, whose biography was my father's first important book. W. G. Ward said of himself, "I have the mind of an archangel in the body of a rhinoceros"; and even if this was to state both extremes rather too crudely, they remained extreme enough to make him an arresting figure and his life both amusing and dramatic. An examiner, impressed by his brilliant construing of a difficult passage, said, when he paused over an elementary question, "Take your time, Mr. Ward, don't be nervous"; he received the answer, "Not nervousness, Sir, pure ignorance." John Stuart Mill, after a lengthy debate with Ward on free will, said handsomely that he felt he had now heard the best statement that could be made on the enemy's side. Many years later Chesterton dug up these old articles and, reading them, declared Ward the victor. This interested me for one reason especially—the resemblance between the two men, W. G. Ward and Chesterton. Both were ungainly in body, swift in mind, both were dubbed buffoons by the serious and superficial, and both were admired and loved by their most outstanding contemporaries. All my grandfather's Oxford friends helped my father with memories that made a really sparkling book, *William George Ward and the Oxford Movement*; the reader saw especially the scene in the Sheldonian: the old clergy hurrying up from their vicarages to vote against Ward's book and Newman's *Tract 90*. The Latin from the rostrum broken by such sentences read out in English from the book as "O joyful, O wonderful, O unexpected sight: we see the whole body of Catholic doctrine gradually possessing numbers of English Churchmen", and above all the appeal to the (then mainly Protestant) Church of England "humbly to sue for pardon and restoration at the feet of Rome". The book was condemned. Ward was deprived of his degrees (and for some time signed his letters almost gleefully, "W. G. Ward, Undergraduate"). The votes were given in Latin; shouts of "Placet!" had shown a vast majority against the book, a small one for the degradation, then came the intervention of the proctors as they shouted, "Non placet nobis procuratoribus!" and with these words vetoed the proceedings against Newman, so that Ward alone left the theatre thrown out by his University and branded as disloyal to his Church—and, as it was felt by many, even to his country, for the Church of England stood for England. Not that he would have cared much about that for, in theory at least, W. G. Ward condemned patriotism, asking why he should love a country just because it happened to be his. Later he was to say, "I have no affection for my children as such, e.g., Bernard." I hope my uncle never heard this, for he shared fully in the near-idolatry his children felt for W. G.

The bitter cold had damaged several, and killed at least one, of the old gentlemen who came by stage-coach or icy railroad to vote. And the snow provided a fitting curtain when the younger generation took W. G.'s side, cheering him loudly as he left the theatre and pelting their "elders and betters" with snowballs.

My grandparents started their married life on £200 a year. Cardinal Wiseman arranged for W. G. to teach philosophy and later theology at the diocesan seminary, and my father's childhood was spent in a small house on the grounds of St. Edmund's College. On the death of an uncle the Isle of Wight property became my grandfather's and was now owned by my father's eccentric (but not brilliant!) eldest brother, Edmund.

How my parents could have borne to move to Eastbourne I often wonder. It was to be purely temporary—the square, sturdy house about a quarter of an hour's walk from the sea, in a tree-lined road like most of Eastbourne, but definitely towny, no view, not much of a garden. It would do until they could find a permanent house; actually it "did" for eleven years. Those eleven years are so telescoped in my memory that I find it hard to get any sort of order into them. Very soon there were three of us; a brother Wilfrid, called Boy-Boy or simply Boy, almost two years younger than I, a sister Theresa always called Tetta, just a year younger than he. I have few memories that do not include these two. Later came Herbert and Leo, known to us three as "the little ones".

There was Nanna in the nursery, plus a series of nursery-maids, a cook, as permanent as Nanna and equally tyrannical, a housemaid, a parlourmaid, a kitchen-maid and a knife-and-boot boy. The garden was probably tended by a "jobbing" gardener—it would not have called for more than a weekly day's work. Most of it was grass on which we played, though there was a square patch of flowers at the side where I vividly remember one glorious white rose tree—among, I fancy, old neglected bushes—and a riot of nasturtiums which appeared to me very beautiful, though less beautiful than the white roses.

Despite the small regiment of servants, Papa and Mama (called in those early days Puppa and Mumma) were supreme in our lives. The walks with Nanna or the nursery-maid were boring, even if we went to the sea; those with Mama we enjoyed intensely. On Saturdays, however, even Nanna could not spoil the delight of spending the three pennies pocket money which would in those days buy a toy, several large slabs of toffee, three dozen bullseyes or similar delights. "Melting your money down your throat", said Nanna severely. On Saturdays, too, we came home to suet pudding and golden syrup for dinner. The usual alternative to the sea was a country walk known as Paradise—or occasionally Papa would take us onto the Downs, where we could watch the sun setting over the sea in a ladder of light that always intrigued me. Mama used to relate one of the stories I told her as I sat on her bed in the early morning. "There was once a Puppa and a Mumma and they went for a walk by the sea. And the sea washed away the Mumma. And the Puppa was in such a state. So the Puppa got another Mumma. And then the sea washed up the first Mumma. And the Puppa was in *such* a state."

This story may have sprung from my perturbation at the departure of a housemaid. "We'll get another housemaid", my mother had assured me, and I had commented, "So if Puppa goes away we'll get another Puppa and if Mumma goes away we'll get another Mumma." My father at this point said, "And if Maisie goes away we'll get another Maisie", at which I howled with indignant rage. (Christened Mary Josephine, I had become Maisie for some reason still unknown to me; I liked the name and have always used it.)

None of this do I remember, but I remember very well going into Mama's room for my lessons. She was much in bed in the mornings, not being strong and often expecting or having just had a baby. A big chart hung on the bed-post, from which I learnt my letters; another was used for religious teaching. At six I could read with ease, and it became my favourite occupation, being pursued in bed and during nursery meals—the book hidden under the table when Nanna looked my way.

The gulf was wide between our attitude to Nanna in such matters, and to our parents. It was naughty to disobey Papa or Mama, but with Nanna you only avoided being found out. I acted out on one occasion the sort of moral story proposed to us in our earliest reading matter. We were playing in a field and Nanna had forbidden us to go into an adjoining wood where trees were being cut down. Off I went, fell over a stump and broke my arm. I must have been very small, for I remember being wheeled to the doctor in the pram, screaming all the way. The doctor set the arm and congratulated me on my courage—which puzzled me then and puzzles me still.

I shared another puzzle with most of the children of my era. Life on the whole was clear-cut, there was right and wrong, you were rewarded or you were punished. But sometimes things happened where you were made to feel wrong and had no faintest notion why. We had a pretty parlourmaid called Helena who knew by heart a great deal of comic verse which I, in turn, learnt from her. The parents were away and a dear old lady, Miss Lewis, was looking after the maids, the house and even, I imagine, Nanna. Much amused by my recitals, she told me one day to say my poems to our parish priest. I was sitting on Father Lynch's knee, he was laughing, Miss Lewis smiling. Then I came to the only line I still remember in which a parson was described as

Tossing old Mollie in the hay.

Father Lynch grew grave; he put me down from his knee with every sign of displeasure. Miss Lewis grew red.

Another time I was challenged on my memory of my brother Herbert's birth. "I remember perfectly", I said. "First Puppa went to sleep in the spare room. Then Mumma got ill and then Herbert was born."

My parents did not get red or cross, yet I felt again in their sudden silence this presence of a mystery. Most of all I felt it when, hearing that Papa's cough had kept Mama awake, I remarked, "If I ever marry I shall make it a condition that I have a bedroom to myself."

An aunt living in the country once offered a puppy to my sister, telling her, however, that she had better have a "little boy puppy", as our parents would not want a kennel such as she had. Going into the garden with the gardener to inspect the puppies, my sister innocently asked, "How do you know the difference between a boy puppy and a girl puppy?" Our governess of the moment turned on the unhappy child and berated her violently. Tetta has told me that many years later she dreamed of the incident, and indeed it shook us both.

What made it sillier in my case was that I was absurdly little alive to such questions. I have no recollection of ever asking them in my childhood or puzzling over anything except the oddness of grown-ups, whom I rather wanted to please than otherwise. I was a very conformist child. I did want to be a boy—but only because they seemed to have more fun and it was so much easier to climb in knickers than in a skirt.

As to my parents, I was reminded many years later of my own early attitude when in World War II a young cousin of mine was proposed for promotion in one of the uniformed services. Interviewed by a psychiatrist, she confessed to liking not only her mother and her sisters but also her sister-in-law. This was held to be so abnormal that she lost the promotion.

I not only liked my mother, I loved her a great deal better than my father or than anyone in the world. I found lately a quaint little letter of mine showing another type of strange idea over which the young of my era puzzled their heads:

> There was something that puzzled me in that book called "Instruction for children". In it they say that a good child loves his father and mother just as much the one as the other. Now I love you more than Papa and I don't see how I can help it.
>
> Your loving little daughter.
>
> P.S. Don't show this to anybody.

This really meant, I think, that Mama was better as the confidante whom my childish egoism constantly demanded. She understood everything and always had time to spare for a long and satisfying conversation. But when it came just to having fun Papa was unequalled, especially as we grew old enough to appreciate his many good stories, his mimicry of Manning or Gladstone, his recitation of Tennyson in the old bard's exact singsong. He would take us for long walks, or to the pantomime, or down to the sea, where Boy quickly learnt to swim, but I did not, being rather afraid of adventuring beyond the shallow waters of the immense sandy beach. I greatly preferred the rocky pools, with seaweeds to be brought home and pressed and tiny creatures to be looked at.

Life seemed full of adventure—perhaps a little too much so, for Nanna especially tended to live in a state of perpetual crisis which communicated itself to us. Half Cornish, half Irish, she was both imaginative and excitable. She waged war spasmodically against the cook or housemaid, and unceasingly against the unfortunate nursery-maid of the moment. The most hardly used of all these girls had been imported from France and Nanna, who had begun her own nursing career in Italy, addressed her in the strangest mixture of languages. "Gabrielle", she would cry on a wet day, "paraperplui per tutte due"—and again I remember, "Quando le dos est tourné toujours le travail est lassé." We were always changing nursery-maids—small wonder seeing they were made the whipping-boys; Nanna seldom punished us. But Gabrielle, poor girl, stayed on longer than most, being a stranger in a strange land.

Away from us only for short visits, our parents certainly pervaded daily life more fully than most parents in our world of those days. Papa had no office but worked in his study, Mama wherever she could find a quiet spot; it took her seven years, between babies, to complete her first novel, *One Poor Scruple*. Papa meanwhile had written the life of his father, published in two separate volumes, *W. G. Ward and the Oxford Movement* and *W. G. Ward and the Catholic Revival*. Wiseman's executors then asked him to write the biography of the great cardinal. The sales of this, and, still more, the reviews in all the national papers, were startling; the W. G. Ward volumes had been a success but this was something quite unusual, and led a few years later to his being offered the Newman biography.

Social life at Eastbourne was on the dreary side and both Mama and Papa avoided it. Mama followed, she once told me, the method suggested to her by one of her aunts: "Return all calls but refuse the first invitation to tea and give no invitations yourself." There was one family called Williams with a Catholic son, who was more intellectual, if possible, than my parents; there were Professor Huxley and his wife, with whom a very close friendship developed. The only playfellows I remember our having were a series of Huxley grandchildren, the family of a clergyman who spent their summer holidays at Eastbourne, and visiting cousins—all these we longed for with a great longing during the period of drought.

By this time, while the "little ones" were still with Nanna we three had a governess. Miss Ridsdale was devoted to Boy and I don't think disliked any of us, but she definitely preferred our parlourmaid and spent much time with her, especially when our parents were away. Once I said, "I think Miss Ridsdale ought to hear our lessons instead of sitting in the pantry with Helena." The others stared at me amazed. Not only were we getting out of lessons, but in all probability Helena would presently come up to the schoolroom with her accordion and we should have a jolly evening. Much as I adored my mother, I never told her about this. I suppose I felt it would be "sneaking", but I don't remember it as a temptation to be resisted; simply it never occurred to me as a possibility.

Miss Ridsdale got her *congé* without aid from me and I remember no other permanent resident teacher. We had holiday governesses, and during term-time Tetta and I went for our lessons to Miss Williams, the sister of Papa's intellectual friend, and Boy to a day school. I enjoyed this unsystematic but stimulating teaching and absorbed a good deal of Greek and Roman history, reading also Kingsley's *Heroes* and other books about gods and men. We must have been a curse to the holiday governesses. Boy was adept at inventing such games as racing round the room without touching the ground; we leaped from chair to chair and ran across the solid schoolroom table. Mostly the governesses were French and had little or no control over us—far less than Nanna, who, unlike them, had no hesitation in invoking the parents. The governesses, like myself, never told. On one of them our worst assault was moral; we shouted, "Vive Dreyfus!" with no faintest idea of anything about him except that he was a character strongly disapproved by our pious Catholic governess.

I remember very few punishments in those years—the ones I do remember I approved of as just. I had my ears boxed by Papa when caught upsetting the dust-pan as fast as the unfortunate housemaid could fill it. I had also just thrown a large stone brought in from the beach from the top landing down into the hall. My mother too would have punished me but I realized even then that she disapproved my father's hastiness. She probably feared for my hearing. In the ordinary way, while Papa very occasionally spanked Boy, corporal punishments were not for us girls.

Boy, like my father, was hasty, indeed violent, in temperament. But we all got on well together, partly because he was so natural a leader that by the age of seven he dominated both sisters, partly because he made, when quite young, very real efforts at self-control. We three regarded the little ones with kindly amusement and encouraged their belief in mythical figures dwelling in corners of the nursery. The only time I remember real trouble in the family was one summer which I think of still as the Horrible Holiday.

Our family on both sides abounded in strong-minded characters. I do not know whether it was my father's mother, his sister or his brother Bernard who imperatively urged on my parents the duty of adopting a cousin left an orphan at the age of thirteen. My mother was intensely reluctant but agreed to have Tom for the summer holidays. At this point I cannot trust a jaundiced memory, for he still seems to me a monster of a boy. Rather nice-looking, with open face and red hair, he appeared on first view an asset to the schoolroom party. But very soon he was enjoying himself by making us quarrel with one another. Now I was his favourite and now Boy, and we were pushed into mutual distrust and quarrelling. I don't think this lasted very long, for my really keen memories are not of our quarrels but of his bullying. I watched him with horror twisting Boy's arm to make him scream and tormenting him into one of those rages which he had already learnt to control under normal circumstances.

Those holidays were certainly abnormal—but the strangest of all as I look back is that, with all we suffered, I believe I still did not tell. I say I "believe" because I am pretty sure that my visible misery was what conveyed to Mama that things were very wrong. No doubt she was watching us more closely than we realized—and Tom disappeared for ever.

As keenly as the Horrible Holiday I remember very happy ones. Christmas was preceded by Boy's birthday in October and Tetta's in November, followed by mine in January. What days of anticipation and of fulfilment those were. I never remember being disappointed in our birthday presents, and it was wonderful to be Queen of the Day, choose one's favourite dinner and decide what games were to be played. As Christmas drew near a huge screen shut off part of the hall or study and one tried to catch glimpses of the tree through the window; it was always different, once with a flight of birds, another year with Chinese lanterns. We met Papa, his arms full of mysterious brown paper parcels; we were shoved away as we tried to peep round the screen. One year, I remember, Christmas was followed by a bitter winter full of delight. The grown-ups would gather in the nursery—the largest and warmest room in the house—and play wild games with us. There were visiting friends in Eastbourne at the time and I remember Mr. Gibson (later Lord Ashbourne) coming to our fireside from bathing in a partly frozen sea, watched by a gallery of spectators. There was Willie Williams too, so absent-minded that Fr. Tyrrell described him as "smoking and swooning in an armchair" oblivious of his surroundings; and there was usually some lame dog on whom my parents were taking pity.

And we would set up a string between two chairs and hit an oblong balloon across it by the hour together in the then fashionable game of Piladex. Scores of balloons were smashed between the hands of the men players and the game would reach a frantic pitch of excitement, till my mother achieved an adjournment to the drawing-room where my father would sing to us. Sometimes it was "The Little Fat Grey Man" or "The Tin Soldier", sometimes the terrifying "Erlkönig", but best of all any song at all from Gilbert and Sullivan, we joining in the chorus. When the D'Oyley Carte Opera Company came to Eastbourne we felt we were meeting old friends, and the excitement of seeing as well as hearing was tremendous. Even more tremendous was our first Shakespeare play. I lived for days thereafter in the Forest of Arden. Other visitors were our two Uncle Edmunds. One was my mother's uncle Lord Edmund Talbot (later Lord FitzAlan), known from his jokes and general jolliness as The Funny Uncle Edmund. The other was my father's eldest brother, The Disfunny Uncle Edmund. He was noteworthy for taking us to a toyshop, sitting at the counter and telling us to choose whatever we liked. I do not know to this day whether we had been in some way admonished, but I clearly remember feeling that I ought not to choose too highly-priced a toy. Still, we did pretty well. Our priest uncle, whose rather dry humour was more appreciated as we grew older, saved us from the shopping embarrassment. When he gave us presents he chose them—but I still remember almost bitterly his once remarking blithely on arrival, "I bought some presents for the children but I left them behind in the train." I remember no present from The Funny Uncle Edmund, yet his were the visits most keenly anticipated.

We too went visiting. In the Isle of Wight lived The Aunt With The Dogs in a small house with an immense garden, designed as several gardens each of fair size and each named after a different friend. Aunt Emily suffered from angina and thought it necessary to lie down for most of every day. She would make her way to a *chaise longue* placed each day in a different arbour looking across lawns or flowers or shrubs to the surrounding sea. She wore usually a satin tea-gown with an Inverness cape and a man's cap. We must never disturb her at her rest and she had her meals alone, but the hours in which we talked to her were thrilling, with the memories of her childhood and her profound interest in ours. There were two shelves of books in the house handwritten and illustrated by Aunt Emily and her sisters, which seemed to me marvellous and which were in fact amazingly good for the work of youthful amateurs. There were all the children's books they used to read which we could now devour, and masses of others, for Aunt Emily had once been a great reader and was still a woman of liveliest intelligence. There were lovely copies of Italian paintings made in my aunt's youth by the best copyists of Florence. A rich father, whose favourite daughter she was, refused her nothing, but probably in those days the cost of these as I thought marvellous paintings was not exorbitant.

The sea was close at hand and we bathed daily; we would walk to Alum Bay over the heather down and gaze at the coloured sands, which we could also buy arranged in various designs in glass bottles. This was at Gubbins', the little village shop first at Freshwater, later branching out to Totland Bay, the new seaside resort just beginning to sprout at Aunt Emily's doors. We were each given half a crown to spend at Gubbins' and this vast sum was laid out over and over in animated discussion before the final momentous decision was reached. One year my fairing was a paint box, for Aunt Emily had fired me with ambition and I began to paint flowers and illuminate poems in imitation of her past glories.

That house and garden is perhaps the saddest of my memories. For year by year it faded, year by year grew less desirable. The gardener each year neglected the flowers more openly. There was an immense vegetable garden and Aunt Emily used to say, "I like a plenty." But every year we got less—for this gardener had found a good market for vegetables in Totland Bay. The house got shabbier and shabbier—rooms we occupied which my aunt seldom entered grew not only shabby but grimy. Aunt Emily read no longer and the liveliest mind grows dull with no food to keep it going. Later visits to the Island became a painful duty, but in those early years enchantment began as we stepped on to the little steamer and the whole visit was steeped in it.

One of the rare moments when I felt we had pleased my father while rather annoying my mother was when my sister and I hesitated as to the relative pleasure of a visit to Aunt Emily or to Uncle Henry. It certainly was an immense compliment to his sister, for Uncle Henry (the then Duke of Norfolk) meant Arundel Castle, a host of cousins, marvellous presents at Christmas, games of hockey, charades and a surrounding beauty which even as a child poured into me on every side. I remember one spring when Uncle Henry lent the castle to my parents for three weeks. We would walk along the paths between the fresh green hart's-tongue ferns and the clumps of primroses, looking out on the wide Sussex countryside, down to the old stone dairy where milk had never tasted so delicious. We would explore the whole house and the keep, learning about Roman brickwork and being instructed by my mother in the different stages of Gothic architecture.

But the Christmas visits were better still, for we loved Uncle Henry far more than the house he had created. Today it would be thought absurd to rebuild a medieval Gothic castle in all its details. If such a thing were to be done, he had both the money and the taste to do it and he had certainly made of it a thing of beauty—studying and planning with all the energy of an energetic and ardent character.

Seen through childish eyes, Uncle Henry was chiefly appreciated as even funnier than his brother, The Funny Uncle Edmund. He was always untidy and when waistcoat and trousers threatened to part we were encouraged to murmur warningly, "Uncle Henry, your contour." He was a small man with a shaggy black beard which made the eating of the soup he was so fond of a real problem. He would roll apples or oranges down a table seating two score guests or more to the happy child who could field them at the other end. He would lead us to the top of the highest tower with a sheet to wave in farewell as departing guests passed by in the train. He would organize charades and act the comic parts in them, he would lead a hockey team and seem as much concerned as we were over winning. On our frequent walks he and my mother would exchange dialogues from Scott and Dickens, impersonating various characters. They had done this since her childhood spent at Arundel after the death of her parents.

My mother's father James Hope was, like my other grandfather, an Oxford Movement convert—but in every other way as unlike him as possible. Ward was impetuous, Hope was cautious; Ward awkward and clumsy, Hope graceful and almost incredibly handsome; Ward was an extremist in everything, Hope a well-balanced lawyer whose counsel was sought on every side. With Manning, he had left the Church of England several years later than the bulk of the Movement converts—as a result of the Gorham Judgement, which had declared Baptismal Regeneration no part of the official teaching of that Church. James Hope married first Sir Walter Scott's granddaughter, then, after her death, Lady Victoria Howard. On his first marriage he changed his name to Hope-Scott, but my mother and her brother and sisters reverted to the name Hope. Their father and mother both died before Mama was seven. Her Aunt Mary had adopted her small nieces and nephews when she herself was only twenty-five, and they lived at Arundel with their widowed grandmother and their very young uncle. When she grew up, my mother shared a visiting card which read, "The Duchess of Norfolk, the Ladies Howard, the Misses Hope"; it was called in the family "We Are Seven."

I think we loved all Mama's living relatives more than Papa's, but it was of *his* dead father that we were supremely aware. Papa loved him devotedly, disagreed with him vehemently, talked of him incessantly. Although Mama sometimes said, "You would think this family only had one grandfather" she realized that the early death of her own parents made this inevitable. She had few memories except of her father's profound melancholy and her own terror of witnessing his tears during the months after her mother's death. One interesting and curious fact I learnt later was that all my four grandparents had been Oxford Movement converts—Victoria Howard putting up a serious resistance when her mother joined the Church and reaching conviction only after many conversations with Father Faber. He received her into the Church when she was eleven!

In the background of Uncle Henry's genuine delight in our company was a tragedy of which we children had only a faint notion. We met occasionally, wheeled through the long passages, a figure of whom we were shy. Boy alone once asked to be allowed to visit this afflicted only son of Uncle Henry's. He had been born deaf and blind and his mother, Aunt Flora, was dead. Her picture, surrounded with flowers, stood like a little altar in the library. Year after year Uncle Henry went to Lourdes to pray for the boy, day after day he watched over him. He would not marry again in his lifetime, feeling it unfair to any woman. None of this I understood yet, nor the hours spent over the self-imposed labours which "the Uncle" (as we called him) took most seriously. He would probably not have accepted some of the later developments in Catholic social thinking, but he had a great sense of responsibility towards anyone who depended on him—relatives, tenants, workmen—and he was ahead of his time in giving old-age pensions to his estate labourers. On our Christmas visits the twenty-foot tree in the great hall was surrounded with handsome presents—on one day for the Arundel schoolchildren, on another for the estate workers. My father and the older cousins stood by with sponges on long sticks in case of fire, for it was entirely candle-lit. Aunt Mary had usually chosen the presents with carte blanche as to the cost.

There was political work as well as social, especially during Uncle Henry's period as Postmaster-General, and he emerged from a morning of heavy labour to a real enjoyment of the fun he set on foot. Before his work he had always heard Mass in the exquisite chapel that was the best thing in all his building.

Aunt Mary kept house for her brother. With them in my earlier years was still Aunt Peggy, the youngest of this large family. She had caught some mysterious disease on a pilgrimage to Jerusalem. The best doctors of the moment could not cure or even diagnose it, and she was slowly dying in the fullest consciousness and considerable cheerfulness. We would visit her by turns in a small room next to the big drawing-room. The thick walls were set with heavy doors, iron-studded, and no noise penetrated from one room to another. One could talk with Aunt Peggy as though alone in the world with her; and child as I was, the experience became something of permanent value. Not that we ever talked of values; chiefly we discussed what I was reading or must, *must* read next. I certainly did not feel the crushing weight that my father foreboded when he warned my mother, "I will not have you priest-ridden or aunt-ridden." Mama's aunts, my great-aunts, were a delight telling me of the past, and, with "that horrid Howard habit of reading", as it was called by one of our in-laws, letting me into whole worlds in life and in books.

Many years later, when most of them were dead, I came to recognize the limitations of those worlds—but after all, what world here below is without its limitations?

My father's strong-minded mother, who had an astonishing resemblance to Queen Victoria, died sooner and is therefore a less vivid memory than my aunts and great-aunts. She lived at Hampstead and we were staying with her as the Queen's Diamond Jubilee approached. She had a carriage in which we were to drive to London for the celebrations, and I remember the dialogue between herself and my father as typical of exchanges on the Ward side of the family. She was fearing the fate of her carriage in the crowds and doubting whether to lend it to us when he remarked, "We brought the children all this way to see the Jubilee", to which she answered, "I thought you brought them to visit me."

Whether we did have the carriage I do not remember, but I recall vividly the room with a view engaged for us and other relatives by Uncle Henry. Aunt Mary was in charge of a delightful day of picnic-eating and rushing to and from the window. I wore clothes copied from those the Queen would have worn at my age (I was then eight)—a figured muslin dress down to my toes with a frilly edge, and what was known as a poke bonnet, of great size.

My father's eldest living sister was made Lady Abbess of Oulton Abbey, Staffordshire, two years later, and I was taken by my parents to be one of the attendants in the ceremony of her installation. It was a very imposing affair and I was told something of the days of persecution, when the community had to go beyond the seas and English girls wanting to enter were smuggled over, against the law, never again to see their native country. I was fascinated by my aunt's crozier and the abbatial pomp dating from medieval days. From Dame Laurentia she had become Lady Laurentia Ward, and the other nuns knelt before her. Still more I was intrigued by the whole question of enclosure and what would break it, persuading one of the nuns to put one foot outside but urging her in vain to bring the other to join it. There were many priests and prelates in attendance, and a lot of gaiety in the celebrations. My companion attendant was another cousin, of the exalted age of sixteen, to which I aspired as something so remote as to be almost unattainable.

The Boer War did not disrupt our lives as later wars have done.

I have come since to see it as the point when the British Empire, in appearance reaching its highest peak, actually began its decline. All the adults of our circle, including Baron von Hügel, were "Jingoes", believing that the Empire was on the whole a strong power for good. "I utterly fail", he wrote to my father, "to see even a little cloud on the horizon, of a race and empire coming, more favourable to a decent, manly, healthy standard of morality; or as determined, upon the whole and in the long run, to see justice and fair play done and shown to all, the Church included. And woe to us, if we seek for more; we want no more and no less."

We did not yet know Chesterton or Belloc and should certainly have highly disapproved their disapproval of the War. Looking from the vantage point of another sixty years of history, there seems something ironical about the whole thing. For those very Boers whose rights they so strongly vindicated had not only dispossessed coloured races with prior rights, but were about to enter upon a period of oppression of them that would shock the whole civilized world. If our imperialist attitude was crudely simple, that of the non-pacifist pro-Boers certainly omitted much of the total picture.

Of these things we children knew nothing. The word "Jingo" came from a song of the previous generation beginning:

We don't want to fight, but by Jingo, if we do,
We've got the ships, we've got the men, we've got the money too.
We beat the Bear before, boys, and we'll do it once again,
And the Russians shall not have Constantinople.

It was a very small animal we had to beat compared with the Bear or even the Eagle, but we were an unconscionable time doing it. The schoolroom atmosphere during the War is best conveyed by one of my letters:

Dear Mama,

Thank you so much for the nice Karki [*sic*] notepaper you sent me. Were those little pictures of the Generals for me only or to be divided among us? May Miss Duval spend one of the shillings you left her on some ribbon for rosettes for St. Patrick's day and for the Oxford and Cambridge boat race and for the relief of Mafekin [*sic*] of which we expect to hear soon. Please answer this as soon as you can in case Mafekin is relieved tomorrow (which I hope it will be).

Belloc's remark, "I have no inner life", often comes into my mind as I think back on my childhood and contrast it, not only with lives of saints but also with such very different memories as those of Renan, James Joyce or Simone de Beauvoir. My own stream flowed far more placidly. I felt no deep emotions as I said my prayers. I doubt if I ever acquired a complex. I could cry heartily if upset, but it was all over in a few minutes. I accepted my parents' infallibility as well as that of the Church but was not deeply concerned with either. On my seventh birthday, with a doll nearly as big as myself in my arms, I met Father Lynch who inquired my age and then commented, "Time to be thinking of our first Confession." I intensely disliked the idea and, though he was very kind and gentle when the horrid day came, I have never got over this dislike. It is much easier today for a child who prepares at seven primarily for First Communion and in this joy can take the other in his stride.

My First Communion came four years later, and according to custom was preceded by two days of retreat at the local convent. My mother shared these days with me, which made them endurable, but for a very talkative child the strain was considerable. It was certainly a bad arrangement and it is small wonder that a flood of what are known as "scruples" swept most small girls at that age. Then, too, there was so much to be scrupulous about; the water swallowed washing the teeth in the morning, the crumb that might have stuck in them overnight, the necessity for confession before each Communion. The natural and supernatural joy could be overcast by all this, but the joy was still very great.

I may be told—with perfect accuracy—that, although the fasting rule was that from midnight no food or drink must be taken into the mouth, crumbs from the previous night did not count, tooth-washing should be disregarded. Also that, since only mortal sins need be confessed, it was absurd thus to link confession with the reception of "our daily bread". All this is true, but not all priests were clear about it. I knew a little boy who was asked by a priest—when he spoke of having (he thought) swallowed some "tooth water"—"Was it distinct from your saliva?" And it was usual for the laity to be told always to go to confession before each Communion. In a period of severity the clergy, too, tend to become scrupulous.

I was much addicted in these years to what were known as "story-books", in particular *The Wide Wide World* and the other works of Elizabeth Wetherall, the Daisy books, and above all *Queechy*. Even then I felt my own insufficiencies; these little girls read the Bible so assiduously, blushed so picturesquely and wept for such altruistic reasons. Fleda, the heroine of *Queechy*, I admired supremely. At ten years old this little American girl converts a rich and aristocratic English atheist. Forcing back the tears that have welled (or sprung?) into her eyes on learning of his lack of faith, she points at the setting sun and asks simply, "Who made that, Mr. Carleton?"—filled with envy I read on : "Mr. Carleton was an atheist no longer."

Fleda gives him her Bible and he promises to read it daily. Ten long years pass by. Fleda's family lose their money and are mainly supported by the heroic efforts of this delicate girl, constantly shattered though she is by blinding headaches—when she lies on a sofa smiling painfully through her tears. But Mr. Carleton comes back from England in search of the child he once knew. In a poignant scene he produces the well-worn Bible. At first, he tells her, her memory was always present as he read, later the book became so much to him as to eclipse all thought of the giver—but now this thought has returned and he will not have it so. He has decided to give her back her book, "and I will not take it again unless the giver goes with the gift." Fleda turns mechanically the leaves of her Bible—her one clear thought that she is keeping Mr. Carleton's book. Slowly she gives it to him: "The book and her hand were held together."

How beautiful this seemed to me. I did not intend to marry (one never does at ten years old) but such a proposal would have been tempting. And if a *Methodist* child could convert an atheist? I remember telling Mama a little wistfully that I liked the way in which in *Queechy* and *The Wide Wide World* the grown-ups talked so much about religion to the children. Our family, though chiefly of convert stock, had some of the traditional reticence of English Catholics. A little later Mama gave me the *Récit d'une sœur*, where the religious romanticism of Albert and Alexandrine satisfied me completely. The young man who had a haemorrhage from racing after his beloved's carriage and eventually died of consumption, the beautiful girl spending the rest of her life in good works and learning to "pleurer son Albert gaiement"—all this was very satisfying.

I add in self-defence that it was only one side of my juvenile literary tastes. I devoured Henty, found *Treasure Island* so absorbing that I neglected all precautions, reading it at forbidden times. Scott and Dickens were read aloud to us and I am sure I was reading my favourite of favourites, Jane Austen, well before we left Eastbourne. Next to Jane I loved Charlotte Yonge and Trollope. I had not yet discovered the detective story, but already my mind was—and has alas remained—over-hospitable. Reading at a furious pace, I would devour anything in the form of a story. One of our readings-aloud brought the most comic illustration that I remember of grown-up reticences on certain subjects. The book was *David Copperfield* and we had reached David's return home from school, when he looked through the window and saw his mother suckling a baby. "Sucking a baby!" exclaimed Boy with a shout of laughter. "She was nursing a baby", my mother said. But Boy repeated, "You *said* sucking!" and continued to laugh uproariously.

My childhood had been perhaps unduly prolonged; with the continued presence of Nanna and no resident governess, a nursery atmosphere pervaded the house, especially when our parents were absent visiting or househunting. I was almost thirteen when at last a permanent home was discovered and bought. We moved to Lotus at the end of 1901, a house on the outskirts of Dorking twenty-five miles from London and about the same distance from Arundel. Christmas and my thirteenth birthday, January 4th, were spent at Arundel in a state of delirious joy. The joy was an amalgam of the usual delights of the place and the background satisfaction in the new home, which we had loved on sight.

Boy had become a boarder at his Eastbourne prep. school and he returned there at the end of January. He had begged that Christmas to make his First Communion, but he was only just eleven and before Pius X had spoken this was held to be rather young. He was told to wait—but a sudden illness took him away from us on the Feast of St. Agatha, Feb. 5th, 1902. My mother and father had rushed to Eastbourne, and when we heard of Boy's death I insisted on going there too. Having gained my point, I pushed away sorrow for a while by reading Jane Austen—but felt it rather wicked to do so. Maude Petre had come to stay with us and showed, I now feel, great courage in taking me, with a heavy cold upon me, to join my parents.

I could never thank her enough for this, after I had looked at the beauty and majesty of Boy's face.

After the funeral I was put to bed in the Eastbourne lodgings and I think it helped Mama to have to take care of me. Aunt Mary was there and Uncle Henry; I heard later that his presence advertised the school and brought many new boys. The incongruities of life begin very early. But my childhood had abruptly ended.

2

DORKING AND CAMBRIDGE

It was hard for my mother and father to take up daily life again after Boy's death. Aunt Mary had the happy inspiration that spring of giving them a present of a journey to Rome, and I went to Cambridge to stay with the Anatole von Hügels. Anatole was the younger brother of the more famous Friedrich. Equally learned in his own line, he was curator of the University Museum of Archaeology and Ethnology. There one could see the "pillow"—a straight piece of bamboo, raised a few inches, on which the neck rested and on which he had slept during his three years in the Fiji Islands. There were wonderful weapons in the museum and strange gods, of whom Anatole had much to tell. He had fascinating memories, too: of absent-mindedly eating all the bananas his cannibal host had intended for supper and his own momentary fear of being eaten in their place; of walking fifteen miles and swimming three rivers to get to the nearest church for confession and being told to come back again on Saturday! He stood his ground and the priest rather grudgingly heard his sins and absolved him.

It is harder to think of Anatole standing his ground in his own interests (even spiritual) than of his placating a cannibal chief. He was, I think, the gentlest man I have ever known. The Austrian accent which both brothers retained added to the charm of his rather precise talk. His chief recreation was a large garden in which he would work by the hour, peering short-sightedly at the tiny flowers in the rockery, each of which he cherished individually. The colours blended marvellously and no plant was allowed to encroach on another; that rockery was the loveliest I have ever seen. The flatness of the country revealed glorious sunsets as we walked to the iron gates at the garden limits. I still wore my black dress—indeed I wore it for a year—but I had not believed I could so soon feel life so worthwhile again.

Isy von Hügel, even dearer to me than Anatole, had been Isy Froude, niece of James Anthony, whom she described as the most prosperous person she knew and the most melancholy. She had many memories of Newman. He had thought her like Hurrell and he gave her, as a child, something of the love he had had for his closest friend. Fifteen years older than her husband, Isy had the liveliest and most youthful mind down to her death at the age of ninety-three. At that age she went to a lecture of my husband's which much excited her, would not let him go to bed but sat up most of the night discussing it, and died the next morning. This, however, was far in the future. Isy was intensely active now and our talks, walks and readings were a source of perennial delight. A fellow guest was her cousin "Willie" Mallock, the then celebrated author of *The New Republic*. This rather philosophical best-seller was suggested by Plato's *Republic*. Mallock's scene was set in a country-house party: the characters were supposed to be drawn from life and were variously identified (Isy was certainly one of them). The ideas were thought alarmingly advanced. Mr. Mallock's appearance was not impressive; he was small, fattish and, I thought, commonplace. But he won my heart the first evening—for after dinner he read aloud, with rare perfection, the scene in *Pride and Prejudice* where Mr. Darcy is writing a letter and Miss Bingley interrupting and commenting. I can still shut my eyes and listen—

"You write uncommonly fast."
"You are mistaken, I write rather slowly."
"I am afraid you do not like your pen, let me mend it for you. I mend pens remarkably well."
"Thank you—but I always mend my own."

Mr. Mallock and I were Austenites and therefore friends. I still like the old name better than the newer Janeites, though Kipling has hallowed the latter by his delicious story and poem—

Jane went to Paradise
That was only fair . . .

Anatole's mother lived close by. The old Baroness, as we called her, was Scotch and very forthright. She told me with extraordinary energy the story of her conversion to the Catholic Church. Already an Anglo-Catholic, she had accepted the full Catholic teaching on the Real Presence in the Eucharist. One morning, staying with less advanced friends, she went to Communion in a neighbouring church. The clergyman spilt the chalice on her dress. In an agony of mind she cut out and burnt the front of the dress and spent the morning in prayer. Going down to lunch she found the clergyman in the drawing-room. "Please forgive me", he said "for my shocking clumsiness this morning. But I trust that with modern cleaning processes your dress will not be ruined."

"I went straight to a Catholic church," the Baroness said, "and asked to be received."

I spent those weeks listening enthusiastically to talk and to reading. Croft Cottage, then a little way outside Cambridge, had a chapel in the house which Catholic girls from Newnham were allowed to attend, and any other Catholics resident nearby. The Anatoles were intensely hospitable and the house was something of a centre for dons, clergy and others. Always inclined to take my colour from my surroundings, I absorbed for the time Isy's prejudices against Girton and Newnham—prejudices, not against education for women, but in favour of what she held education should mean. "They stop all intelligent conversation," she would exclaim indignantly, "by saying 'that's not my period'." It still *was* the period when girls had to fight even to be allowed to follow lectures and take examinations. They could not receive degrees either at Oxford or Cambridge. As a result of all this, they were inclined to be on the defensive and to act as the "bluestockings" they were accused of being.

Isy was one of the most cultivated women I have known, but she took her culture lightly and it held its proportion in a full and complete life, of which the chapel was as much the centre as it was for my relatives at Arundel. But at Croft Cottage the intellectual interests of the Church were thought of more—as was natural enough in a University town—and I felt my own mind opening its windows.

It seemed far more than a few weeks later that I was at Lotus again, and Mama and Papa were back laden with presents for us all. My sister and I went to the local convent daily and were soon joined by "the little boys". There was no more schoolroom and Nanna very gradually lost her hold upon us. She remained with us until her old age, making it exceedingly difficult for my mother to engage or retain maids. We learnt that the question was asked at various London employment agencies, "Is that the family with the old nurse?" But we all loved Nanna dearly.

From one garden to another—for the Lotus garden, sloping down by terraces, was as attractive as that of Croft Cottage, though totally different. Azaleas and roses, bamboos and silver birches gave bold colour effects and framed a wide view over the Surrey hills. My mother gardened ardently and we all helped, being financially rewarded for the duller labours of watering or weeding. On Sundays there was no weeding, and watering was cut to the essential minimum—but we were not paid for it! There was also a series of gardeners, one of whom, an ex-sailor, taught me singlestick. He had, however, to be dismissed for misbehaving with the kitchen maid. I don't know how far I was aware of this, but I well remember the shock I had on learning that the daughter of a highly respected Catholic couple in the parish was about to have a baby without preliminary marriage. It sounds exaggerated, but I am sure it is not, to say that a dark cloud hung over everything for some days.

The process of growing up went on in pleasanter ways at a great pace. Now my sister and I were constantly with our parents and met all their friends. In my earlier memories of Lotus the permanent local Catholic group stand out. Two old Belgian priests ministered to our spiritual needs: Fr. Volcryck was parish priest, Fr. Petitot convent chaplain. Fr. Petitto spoke a strange language; he had forgotten his French, he said, and he certainly had not learnt English. Fr. Volcryck spoke very fair English, but would make the oddest mistakes. I remember a sermon on Mary Magdalene: "She was, I regret to say, a public singer and she lived a life of dissolution." A funny old Irishman with a Greek wife, living next to the convent, would occasionally prompt or correct Fr. Volcryck from his seat just in front of us. One sermon led to the mention of a bat, and as the preacher hesitated we heard Mr. Loughnan's loud stage whisper "tennis bats, *tennis* bats". As we left the church Mr. Brookfield, a retired actor, would highlight the scene and invent further incidents.

The Brookfields made pleasant neighbours, Sir Hugh Clifford was an exciting one. Like Anatole, he had been in many lands and he specialized in stories of werewolves and tigers—men who could change at night into wolf or tiger, returning in the morning to human form. I think he believed these stories firmly; he loved to tell them and we loved—though at night sometimes nervously—to listen to them. Other people came and went: Henry Harland, author of *The Cardinal's Snuff-Box*, a now forgotten best-seller, with his wife, rented for a while the house nearest to ours; Mrs. Belloc Lowndes,

Belloc's sister, spent one summer in Dorking; and our own house, especially at weekends, was often filled very full.

There was one family of whom we saw a great deal. Mrs. Clutton, old, white-haired and very beautiful, was the daughter of one of Newman's converts, George Ryder. She and her two sisters had been known as "the beautiful Miss Ryders". Now a widow, she was living at Dorking with two daughters—Beatrice, called Bice in Italian fashion, and Cissy, an invalid sister—always there, and another, Kitty, a frequent visitor. Bice, too, was very lovely; my mother felt her to be like a Hardy heroine, specifically the heroine of *A Pair of Blue Eyes*. Kitty, also handsome and several years older, was a sardonic character. She had never recovered from the experience of education in a convent where the nuns had all been trained in a French novitiate. I remember her telling my sister and me how she had to wear a bathing-dress when she took her bath. "But weren't you *alone*?" we asked, amazed. "Yes, but the nuns said the angels were watching me."

Another time she told us she had complained of a bad egg and the nun told her to eat it in seven mouthfuls in honour of Our Lady's seven sorrows. "I should have thrown it at the nun's head seven times", was my sister's indignant comment.

This sort of nonsense had bitten more deeply than it deserved into Kitty Clutton. Her brother had married Maud Petre's sister, and she found her sister-in-law's sister and their friends a welcome relief from the smothering French piety of her school. The exaggerated sneer that one so often noticed later on Modernist lips was not without relation to experiences of this kind.

There is something about faded beauty and great sweetness of manner that has always irritated me—often, I expect, unfairly. I preferred Kitty, with all her crudeness, to her mother. She said all she meant and a little more—a fault with which I have a congenital sympathy. Mrs. Clutton was what is sometimes called "a man's woman". She was devoted to my father, but in her attitude to my mother I always felt a touch of exquisite and probably unconscious felinity. When later I knew Lady Ritchie, Thackeray's daughter, I recognized the same note struck more definitely. "How glad I am", she said to me one day, "that Albert was in love with Amabel —but married Emily" (these are not the real names, but she spoke of real people—and I was very fond of "Emily"). I have an idea that, even if a Girton girl was too closely confined to her "period", at least she had less leisure and less tendency to cultivate such sayings.

For Mama the loss of Boy had been crushing. She told me many years later that she had felt wine to be a real temptation in those months for the relief, even temporary, of her gnawing grief. I think it must have been Boy who sent her one of our best friends. In those last holidays he had told us of the priest who had preached a school retreat—Fr. Maturin. He laughed over the mannerisms we all learnt to know later: the whispered opening, the sudden swing that suggested a confiding of the heart of the sermon to the pillar behind. He even insisted that Fr. Maturin, when worked up, had blown his nose into his hand. But Boy had been tremendously impressed and conveyed the feeling to us all of a considerable experience.

That summer Mama decided to follow one of Fr. Maturin's retreats and very soon he was established as the friend who would run down from London with little or no notice and stay as long as his work allowed. Fr. Maturin was that unusual thing, an Irish convert. Still more unusual, he came from a clerical and High-Church home, his father being the Vicar of Grangegorman. He was descended from Charles Maturin, whose rather horrific stories bore the same stamp as those of Mrs. Radcliffe—from one of them, *Melmoth the Wanderer*, another relative, Oscar Wilde, got the name under which he chose to live in his last years in France. Fr. Maturin had inherited a considerable power to make one's flesh creep with ghost or horror stories. He was not attached to a parish but preached, lectured, wrote and had a great host of spiritual children and converts under instruction. Boy's bedroom had been made into a chapel, and a visit from Fr. Maturin meant daily Mass in the house. The friendship with my father was as close as with Mama, and the two men would talk together by the hour. And in the evening Gilbert and Sullivan reigned once more, or Fr. Maturin told us ghost stories.

I have told at some length in an earlier book[1] of my small brothers' imitations of Church services and my mother's prohibition of sacred words. A curious liturgy was composed, partly from Latin names of plants ("Gypsophila paniculata, ora pro nobis"), partly from their

[1] *Insurrection versus Resurrection.*

own imagination ("Naughty be the robbers, naughty be their naughty name"). How this started I cannot imagine. Many children copy what they see but this was certainly spontaneous and not encouraged by our elders. It went on till the boys outgrew it, when its place was taken in Herbert by a passionate devotion to history, in Leo by a serious interest in Church affairs and in world politics, which he constantly considered in their bearing on religion. By the age of eight he had made up his mind to be a priest and this determination never wavered. Neither boy cared much for sport though Leo was quite willing to play cricket or tennis if called upon and was a good swimmer.

The mock services were considered exquisitely funny by Stuart Collingwood, nephew of Lewis Carroll and possessed of something of his humour, who had become a Catholic and spent a good deal of time at Lotus. He catalogued the library and was usually to be seen, pipe in mouth, carrying an incredible number of books up or down stairs. He called himself my father's *scriba privatus* and wrote in a mixture of Latin and English mocking comments on his work or on the events of our daily lives. *De Homine Quodam Novo* was his contribution to the Life of Newman. *The Ethics of Combustion or If I were Pope* by Cardinal Merry del Val was his contribution to the Modernist rows that raged around us, and he affected to consider himself the hero of one of my mother's books.

For four years my sister and I walked down one steep hill and up another—twice a day when we had lunch at the convent, four times when we came home for it. My mother had kept our religious teaching in her own hands, but I cannot say much for the rest of our studies. I understand that the school is now totally transformed and of course all my old teachers are dead. But the nun who dominated the scene, Sister Domitilla (known to us as Dom), was an unfortunate type of headmistress. Her one aim was to have the greatest number of successes in the Oxford local examinations. I remember our once taking the same Shakespeare play two years running as part of the "cramming" whereby high marks might be achieved. Dom became so hysterical that my mother, disliking cramming and even more disliking hysteria, forbade us to take the examinations—and this I think was a mistake. I don't remember minding in the slightest at the time but, granted that the system was a bad one, we should still have got more education if we had made the best of it. Little incentive to work was left if we saw everyone else winning results from which we were debarred.

However, I did get one thing from the Dorking convent. We learnt by heart the three Synoptic Gospels, the Acts of the Apostles and great parts of *Julius Caesar* and *Henry V*. I had a good memory and the more it was exercised the better it got. For my own pleasure I was now learning Browning and I could recite *One Word More*, *Rabbi ben Ezra* and long passages from *Saul*, *Karshish* and my other favourites. One night I remember being told I could "stay up" as long as I could go on repeating poetry—but the parents were crying for mercy long before I capitulated.

Dom had a horrible French accent which I caught and never lost; but, as I cannot remember the time when I could not read French, I imagine she taught it fairly well. A very intelligent lay mistress gave us elementary German; and Reverend Mother, whom everybody loved but whom I regarded as under Dom's thumb, taught us music—a painful experience for her in my case, and for me too since she rapped our knuckles with a ruler at each false note. Summoned to the parlour for an interview, Dom would put us on our honour not to talk in her absence—we all agreed that she had no right to do this and did not dream of taking it seriously. We were day children and most of the girls were boarders, so I suppose I got no deep insight into the religious and moral side of the school, but I made a number of friends and I must say that despite the silliness I got an excellent impression of the moral atmosphere. Some of the boarders felt keenly the way one could never be alone, and the one place with a bolt (which was the lavatory) they had dubbed "the camp of refuge". Dom, one day catching this phrase, said, "I hope that means the Sacred Heart, my dear." Poor little thing, she meant so well. She was overworked and not strong; she would move one's heart at first by weeping over one's transgressions—but, as my sister remarked, once was enough. It became a game to jump as one passed the parlour so as to get, through the high-up glass panel, a glimpse of the girl who was the current recipient of Dom's tears and see how she was taking it.

Probably the influence of Mother Prioress was stronger than I knew among the boarders, who all spoke of her enthusiastically. I remember a new girl from the West Indies who tried to regale us with stories of her conquests—nobody seemed particularly shocked but we were frankly bored and thought her conceited and "soppy". How far that was just the reaction of myself and my group of friends I cannot of course know, but I would take a bet there was a healthy atmosphere in the convent. The teaching, my sister adds, had already improved before she left and she further maintains that she was always happy there and that my view is a jaundiced one!

The age of sixteen was something of a climax for me. The Bishop was coming to Dorking and I was to be confirmed. My mother had prepared me for First Communion with Mother Loyola's book; now she used her *Soldier of Christ* in preparation for Confirmation, and while late First Communion still seems to me deeply sad, I feel there was a lot to be said for adolescent Confirmation. It came at the time when strength was specifically needed; true, the grace given can always be stirred up, but Confirmation does seem to become a forgotten grace when given to tiny children who understand little or nothing of what they are receiving. Confirmation at my date was a great event, much looked forward to, greatly prepared for. And I asked Isy von Hügel to be my godmother.

But before the great day came something else happened that was also to affect my future. Mama's aunt, Anne Kerr (*née* Howard), came from Scotland to stay with us, bringing her youngest daughter Minna, about one year older than I.

My cousin Minna was tall, slim and golden-haired and, I thought, perfectly beautiful. She was already in my eyes a woman of the world, and her mother and mine were very close. She too was just about to be confirmed, and from London, where she had stayed with Aunt Mary, she brought the atmosphere of the London Oratory. What name was I taking for Confirmation—Philip, of course? I had decided on Paul and Francis, but now enquired into the possibilities of a third name, out of devotion, I fear, not to St. Philip but to Minna. I copied her handwriting, her tricks of speech. We had always spoken of "Aunt Mary" or occasionally "Aunt Maisie", as this aunt was my godmother for whom I had been named. Now I began to call her "Aunt Polly", which was the Kerrs' name for her. My father's merciless teasing over this special vagary brought me more or less to my senses, but Minna had sowed the seeds of something more important.

That autumn she was going to "complete" her education by a year or so at the Cambridge convent of the Mary Ward nuns—the nuns of the Bar Convent, York, Mother Loyola's nuns—and I was seized with a passionate desire to go there too. My parents granted my request and the next event after the Confirmation was getting ready for a short period at boarding school.

I am always thankful I had that time at Cambridge. The school was a very good one. Mother Mary Salome and Sister Mary Aquinas were both first-rate teachers and both had the power of evoking enthusiasm. Then, too, Mgr. Nolan, head of St. Edmund's House, who many years earlier had taught Latin to my mother, now volunteered to teach it to me. He also formed a tiny class of Minna and myself—who were a little older than the other girls—for Scripture. The Scripture was disappointing; he took us verse by verse through the Acts of the Apostles, so slowly that perhaps we did two chapters in a term, giving us no broad ideas or pictures, but a rather tedious detailed commentary. Far different was the Latin. He was a true scholar and loved to teach me as much as I could take. He was always lamenting my backwardness. We read Horace and Tacitus. I was given great chunks of syntax to memorize and made to write Latin verses, which were, of course, unspeakably bad. I was constantly torn between the demands of my different teachers, all piling on the homework! Mgr. Nolan always won. What a change it was to have almost more than I could handle, and all of it so interesting. I got permission to study in bed before the rising bell—which I think was at seven—and Mgr. Nolan muttered alternately that I was a year behind and that I had the makings of a classical scholar.

Croft Cottage was near for Sundays and holidays and sometimes Mgr. Nolan took us out. There were lectures in the town, there were the striking sermons of Mgr. Robert Hugh Benson at the parish church which we frequented, having only an occasional weekday Mass in the convent chapel. And each morning classes began with a lesson in religion given by Mother Mary Salome, who was the Reverend Mother, and for whom I developed a profound affection. This began rather oddly. Mgr. Nolan wanted one day to take Minna and me on the river. Now the school rule was, only parents or those authorised by them *in writing* could take pupils on the river. We were annoyed but decided we had better obey; he was furious and an unpleasant afternoon was spent by all. I decided to open my mind to Reverend Mother and tell her what an insane rule I deemed it. After a moment's thought she said, "Perhaps you would like to know why the rule was made? Mgr. Nolan once took out some girls, upset the boat and almost drowned them."

Another time Reverend Mother said with a smile: "If I say anything different from what your parents have told you, your disapproval is very obvious. I like you for this but you will learn in time that there may be two quite good ways of looking at a thing."

I don't remember much of our religious lessons—I think now that it is quite probable the girls from York were right who told us that Mother Loyola was far more interesting, but although Mgr. Nolan's was the strongest intellectual influence, Mother Salome and Sister Aquinas taught me much—and best of all, exorcised the cynicism implanted by my previous experience. Our school was a tiny one—only a dozen girls, all around the same age. I think it was projected as what would in America be a junior college, and we all got individual attention. Of my schoolfellows two became Carmelite prioresses, one (another cousin, Minna Stewart) a Sister of Charity, so our proportion of successes in the spiritual sphere was fairly high. Minna was to die young, but in her funeral procession was a multitude of sick and poor whom she had succoured. At York, which I visited, were relics of the Martyrs and lively memories of Mary Ward, towards whom I developed a devotion. But the nuns were not enthusiastic over our delighted discovery that the first nuns of the order were dubbed "galopping girls" and "apostolical viragoes", by the old-fashioned English clergy—who disapproved of them as "Jesuitesses", and as the only nuns who had no enclosure.

My mother had withdrawn her objection to examinations in the peaceful air of St. Mary's Convent. I vividly remember sitting for the Cambridge Senior, I being the only one in that vast room taking Latin, and being seated between the only two examinees in what I thought of vaguely as Science. Everyone else in the room was doing freehand drawing—a fact which had caused some slight annoyance to my teachers. Drawing was one of my "strong subjects" and it was impossible to take both it and Latin. The two science girls came from a Government high school and struck me as looking profoundly interesting, but I had no opportunity to break the ice, which would definitely have needed breaking.

3

GROWING UP

MGR. Nolan held a post-mortem on my Latin paper and decided that I had failed. I had had a stab at the hardest "unseen" and he wailed over my folly in not having done the easiest one. When, on the contrary, I gained a distinction in Latin, he kissed me solemnly and decided that I *must* go on to the University. It is comic to remember how shy he was, how embarassed I, and how disapproving my parents over this very avuncular kiss. But the University was the serious question.

I imagine had I fought for it I should have won, but it was a curious case of my father repeating with me, in all unconsciousness, the same kind of mistake his own father had made with him, for he had lost Oxford owing to the fanatical opposition to Catholics going there into which Manning had been pushed by "Ideal" Ward. Many years later, reading the report of the Commission of Higher Education in Ireland, I noticed that Wilfrid Ward was the only commissioner who never asked a question about women's education. The conventional thing at that date in our world was to send your sons to a university and to present your daughters at Court and give them a London season. My parents could not afford to give a ball for us but they did take a house in London for a couple of months every year, my sister and I were both presented, and we went to a good many dances.

It was not the kind of life that suited me, but I lacked the strength of mind to carry through the plan with which I had left school. The parents had not said that I could never go to Oxford, but only that I should wait, live at home for a while, be presented and then we would see. I bought a lot of books, intending to read French and Latin steadily with a view to a London degree if Oxford proved out of the question—but I did not get far with them, and the next few years were dissipated in a mass of incoherent activities. A neighbour had taken up artificial flower-making and I learnt how to make Parisian blossoms in silk and velvet. I superintended for her a group of London slum girls who were being taught the art, and suffered some embarrassment as they shouted into the Dorking streets from the window of our workroom and tried to make friends with the astonished citizens.

I stayed for several periods at a settlement at Mile End supported by Aunt Mary and carried on by a group of her friends. One of them, Sybil Smyth Piggott, had been a hunting, sporting character and gave up her horses to live permanently in these grim surroundings. I admired her ardently, especially in her care for retarded children, whom she had the most astonishing power of developing, especially religiously, preparing them for First Communion with endless patience. After my sheltered upbringing it was strange to listen to the stories of a woman whose husband had kicked her in her pregnancy and induced a premature birth. So green was I that I arrived at the church during a mission escorting a drunken woman who had promised to go to confession. But I soon learnt better . . . We supplied dinners to the poorest school-children and took our turns in serving them—and the poverty was indeed frightful. I suppose we were very paternalistic, but it all seemed a good thing at the time. And when these private activities did draw Government attention to a shocking state of things, the Government found no better remedy than paternalism of its own.

For a period I was my father's secretary—but my mother grew afraid that he was overworking me. He did indeed have a tendency to want things done suddenly at odd hours, but on the whole I enjoyed it and I think it would have been better to let it go on. I still remember some brass candlesticks I bought with my first earnings, and overwork would have been more satisfying than the desultory life I was falling into.

Two sisters (Lady Cory and Lady Carew, if I remember rightly) were deeply concerned to save debutantes from idleness by teaching them what I think was called Jacobean embroidery. Tired by then of slumming and of Parisian roses, I became Lady Cory's pupil and with my sister sat at a huge frame like a loom, and embroidered a vast cushion. Becoming ambitious, I decided next to do a picture, and chose the well-known "Disciple kissing St. Catherine's Hand". An artistic friend painted the faces on silk and the whole effect was excellent until the picture was taken off the frame. But alas, just as I had once made flowers that fell apart because I could not wait for the sole efficient adhesive—gum Arabic—so now I had bought the canvas at the wrong shop and it shrank and crumpled. We had to nail the thing to a board to keep its shape—very discouraging after weeks of work, so I turned to something else.

I attended university extension lectures, wrote papers on the history of Florence and won a prize. I gathered a group of neighbours to read Dante together in Italian with a convert clergyman as our guide. This was largely an expedient to help him financially, and when he refused payment it petered out.

I worked vigorously for any bazaar that came up, knitting bed-jackets and adorning them with contrasting ribbons, making pin-cushions shaped like sausages and similar inanities.

I played a lot of tennis and read a great many novels. At one point, I even dabbled in politics, doing some canvassing at an election for the Conservative Party—an example of my tendency to accept the ideas around me until somehow jerked into thinking for myself.

My father took the editorship of the *Dublin Review* the year I left school, and would give my sister and me an occasional book to review. There was a general assumption that I would write and I struggled vainly to imitate my mother by producing an interesting story. The idea of a training for work in some other field than fiction was never suggested and I still shudder to think of my first incursion into biography. Father (later Archbishop) Goodier had initiated a series of popular Catholic books, including the lives of the saints. I was asked to write the life of St. Bernardino of Siena. I read busily in the British Museum but I had not the faintest idea of finding out which early documents were reliable. I quoted impartially from contemporary records and from things written a century later. Probably I called both "the old chronicler", for this was the fashion in the school of hagiography to which I was accustomed. But one thing I did attempt to do: write of Bernardino as a real person, not as "the servant of God" whose virtues precisely resembled those of all other servants. I saw him and I hope showed him as an individual.

It would indeed be a mistake if I conveyed the idea that my parents did not encourage my activities—eagerly and impartially they encouraged almost everything I attempted. Only once I remember my mother's criticism, when I had picked up a meretricious craft whereby bits of glass and china were somehow fixed in a sort of mosaic on pottery vases and bowls. I had been doing this enthusiastically after an attack of pneumonia and when I was well again my mother said, kindly but with most just reprobation, that this craze had been part of my convalescence. Anything thoroughly inartistic she could not bear, but she was delighted at my lessons from Marianne Gibson (later Lady Ashbourne) in flower-painting. I also took lessons in script so as to improve the illuminating I had done as a child and never quite abandoned.

The trouble was (and it became a real trouble) that our parents, while far too easily delighted by our efforts, lacked totally any sense of educational direction. Obviously, by the time my five-year-younger brother was ready for Oxford, it was too late to think of it for me. How the years had drifted by—and I was becoming hopelessly an amateur; dabbling at writing, dabbling at art, dabbling at social service (then called works of charity), dabbling even at theology and mysticism in my undirected and omnivorous reading.

Social life of various kinds was much interlaced with my scattered efforts at self-employment. But it was not altogether easy to be the daughter of an exceedingly popular father and to belong at the tail end of an important family, however clannish. Out visiting with my father I was always happy with his contemporaries, listening and talking. But when left with the girls of my own age, I became conscious of being badly dressed and unskilled in small talk. A famous hostess of the date once remarked how good a London season was for a girl—she got kicked around thoroughly. I disagreed then and I disagree now. I was not much kicked around, but girls are sensitive beings and I doubt if snubs, perhaps even imagined snubs, are particularly good for them or help them to develop into well-balanced women.

Very enjoyable was my first solitary grown-up visit. It was to the British Embassy at Constantinople. I spent a month there with my Aunt Minna and my uncle by marriage, Nicholas O'Conor (always called Feargus, after the Irish rebel), who was ambassador. Abdul Hamid (known as Abdul the Damned) still held his throne as Sultan. There was a separate harem life and I had the luck of going to a Turkish wedding, besides rambling in the bazaars with a resident English woman who knew many of the veiled Turkish ladies. Dogs swarmed in the narrow streets, many of them diseased and horrible, the bazaars were full of delectable things to buy, and on a visit to a silk factory I was presented with a dress length of glorious yellow silk. Years later I learnt the fascinating story of the silkworms smuggled out of China and brought to Constantinople in the days of the Emperor Justinian.

We were taken also to his great church of Sancta Sophia, now a mosque, with vast hieroglyphics on the walls, which, together with the slant of the carpets, gave the whole building a sort of crooked turn towards Mecca. The mosaics were painted over but nothing could spoil the magnificent proportions. We visited one little mosque-out-of-church where the mosaics had been left visible—but it was later at Ravenna that I really learnt what mosaics could be. I appreciated more the beauty of the Golden Horn, the curiosity of the howling dervishes at Scutari and the glimpses behind the Turkish women's veils. I was madly ignorant of Eastern history, even Church history as far as the East was concerned, and although I knew that this was old Byzantium the fact made little impression upon me.

I enjoyed life at the Embassy and especially the society of my three cousins, whom I had known in brief periods at Eastbourne but who had been young enough to be chiefly my sister's companions. Now we all became fast friends.

The young enjoy quite specially the friends they have made for themselves, and among my happiest memories are long visits to Billing and Brigg—the two homes of Gervase and Winnie Elwes. They were the youngest parents of a large family I have ever known. They had married while Gervase was still at Oxford; from there he entered the diplomatic service but soon left it to become a singer. He used to sing Gerontius most exquisitely and always made of his preparation for the role a preparation for his own death—which actually came suddenly through a fall from a train. There was no faintest streak of morbidity in Gervase but an extreme simplicity of character, deep devotion and a great modesty about his work. He would never have fought for his own hand, and was loved by all his fellow artists.

Inheriting a large property in Lincolnshire and a smaller one in Northamptonshire, he might easily have settled down into merely a useful country squire but for his wife, Lady Winefride, sister of Lord Denbigh and a character who can only be described as dynamite. Even those coming to know her in old age recognized that there could be no stagnation in Winnie's neighbourhood. We had always to be doing something: playing tennis, acting charades, driving many miles to visit neighbours or to hear Gervase sing in some cathedral. Winnie drove herself so hard with social and charitable activities that sometimes merely sitting down lulled her into a deep sleep. I remember sitting next to her in Lincoln Cathedral while Gervase was singing in the Matthew Passion and seeing her wrapt in slumber. I suffered shame on that occasion, when the sons of the family one after another kindly offered me a score—every one of them, almost to the babies, could read music. But you could not really feel uncomfortable with the Elwes family; the eldest, Geoffrey, was almost my contemporary and, adopted as a sister by them all, I enjoyed every minute of my visits. The youngest four made a delightful quartet singing and acting. "Has anyone here got a sense of pitch?" Richard once enquired at about the age of six when he wanted a note to start their song. I felt almost like the old ladies who were looking about vaguely, thinking this must be something they had left at home—but it was not too late to try to learn.

Asked how many children he had, Gervase used to say, "Six boys and then I lose count." At the tail end came two little girls, quite babies the first time I stayed with them. "Tous légitimes?" a French acquaintance once asked, as he looked from the young father and mother to the eight children and back again in renewed amazement. And indeed Gervase and Winnie were as nearly an elder brother and sister to me as their children were younger ones.

A little later when my brother Herbert was at Balliol, visits to Oxford were a great delight. Walter Moberly taught me to punt and I spent many hours on the river. There were four Moberly brothers, one sister, Violet, and Mrs. Moberly, whom I loved dearly. She always wore, as I recall, a widow's garb and rode through the streets of Oxford on a tricycle. Knowing the Moberlys was an introduction into a new world; not wholly new—for years I had known Mary Church, daughter of the Dean of St. Paul's and my mother's contemporary. I had with my father stayed at Temple Newsam and Lord Halifax had been very kind to me. I knew also various Anglican bishops, and had even, with both my parents, spent a weekend at Farnham Castle, then the home of Bishop Talbot and his family.

But to know people as one's parents' friends is one thing, to know them as one's own quite another. Walter Moberly, though a few years older than I, was almost a contemporary and became a great friend.

He had taken a Double First and was at this time a tutor at Lincoln College. When for a period he lectured at Glasgow University he told me how refreshing, after the polite silence of Oxford undergraduates, he found the students' habit of expressing their feelings. When they enjoyed him they applauded, when time was up they shuffled their feet. (Another Oxford friend of ours, Professor Phillimore, reacted differently: "I am sorry, gentlemen," he said, "I have still some pearls to cast.") Walter later won a D.S.O. in the First World War and has since become famous by his brilliant analysis of the diversities and problems of Redbrick and Oxbridge, by his management of the Universities Grant Board and above all by the work, done after the normal retiring age, at Cumberland Lodge. This postgraduate centre was established with one special purpose, which Walter had very greatly at heart. The immense danger of education today is, he believes, specialization carried to a point at which the student in one field becomes incapable of exchanging ideas with those in others. Far less can he integrate his own particular discipline in a larger whole. His danger is to become unconscious of the universe. Cumberland Lodge was created to bring together the students of various branches of science, various periods of history—but above all the historian and the scientist, the scientist and the theologian.

Queen Mary took a very special interest in the scheme and it was in the Henry III Tower at Windsor Castle, lent by her, that my husband and I stayed with Walter and his wife half a century later than those boating days, and were able to glimpse his fascinating work.

Walter's grandfathers had both been Anglican bishops and, as a cousin of his once said to me, we were all grandchildren of the Oxford Movement. Through his eyes I saw much of the best thought and life in the Church of England. He was more modern in social outlook than my father, yet entirely approved by him. My father used to speak of him sweepingly as "by far the ablest of the younger generation", so a seal of parental approval was set on this friendship; and this was something which I always continued to value.

With Frances and Gilbert Chesterton the friendship I made was perhaps to mean the most in my life. In those years no one who read anything could miss Chesterton. He was writing in every periodical. His books were pouring from the press. My mother and I were madly excited by his studies of Browning and Dickens. My father was swept off his feet by *Orthodoxy*. We must, we felt, get to know this man and we cast about for an introduction.

My first meeting with Gilbert and his wife was at what were still called the "lodgings" of the Governor of the Tower of London. I had been to the Tower before but never to this part of it; mine had been a pilgrimage to the prison—of St. Thomas More, beheaded on Tower Hill by Henry VIII for his faith, and of my ancestor Philip Howard, imprisoned by Elizabeth I.

Allowed to see neither his wife nor what I had almost called his posthumous child, it was eleven years before the death came which he had rehearsed so often, writing on the prison wall, "The more suffering with Christ in this world the more glory with Him in the next." St. Thomas More had wanted a merry meeting in heaven with all he had known on earth and I feel sure meeting him must have been for Philip a bit of the joy that the glory of heaven includes. And now here I had what was certainly a merry meeting with the man who was in our age supremely the spiritual and intellectual heir of More. But Frances Chesterton was singularly unlike Dame Alice.

Having written two books about Gilbert Chesterton and his wife, I can only hope that any readers I have kept up to this point will not feel it a mean trick if I refer them to *Gilbert Keith Chesterton* and *Return to Chesterton*. The little I have to say about Gilbert in this book will occur in a later chapter where I shall be discussing Hilaire Belloc and that mythical animal the Chester-Belloc.

I was not very good at changing my wavelength with these various friends, and I remember Winnie Elwes saying one day, "My dear, you really must not do it! Young so-and-so says he can't ask you to dance, because last time he danced with you you asked him what he thought of Gladstone's moral character." This happened to be a favourite topic of discussion with Walter, who, brought up in Liberal circles, objected strongly to my father's endorsement of Labouchère's remark, "I wouldn't mind Gladstone playing with three aces up his sleeve if he didn't try to convince you that Almighty God put them there." But Winnie of course was right—the topic was ill-chosen for a young guardsman.

Halfway between London and Arundel, Lotus became the sort of small-scale social centre which my parents wanted for themselves and for us, but which had never seemed possible at Eastbourne. It was astonishing how much the slight difference in distance from London meant. But it was the garden also, the lovely view, the more spacious house. In London in the winter, Sunday afternoon still meant for me either staying at home with Mama, while men friends visited her (I remember vividly a little heap of silk hats in the hall), or else going out with Papa to call on the women whose husbands might at that moment be talking to Mama!

But the weekend habit was beginning and spring and summer filled and sometimes overfilled our spare rooms at Lotus. My sister and I would double up; Mama, notorious for absentmindedness, came at least once without knocking into my usual bedroom to discover a male guest in the bed and retire in very Victorian confusion. Confusion was, I must confess, something of a keynote in our lives. The preparations for a "real party" were strenuous; a very untidy house must be tidied, Nanna prevented even more firmly than usual from hanging what were not yet nylons to dry on the balcony, flowers picked and arranged in large quantities. This I loved doing—but Mama could hardly bear to see her borders depleted; flowers were to her lovely things to be enjoyed and admired as they grew—the cutting of them was a sacrilege. Papa's study remained untouched. "It isn't as if he only wrote novels", Nanna remarked scathingly when Mama tried to tidy it a little.

Some weekends stand out specially in the memory: Gilbert and Frances Chesterton meeting George Wyndham; George with Gervase and Winnie Elwes, George again with Lord Hugh Cecil after the tragic ending of his campaign in Ireland, pacing the room as he talked until two in the morning; Belloc reciting his *Cautionary Tales* before they were published; old Lady Blennerhasset with her memories of the historian Döllinger, certainly the greatest scholar in the group which left the Church in protest when Papal Infallibility was defined.

Weekends were over all too soon for me; but my father agreed with Jane Austen that a visit was "perfect in being much too short". Some of our friends stayed for a week or two and he would murmur a little peevishly that they did not understand work—it was hard to flee to his study as was his wont the minute after breakfast and remain buried there till we had nearly finished lunch. He was willing to sacrifice this in the holidays—still making our Christmas trees and stage-managing during our occasional bursts of acting fever. Leo really *was* an actor, the rest of us fair enough for young amateurs. The fun for me was making the play, which we did by weaving together scenes, speeches and shorter quotations from Shakespeare, Sheridan, Pope, Tennyson and all our other favourites. *Sleeping Beauty* one Christmas was followed by *Cinderella* the next, and there were repeat performances of this in London.

My father enjoyed, too, almost as much as ourselves the visits of our growing circle of cousins. After Uncle Feargus' death the O'Conors had come home to live and they were with us the most frequently of the cousins. We all enjoyed the same things—singing round the piano, acting charades, going for long walks, playing tennis and playing the fool. It is odd what pointless things one remembers: Muriel and Eileen discussing a young man guest with considerable verve and realizing next morning that there was a blocked-up door between the rooms and he had heard every word they said; the helpless giggles with which we all listened to Mama when a hungry boy cousin asked for a little more meat, and she murmured as she carved it, "Oh the little more and how much it is." Her distress at her own lapses was quite ineffectual in checking them; rumour had it in the family that she had once signed a letter to the local doctor "Your loving Jo", and we were ingenious in noting for *her* embarrassment real or imaginary signs of *his*.

Chesterton said of the Browning love-letters that the reason they should not have been published was the very opposite to the one usually given. Robert Browning had told his love in "One Word More", Elizabeth hers in *Sonnets from the Portuguese*. The letters were full of family jokes and incomprehensible allusions, which obscured rather than revealed. There was far more besides in the Browning letters, as in all worthwhile letters, but it is true of most recollections certainly of ours. I can laugh over them still with my cousins. I cannot tell my readers what they meant to us all.

In those days of ample staffs and large houses we did quite a lot of "country-house" visiting, including of course, Arundel. From there I was taken to my first ball, at Petworth, and enjoyed the famous Turner collection more than the dancing, which I always did badly. Uncle Henry had married again just before I left school, a cousin we knew already, Gwendolen Maxwell. We called her Aunt Gwendy. As I grew up, she gave me some lovely clothes and jewellery and invited me to amusing parties. In Scotland with my father I stayed with the Norfolks at Kinharvie, with the Balfours at Wittinghame, with a Hope cousin at North Berwick, at Fort Augustus, where my eccentric Uncle Edmund was frequently in the monastery. He would take the monks out for very long drives, having first, with tender attention to their health, made them drink his own favourite purgative, Seidlitz powders. They would also be invited to stay with him in the Isle of Wight, where the normal pattern of country-village churchgoing became madly disrupted by "the Squire's" presence. The High Mass might last four hours with Edmund as master of ceremonies, or prolonged Vespers would display him in a cope. It was all correct by the rubrics, which he knew far better than his monkish guests. When he felt he had kept them long enough at their psalms he would bow deeply before one or another and offer refreshment: "Ite in coenaculum meum ubi invenietis vinum paratum."

Visiting this uncle in the island was rather terrifying. But at Fort Augustus there was my father as protection and the compensation of the glorious scenery. My father would hardly ever stay more than two days at any one place. On we would rush—to Kinharvie, Abbotsford, North Berwick, Woodburn. Of this, home of the Ralph Kerrs, Fr. Sebastian Bowden used to say approvingly, "Mass in the house, cup of tea with my thanksgiving, golf at the front door." And my father was only perfectly happy when golf could form a part of the daily round. Philip Kerr (later Lord Lothian), himself a brilliant player, gave Papa an adequate number of strokes for an exciting game—but I always felt that with Philip, as with his other friends, Papa's preference for golf over tennis was fundamentally a preference for conversation. Neither of them, I thanked heaven, would spend the evening recapitulating each hole, as did almost everyone I met at North Berwick. There we stayed longer than at most places and I considered it a most tiresome ritual at Lucy Hope's house that we were expected to get up and rush to the window each day to watch Arthur Balfour, philosopher and Conservative Prime Minister, driving off from the first tee (if these be indeed the terms used in that depressing game which, at North Berwick, was talked across you each night at dinner if you could not talk it yourself). Papa and Philip talked much on politics and philosophy, but golf they were content to play.

The mania for good talk that had seized me was not shared by most of my girl contemporaries. My romance for Minna Kerr had been a rather onesided affair and settled down after we left school into a calmer friendship. She did not share any of my enthusiasms and would certainly not have endorsed my preference for an evening at Lady Bell's over a dance. Lady Bell was the mother of Gertrude Bell, who became so famous in the Arab world, and it was fascinating even in those days to watch and listen to Gertrude talking to the men who clustered around her. And I remember the amazement of one of my friends as I pointed out my even choicer subject of admiration: Lady Gwendolen Cecil. She and her brother were among the great talkers of the period and her life of her father, Lord Salisbury, made her later more widely famous. My friend gasped out some words about a dress on which a good deal of breakfast had been spilt; I had not noticed and should hardly have cared.

I feel hideously like Jane Austen's Caroline Bingley in stating a preference for conversation over dancing and I seem to hear her brother saying, "Much more rational, my dear Caroline, I dare say but it would not be near so much like a ball." There were certainly moments—when the last reel was being danced at the Butes' by all the young men in kilts; when the curtains were drawn back to let the sunlight in at four or five in the pre-daylight-saving morning and we all sat down to bacon and eggs at Norfolk House. But my own double mind was the real trouble during these years. I did not care enough for social life to work at it—to improve my dancing, to listen to boring partners as if they were interesting, to keep my weight down and take trouble to dress well on a moderate allowance. Yet I had not the resolution and steadiness of purpose to find a line of my own and pursue it.

What would I not give today to have again the precious hours and days I valued so little then! It is nostalgic to think of a time when housework and cooking just happened—only a tyrant or a fool of the first order had any serious trouble in keeping servants. Even with old Nanna to annoy our household, I never remember our being shorthanded. One friend of ours declared that his footman's morning greeting was invariably "Tea or Holy Communion, sir?" and either choice was the beginning of a day that should, I feel, have been carefree. Rooms were tidied when you left them, your clothes brushed and mended when you took them off. "Those spacious days", a friend of mine once called them and, although they were only spacious for us, I gasp today to think of the ingratitude that failed to appreciate *how* spacious for us they were. Another friend said once in defence of writing her first book, "It saved me from wasting time", and I think with horror of the time I wasted in those days.

Girls are, I know, overworked today. The job taken on leaving school can mean hard toil, the fun in the evening costs a lot in loss of sleep. But I think for the most part they are happier than I, at any rate, was in the leisured life which left too much room for the narrower choices but precluded—unless you were very strongminded—a larger one. The blame for these unsatisfactory years rests on my own shoulders and I have often repented of them. I doubt if I should do any better if I were wafted back half a century into that same old cushioned and limited section of a large and very ill-arranged world. But I sometimes cherish a fancy that the psalmist's promise is fulfilled and that in an old age of unusual health and strength there has been given back to me something of "the years that the locusts have eaten".

Around this time a Lady Groves had written a book on social customs at which Chesterton poked fun very brilliantly. Rereading his essay, I felt it could be applied to all the more recent talk of U and non-U. How little those things have changed in half a century. Some of the old shibboleths have been dropped, some new ones picked up. The important thing seems to be that shibboleths should exist—and not merely to exclude those who cannot pronounce the h. It was held almost indecent in my youth to refer openly to social distinctions, but they were a more solid, if invisible, barrier than they are today. Yet if a word must be found the one then used—"gentry"—seems to me much more elegant than "U", and more expressive.

The Chestertons' milieu was far more new to me than that of the Moberlys, though I did not at first fully realize why. Much later, when I was writing Gilbert's biography, I remember talking to Charles Somers Cocks, a Foreign-Office friend, who had known him, and who went into gales of laughter over the thought that Gilbert's father had been a house-agent. This fact did not strike me as funny, but the laughter pinpointed something I was groping after, which

Gilbert himself has admirably stated from the opposite end. My parents would not have laughed at the thought of a house-agent as an author's father—although my mother was a little surprised when Gilbert once said to her, "You and I who belong to the good old upper middle classes." Papa struggled (in vain) to get Gilbert made a member of The Club and was furious at the attitude of many of his fellow members who rejected the idea on social grounds. But even my parents took for granted that you "knew" certain people and did not "know" others. If you were county, you were not town —especially when the town was as nearly suburban as was Dorking. My mother made an exception of the Catholic neighbours, and I remember her maintaining against one of our relatives that it was a duty to lower social barriers with people who worked with one in church or charitable activities. "They ought not to expect it," was the argument. "I ought to give it," was the answer—but it was a gift that might in those days cost something.

Of course with my parents there was the special difficulty of living so near Dorking that interruptions to their writing were of horrid frequency. Before the days of cars or telephones, a drive in a carriage took you to country neighbours for a prearranged lunch or tea. The town once admitted might become a flood. All this was true, but it had reached my consciousness in the form that while I might bring the convent boarders to tea on a Sunday I must not play with the doctor's daughters. When I "put up" my hair and became Miss Ward I was told to be *very* nice to the Catholic neighbours but to avoid the use of Christian names. When a young married woman proposed that we drop the "Miss" and "Mrs." I felt totally incapable of obeying both parts of this instruction. But as "Irene" (for this was the name of the girl in question) went on talking I realised that mine was not the only world putting up barriers against a world supposedly inferior. She began to describe some club from a London suburb against whom she had played tennis. I could not see from her description wherein the difference lay between her own club and the other, but she called them frequently "the poor things" in a voice of pitying condescension. And another Catholic neighbour had been reported, when we gave a tea to the local Children of Mary, as saying that she was happy her daughter should come to Lotus but not if some tradesman's daughters were coming too.

In America this snobbery is less pervasive. Strongly rooted in certain circles—in Boston, for instance, and Philadelphia—it is not only laughed at by most of the country but somehow shows its own intrinsic absurdity more plainly. I once got a telegram asking me to lecture to "Boston's best. No fee." And I heard a voice murmur at a Philadelphia tea party, "They talk on street corners—these gentlefolk." But Boston's best would scarcely count in Chicago, the famous Philadelphia names of Biddle or Drexel get confused with pretzels and scrapple, that strange Philadelphia food. And Boston's best cannot compete with the many other groups in that city who are willing to pay a fee. It might be argued that America's real danger, money snobbery, is worse than anything in England. Australia has shaken off both, I think, to a much greater degree; I certainly know no country in which I have been less aware of display of wealth or divisions based on birth or education, more aware of an all-embracing friendliness. But *no* country, I suppose, could pass a strict test 100%—the question is one of larger or smaller groups who could within the general society.

My mother was right in her feeling that only one thing could totally bridge this strange gulf that society has dug between human beings, but wrong in thinking it could be done in an artificial fashion that weighed and measured. Chesterton said once of racial and social barriers that the way to destroy them was not to try and hack them down, but to ignore them as a child does. This was exactly what Gilbert and Frances did, and I learnt a useful lesson on my very first visit, being asked to share a room with a coloured friend of Frances. My sister and I had demanded separate bedrooms at home and I disliked sleeping with anybody but, O shameful confession, I felt quite specially annoyed at the thought of a coloured room-mate. One of the avenues opened for me on that visit was towards the interracialism which today would seem to me as obvious as breathing. But in practising it with such simplicity my hosts were ahead of many who were thought to be pioneers in race relations but who had not yet uttered the word "integration".

4
THE MODERNIST CRISIS

I am told that once, in early childhood, I remarked to my mother, "When I'm grown up I shall travel about with Puppa", to which she said, "Then what shall I do?" and I answered firmly, "You will go to heaven." Despite the fact that Mama came first in my affections, I valued very specially trips abroad on which she was as happy that I was taking care of him as he and I in our companionship with one another. For an element that must not be left out of these otherwise unsatisfactory years was my close sharing in the activities and anxieties of my parents. I might perhaps have managed to shape a separate life for myself had I been less deeply involved in theirs.

Initiation into foreign travel had begun in childhood with Chartres and Paris. I was taught French history with visual aid from Notre Dame, the Sainte Chapelle, the Tuileries, Versailles, Napoleon's tomb. I have always found this way of learning intoxicating and my parents gave me many opportunities. They took me abroad themselves, they sent me with friends. One year I was joined as a third with Miss Thesiger (aunt of Ernest Thesiger, the actor) and Hersey Wauchope for an exciting month in Florence, meeting my father afterwards for a return journey through the Italian lakes and Switzerland.

Those were the years of Modernism, of my father's editorship of the *Dublin Review*, of his writing of Newman's life. I shall never forget one holiday in 1911, when the Newman *Life*, its immense intrinsic problems increased by criticisms from men who knew little of them, had brought my father to a point of nervous exhaustion that made my mother and me feel a change to be imperative. I went with him to France and was awakened night after night by a shout that penetrated the wall between our rooms, as he struggled out of a nightmare. To George Wyndham he wrote on this trip: "I wonder if you will feel at 55 as I do that *quite suddenly* old age has begun. I did not feel it when I turned 54. It has all come quite suddenly in a few months."

My mother and I were convinced that the five years 1906-1911 had been enough to explain a change that reached its climax as the Newman biography neared completion. Although not for long my father's secretary, I was sufficiently the confidante of both parents to have lived those trying years in a close mental companionship from which some of my own "ploys" may well have represented an occasional mental holiday.

The year I had left school was also the year in which my father's editorship of the *Dublin* began and my mother published the most important of her novels: *Out of Due Time*.

A few words are necessary here about the historical background. When Newman and my grandfather came into the Church they came at a moment when the long siege, first by Protestantism and then by secularism, had left dire results. Not in England alone but throughout the Catholic world the study of theology, history, the Bible, had long been approached more as a matter of arming the student against attack than as a deepening and widening of his Christian knowledge, and of his own intellect. Professors as well as students were living in a world shut away from all modern thought and progress and the Church was therefore making no impact on the world in which it actually was. The greatest Christian thinkers had been set aside. Lip-service was paid to St. Thomas and the Fathers, but in fact they were ignored; manuals were all the fashion, which, professedly expressing "the mind of St. Thomas", had little in them of any mind at all and were merely repetitions at third or fourth hand of what somebody many years before thought St. Thomas' mind to be.

Newman quickly realized and deplored this state of things. "We are living", he said, "on the intellect of a former age." And again: "We must lay again the foundations of Catholic thought—and no foundation is above the ground." Quietly then, sadly often, suspected of heresy, working, as he put it, "under the lash" of Catholic criticism, Newman began this giant task. Other men had started it also, all over Europe, and results were beginning to show during the pontificate of Leo XIII, especially in Church history and Scripture studies. The Pope encouraged these pioneers, acceded to Cardinal Mercier's request that at Louvain theology should be taught in the vernacular, and urged a return to St. Thomas instead of the use of inferior derivatives.

But towards the end of his long life, Pope Leo, it was said, began to feel alarm at the excesses of certain biblical scholars. "What is happening?" he was reported as saying: "Where will it end?"

His fears were justified in the next pontificate as Modernism began to declare itself more openly. In speaking of Modernism, I use the word not as it is often used today, but as used in the papal documents of the period for the bible of a heresy. Very roughly put, the heresy was that of naturalism: an emptying out in every field of the supernatural, but affecting especially the Catholic view of the Bible, of the Godhead of Christ, and of the nature of God Himself. The Bible, Modernists claimed, was to be regarded and treated exactly like any other book. Therefore in a period when "higher criticism" was rife, Christians would be wholly unprotected against views so extreme that the successors of these same critics did in fact abandon them.

To phrase it as simply as this is of course what is called hindsight; most people were at the time far too confused to see the issue so clearly.

For me, much later, the early Church, for my father the thirteenth century, served to illuminate it. In both periods Christ's revelation had been faced with human systems of thought and also with the language which men had chosen to express those systems. In both periods the Catholic thinker had had to learn the language in order to express in it his own far greater truths. In so doing he might sometimes make mistakes—as did Origen, as did Tertullian. But if he would not make this attempt, a whole generation might lose the revelation intended for all mankind.

The Modernists appeared to be asking for the same thing as Catholic thinkers. But their claim for a reconciliation between the Christian revelation and modern thought was really totally different; rather than learning a new language they were giving up the ideas that the old language enshrined. They would still say the Creed, having abandoned its meaning. And this created the problem which made the fight so obscure, made it so hard to distinguish friend from foe. The Catholic who began by accepting at face value the *credo* of the Modernist ended by suspecting any Catholic a little more intellectual than himself, who uttered ancient truth in words he had not learnt in the schoolroom.

Nor was the Modernist created out of the Catholic suddenly; year by year, or, at the shortest, month by month, he allowed the presumptions of Scripture criticism, the anti-miraculous view of life, to grow upon him. And he was helped in so doing by much of folly in popular Catholic devotion on which he riveted his gaze. The fullness of the Liturgy might have saved many who found scapulars, medals and the Rosary made more important than the Mass, private revelations dwelt on more than the Gospels, La Salette talked about by Catholics more than the Trinity.

There is no question that Fr. Tyrrell and his friends were working themselves into a kind of frenzy over all this instead of trying to remedy it. They diminished theology to its utterly minor elements when my father was begging only for more theology and better theology. But to ask for anything whatever was suspect in the eyes of the narrower sort. And while my father was in anguish when he read Tyrrell's final book, *Christianity at the Cross-roads*, there were those who claimed smugly always to have realized whither he was tending. "What", wrote Tyrrell, "are the categories and concepts of Jesus to us? Are we to frame our minds to that of a first-century Jewish carpenter, for whom more than half the world and nearly the whole of its history did not exist . . . Would the military genius of the past tie us down to his weapons and methods of warfare?"

The Christ of history was in Modernist eyes a man of genius conditioned by the age he lived in; we are back at Arianism, with the difference that the Arians at least believed in God the Father, Creator of heaven and earth, while the dissolving view of the Modernist philosopher saw God almost solely as immanent in creation. I remember an early book of Maude Petre's in which a beginning of this attitude greatly startled my Aunt Emily. She had always made a point of avoiding these subjects with her friend and keeping at a level of cheerful chatter. But now, rather drawling out the words and giving them deliberately a rhyming sound, "Maude, Maude," she asked, "did you say you were equal to Gawd?"

"What", I queried, "was the answer?"

"Well," said my aunt, "it boiled down to the fact that that was more or less her idea."

This was the effect of Modernism as received by the average Catholic—and indeed its ultimate effect on the outlook of its leading exponents. The three large volumes of Loisy's letters give a melancholy picture of a gradual descent terrifying to witness for one who lived through those years, and the terror is reflected in the letters of one of his closest friends, Baron von Hügel. The Baron, who in Scripture exegesis went all the way with the Modernists, was philosophically poles apart from them. He had an uncanny power of dividing his mind into two compartments, of which the right seemed not to know what the left was about. His friends said he would pass from writing Scripture criticism logically destructive of belief in Our Lord's divinity to an hour of rapt adoration in front of the tabernacle. In his last years the right compartment appeared wholly dominant, but at this time the intensity of his sympathy with the scholars and students in the Modernist camp was too keen for him to see the difficult problem they presented to the authorities of the Church, the immense danger they were to the very existence of Christianity.

The Modernist atmosphere was all around us at Lotus; the Ashbournes especially seemed always to have one or another, French or English, staying with them. Not of course Modernists only: Duchesne, as well as Bremond and Fr. Tyrrell, was brought to visit us while Maude Petre was a close friend of Mama's and the Baron of my father's.

It seems absurd to feel, as I often did, that had Fr. Tyrrell's chin been different the course of events would have been changed or at least modified. The almost total absence of this feature surely expressed or at least symbolized a weakness that one quickly realized. He reflected almost like a looking-glass the ideas of a stronger personality in his company. Later he had thrown himself into the full stream of Modernism, but there were points when we first knew him at which he might well have halted and held others back. There was in him a deep piety, an intense sympathy, which drew to him sufferers from the harshness and narrowness of so many Church authorities, sufferers from the inevitable trials of conflict between the visible tangible realities of earth and the great reality of a world still hidden from us. So many troubled people were sent to him for help that he said once he sometimes felt like a specialist who never met a healthy mind. My bishop uncle (certainly no Modernist!) had found Tyrrell's early books of immense help for himself and others. Fr. Tyrrell might well have been another Fr. Maturin but for the weakness between mouth and neck.

Von Hügel was totally different. His deafness set him apart; he would partly but never wholly emerge from his private world with an exquisitely polite "Please?" to offer you a little instrument like a telephone for your reply to his remarks. This hearing aid did not always work, but I never felt it made the slightest difference. While Tyrrell reflected the mind of others, Von Hügel threw on to them the powerful reflection of his own. He found it almost impossible to believe that anyone of intelligence and goodwill could really differ from his views. At one end Loisy, at the opposite end my father, pained and startled him when they did succeed in making him realize the facts of life as regarded their own outlook.

My father, though a close friend and great admirer of the Baron's, had always felt his critical views to be exaggerated and unsure, but deemed himself too little of a scholar to be able to discuss them. His own general position was precisely Newman's, and he came to feel in relation to Von Hügel what Newman had felt with earlier liberals —great sympathy with the desire for breadth and depth, great doubt as to much that the Baron urged and above all as to the fashion in which he urged it. He saw on the horizon a danger the Baron long refused to think possible—the Loisy of the later letters, the Tyrrell of *Christianity at the Crossroads*. He believed the ideal way to meet this danger was open discussion, but when authority eventually met it by condemnation in the shape of the encyclical *Pascendi* he submitted. The Church, he reminded himself and others, had, in Newman's words, to scatter the enemy before she could divide the spoils.

But when my father took over the *Dublin*, the encyclical was four years in the future, and his aim was to gather in all Catholic thinkers and scholars, besides many non-Catholic Christians, and make the review an organ of real value in expressing a large Christian humanism. He was for several years astonishingly successful. Not only was the *Dublin* full of interesting and original articles, but it was widely acclaimed in the world of letters and the circulation multiplied. At the same time my father was engaged on the life of Newman, kept up an immense correspondence with his friends, and led a full social and family life.

All this was reflected in my mother's novels, and above all in *Out of Due Time*.

The book had begun in her mind as a study of De Lamennais and the *Avenir*, but as it grew it became a curiously prophetical picture of the Modernist scene in England, of the stresses and strains on friendship resulting from the different attitudes of men and women passing through what was in fact a major crisis in the history of the Church.

Fr. Cuthbert once described my father as a "man of affairs of the intellect", and one of his chief interests was the analysis of the various parts played in the Church by thinkers and rulers, of the place of dogma and of devotion, of progress and of obedience. In two articles entitled "For Truth and for Life" he drew out this analysis in the *Dublin Review*—largely for the help of those who were feeling at the moment the difficulties engendered by general suspicions, among the less intelligent, of any effort, however loyal, to make the Church's teaching more intelligible to thinkers and in general to the modern world. My father had, as a young man, spent some years in a seminary, before discovering that he had no vocation for the priesthood. One of his former professors, Mgr. Croke-Robinson, joined Archbishop Bagshawe (aged over eighty and reluctantly retired from his see) in a threat to denounce his old pupil's articles to Rome. In his strange letter, Mgr. Croke-Robinson did not quote a single word from the articles. But he put into inverted commas, as though from them, what *he* deduced as my father's meaning. His own unusually keen sense of the Faith, he remarked, "smells the rat in your reverent and deferential and clever periods":

> "The Church will have to do this or avoid that". She "must wake up". "She is not up to date"—"She is not blessed at present with the best available intellect or erudition"—"Rome wants sweeping out of a horde of mediaevals, unintellectuals, fossils, laggards—to be replaced by modern intellectuals, men abreast with the advance of modern thought etc. etc." All this I can read as plain as a pike-staff in your writings.
>
> See how awfully hard it is to be a little child for those of intellectual gifts! . . . How hardly shall "intellectuals" (as well as rich) enter into the Kingdom of Heaven! Besides which consider the terrible danger of the deceitfulness of the heart, the subtleness, quite awful, of intellectual pride, and so on . . . Look at the wrecks of intellectuals strewing the path of Holy Church on either side and all along the line . . . as the White Throne is not far off I could not face it peaceably unless I had remonstrated with you, I hope in all charity and without offence.

This letter is typical enough of the "orthodox" battering that my father was receiving, especially in its allusion to his "reverent and deferential and clever periods". Cardinal Merry del Val said of him that his theology was acrobatic and that when he fell he would quickly recover his balance and convince everybody that he was all right.

Obviously neither of these men came into the category of thinkers; those who did, such as Bishop Hedley and Cardinal Mercier, Dr. Barry, Fr. Thurston and many others, understood and were themselves trying to do the same work as my father. But it was a difficult time for the thinkers, owing to the betrayal of the Church by some among their ranks and the consequent shaking of authority's nerves. As each of the leading Modernists poured out literature under eight or nine pseudonyms, the general impression was of far greater numbers than they really mustered.

My father had hoped that Scripture scholars and philosophers, especially in France, were bringing about the revival of Catholic thought which Newman had longed for—and indeed this was true of many. But with the defection of Loisy, Houtin, Hébert and others, suspicion was beginning to fall on men as deeply loyal and Catholic as Lagrange, even on Cardinal Mercier himself.

The Modernists and their sympathizers, especially after the appearance in 1910 of the encyclical *Pascendi*, were as concerned to bring suspicion on all loyal Catholic thinkers as were the obscurantists. They wanted it to appear manifest that no one could continue to think and remain a Catholic. Above all they wanted Newman condemned—and Wilfrid Ward with him. To them, as to their opposite numbers on the Right, the subtle distinctions that must be drawn between truth and those exaggerations of one part of it at the expense of another which are called heresies, were mere special pleading. For them, too, my father was just an acrobat.

"Is it true", Fr. Tyrrell wrote, "that Wilfrid Ward is saying that if you read the Encyclical as it ought to be read, back before onto a looking-glass, it contains a very cautious approbation of Newman, and only condemns Loisy and me?"

And again: "I believe Ward says that *evolution* but not *development* of doctrine is condemned and that we should distinguish between mod*erns* and moder*nists*, as is quite plain if you read between the lines and alter the punctuation."

My father spoke of himself in those days as "distracted"—and it was small wonder that he felt so, under the three-way pull of Modernists denouncing him as a coward, obscurantists calling him Modernist, and large numbers of ordinary Catholics, loyal but puzzled, appealing to him for help. "I am almost as isolated", he wrote, "as J.H.N. was in 1862, but cannot act otherwise, and I take some comfort in imagining that he looks on and approves."

Years later, I noted a remark of Chesterton's which would have cheered me much at this time—for my father was being called a "trimmer" by both sides. How absurd it is, says Chesterton, that this word should have become one of abuse. For a trimmer goes to the side of the boat that needs him; by his act its balance is restored. This indeed was what Wilfrid Ward was doing, and it was ironical that from this his troubles sprang. For he was an incredibly rash talker, and by no means only to those who agreed with him. Like Chesterton's ideal trimmer, he was always trying to restore the balance. To Modernists he stressed the duty of obedience, to rulers the duty of forbearance, to theologians the duty of explaining.

A papal encyclical is as seldom written by a Pope himself as a royal proclamation by a sovereign. *Pascendi* was an intensely theological document, obviously written by a professional theologian and in highly theological language. (We heard Cardinal Billot's name mentioned and that of Cardinal Vivez y Tuto.) It was impossible that the man in the street should understand it without help from the theologians—and that help was not forthcoming. Not particularly well translated into English, it was hurled by the Catholic newspapers at the heads of the faithful and spoken of from the pulpit as though so limpidly clear that to be puzzled by it spelled disloyalty. Moreover, the lists of penalties directed against crypto-Modernists in seminaries and elsewhere filled "with dismay and perturbation" even so intensely loyal a Catholic as Uncle Henry. He went on to say that even from the point of view of human prudence, "the Holy See knows its own business better than I can tell it; especially, as being ignorant of the disease I am no kind of judge of the remedies needed. I *cannot doubt* that what has been done will lead many into temptation and blind the light from others, but it often happens that a battle must be fought though it is seen beforehand the loss must be terrific."

This loss both Papa and the Uncle desired with all their hearts to minimize; and my father at least thought this could be done if theologians would explain to the ordinary Catholic (a) what the encyclical meant in modern English, and (b) its relation to the general teaching of the Church and to the heresy it was condemning.

All his theologian friends recognized that the encyclical needed theological exposition for its understanding, but none of them would say this publicly. Explaining could be taken to mean explaining away, especially following on a chorus from Press and pulpit declaring how joyfully the encyclical had been received—and presumably therefore been already read and understood!—by all. It was in fact as complex and difficult for the lay reader as the heresy it was combating. But a real heresy-hunt was on, and to try to help people to read it aright was to lay oneself open to the huntsmen.

We were far better off in Westminster than were many, for Cardinal Bourne was no heresy-hunter and was careful to point out from the beginning that England was no Modernist centre. By and large he supported my father, but with a caution of word and manner doubtless rendered greater by the rashness of this layman, which must have made him shudder. Nor did he shudder alone. My mother and I did our uttermost to keep my father from writing rash letters and saying rash things. He was living at fever pitch and our nerves too were shaken. We were only really happy when we could send him off to Cardinal Mercier at Malines, where he could speak his full mind to a fully sympathetic listener. But my father, on his side, could never understand anyone who did not say everything to everybody. And this was strange in a man whose articles and books were remarkably well balanced and who recognized in theory the problems of authority as well as those of thinkers. "He talked very frankly," runs a letter from Malines to my mother about the Cardinal, "becoming more and more open as time went on. His general position seems to be just the same as mine, but there is in him and the Louvain people a curious standard of frankness (or want of frankness) in dealing with Rome. He thinks the Roman theology quite impossible: but though he is hand and glove with the Pope he clearly does not give him the least inkling of this view. He advises me to be very careful in Rome, and says they want very thorough loyalty. I don't see how I can with sincerity speak at Rome as though the Encyclical arouses in me a feeling of enthusiasm when it does just the reverse. The more I found the Cardinal in agreement with me the more puzzled I was on this point."

In a letter to Cardinal Rampolla, my father said of himself: "To speak rashly has always been my fault and my misfortune." This letter gave an excellent summary of his position, and I have always regretted that by the advice of Cardinals Mercier and Bourne it was never sent. The recipe seems to have been left untried of laying before the Church's rulers a clear and at the same time respectful statement of what those things were that troubled men of intelligence who were also obedient. The rebellious shouted, the obedient did not dare to whisper.

When Bishop O'Dwyer of Limerick offered to write an article showing that the encyclical did not condemn Newman, and added that the Editor could of course reject the article if he did not like it, my father was delighted. The Bishop had appeared so fully to see and share his own attitude that he expected from him a treatment of the problems that would calm the troubled. Uncle Henry sounded a note of caution—did Wilfrid, he asked, really know what line the Bishop would take? Himself no philosopher or theologian, the Uncle had seen the encyclical as the firing of a gun in a mortal combat. It might well have been necessary, he said, if the evil were so great a one as the document indicated, but after such a shot the nerves of the gunners themselves would be shaken. Throughout he had advised my father to go quietly, cautiously. Now he advised him to make sure whether this offer might not prove a gift to be feared.

Wilfrid Ward, alas, proceeded, as it seemed to me, to do everything likely to drive his notoriously violent-tempered friend into a passion. Day after day he wrote letter after letter pressing on the Bishop his own view of what was needed. I have always thought it possible that, if he had not done this, his final suggestion that the article should be printed with the omission of the first eight pages might have proved acceptable. For those eight pages contained precisely what he had already explained *ad nauseam* that he could not print—the usual cries of enthusiasm for the encyclical which he had deplored in other Catholic periodicals. Above all, the Bishop made use of such expressions as "insidious and treacherous spirit", "cheat and hypocrite", "jugglery of thought", which appeared to hit at all those people who my father knew were not disloyal but were deeply troubled. As it was, the answer was a postcard:

Dear Sir,

Your proposal is simply shocking and I decline to accept it. I shall publish the article as a pamphlet in London and state its history.

But when he did so, the Bishop put at the beginning, albeit in a rather grudging tone, those very explanations my father had vainly besought in his far-too-numerous letters. Cardinal Bourne was much worried by the incident, but although writing my father a letter demanding that he state publicly his own responsibility in the matter, he did not, as we had feared, demand his resignation.

To return to the point where I began this chapter: my father's sudden ageing while writing the Newman biography in the midst of the Modernist storms. He was encountering for the first time a situation of great intrinsic difficulty for which by temperament he was peculiarly unfit. His own mother had asked not to see his father's biography before it was published. Cardinal Wiseman's executors had not asked a question or raised a difficulty. The case of Newman was very different and the anxiety of the Cardinal's executors is easily understood. Today Newman ranks to all intents and purposes as a Father of the Church, but at that date many theologians, and all the men who had studied under these theologians, suspected him of being at least what was called materially heretical. I heard this said again and again in my youth—very occasionally I meet it still. But note: all Newman's own sons—the Birmingham Oratorians—had been educated in the rigid scholasticism out of which such suspicions grew. They trusted Newman himself but for the most part could not follow his line of thought. Whenever my father did so in his own words, not Newman's, they became suspicious. He would have to rewrite, giving a page of quotation to what might have been said (had been said!) in a sentence. Even in an era of long quotations he realized that his were becoming over-long, threatening the artistic balance of the book. The nervous tension aroused was in part the inevitable result of the Modernist crisis but in part his own fault. Lack of caution in conversation, a real terror lest Newman's orthodoxy should be called in question at Rome, was, they reasonably felt, the very way to produce such a disaster. "Your good name is his", Isy von Hügel had written to my father—and she begged him to go more quietly, more carefully. The defect of his quality—his eagerness to help the Catholics of their own age who so sorely needed help—was certainly a rashness which alienated the men who *might* have trusted him had they understood Newman well enough to understand Wilfrid Ward.

Might—or might not. For there was another problem that always remains for a serious biographer. The wife and children of the layman, the spiritual children of the priest, tend to want his face painted without shadow. Wilfrid Ward adored Newman so much as to speak of his own well-loved father as intolerable in his relations with J.H.N. But my father wrote a biography. What a family desires is a panegyric. (I can sympathize with them, for *my* hackles rise at criticism of *him*!) But he did try, even when writing his hero's biography, not to fall into this gigantic error, not to commit this sin against art which is also a sin against truth.

The publication of the Life of Newman in 1912 relieved the atmosphere as far as our family was concerned. The paean of praise led off by a *Times* leader was refreshing. A letter from Cardinal Gasquet, living in Rome, assured the author that the authorities were as little likely to condemn the Newman biography as to condemn an encyclopedia. It was so obviously a truthful and unbiased record. And being truthful, it showed Newman's joy in the Church herself—"This *is* a religion"—as plainly as the high tragedy of his human drama.

A year after the Newman biography, in the introduction to a collection called *Men and Matters*, Wilfrid summed up the problem of the Catholic thinker in every age. The Modernist wanted to keep the language of Revelation while emptying out the divine content. The believer wants to express that Revelation in words understood by the world around him. "Catholic theology is the great intellectual defence of the Church." The Fathers in the fourth century, St. Thomas in the thirteenth, had made Revelation intelligible to their contemporaries. "We can no more afford now than we could in the fourth century or the thirteenth to lose contributions of value in the difficult enterprise of meeting the anti-Christian thought of the day."

Shot at though he was by both extremes, my father had not been silenced, and Von Hügel wrote in obvious surprise, "As a piece of writing that has passed the Censors in these our times, it possesses a certain remarkable breadth of its own."

An aunt once told my mother how amazed she was at our frequent trips to the Continent: "How can you afford it? You must be a very good manager." It was indeed one of the best things my parents gave us. You can always afford what you want very much. We did it by going cheap—and cheap was in those days very cheap. I remember a *pensione* in Siena with excellent full board including wine, at six lire a day (then between four and five shillings). There my father and I stayed for a month, passing on to Florence, where I taught myself to look at paintings with Ruskin's *Mornings in Florence*. And it was a good way. As a guide to Matisse, Ruskin would be pretty useless; but I learnt a lot from him about colour and line and, with my father's enthusiastic co-operation, a good deal about Church history, especially from the frescoes in the Spanish Chapel.

Besides my trips alone with Papa, we used as a family to spend part of most summers on the Continent. Several times we went to Switzerland, twice to St. Enogat in Brittany. Not yet absorbed by Dinard, it was an attractive village with wonderful views and beaches. The first year we went I found it enchanting, but the second summer was the solitary instance I remember when "going abroad" seemed suddenly to have lost its charm. We had seen all the sights and views within a walk and made all the expeditions. We had seen the Corpus Christi processions and some of the Pardons—and it rained, how it rained. Each night the moon and stars appeared, but in the morning it was raining again till night. And my sister and I quarrelled, which we had not done seriously since we left the nursery. It was high time for taking stock of myself, but I only decided that I was bored with Brittany and wanted to go home. I was not very well that summer and my mother thought this a good idea. I went to Aunt Mary, who took me with her to Sheffield where a new Carmelite convent was to be opened—on land given by Uncle Henry, for he owned a great deal of land thereabouts and had a few years earlier been Lord Mayor of Sheffield, with Aunt Mary as Lady Mayoress.

We went over the convent before it was enclosed and I thumped the hard straw beds which humped in the middle so that I could not imagine how anyone could lie on them without falling off. Two of my old schoolfellows were sleeping on such beds already in two different Carmelite convents. I shuddered at the idea and the shudder must have shown on my face, for the photographs taken of

Aunt Mary and myself were, my family declared, a lifelike proof that girls were walled up in convents and had great difficulty in escaping.

Without any of the analysis I made later, I had begun by now to be puzzled at myself. I had everything to make me happy yet really fundamentally I wasn't. I enjoyed an immense number of things in life, but I had a vague unsatisfied ambition and, of all incredible things to look back on, time often hung heavy on my hands.

After August 1914 I never suffered from that particular complaint again.

PART 2

SECOND QUARTER-CENTURY

1913–1939

5

FIRST WORLD WAR

BELGIAN refugees fill the horizon as one looks back at the first months of the First World War. The ordinary citizen certainly believed that we had gone to war simply because the Germans had invaded Belgium—we felt we could not do too much for these people driven from their homes. Dorking became very much of a centre. Our two Belgian priests were dead but Fr. Volcryck had built a church, much too big for the congregation, largely with Belgian money. And there was a half-Belgian family who had come to live there of recent years: James Dessain, married to a very dear friend of mine, Lucy Devas, and brother of the Burgomaster of Malines.

James was an absolute godsend in this situation and it was one of his relatives—I think the Burgomaster himself—who took charge of the large numbers who came to us. Some were received into families, for others empty houses were taken and furnished by an energetic committee. Thanks to the Dessain family we escaped most of the troubles that other towns suffered. "He went down and scolded them in French and Flemish", an irate host remarked with satisfaction when he had begged the intervention of Monsieur Dessain with a troublesome guest. The influx was bound to bring with it difficult elements, and I am afraid it is very English (or perhaps merely very human) to embark with enthusiasm on a project and then suffer from reaction. Even at Dorking the grumbling that swept the country over "those Belgians" began to be heard after a few months, but on the whole they integrated surprisingly well with the population.

My brother Herbert had been in the Officers' Training Corps at Oxford, whence, after hardly any training, he was given a commission in the Fourth Devons and shipped off to India. There, no doubt, the training would continue—and we presently heard with amazement that he had been made Quartermaster. The vision of Herbert dealing with clothes and stores was startling, the thought of India reassuring.

Oddly enough, the moment of expansion in the Ward family fortunes dated from a Quartermaster-General over a century earlier. But alas, there was no hope that Herbert would remake them; he was more likely to dissipate his substance replacing saucepans and pillow-cases lost, stolen or strayed. Leo was still at school and when, the following year, he volunteered, was turned down on health grounds and went instead to Christ Church. My sister, immersed in reception work for the Belgians in London, went on when that came to an end to work for the Red Cross, as secretary to another great-uncle, Edward Stewart, who was one of its most important organizers. He received at the end of the War a much-deserved K.B.E. for his work. Later, at the Recreation Huts for soldiers in Calais and Boulogne, Tetta was to see far more of the War than I ever did.

I wanted desperately one thing only—to nurse wounded soldiers. A tiny hospital was opened in Dorking, but we received only convalescent cases and my work as a "nurse" was almost entirely washing dishes and scrubbing floors. A soldier watching me kindly suggested that I might get better results if I wetted the floor before applying the brush. My sister had shown equal ignorance when first called upon to make tea and an old lady had murmured, "It's time there was a war." A war, two wars, have been too heavy a cost, but any girl today could make tea or a bed, could sweep and scrub even if she could not make Parisian flowers and had never heard of Jacobean embroidery.

I made my first bed at the Italian Hospital where I was accepted as a V.A.D. nurse early in 1915. In my ward there were twenty-five beds to be made before breakfast every morning. The hospital was under the care of the Sisters of Charity and their wide white caps were a familiar and pleasant sight, for I had a very specially loved great-aunt who was one of them at their Mill Hill orphanage. The nurses were something of an afterthought and our quarters were bad. We slept in cubicles; I always wondered how the night nurse could sleep at all, and often had to reproach myself if I ran up hurriedly during the day to fetch something. We had one very small sitting-room for eating and recreation. It was in the basement and there was a basin on a stand to wash our plates in after a meal. Mass was at six. After it one could drink a glorious and most welcome cup of coffee in the kitchen before going on duty at seven. Breakfast at eight, two hours off in a day that ended at seven in the evening; by that time I was utterly exhausted. It was not obligatory to go to Mass; my first appearance on weekdays would probably be in the kitchen a few minutes before seven.

But I enjoyed the life enormously. The hospital was intended, as its name implies, for Italian patients. The floor above ours was entirely Italian, our floor had some Italian patients but the largest ward had been offered to the Army. As the nursing was first-rate, really bad cases were sent there. I remember the return of a doctor from his holiday; "When did Number 11 die?" he asked, for he had left him in a desperate state. I pointed to the bed where an unrecognizable Number 11 was sitting up engaged in lively badinage with another soldier. Sister Pauline was a marvellous nurse and an astonishing character. She had been a district nurse and was called on, when actually in the novitiate, with the request that she should become their head for the whole London area. She was in charge both of the soldiers' ward and the women's on the same floor, helped only by one trained nurse and myself (besides the rather old nurse who by her own choice did night work all the time). There was a delightful ward-maid from Argyll and the Isles with the loveliest accent I have ever heard (Sister Pauline later had her trained as a nurse). This was at first our staff, but to it were soon added V.A.D.s sent two at a time by the Red Cross for periods of a month or two to give them some experience before going on to military hospitals.

I was myself technically a V.A.D. but after a very short time Sister Pauline put the trained Irish nurse in charge of the women's ward and me of the soldiers'. I remember a childish pride in being a staff nurse and a corresponding vexation when Mama, who could never get a phrase right, proclaimed triumphantly that I was "on the staff of the hospital". (She made the remark, unfortunately, to Mgr. Nolan, who answered in tones as near thunder as his voice could produce, "She might have been a classical scholar!") I had little experience in training anyone and I remember with a shudder the procession of V.A.D.s and the difficulty in remembering to tell the same things to each one in the succession. I got a sharp lesson, but she a sharper, when one of them put down a boiling dish of instruments on a large plate-glass table. Even in those days it cost her five guineas, and after that I did remember to say, "Never put hot things down on glass." I was not the only stray intellectual wandering about, and hospital experience was an invaluable training in practicality.

Half-days off were usually spent with Aunt Mary and I sometimes stayed the night. After the Second World War it seems absurd to speak of the bombs in the first. But there was enough danger to cause the more timorous to take shelter, and this they did almost entirely in the London Underground, bringing down their bedding and establishing themselves for the night along the platform. It was a curious sight, and I found it interesting as I went to and from Egerton Crescent to watch the family parties and speculate about the homes they had come from.

One morning I went back to the hospital after spending a night with the Aunt and found a state of frantic excitement. A bomb had actually fallen in the square, damaging the statue of Queen Anne and causing the death of an Italian patient with heart trouble. The soldiers had certainly enjoyed it and I felt defrauded at having missed the excitement. After that we were told to go down to the basement when the sirens sounded. But I soon ignored the order; after a day's work bed was better than a cellar, and I thought too much fuss was being made over a single bomb.

At last we acquired a V.A.D. who became fully a colleague, only differing from me in working shorter hours. Richie Thorpe was a sort of connection, for her first cousin Mairi McDougall had married my half first cousin Walter Maxwell-Scott. She was as Scotch as well might be. Sister Pauline was too, and my own Scotch blood responded warmly to them both. The men were altogether delightful and we soon felt the importance of amusing as well as nursing them. We watched hospital visitors beside the beds and sardonically noted the tall stories the soldiers told them. Nursing the men, one did really get to know them—and the first thing we learned was the total unreality of the newspaper picture. These men were volunteers; conscription had not yet begun. But they were very far from that straining at the leash, described by the *Daily Mail*, to get back to the Front. They had been in hell and no man wants to return to hell. Their courage remained and their gaiety—and this was something tremendous.

I sent for the old acting clothes from home and it was amazing how easily some of the younger men could be dressed up as girls—"After six weeks on a milk diet", one of them explained ruefully.

There are always one or two born actors in a large group and, choosing a time when the majority were convalescent, we put on the usual kind of show that got photographed and praised in the usual kind of way.

But I became unpopular with the old Italian sisters upstairs. I had, in the stress of the circumstances, borrowed at least one dressing-gown from the Italian men's ward and an emissary had to be sent to recover it. It was a reminder of a problem always with us, for the Italian sisters not only always seemed to be old; they had also never grasped the elements of the English language and their only idea of nursing was the administration of aperient medicines. Nobody got quite so angry with them as the Italian visiting physician. I have seen him almost purple as he tried to read a temperature on a chart which, for the sake of "holy poverty", had been kept in pencil, rubbed out and used repeatedly for a series of patients. "No one", he was heard to mutter, "over a hundred should be in charge of a ward." An unfortunate young Irish sister was then installed as a buffer between the two Italians. But the oldest nun of all was retired—and put to answer the telephone. We could see her standing tiptoe on a stool to reach the mouthpiece. We could hear her: "Pliz? Zis is ze Italian 'ospital. Pliz?" The dialogue seldom seemed to get much further.

I always regarded the efficiency of the hospital—for it was efficient—as a miracle of Sister Pauline's. If the dispensary sister got ill, there she was dispensing the medicines; she took the theatre sister's place and rapidly trained us to be efficient assistants. Sisters of Charity get up at four and Sister Pauline was often now not getting to bed before midnight. A "late sleep" meant till five-thirty in a dormitory where the others were all dressing at four. She did most of the paper work—and what added to her difficulties was that she was never officially matron. The old Superior (who meant excellently but knew nothing of nursing) kept the reins in her own hands, which meant that the most plausible sister was likely to get her word in first, often with unfortunate results.

I reached one conclusion in my time at the Italian Hospital which I have never seen reason to modify. A real vocation to the religious life is a marvellous thing and I grew daily in veneration of Sister Pauline. But there are in every community some who have no special vocation but have just happened to float there. Had they fallen into a congenial profession they would probably have stayed in it, had some man wanted to marry them they might easily have married him. I became profoundly convinced that the habit does not make the nun.

Sister Pauline had to have an operation. She was up again and at overwork terribly soon. Richie Thorpe and I were convinced that the surgeon who had operated knew nothing of the situation. We decided to doff our uniforms and ask in the ordinary way for an appointment. I was trembling as he looked at us and said, "Which is the patient?" for I had undertaken to open the matter. He was at first furiously angry, but by the end of the interview we realized we had made an impression. As we rose to go we unobtrusively laid three guineas on the table as a fee for our "consultation".

Things did improve, as I learned from Richie, but I had no opportunity of seeing for myself. I happened just then to catch influenza and as soon as I was out of bed the Superior told me firmly that I was not strong enough for hospital work. I have always been as strong as a horse, but unfortunately the surgeon, losing his temper recently at being offered a blunt instrument in the course of an operation, had cursed the hospital circumstantially, concluding with the remark that V.A.D.s called on him and interfered with his business. Richie, I am glad to say, remained in the hospital. The Superior (quite rightly) had decided that I was the ringleader in an action she must have found hard to qualify in language suited to her dedicated state.

I have put this account of my life at the Italian Hospital together, though in fact it was divided sharply into two periods by several months at home during my father's last illness. He had gone to the States on a second lecture tour, his first in 1913 having been so successful that innumerable engagements were lined up for him. He returned, apparently in normal health, to face a peculiarly heavy trial. I have mentioned my eccentric uncle, who was the eldest brother. Just after my father's return he died under an operation. Owing to my grandfather's breaking and never renewing the entail on the Ward property, he had the legal power to dispose of it as he chose. "Edmund will do the right thing", his father had said, but this was a bit of unwarranted optimism. I am convinced that Uncle Edmund, while probably not certifiable, was not clear enough in mind to be fully responsible. As a child I remember his strange rages and his conviction that Fenians were concealed in his garden. I have always fancied there were three motives for the will he made, leaving money to every Catholic bishop in England and immense sums to various diocesan charities. He also left money to my mother, to his sister the Abbess of Oulton, and to each of us—and annuities to Bernard, Emily and Gertrude. The estate was a good one, but he madly over-estimated its value. These sums could not have been found at all, had not money during the War depreciated and land risen in price. Even so it meant selling almost the entire family property. In his will Edmund stressed his fear of hell and I think that consciously he was dwelling on the idea that vast charitable benefactions would bring many prayers for his soul. But subconsciously two other motives were working.

All men love power and Edmund's form of exercising it had always been his money. In this will he was making us almost independent of my father, he was taking away from him this special power, he was using it himself to do last important acts of generosity. All the bishops would bless him; through him Aunt Agnes's convent was now endowed; his brother and his two sisters would live on his benefactions. And in a last not insignificant gesture he named my father residuary legatee of a ruined property. In those days it was axiomatic that land coming from your ancestors went on to your male heir, but Edmund had always been furiously jealous of a younger brother who had made his the name that was known. He had been asked once too often, "Are you Wilfrid Ward's brother?" and this, I think, was the main subconscious motive for the will.

We learned the situation only as it was read after the funeral: fairly quick at mental arithmetic, I added the twenty thousands, five thousands, two thousands—and brought them out (correctly, as it chanced) at twice what his brother Bernard and the lawyer had indicated to my father. Bernard, of course, had not seen the will, and the lawyer, who had been terrified of Edmund, was still shaking like a jelly.

Those were weary weeks that followed. Papa had never expected to outlive his brother but had thought confidently of the family future. Also, he loved "the Island", where I imagine we would always have lived had Uncle Edmund been a different type. We discussed the question of contesting the will and it was I who first uttered the unhappy word "compromise", of which I was to sicken as time went on. What made it all so awkward was that my father was a devout Catholic and very far from enjoying a fight with bishops. The lawyer he at first engaged struck me as rather brilliant, but naturally enough he wanted to use such points as the insistence laid in the will on the funeral sermon being preached by a priest who believed in hell. Today, Edmund declared, most of them do not and the choice must be carefully made. Naturally, a Protestant lawyer rubbed his hands with glee as he thought of the effect of this upon the public. And he said, sensibly enough, that in his view the only hope of winning a compromise lay in collecting strong evidence that we might be able to overthrow the will altogether. With his complete agreement my father changed lawyers, hoping that a Catholic, himself in touch with many of the bishops, could so handle the matter as to effect a compromise without public scandal.

We were slow to see something more wrong with my father than the effects of mental strain inevitable in a man of his temperament. He visited the lawyers incessantly and must have driven them half mad with his imaginative and over-intellectual analyses of motives and possibilities. He went for long walks night after night; he began to look haggard and my mother begged him to see a doctor. Sir Berkeley Moynihan, who had performed a successful operation on Uncle Henry a year or so earlier, could discover nothing seriously wrong and a month in a nursing home was followed by a visit to Buxton.

As the weeks at Buxton passed, it was my father himself who first realized he was a dying man. With the strong resolution of which he had always been capable, he turned from the thoughts of the lawsuit. He could not get up for early Mass but he climbed the hill to the church each day and spent a long time in prayer. He read daily the chapter in the *Imitation*, "The Royal Road of the Holy Cross". Our lawyer was meeting the lawyers of the bishops and of our abbess aunt to discuss the compromise; when we heard of its total failure, Papa neither got angry nor attempted to see his lawyer and discuss other possibilities. He was losing weight alarmingly and we went to Leeds, where Sir Berkeley decided on an immediate exploratory operation. This revealed an inoperable cancer, but Sir Berkeley was of the opinion that another six months of life were probable.

I have told the story fully elsewhere of the six weeks that actually followed: my father's acceptance of God's will was total and his repentance profound for a life on which we could only discover venial spots. Mama and I were with him all the time. Tetta returned from France and Leo came frequently from Oxford. We went south again—but not to Lotus. Obviously, professional care would be needed and Papa was installed in The Nook (a rather remarkable nursing home at Hampstead), Mama, Tetta and I taking lodgings close by.

This was not an altogether unhappy time. We were able to be with him constantly. He would dictate to Tetta or to me the moving letters, some of which are printed in *Insurrection Versus Resurrection*. There was a sense of what our family life had meant, there was a mixture of joy and sorrow in watching the parents together. The dust of daily life sometimes obscures underlying beauty. Now suffering had blown away the dust. After much meditation on the Cross it seemed fitting when death came to my father on Passion Sunday.

For a while everything was indeterminate. I was nursing again, Tetta was with Mama and working at the Admiralty. What would now be called "compassionate leave" had been requested for Herbert, that he might come home from Mesopotamia and decide whether or not the lawsuit should go on. "Go home, my boy," said his Colonel, "and fight all those bishops." At this point the rather absolute Ward mentality of the older generation played an unhappy part. Bernard Ward and his abbess sister had both taken a strong line in favour of Edmund's will. I think they thought of the family treasury as practically inexhaustible, and they were horrified at my father's attitude. Uncle Bernard visited him on his deathbed and full affection was shown between them, but the will was not mentioned.

Now Uncle Bernard assumed, with complete Ward crudity, that the lawsuit would of course be dropped—and this enraged my mother and to a lesser degree myself. Were we tacitly to agree that my father had been wrong, and to tell the world so by our action? The decision of course rested with my brother.

Bernard's bark proved worse than his bite, for a compromise was reached, largely through his effort whereby something was saved from the wreck. Soon after this came my break with the Italian Hospital which put me briefly out of work.

For some time, as I now realize, Sister Pauline had been concerning herself about me, and not merely about my work. She had, early on, suggested that I take the women's ward and let the other nurse have the soldiers. The ward was smaller, I would learn more about nursing without being overworked. But I was intensely eager to nurse soldiers and I rather enjoyed being overworked. Quiet thinking and above all praying had borne little part in my life for a very long time. I went to Sunday Mass, of course, and to the sacraments, but because I thought so little I did not realize that I was not praying. Sister Pauline did, but the finger with which she touched me was too delicate. I really needed batting over the head. My father's death had done this but for a few months I was too stunned for any visible results.

And then came a visit to Aunt Emily, during which, I suppose psychologists would say, certain subconsious elements in my mind rushed to the surface. This may well have been the way of it; God, after all, created the human psyche.

Aunt Emily had talked the entire evening of the past glories of the family. Poor dear, living in the midst of lands for sale, it all came specially hard on her. I went to bed with the words "a noble property" ringing in my ears. I could not sleep and suddenly in the night I felt overwhelmingly that the whole great world, visible and spiritual, could not be narrowed to the proportions of a silly old estate.

I reached for my New Testament and opened it blindly. "The Spirit himself", St. Paul was telling me, "giveth testimony to our spirit that we are sons of God. And if sons heirs also, heirs, indeed, of God and joint heirs with Christ; yet so if we suffer with him that we may be also glorified with him."

What in the world had I been thinking about all this time—what was the matter with me? "For the expectation of the creature waiteth for the revelation of the sons of God. For the creature was made subject to vanity, not willingly, but by reason of him that made it subject in hope, because the creature also itself shall be delivered from the servitude of corruption into the liberty of the glory of the children of God."

"Not willingly", I kept repeating to myself as I thought of my inanities. Not perhaps so much the estate, for that had not been deeply personal, as what I now called the "mucking about" of the last few years, including my foolish ambitions at the hospital. That night I really prayed. The next day, passing through Horsham, I stopped at the church and made a confession poles removed from the superficial catalogues that had become my habit.

Just after this Aunt Gwendy happened to remark that a V.A.D. was wanted for a tiny hospital for incurable soldiers that she had opened at Littlehampton. It seemed ideal for the solitary stock-taking, the start of something new, that I was feeling after. The more she pointed out how dull it would be, that I must not take days off to run over to Arundel, that I would be no staff nurse but only a V.A.D., the more I felt that this was the right thing. My sister being with Mama I had no hesitations on her score, and at Littlehampton I spent at least the next six months.

Nothing could have been a greater contrast to the Italian Hospital. There we had discharged old patients and received new at least once a week. Here in six months one man died, one new case arrived. Visiting was freely allowed, but not many soldiers' relatives could come as far as Littlehampton. At the Italian Hospital there were few men who could not hope for recovery, here we were hopeless of every case save one. The difficulty was immense of keeping a cheerful atmosphere. Constant changes of patients had been, though I had not realized it, almost equal to a change of scene. How thin my poor little jokes wore, how empty we all got of ideas that would cheer our patients. It may well have been in part observation of this little hospital that caused Aunt Anne Kerr later, initiating the idea of St. David's Home for incurable soldiers, to realize that it must be established close to London.

I remember only one visit to Arundel during those months—before I went there in February 1917, for Uncle Henry's funeral. Mama was staying in the house and we walked together along our favourite paths, looking back a little sorrowfully. I have not said much about the wartime background but it certainly added to that sense of the end of the world which we were both feeling. Herbert was back in Mesopotamia. Mails were rare, boats often sank and he was anyhow a bad correspondent. "We must learn to look forward, not back", Mama reminded me, but the young find it desperately hard to stretch their vision into the world to come without some foreground of happiness to be hoped for here and now.

6

THE CATHOLIC EVIDENCE GUILD

After Uncle Henry's death, the hospital at Littlehampton came to an end. Leo, after being repeatedly rejected as a volunteer, was conscripted (classed 3b) and Mama and I decided to make what home we could for him during his training in an officers' cadet corps at Cambridge and later at Southampton, where he was quartered for quite a period.

The rest of the war years are rather blurred in my memory; we moved about so much; were now back at Lotus entertaining Canadian priests and what seemed a whole regiment of Catholic Highlanders; now in lodgings, now in rented houses in London. In 1918 my sister was married at the Oratory to Francis Blundell of Crosby and became a "Lancashire Catholic". They are quite a special breed, being neither Irish nor convert, but deeply rooted in England's Catholic past. The priest's hiding-hole at Crosby had been transformed into a cupboard but the village has kept the stone crosses, so rare in England, and deep in the woods is the Harkirk, to which people come on pilgrimage. It is a tiny chapel built with stones that were piled over the hidden graves of Catholics buried in the persecution years. Some of the stones have faint, broken inscriptions discernible on them. Francis' grandfather had found them lying about and tried twice to build them into a wall. Twice the wall fell down; he dug beneath and found the bones, over which he erected the chapel. Besides this tiny shrine, the solitary church in the village is Catholic—for this has remained a little pocket of pre-Reformation England. No Irish immigration, no converts, certainly no "Italian Mission". It was in Normandy that I later walked through a village where I found the Blundell arms over an archway and heard that the local château was owned by a man called Blondel—the name linked with Richard Cœur-de-Lion, which has become as English now as it once was Norman. But probably the farmers with names like Lightbound or Leatherbarrow are descended from the Saxons, who were there even earlier. I found much to speculate about in Little Crosby and came to love it, but in my own life it belongs to a later chapter.

Besides the party that followed Tetta's marriage, there was at the house we had rented in Ovington Gardens a reception for Muriel O'Conor's wedding with Charles Nevile of Wellingore, Lincolnshire, where his brother was managing his estate and himself farming many acres. Muriel and Charlie's home was for many years in the Sudan, though she was often back at Wellingore as one baby followed another. All three O'Conor sisters were married within one year; Eileen to Prince Matila Ghyka, then naval attaché at the Rumanian Embassy, and Fearga to a cousin of hers and ours, Malcolm Maxwell-Scott.

In a book of this sort a "family tree" would seem absurd, but the ramifications of my mother's family perplex and bewilder the outsider. It amused her to say, "My uncle's wife is my sister's niece"—but it would have been fairer to have said "half sister's". For her father had married twice, so that she and Aunt Mamo Maxwell-Scott had the same father but different mothers. The Maxwell-Scotts and ourselves had a grandfather but not a grandmother in common, Uncle Henry Norfolk was our great-uncle, but not theirs. Aunt Mamo had married a Maxwell, whose niece had later married Uncle Henry. It was not really difficult to work this out, though it might need pencil and paper! The relationship had arisen from a fresh angle when Fearga O'Conor married Malcolm Maxwell-Scott—for they were half first cousins; the dispensation needed for the marriage was given amusingly enough on the ground that Fearga had reached the alarmingly advanced age of twenty-seven.

Mama and I had to live the rest of the war out doing what jobs were asked of us. We decided on selling Lotus, since Herbert on his return would certainly want to live in the "Island". So the Isle of Wight is always called by its natives, and Islanders have, too, a special character. They are amiable and leisurely; I have heard them described as Irish Baptists. We spent a summer there but for the moment our headquarters became London, where we were ever more constantly aware of the war.

English Catholics tend to be violently patriotic and the Pope's efforts to make peace were not much appreciated by their country. A jibe was printed in *Punch* of which two lines ran: "The Pope is in his Vatican, He's thinking of the Pope." But even those who were afraid of a peace not based on total victory were prepared to pray for one that was—at the Oratory one Rosary now succeeded another during a great part of the day. The enthusiasm evoked by the various Rosary campaigns springs perhaps in part from the layman's subconscious awareness that he has lost his proper share in uttering his worship. When the Dialogue Mass is fully and firmly established the Rosary, proper really to private meditation, may get back where it belongs. Anyhow, we all gave it forth with great gusto, at the Oratory, the Cathedral, and elsewhere. And perhaps this is the place to ask the questions: Did the First World War really bring with it a religious revival—and what was the condition of the Catholic body itself?

There is no denying the materialism of the world into which the war broke, nor that there was a reaction as the result of suffering and death towards a greater emphasis on the spiritual. But I wonder how deep this went. People were seeking for solace on any plane. Angels were alleged to have been seen at Mons; Russian soldiers were alleged to have passed through England. Both stories were half believed; both brought a vague comfort.

The witness of the chaplains who had served in the Army and in the hospitals was for the most part negative—there was certainly no anti-clericalism; the chaplains had distributed cigarettes and written letters home, and the men had been friendly and grateful. A book appeared to which chaplains of the various denominations contributed, but the Catholic contribution was finally refused and became a book on its own.

Our chaplains had much to tell of the desire of the Catholics for the last sacraments, of the numbers of others asking for baptism. It looked as though a unique opportunity was offering for the Church, but we had later to echo sadly enough what Newman said seventy years or so earlier: "The Church must be prepared for converts as well as converts for the Church." No one had yet begun the serious examination of Catholic education to which it is being subjected today. There was little talk of lapsed Catholics, but it did gradually become evident that the splendid deathbeds of our soldiers gave no evidence of their ability to show these outsiders what it was that enabled them to die so well or why the Faith made living better for Catholics than for the rest of the world.

There was not in England the reapproach to dogma which had begun so vigorously on the Continent, there was no beginning of a liturgical revival, there was nothing offered to the layman after schooldays were over except pious confraternities or clubs with entertainment value which, it was hoped, would keep Catholics together and result in Catholic marriages.

When the War ended my brother Leo was soon demobilized and at once offered himself to Cardinal Bourne as a priest for the Westminster diocese. Before going, by the Cardinal's advice, to the Procure de Saint-Sulpice in Rome, he was a good deal at home. One day he rushed into the house in wild excitement. "There are Catholic speakers in the Park," he said, "and one of them is magnificent."

The soap-box orator is an acknowledged figure of fun. The Communist sings:

> Long-haired preachers come out every night,
> Try to teach us what's wrong and what's right.

The doctor at a hospital where a speaker was taken after an accident called him "that crackpot"—and when a priest friend repudiated the title, he reiterated, "I've listened to them. They're all crackpots." And indeed, looking at many of the fraternity, one sees his point. *Our* fraternity it was to become; but we were not, we hoped, eccentrics. We were, in fact, attempting something new: not hymn-singing, not emotional appeals, but the development in terms understood by the man in the street of a philosophy of life suited to all men.

The pioneers went to Speakers' Corner, Marble Arch, a well-known spot for the ventilation of ideas. From a row of platforms every possible opinion, political or religious, could be heard. Our new society was called the Catholic Evidence Guild, and a New Zealander, Vernon Redwood, was the founder. Permission had been obtained from the Cardinal and women too might speak.

The idea that training in dogma was necessary did not seem as yet to have occurred to anybody. Leo and I at once joined the Guild, and we shortly afterwards collected one of the best speakers it was ever to possess, Jack Seymour Jonas. He was a convert to the Church and my mother and I, seeing him one morning in uniform at Mass and noticing his Australian hat, thought he might be lonely and invited him home to breakfast. He was, in fact, English but had joined both the Church and the Army in Australia.

A good deal of snobbery is intellectual, but one learns in the Guild atmosphere how little education and intelligence need coincide.

Our best theologian was a charwoman who had not an "h" in her vocabulary, but had a profound knowledge of theology, largely self-taught. Our best scholar—a man who could competently meet problems arising from Hebrew and Greek texts—went to school to her for theology. Other speakers were boys and girls who had left school at fourteen; there were, and still are, teachers, typists, bus-conductors, nurses, scientists, housemaids and professors. We have everybody in the Guild. The united study of theological truth provides a *mental* culture that draws together people separated by degrees of general education.

The main reason for this special quality in the Evidence Guild lies with the crowd. The object of the Guild is to teach anyone who wants to listen about the Catholic faith. We gather our audiences in Hyde Park in London, in the Bull Ring in Birmingham, at the Pier Head in Liverpool, in the Domain in Sydney, on Wall Street or Times Square in New York, at street corners everywhere. And not with speakers only, but with listeners too, we get down to the bed-rock of humanity and discover in day-to-day experience how much more important it is to belong to the human race than to any special section. Our chief novelty as street speakers was that we aimed at the mind, not the emotions, but our founder was also our cross! Full of ardour for the Faith, with a very bad temper, his aim was to give testimony; and, although our rules forbade attacks on other religions, Mr. Redwood could not resist them. Standing on the platform looking down at a rather violent woman heckler, "My dear friends," he began, spreading out his arms, "We love you, every one. We are not out here to attack any man's religion, but Protestantism never saved a cat . . . Stop cackling, you old hen."

But if Mr. Redwood's speaking filled us with shame, most of us also became ashamed of ourselves. It was easy to prepare a lecture along the well-worn lines of Catholic apologetic—but as the questions beat down like hail I began to realize with horror how little I knew after a normal, indeed rather above the average, Catholic education. Listening to some of the other speakers I realized that they knew even less than I.

Some provision had been made for training us, but the Guild experiment was so new a thing that all it called for had not begun to be realized. Dr. Messenger, appointed Director of Studies by the Cardinal, had arranged for lectures at our headquarters, the old

Army hut in the grounds of Westminster Cathedral. Here various priests lectured to us, speaking usually well above our heads, no questions were ever asked *of us*, no examinations held to decide if we were qualified to speak. And the lectures were unconnected, not a course.

I am not sure of the date at which Dr. Arendzen succeeded Dr. Messenger, but it must have been fairly early on. For when a group of us—Mark Symons, James Byrne, our charwoman Louisa Cozens and I—got together to try to devise some real training system, it was from him that we got encouragement and support. Himself a member of the Catholic Missionary Society, who lectured in halls to non-Catholics, Dr. Arendzen realized something of what we had to meet out of doors. Years later, I found a letter in our archives in which he begged Mr. Redwood to consent to an examination for speakers. The trouble was that no examination was thinkable which our founder could have passed! Dr. Arendzen probably realized this, for the decision come to was that the first group of members (in which I happened to be included) need not be examined, but that all joining from now on must pass a test—which at first was very general and lamentably easy.

We had begun with a weekly meeting on Sundays in Hyde Park. But it was obvious that only "good" speakers could be put up there. The heckling was fierce and the questions often difficult. And Catholics came in crowds and were only too apt to report us to Archbishop's House for heresy if they thought we had made a mistake.

Young speakers were flocking in and we soon realized that part of their training must be done on the outdoor platform. *Nobody can learn to do a thing well except by doing it.* We decided to open pitches in more remote parts of London and to let the new young speakers begin under the care of a senior who could get them off the platform if they were out of their depth and could, as chairman, answer the more difficult questions.

Meanwhile a small group of us had drawn up an outline of a dozen or so lectures on subjects beginners could soon handle and had established a second night for intensive preliminary indoor training. We still attended regularly the lectures arranged for us each Wednesday, while on Tuesdays we gave simple talks suitable to an outdoor audience, carefully prepared by a senior, with questions we had had out of doors *to be asked of the class.* Time must be left not only for questioning the class, but for making each of them talk for a few minutes. Much remained to be done in developing the training, but we had already learned something from meeting the unbeliever in flesh and blood.

For the seniors Dr. Arendzen's lectures were the best possible; he not only knew theology at a depth and with a richness I have seldom seen equalled, he had also met these men we were meeting and could give us dogma in modern English, making it accessible to us and to them together. Born in Holland in 1873, he never lost his Dutch accent, yet it was he who first taught us to speak to the Englishman of today in a language he can understand. A considerable scholar, he held high degrees in Semitic philology, and divinity, from Cambridge, Bonn and Munich. He wrote learned books and articles for the *Jewish Quarterly*, *Journal of Theological Studies* etc., but he also wrote popularizations which we could use on the street corner.

He would come down to our headquarters and ask what subject we wanted treated that evening. Ten minutes was all he asked to prepare whatever we chose and we would watch him in a corner of the room while everyone talked around him, preparing with incredible grimaces the finished lecture that would immediately emerge to be followed by a barrage of questions.

His absentmindedness was notorious and we loved especially the story of his housekeeper coming in after awaiting in vain the summoning bell to remove his soup. He was sitting in front of an untouched plate, but starting up on her entry he dipped his finger in the soup, made the sign of the cross and left the table, his dinner uneaten.

Unfortunately, Dr. Arendzen could not often be with us and many of the priests he sent us could not do this urgently needed task of translation. We must learn somehow to do it ourselves—and the available books were depressing me more and more. The slogan with which we had begun our work—to go out and defend the Faith—was showing itself as less and less adequate, yet that is precisely what so many books of apologetics did. "What is the answer to this objection?" "How do you reply to that attack?" It was profoundly unsatisfactory, especially as we tried out the traditional answers on a crowd whose reactions turned out to be quite untraditional.

Our textbooks demolished on paper in a few sentences Luther and Calvin, Hume and Locke, Ingersoll and the Archbishop of Canterbury—but we had to meet Brown, Jones and Robinson in person, and we never found they would stay put after our first glib answer.

Nor did the books allow for a further problem of which our training had to take account. Even Dr. Arendzen's experience had been almost wholly in churches and halls; in other words, speaking to a captive audience—come because they were already interested, but captive still. He himself was so fascinating that any audience would have listened—if they could have heard and understood him. His voice was bad and his accent baffling. We, with all our eagerness, had to strain to follow his lectures; what would an outdoor crowd have done? We knew the answer only too well: they would have walked away.

We passed rather quickly from the slogan "Defend the Catholic Church" to the somewhat better "Prove Catholic doctrines". Our approach was still that of apologetics rather than of theology, but we were moving in the right direction and should have moved faster had we all been moving together. There was now a growing group of speakers who realized the need of study and were prepared to devote time to it. We were also organizing a rapidly increasing number of meetings. We decided to divide these speakers into groups (known as squads), each under a leader and responsible for a certain number of meetings a week. We found also that Hyde Park on weeknights was a first-class training ground, with few Catholics, few silk hats and few educated questioners, all of which elements were present on Sundays. Other nights there were just ordinary listeners and organized opposition secularists, and the dear old Protestant Alliance.

This society, now moribund as far as Hyde Park is concerned, derived its support (we fancied) from retired colonels and old maiden ladies. For some obscure reason we also decided that most of them lived at Cheltenham (although there was a minority vote for Bedford) and that many of them would die of shame if they could see what their money was paying for. "Standing firm for the Lord", it was called in the Protestant Alliance magazine. At the platform it meant constant interruptions, shouts as we made the sign of the cross—"North, South, East and West"—further shouts of "Liar" or "Twister!"—and a good deal of really unpleasant language, especially on the subjects of the Blessed Virgin and the Eucharist.

There could not, in Hyde Park, be physical violence, as the police were never far off, but outlying pitches in those days were quite exciting. Pennies were given by our hecklers to little boys who, on occasion, ran pins into our ankles or tied our shoelaces to the sides of the platform. A ripe tomato might be thrown or a drunk would shake the platform violently. One of our speakers was shaken off at Wood Green; his immediate resumption of the meeting brought him afterwards one convert ("There must be something in it") and one Catholic to train as a speaker.

These things did not happen every day; the worst hazard at Wood Green was an empty street, and that we all dreaded far more than the rowdies. For beginners it was important to alternate the two types of meeting, and we had plenty of both, the exciting and the dreary.

My own squad took charge of Hyde Park Saturdays from 5 to 10 p.m., Finsbury Park Sunday afternoons and Highbury Corner Sunday evenings. We were so enthusiastic that normally we all attended all three meetings, having tea at Lyons' in between discussing the questions we had answered or failed to answer.

The main problem, even in Hyde Park, was how to be interesting enough to keep a crowd. And this problem was for some time solved mainly by personality and light relief. There were other speakers at all places where we spoke and the rule seemed clear—the best speaker gets the crowd. Every meeting was a fight for existence.

One day I was asked to take a new speaker into my squad. He had been allocated elsewhere, but the pitches were geographically inconvenient to him and he had asked for a change. We had already met briefly at a Guild Bazaar at which this new recruit was selling goods at a stall justly labelled "Jumble". He tried to sell me a horrible pair of scissors, the blades crossing each other where they should have cut. I said "Have you no better scissors?" To which he answered, "Madam, there are no better scissors." He had sold those scissors three times and the purchasers had given them back to be sold again. I, being more stingy, merely refused to put down any money. I shall never forget the sense of relief with which I listened to his first speech. One junior had spoken bitterly of my "little squeak of a voice" which held a crowd when his loud one could not. But far from losing my crowd, this new speaker was increasing it.

Nor should I have to criticize his subject-matter—apart from a regrettable tendency to pull the leg of a very disagreeable and illiterate heckler who was lending himself with uncanny skill to the operation. Good heavens, my new speaker knew Latin and was correcting the heckler's garbled quotation! I sighed with relief; now I could sometimes leave a meeting to be chaired by another. That night I sent a postcard to the new speaker, Frank Sheed, in which I said *Deo gratias* that he had come all the way from Australia to join the Catholic Evidence Guild.

Our squad now leaped ahead. Nobody else was taking the outlying pitches very seriously. Redwood thought only of Hyde Park. Jonas took a squad only out of kindness of heart; he was bad as an organizer while miraculous as a speaker. Any meeting at which he was present succeeded brilliantly. But it was quite likely that he had sent a beginner to run another meeting all by himself. The future of the squad system lay with me and my new lieutenant, and within six months we decided to divide our squad into two and open some new pitches. Six months more and we were able again to divide—Maurice Burns taking half of what had been my half, and Mabel Jones, half of Frank's.

The real meaning of the squad system is not always understood; it is not—and as one says in America, I repeat *not*—simply a timetable affair, a method of fixing meetings and seeing that all the members make their speeches. This is a very minor matter. A squad exists to encourage speakers in their quite inevitable fits of depression, to criticize their speaking constructively, encourage them to take tests and attend classes regularly and to provide a social life that will integrate them into the Guild. Frank Sheed especially promoted this by organizing squad teas—held at first in the training hut, with each member of the squad bringing something to eat. We girls jeered when on one occasion almost everyone brought bananas; we would show this male squad-leader! But the competition between squads was always friendly and one of the best effects of the system.

Meanwhile, on the platform we were getting puzzled at not producing more results. We knew our speaking was improving. The classes were turning out better material, there were now tests on each individual subject and practice classes for beginners every Friday. We did not feel on the whole that we failed in developing our proofs even on such subjects as the existence of God—anyhow, we did not often lose the arguments. Our crowd let us know fast enough when we did. But somehow we were not making converts, and we were still wearily working at finding snappy introductions to keep the attention of our audience. I remember a beginner once opening with, "Ladies and gentlemen, did you ever see a corpse?" After a moment's silence a disgusted voice from the crowd said, "Purgatory" and this was, in fact, his subject. "Purgatory", "Confession" and "the Pope", all had some entertainment value; and, interestingly enough, such conversions as we heard of came more often from lectures on Confession than on any other subject. But some of the comments on our efforts were disquieting—and it can hardly be too much emphasized that we outdoor speakers are the only people almost morbidly aware of exactly what our audiences are thinking. "All right," said a heckler one day, "you say Christ claimed to be God and proved His claims were true. So what?" That "So what?" rang in our ears even more than an old woman's comment, "Young man, you may talk till you're black in the face, but you never will convince me that your Pope is God."

We considered these two remarks a little gloomily. The second showed that, although in fact the speaker had given a lecture on papal infallibility theologically correct and quite clear to a Catholic, it had taught this particular member of the audience nothing whatever about what it meant. This must be equally true with the "So what?" after the lecture about Christ's divinity. No one seeing *what it meant* could have remained so indifferent, so bored. Gradually it dawned upon us: our two problems were one and the same; we must interest the crowd, not by remarks on the side, but by the intrinsic interest of what we had to tell them. And it was no use to prove a doctrine to them if they did not understand what it meant.

We only saw this gradually and as we saw it we passed on to our third slogan: from "defend" we had moved to "prove", but it was a far bigger step to move from "prove" to "explain". It was useless to prove Christ's claim to Godhead to men who knew nothing about the God He was claiming to be, and whose whole idea of Christ Himself lay in some odd line of a hymn they had learned in childhood such as, "Gentle Jesus, meek and mild". We must show them the Christ of the Gospels as He spoke to Pharisees and overturned the tables of the moneychangers as well as when He looked on Peter or Magdalen to forgive them. *This* man was God.

It was useless to tell people about papal infallibility when they had not even begun to take in what revelation meant or how infallibility was its guardian—when most of them set no value on truth at all in the religious sphere, which was for them only a matter of sentiment.

It was useless to prove to them that God existed unless they knew something of what God meant; there must be at least some dawning in their minds of the doctrine of the Trinity. This was true above all for the Jews, of whom there are always numbers in every crowd and whose minds are among the liveliest we have to meet.

It was years before we would see all this clearly, but early on we began to grope in the direction of getting more theological reality into our speeches, of understanding better the mentality of our crowd so that they should be interested not by our oratory but by our subject-matter, above all of learning more and more of the dogmas we had to teach and developing better methods of teaching them.

We had felt from the beginning that each speaker must develop along the lines proper to his own mind, but it would take some time for him to discover this. Meanwhile he must talk about something with which he was familiar while continuing to learn simultaneously from classes indoors and from hecklers outside. Beginners could talk on the visible Church, confession, the Pope, the Bible, on the Church, the use of images—and in the early days there were plenty of questions on these subjects. Later on one type of mind would go deeper into history, another revel in theology. But it was a stumbling-block in the path of the Guild's progress that so few people joined us whose education had progressed to a university level; even today after forty years I could count the Oxford and Cambridge speakers in Guild history on my fingers.

But how many first-rate minds there were, among speakers and crowds, who only needed the impetus and guidance that we were learning how to give them! Our theological charwoman was not the only example of mental power of a high order self-developed or awaiting development.

Learning how to train the crowds' teachers would have been easier and faster but for other factors. Ours was not the only society

Mr. Redwood had founded—there was also the "Fellowship of Freedom and Reform"—the object of which was to fight against Prohibition. Whether or not there was any real danger of this in England, the brewers were willing to pay men to speak against it, and salaries for this were offered to our most promising Guildsmen, most of whom refused them. Mr. Redwood, convinced that Prohibition was anti-Christian, held this society to be a crusade in the same way as the C.E.G. There could be no meeting of minds between our group, endeavouring to penetrate the Church's doctrines and to teach them, and a man who could say, "Don't you want to do God's work all day instead of only in the evenings?" He would not or could not face the fact that this new society was paid by the brewers, that speakers were more than hesitant about appearing on its platform side by side with their Catholic one, that some of us felt such a combination spelt disaster for the Guild. We had now to turn with sighs and groans from the development of our work to a fight for its life as an organization.

The Guild Master can only hold office for two consecutive years. In 1920 Mark Symons succeeded Vernon Redwood. His sympathies were entirely with the theological party, but in 1921 the yearly elections would take place once more and it was certain that the Freedom and Reform group would put forward another candidate. The number of speakers and pitches had grown that year at an amazing rate; had the election rested with the speakers there would have been no problem—they were almost 100% with us. But there was a vast mass of associate members, dubbed by us "Pay and Pray", subscribing to the Guild funds and promising us their prayers. They outnumbered the speakers greatly; they were almost 100% behind Mr. Redwood and each of them had a vote. As the speakers increased and the work developed, such a situation became fantastic, but the only way out appeared to be for us to persuade the associate members to disenfranchise themselves. We planned most eloquent speeches but felt little hope of prevailing. And then the Cardinal intervened.

By the constitution of the Guild the lay officers were and are elected by the members, but the bishop of the diocese is the president and he appoints clerical officers—the Director of Studies, clerical secretary, and examining chaplains. The C.E.G. is diocesan in character, each diocese having its own guild. Cardinal Bourne's was the first guild in England and none could have been more fortunate in its president. A certain reserve and coldness of manner masked the immense courage and generosity of which the Cardinal was capable. There was much opposition to the very idea of the Guild among old-fashioned clergy and laity—it was a danger to the Church to have laymen speaking publicly, a degradation for the Church to resort to these Salvation Army methods. Quietly, with an occasional pull that reminded us he held the reins, the Cardinal supported us. When we published the first edition of our *Training Outlines* he wrote the introduction—suggesting that priests might find the book useful in preparing their sermons. It is hard today to realize how revolutionary such a remark appeared.

It would be hard to exaggerate the debt we owe to Cardinal Bourne, especially at this crisis in our existence. I had been well aware of his close attention to what was happening in Hyde Park, through one of his secretaries, Mgr. Jackman, who would ring me up from time to time to ask abruptly, "What's this I hear about the meeting last Sunday?" I knew too that the Cardinal would himself listen from time to time and that he was on the whole well satisfied.

And now Mgr. Coote, his other secretary, announced that His Eminence wished to have the case for a change in the constitution and the case against it laid before him. Anyone who liked might write him a letter on the subject. The speakers' party sent about fifty letters, the other party only three or four. So Mgr. Coote told us, after communicating the Cardinal's decision, that thenceforward only active members should vote.

This announcement was made at a Wednesday-evening class and pandemonium followed. James Byrne was chairman at the lecture and one of the opposition party—a young Cathedral priest—tried to pull his chair from under him. Laymen stood up—one of them a convert clergyman—shouting that they would appeal to Rome. The idea was pure comedy, of a congregation of Italian cardinals—or perhaps the Pope himself—appealed to against the English cardinal's decision about the society he had created.

A week later came the elections. It seems very odd today when the problem of names only arises if there are three Jims or two Margarets of whose second names one is not certain, but I find it hard to remember the first names of most of our early speakers. We called the men Sheed, Symons, Byrne, the girls Miss this or that.

And when two names were alike, Byrne and Burns, we distinguished between them by (for example) calling the former "Big Byrne". Big Byrne was one of our ablest speakers and trainers, but given to language held in those days to be unsuitable in the presence of ladies or the clergy. After a particularly explosive sentence a priest said to him, "That's not the way to talk", to which he replied (unanswerably), "It's the way I talk." Frank Sheed was lecturing one Wednesday in our hall when he heard voices behind him. Byrne was in the chair, and Redwood had got on the platform and was speaking in an angry and powerful whisper, "You dare to call me a bloody liar—me a daily communicant!" Byrne's reply was brief: "They're the worst." Frank continued to lecture about the Incarnation.

It is one of the Guild's most signal triumphs that we were able to use Big Byrne's remarkable talents and to prune his language just enough for platform purposes. Indoors he remained uninhibited and it was a marvel that after his speech in favour of Symons our gentle and admirable Master was re-elected. For at this point a message arrived from Mgr. Coote to say that no election speeches were to be made, so the other side had no chance of committing themselves by rash words.

At this time the constant anxiety about what he would do or say next obscured for me Byrne's great value as one of our founding members. We could no more have done without him than without Miss Cozens. It was not only the mental power he put into planning the classes; his very violence on the platform had an odd but most useful effect on the crowd. The term "wowser" belongs to Australia, but the suspicion of humbug is linked with religious lecturing in every country. Byrne's language took the Guild out of that atmosphere altogether. No "dearly beloved" about him. He could not have dressed truth up to make it look nicer; he could not have concealed a scandal in Church history. We certainly did not want our speakers to use the word "bloody", but Byrne's vehemence did break down the suspicion that we were another lot of "do-gooders", refusing to face the realities of this world and pointing from an unreal earth to a mythical heaven.

When our speaking first began the Guild was defined as a society of lay men and women. It was believed (mistakenly, as it proved) that it was possible, without experience of street speaking, to train street speakers. Hence it happened that for many years the priests who spoke outdoors did not do the training or examining. The first was Fr. Arthur Day, S.J., and we never had among the clergy a more wholehearted Guildsman. He haunted the platform at Marble Arch, speaking not only on Sundays but on week-nights, staying on after speaking, talking things over with hecklers and lapsed Catholics. After him Fr. Dukes carried on the same day-to-day apostolate. I shall never forget the old lady who had been a nun for twenty years and out of the Church for twelve. She came one day to the pitch and blasphemed the crucifix so vehemently that our outdoor secretary said, "That woman must once have been a Catholic." Day after day she came back, at last capitulating to grace but stating that only to Fr. Dukes could she make the confession of those many years. She made her general confession and not long after the Guild, on pilgrimage to Rome, brought back for her the Pope's blessing. Despair had been her problem rather than the loss of faith, and it was wonderful to see her now happily preparing for death.

The struggle with despair brings to mind a priest who from his more brilliant gifts has overshadowed in people's memory Frs. Day and Dukes. For Father Vincent McNabb used to maintain that the loss of hope was *the* great tragedy of our world today. He would point out in the retreats he loved to give us that when the priest cries out at Mass "Sursum corda" the people answer, with a touch of indignation, "Habemus ad Dominum." He longed that the heart perpetually on high should be the mark of the Guildsman. Someone once quoted, "He who fights and runs away will live to fight another day." "No, he won't", said Father Vincent. "He'll live to run away another day." My memories are even more abundant of what he did for us speakers than of his great apostolate to the crowds. He loved to preach on St. Peter's epistles and I realized as never before the meaning of the "kingly priesthood" in which we all had our share. Intensely democratic even in the spiritual sphere, he would remind us that no private revelation given to the highest saint was equal to the Our Father, which Christ had given to us all.

Father Vincent would do the strangest things. I was startled one day, kneeling for his blessing, when he too dropped to his knees. There we knelt a while, side by side, talking eagerly. But it was something again to see him kneel in Parliament Hill Fields and kiss the feet of a particularly nasty heckler. The first time this happened the man was stunned, the second time he rallied and said, "Get up, McNabb, you're only play-acting." And as Father Vincent dusted the earth off his habit he said quietly, "Well, well, it's hard to tell, isn't it?"

But how the crowd loved him! Once I am told they ducked in the pond a heckler at Hampstead who had gone too far. "You're going to hell, McNabb," the man would shout, "and you know it." At Regent's Park the old lady whom he addressed as "Mother" became known to us as "Mrs. McNabb". She was difficult for the rest of us to cope with. "Thou shalt forgive thy brother", she would shout in stentorian tones, "until seventy times seven—and not once more." At this point we were lucky if her teeth fell out (as they generally did), for this gave us the chance of being heard while she was adjusting them. But she would always listen to Father Vincent.

A Jew, Edward Siderman, who has heckled us now for forty years, wrote a book about him, called *A Saint in Hyde Park*. It gives a most vivid picture. All through the year Father Vincent would walk in his Dominican habit from Haverstock Hill to Marble Arch or some other pitch. He told us he often heard an argument going on as to whether he was a man or a woman. He knew all the pitches, but Marble Arch was where he spoke oftenest. And once a year he became the chief inspiration of one of our most important developments: the Hyde Park Retreat.

During Holy Week we decided ordinary meetings should be superseded by a series of sermons. There would be no questions, we hoped, no interruptions. And on Good Friday we showed some very large Stations of the Cross, our men speakers taking turns in holding them aloft on one platform while the preacher spoke from the other. Down to his death Father Vincent always preached these stations. His well-worn Bible was stuffed with notes he had made in preparation; like all his speaking, this was intensely scriptural. The Stations lasted an hour and a half, the crowd grew constantly. One year the police estimated 5000, and his unaided voice reached to the edges of the crowd and beyond it to casual passers-by, who would at least look briefly at the pictures and catch some few words of the meditations. For they were true meditations and very few in that multitude were wholly deaf to them or to the singing by the Catholics of the verses beginning, "God of mercy and compassion, Look with pity upon me."

After each station this hymn was sung and an act of contrition repeated. But the realization of what sin is and the motives for sorrow became even more powerful when on the following day Father Vincent examined the crowd's conscience for them. Taking the Ten Commandments, he would tell them he wanted no word of confession from them but only that they should look at themselves and tell God that they grieved over their failures to their fellow men and to Him their Creator.

But a priest friend of mine heard the confession, as he walked through the Park, of a Catholic out of the Church for thirty years, who had looked and listened on Good Friday. Nor was this a solitary instance; we would prepare for Father Vincent and our other preachers by begging the prayers of contemplatives everywhere, and especially at the Tyburn Convent near by, where in perpetual adoration of the Blessed Sacrament, nuns pray always for England's faith on the spot where the Martyrs died for it.

Retreats still go on in Hyde Park, the stations are still made, but no-one, for me, has ever replaced Father Vincent.

7

TOWARDS CHANGE

I could not give as much time to the Guild as I should have liked during the first two years of its existence. Family life still had its claims, and while my brother Leo was at the Procure de Saint-Sulpice in Rome, Mama and I spent some time there. We met Mrs. Strong of the British School and were initiated into the splendours of Baroque. Hearing her recite Browning in St. Peter's was a memorable experience. "Earth breaks up, time drops away"—written by him of Mass in that central church of Christendom—comes true in such moments. But Rome was much more than a series of great moments. It was a mounting power, almost a pressure of history on the mind. Even at the Cambridge convent I had been taught history badly and cared little for it, but in a tiny way antiquity had come to me through the Classics, the Church through her worship and her saints. Here in Rome it all came alive and I felt like a friend we made who had lived there forty years: "Every summer", he said, "I visit other cities. I exhaust them all but Rome is inexhaustible."

A period followed when my mother lived with my eldest brother at Cowes, and I went up and down between there and London. It was the oddest contrast. Egypt House, which now belonged to Herbert, was well known, having been for more than a century a social centre rented by various hostesses for Cowes Week. Traditions abounded, especially of Edward VII. We were told how he had driven a donkey up the stairs at Egypt. Several ladies in the town would hint delicately concerning the King, their mothers and themselves. The place had a faded air outside its famous week, but Egypt itself is very lovely, especially when the fruit trees are in flower. From the top of the garden you see through the blossoms the attractive red-brick house, the lawn and the sea. You walk through a narrow picturesque street, hardly ever losing sight of the water, or up a steep hill to the larger house, Northwood Park, an example of very good work of a very bad period, then empty, later presented by my brother to the town of Cowes.

The whole island is within an easy car drive, almost within a walk, and I was soon heartily sick of it. Social life there bored me—and I was still too little provided with the "resources" of which Mrs. Elton used to boast. I wanted a definite purpose for reading or study—in fact, I was craving for the Guild. Mama fully sympathized and there followed a series of arrangements for me in London, including a period as a paying guest with the John Bolands in St. George's Square, whence I could easily get to our training centre, to Marble Arch and elsewhere.

John Boland, as a young man, had won the tennis doubles at the Olympic Games. For many years he had been an Irish Nationalist member of the House of Commons, but Sinn Fein had finished his parliamentary career. He was now living in London with his delightful Australian wife and a large family. Eileen Boland was a woman of intense energy, much of which she devoted to the Catholic Truth Society, founded thirty years earlier by Cardinal Vaughan, then Bishop of Salford, and James Britten, who was still its secretary. But he was getting old and Mrs. Boland and I did not really do a wise thing by bringing into the picture another old man—Mr. Reed Lewis. An American settled in England, he had collected a large and excellent Catholic Postal Library with many borrowers and the slogan, "No fees, no fines, no formalities." Donations and his own generosity kept the library going and we believed that a marriage between the pamphlet-producing C.T.S. and this free library would have the happiest results.

Frank Sheed had left Australia, as he thought only for a year. He had taken an arts degree at Sydney University with First Class Honours in Latin, French and English, and was reading Law. Halfway through his law course, he had decided to visit Europe—once practising at the Bar, it might be impossible to get away. He half thought of going to a German university for some more Latin—the New South Wales Education Department would have financed him. He had no intention of staying on in London. It was the Guild that caught and held him there. It drove all ideas of further university study out of his head. If he wanted to stay in London, he must get a job—perhaps with a law firm, perhaps teaching. An organizing secretary was wanted for the Catholic Truth Society's Forward Movement. Still with a year's absence in mind and every intention of returning to Sydney to go on with law, he took the job. He stayed in it for four years.

Obviously the movement had to begin by increasing its membership, and it was Frank's idea to get priests to give special sermons in churches up and down the country. Money was plentiful after the war, and the society did not ask for a collection then and there. We merely distributed membership forms—and the number that came in was phenomenal, both at ten shillings a year and at a guinea.

In the provinces there was more interest in the Guild than in the C.T.S., and Frank and I were both asked to talk about it, to help start it, to return for the opening of classes and initial outdoor meetings; Manchester especially we nursed assiduously, going up by a night train to get an extra day on the job. Birmingham we did not start (I think Fr. Hugh Pope did) but we spoke there in the Bull Ring. Jack Jonas and I spoke at a first meeting in Liverpool; Frank and I again at Leicester, where no platform was available for the first outdoor meeting and we stood on the widest edge of a horse-trough in the market place.

I remember classes and outdoor meetings at Newcastle, Derby and Nottingham. The Londoners' questions were all asked by the Derby crowds. Later I would find the same thing in America and Australia. Both the prejudices against the Church and the difficulties presented by religion are the same wherever you go. An experienced Guildsman is amused by the conviction firmly held everywhere by fellow speakers that *their* crowds are different, *their* situation unique. Liverpool and New York citizens have assured me with equal fervour that no Londoner can understand their people. And from somebody in every city we heard two objections with which we presently began to open our own propaganda meetings: "The time is not yet ripe", and "The local conditions are peculiar."

That year, 1922, the C.T.S. bought the library and I became honorary librarian. But the reckoning of finance at the centre was so sketchy that the promised gift of every pamphlet published to every guinea subscriber looked like ruining us. Expensive offices had been taken. The library had to charge a fee to pay its rent and buy new books; further libraries throughout the country, though promised, never came into being.

Another problem was the relation between London and the provinces. Representatives came to the meetings from the three chief branches: Birmingham, Manchester, Liverpool. Mrs. Boland, Frank Sheed and I knew them well, and our sympathies were with them when our then chairman, Bishop Bidwell, would delay discussions of their resolutions, regardless of (or because of) the fact that they had trains to catch, or would ignore their very legitimate grievances against the parent society. There is such a thing as London provincialism and our chairman was a bad case of it. He *could* not see that anything really mattered outside the metropolis. Fr. Maturin had once told me he could never look at Bishop Bidwell without thinking that his head was exactly like an egg, and longing for a spoon to crack it with. In those days I derived comfort from this "conceit"—and even more when, climbing the stairs for a reception at Archbishop's House, I heard a Spanish relative of his call out, "Hurry up, Manuelito!" But however small he was, however egglike his head, he was very powerful as our chairman, with the kind of blocking power that a man skilful at the game can always command.

In 1924 Frank went back; his law course must be finished and at that time his prospects in life appeared to be linked with being called to the Bar. Before he left England he asked me to marry him, and I asked for time to think it over.

Why I needed to think it over the Lord alone knows, but thought was not easy in the weeks that followed. Before Frank left, there had been considerable stirring of anti-feminism in the Guild. Sometimes this took quaint forms. Two speakers married, the wife at once stopped speaking, and when Frank asked the husband why, the dialogue ran:

"I can't imagine Our Lady on an outdoor platform."

"*I* can't imagine Our Lady married to you."

More serious was the suggestion that women should not hold office, which Frank countered with the remark, "The best man must always have the job, even if that man happens to be a woman." We both agreed, however, that the Master of the Westminster Guild ought to be a man—at that date especially, it would have been an awful proclamation of the poverty of the land had we been unable to produce a capable man. Frank had succeeded Mark Symons in 1922 and 1923, and Leslie Squire succeeded him.

Squire was the most distinguished scholar the Guild ever had. He had taken honours in Hebrew at Oxford. He was an able speaker but so shortsighted as to be almost blind; it was curious to watch him moving a book before his eyes as he peered from word to word. Wholly free from a not uncommon male littleness, he did not attempt to conceal his reliance on my practical advice and organizing, and the anti-feminist party took alarm, with one comic result. Having no man of real distinction, they put forward a first-rate woman to contest the position of Chairman of the Practical Training Committee with me. Although she spoke a great deal out of doors—and most brilliantly—she never came to classes and was not familiar with the training system. Our youngest members became terribly party-spirited on both sides, her supporters putting a notice on the board that if elected she would come regularly, mine pinning up the retort that whether elected or not I would always be there.

On the night of the elections, although I won by a large majority, I was loudly accused of cheating by several young men. My nerve was not, I think, shaken, but my spirits were. Morning after morning I woke up with my face streaming with tears; it took me absurdly long to recover.

It is a strange thing in human nature that a difference in principle can never be merely that. Personalities must come in, and I think mine was often aggressive. When Barnabas wanted to take Mark on his second missionary journey and Paul disagreed, there arose, we are told, a "paroxysm" between them. It is a comfort for us lesser folk to realize that our work for God may be "clouded by too much opinion", as Belloc has so well put it, and may, none the less, remain His work.

Everyone was rather unhappy after the election, and anxious to make amends. The year went much better than I had expected. The men I had to work with were all real Guildsmen and in the committees we found ourselves ready to agree on most of what was to be done. But the loss of our most energetic speaker and organizer meant hard work. I told my mother of the question I had been asked and we went together to Lourdes to beg Our Lady to help me with the answer. On our return I sent Frank a cable in Latin hoping to baffle the Post Office.

The rest of that eighteen months was very happy. Leo had left the Procure after less than a year to try his vocation with the Jesuits. After two years there he had emerged in a state of shattered health. Mama and I felt it a matter of prime importance to help him to rebuild his life. I broke my work in the summer in order to join him in the mountains at Chambery. On the way I stayed a night with the Bolands at a little place called Wissant not far from Boulogne.

Through my bedroom window came "murmers and scents of the infinite sea". After a London street the sound was sheer enchantment. The Bolands' cottage was a hotel annexe with a tiny garden crammed with herbs and vegetables. Strange how well I remember those sounds and sights and scents. There are hours in life of a strange liberation, a realization of its possibilities, that must be akin to heaven when we get back our risen bodies. I spent the next night in a cathedral town, the name of which I have forgotten, ate an omelette, *petits pois* and Gruyère cheese, listening to the bells and gazing across the square at the cathedral. Every sense was satisfied. The next day I looked for the first time at snow mountains, crimson in the sunset.

Neither Leo nor I was a climber but every day our walks—which appeared to me remarkably like climbs—grew longer and steeper. We revelled in the mountains and I went home full of ambitions and plans for a happy and fruitful future.

8

INCIPIT VITA NOVA

After this holiday the months whizzed by. The library was prospering and I found a successor for myself in a Guildswoman, Dorothy Banks Warner, who made a splendid job of it. Gravenor Hewins, son of the founder of the London School of Economics, an Oxford man and an able lawyer, had become Master of the Guild with everybody's good will.

While Frank was cramming his two-years-in-one for his final law examinations, he had also started the Guild in Sydney and spoke every Sunday in the Domain under a huge Morton Bay fig tree. When thirty years later I stood under that tree myself, I envied the Guildsmen of Sydney. It was not fair they should have such a perfect umbrella in so sunny a country—and yet it was, for the tree was really a parasol against the fierce sun for speakers and listeners. It is, too, a sounding-board adding volume to the voice. Frank left a magnificent Guildsman in Sydney, whom he had trained. A distinguished barrister, Peter Gallagher later refused a judgeship because if he took it he would no longer be able to speak in the Domain. What made this more remarkable was that the Guild in Sydney encountered even more difficulties than in London, and has never grown to be more than a small, little-considered group. Peter had lost an arm in the War, he was a gentle man with no pushfulness, though with much of the native Australian energy. He carried on for more than thirty years and his untidy figure and friendly face as he stood under the fig tree is my clearest memory of my first introduction to the C.E.G. in Australia.

During his time in Australia Frank was impounded by Sydney University to debate against a visiting Oxford team: Malcolm Macdonald, Douglas Woodruff and Christopher Hollis. The last two came to listen to him in the Domain. Douglas enquired if he knew Maisie Ward and remarked that he supposed one day they would both have to be doing this themselves. I wish they had!

Meanwhile I was flat-hunting; not so hard a task then as today but still formidable enough. But we were wonderfully lucky. Albany

Mansions faced Battersea Park and was backed by grass and trees. We were to be married from Egypt House, my brother giving me away. One aunt accompanied her gift of silver with the admonition to have Frank's crest put on the spoons and forks at her expense. I smiled at the notion of my Australian's crest; I wonder why I did not think of a koala bear, a kangaroo or even a heraldic waratah.

It was a curious feeling being engaged all by myself, getting everything ready, receiving my engagement ring by post; we had written by every mail ever since Frank's departure but there was no airmail in those days and letters came very slowly. I hardly know what I should have done but for Mama. Leaving her, even though only for a flat across the river, was the real rub. I remember telling her of Mrs. Moberly, who, after her daughter's death, said she felt widowed over again. And Mama had answered, "I should feel the same." Mother and daughter can, I believe, get closer together than anyone else except husband and wife, and Mama told one of our dearest friends, Catherine Ashburnham, that she felt tempted to jealousy for the first time in her life.

Strange that I have not mentioned Catherine sooner. She was a fascinating person with talents enough to scatter her abundant energy almost too widely. Had she been a boy she would have been Lord Ashburnham and I felt like Mrs. Bennet in *Pride and Prejudice* about the nature of an entail when I first learnt that her large property must go to a cousin of the name of Bickersteth.

Catherine, when I first knew her, was living in Wales, where she had built up a Catholic mission, playing the organ on Sundays, seconding the priest's efforts in every way and tearing round the country on a motor-bike. Staying in London, she had joined the Guild, was above the average as a speaker and could even have become a great one. When she moved to Ashburnham she became absorbed in the place, having her friends to stay and making it a centre for Grail Camps and other Catholic activities—but also restoring the pictures, winding the (I think fifty) clocks herself, caring for every detail in house, garden and estate. We had dug her out for my wedding and it was a joy to think that she had promised to stay on with Mama at Eygpt after my sister and the aunts and uncles had departed. Some of the relatives had arrived; I had met the beloved "Funny Uncle Edmund" and his wife at Cowes pier.

And Frank's ship from Australia was nearing port—not, alas, our neighbouring port of Southampton.

Our English railway system is such that I had to go to London in order to get from the Isle of Wight to Plymouth, where I met him. Back through London to the Island again, and Frank underwent on the eve of his wedding an experience that would come to me more than a quarter of a century later—meeting some twenty new relatives all together. And here I must allow myself a digression which explains problems in Guild and family alike that I should perhaps have discussed earlier.

The chief of these, underlying many Guild rows and always present for English-speaking Catholics, was nationality. My very English uncle Bernard Ward, who was a first-rate historian, found himself regarded almost as a traitor in old English Catholic circles for making obvious statements about the Irish Immigration—its proportionate numbers, the degree to which it had strengthened English Catholicism. On the other hand, the Irish, with equal unfairness, moved these very English Englishmen to wrath by assuming that only the Irish could really be Catholics at all. "This godless country" was a phrase heard only too often from the pulpit in warning to the Irish who had left their country for ours.

I had long broken with my family's Conservatism by becoming a Home Ruler. They did not take my politics very seriously; nor did I, but staying with the Bolands clarified my views still further about Ireland. John Boland had been Redmond's secretary and the Nationalists had appeared just before the War to have achieved all that most Irishmen wanted; the Liberal Government had promised Home Rule—and had then disgracefully yielded to the Ulster threats of rebellion. I still believe that had Home Rule been given then Ireland would have been today contentedly integrated within the Commonwealth. Anyhow, Sinn Fein followed the Liberal betrayal—and I was now witnessing the absurdity of Catholic Conservatives appealing to the Nationalists to rally Irish loyalty to England. Eily Boland, much less placid than her husband, would come home raging over the whole situation, "Can't they see", she would say, "that the Irish hate us now more than anybody?" Their position was certainly a difficult one, but it was for a long time held by immense numbers of Irishmen. "Ireland is my mother," Father Vincent McNabb used to say, "England is my wife." There really was a dual loyalty, especially in those who had lived in both countries, and had, as they believed, served both countries in Parliament or still more in Army or Navy.

To be a Home Ruler meant to be in alliance with those many Irish who held that the fullest national development was compatible, not with Unionism, but with an Ireland having its own Parliament in Dublin for home affairs, sending its representatives to Westminster for matters imperial. Such was the faith I still shared, and I well remember the shock with which I heard Frank say that one of his reasons for coming over here was a hope to "get mixed up in the troubles" then going on in Ireland. I loathed the Black and Tans with all my soul, but I still thought of Irish rebels not as patriots but as traitors.

Frank and I were, however, in deep agreement to let no political issue affect our work of spreading the Catholic faith. We discovered with pleasure that we had arrived from opposite ends at the same conclusion—all politicians broke their promises and it was not worth voting for either party. For a first-rate man *in* either we might have voted, but that was a different question. Anyhow, from this detached standpoint we really did succeed in keeping political peace in the Guild, he arguing with the Irish when necessary and I with the English.

I had been very doubtful how the family would take my Guild activities. Mama, of course, was marvellous: she herself trained as a speaker and spoke outdoors. I may say that that took enormous courage. If I, fairly young and becoming increasingly rebellious against convention, still felt faintly embarrassed when I glimpsed under a silk hat the face of an amazed acquaintance, what must it have been for her in her late fifties, traditionally educated, wearing the widow's dress that was still customary, a heckler shouting at her "Widows is wicked", when she saw one day in the crowd a friend from the Foreign Office valiantly endeavouring to pretend that he did not see her!

Mama did not join the Guild at the beginning and my first intimation that my aunts had heard about me came from Aunt Anne Kerr, who told me with a smile that a hat I was wearing looked just like a Salvation Army lassie's bonnet. So, the murder was out; I knew Aunt Anne would be sympathetic, but after all she lived in Scotland! And then, to my amazement, Aunt Philippa Stewart began attending our meetings. She had always, she said, prayed for the conversion of England and this was the first time anybody had done anything about it. For good or ill Aunt Philippa's reactions were always exaggerated and for a while I glimpsed her approving countenance day after day in the crowd or in the Hut.

And then came the catastrophe. The Lord Mayor of Cork had gone on hunger strike in protest against the treatment of political prisoners. Theologians were arguing as to whether his death was or was not suicide. I never heard them use the argument which convinced me it was not. No suffragette had ever been allowed to die. They had always been forcibly fed, despite all their protests. So Terence McSwiney was running a risk of death, but not committing suicide. One day our Secretary, giving out the notices, asked our prayers for him. I have never been able to see how it could be wrong to pray for a man because you thought *him* wrong, but doubtless our Irish Secretary's own feelings were made plain enough in the announcement. Aunt Philippa walked out, caught Dr. Arendzen on a bus and expressed her views with considerable vigour. She never came near the Guild again. Curiously enough, this was the last "political demonstration" that could even be suspected in Guild history.

And now I was marrying an Australian who, although his grandfather had come from Aberdeen, was three-quarters Irish in descent and certainly no Conservative. Amazingly Aunt Philippa took to him with an instant affection which never grew less. But as the family assembled at Cowes for the wedding day my mother and brother were worrying not about the bridegroom but about the bishop. Our then Bishop of Portsmouth was Irish of the Irish. During the War he had written a pastoral so violent in its attack on England that I had gone to the sacristy afterwards and told the priest I had found it hard to go to Communion after listening to his words—and if I, why not others? The Isle of Wight was, after all, English.

Nothing better shows the gulf between us than the fact that our priest was *amazed* at my reaction. "I thought you would agree", he said and then: "He only attacked the Government." But when at last I made him understand, he promised if any more such letters came from Bishop's House, he would read them only in the evening at Benediction and announce in the morning what we had ahead of us.

I don't suppose the bishop was aware of any of this; he and my brother worked well together on local affairs and were very friendly. Herbert, unlike many Conservatives, united strong views with a real enjoyment in meeting opposition. Now the bishop had offered, our episcopal uncle being dead, to marry Frank and me. Not only Aunt Philippa but also another aunt had expressed a fervent dislike of being in the same room with him. The worst to be feared from either of them was a glacial manner which he would, we hoped, think just typically English. Fortunately the house was a large one. Before and after dinner we kept the bishop in the billiard room, the aunts in the drawing-room. During dinner my brother had the aunts at one end of the table, my mother the bishop at the other end. Ireland was not mentioned and the evening went well.

How I enjoyed our wedding. The little church, built by a French *émigré* priest, is very simple and dignified. The schoolchildren were grouped around the steps and in the church carrying bunches of primroses, the sun came out when it ought. The wedding breakfast was a real meal eaten at tables and almost everyone present was a dearly loved friend or relative. Kathy Howard was my one child bridesmaid and Gravenor Hewins was Frank's best man.

We had a great packet of letters from Mr. Belloc advising us how to plan our honeymoon, especially in regard to food and drink. Our first dinner must positively be eaten at the Vendanges de Bourgogne in Paris—which we always located by its nearness to a statue which, though a female figure, reminded us of Nelson's Column. We used to call it Lady Hamilton. Belloc's directions ended with France. For Venice and the Lakes we depended on the commonplace guidebook and the high-souled Ruskin. Frank in Venice threatened an early divorce with Ruskin as co-respondent, but the Lakes cooled my artistic fervour.

We finished our honeymoon by arriving at Grayshott just in time for the Whitsun Retreat. For the first time I was at the hotel instead of in the convent—and I felt that life was, as usual, unfair to women if they were not married. As silence fell within the convent walls the inhabitants of the pub were having their first drink. Certainly we made better retreats in the convent—but after all, the Guild vocation was not a silent one.

After my first cable to Australia many letters and cables had been exchanged discussing the future. I have told in *Insurrection versus*

Resurrection something of my mother's reasons for desiring a new Catholic publishing house. She felt keenly that each author was at present working on his own and was, moreover, almost compelled to publish with a non-Catholic firm. The existing Catholic houses dealt almost exclusively with prayer-books and works of piety or else, like Herder's, with immense books for the specialist. She and my father had been well served by Longmans, but she was convinced that intelligent Catholic books would be multiplied, that their impact would be far greater, if a Catholic publishing house could emerge with a mind behind it. The whole field needed surveying, with writers encouraged to fill the obvious gaps. Continental writing should be examined for books worthy of translation. The quality of a book must be the *first* consideration, whether it would pay the second. The ideal publishing house was vivid in my mother's mind; whether it could be realized was another question.

From a personal point of view Mama had wanted to keep me in England, but she also wanted an occupation for Leo: he was to have been the Ward of Sheed and Ward. But his heart was never in it. Underneath the hard struggle against blinding depression, the constant headaches, the sleeplessness that had followed his breakdown, Leo had never quite given up hopes of being a priest. Doctors and spiritual directors alike had advised him to put it out of his mind. Docilely he tried, even at one stage proposing to a girl whom he liked immensely but who refused him on the ground that she intended to be a nun. (She later married and had three children.) As far as I could judge his fundamental reaction was relief. He never, at the worst times of his breakdown, missed the daily Communion, so much harder after sleepless nights then than today. The depression was the worst thing to deal with, and Mama herself often seemed like breaking down during the last years of her care. But in between its overwhelming onsets we had the old Leo with us again, full of energy and optimism—and a great joy it was to have him.

Hilaire Belloc, editing for America a series of small books which depicted different aspects of the Church, asked Leo to write one. His own was called *The Catholic Church and History*, G.K.C.'s *The Catholic Church and Conversion*, Leo's *The Catholic Church and the Appeal to Reason*. Mr. Belloc was delighted with it; I am only sad that I have lost his letter of warm praise, which was echoed by the reviews. The *Church Times* startled us by its comparison with the Chesterton book, for the review said that Leo's was "in some respects the more solid piece of work". The review continues:

> Speaking of two streams of tendency in modern thought, the German optimistic evolutionary doctrine based on man's greatness, and the French and Russian pessimistic determinism based on man's misery, he shrewdly remarks that the Catholic Church acts as a psychoanalyst towards the human race, reminding it of something which it has almost wholly forgotten, and this is why its religion is able to fit the facts.

The reviewer complained, indeed, that this work of the Church was not confined—as Leo appeared to suggest—to the Roman Catholic branch of the Christian Church, but the analogy struck other reviewers and the book gave him a brilliant start, had he wished to make letters his career.

I think both my brothers were hampered in finding their line by the general assumption that it must lie in writing. Leo's reviewers spoke of his father, spoke of his grandfather, Baron Von Hügel greeted this "new Leo Ward" as their worthy successor. As I see it, both Herbert and Leo were far more men of action than W. G. or Wilfrid. Both had good minds which they would have used from the first in practical issues but for this general overwhelming idea, that they must take up their literary inheritance. Their later careers seem to prove the truth of my theory. Herbert had already done much work for the Save the Children Fund—work which took him through the Near East and gave him the opportunity of studying the rites of the various Eastern Churches and renewing the friendships he had made in Mesopotamia during the War.

Deciding to settle in the Isle of Wight, he next began to serve on all its leading public bodies. He used to tell me that it was the lack of middle-aged men with time and energy to spare that brought about his early appointment as Vice-Chairman of the Cowes Urban District Council in 1930. Two years later he was Justice of the Isle of Wight Division. Successively he became Chairman of the Isle of Wight County Council and of the Juvenile Court, and Deputy President (Princess Beatrice, the Island's Governor, being President) of the Isle of Wight Branch of the Red Cross Society.

This job, which he held for close on twenty years, was especially interesting and important during the Second World War.

But among all Herbert's activities what interested me most and would furnish rich material for the book he will never write was the chairmanship and membership of various boards of prison visitors—Parkhurst, the Island's central prison, Camp Hill Prison and Portsmouth Prison for Preventive Detention. Either novelist or historian could with advantage listen to the memories of a man who has been too busy dealing with human lives to sit down and write about them.

As to Leo, he was to make more than one abortive beginning before discovering his vocation as a missionary. Perforce he had had the short experience of military life, then the effort to become a Jesuit, now he was attempting literature and making as he did so a host of friends. But even in what he was writing now, Leo showed his bent for practical rather than speculative thought. By nature an enthusiast, he poured out all his powers of enthusiasm upon the Church. He had been an evangelist since at least the age of four, when I discovered him baptising our dog, using, as I informed my mother, "the correct form and matter". I remember being relieved that she did not consider it a sacrilege but only said she hoped we should see an improvement in Gyp's behaviour. Two years later, Aunt Mary, taking care of us when Mama was away, wrote to her: "England being Protestant weighs a good deal on Leo, and he asked me if I did not think it would do if some very strong man were to persuade the House of Commons to become Catholic. I was obliged to confess that I did not feel very sanguine as to the plan."

Finding this letter delighted me, for it mirrored so perfectly the Leo that was to be. Souls were intensely real for him and he was only too apt to think that every action of his might affect them for good or ill—usually for ill. He lived in a state of distress over his mistakes, and of violent efforts to repair them. He would write endless letters to individuals, he would dash into newspaper controversies.

I only realized how much Leo had read, how especially familiar he was with the scene in France, as I turned over lately some of his old letters and newspaper cuttings. He wrote a small book for Sheed and Ward on the condemnation of the Action française (with which condemnation he was in strong agreement). He was amused but horrified by some of his French friends. One of them was justifying his own resistance to Rome when Leo interjected, "You are not much of a Catholic." His horrified friend replied, "How can you say such a thing? The Church has always been one of the most glorious ornaments of our nobility." The thought of the Church as a tiara on the brow of the French nobility was altogether too much for Leo. But in England too this little book involved him in controversy. I found among his papers an endless correspondence in the *Outlook*, which illustrated a fact that has always struck me as curious.

By and large the English intelligentsia likes liberal ideas. The harshness of Jansenism, the State absolutism advocated by the Action française, would alike be repugnant to it. But it *dis*likes the Catholic and Roman Church so much more than anything else that it will espouse the most illiberal ideas once the Church has condemned them. So it had been with Jansenism; so it was with the Action française—which desired to overthrow the French Republic and enthrone a monarch whose outlook would probably have been not unlike that of Mussolini.

Leo had struck up a vehement friendship (all his friendships were vehement) with Don Sturzo, the Italian priest-leader of Christian Democracy in Italy. He buzzed to and fro (thus his family characterized his movements) from France to Italy, from Italy to England. He spoke for the C.E.G. and was suggested by Mgr. Coote as the properest person to write a monthly diary of its activities for the *Cathedral Chronicle*.

We were a closely-knit family who could disagree without quarrelling, and in this matter of politics each one of us had a different outlook. My sister helped her husband in his political work. She was a Conservative, not fundamentally much interested in politics. But when Leo said in a moment of exasperation, holding his two fingers an inch apart, "You whose range of interests is so wide", I remembered *him* as we entered Switzerland during a glorious sunrise, with his eyes glued on the book he was reading! His own apparently wider range all converged on one topic; outside that and music, he did not go far afield. He swam and walked for exercise but he never watched a game and if he played tennis it was only to oblige. He hardly looked at flowers or scenery. He read no modern novels.

Herbert would have assented wholeheartedly to those French

Catholics who were talking of the layman's duty to build the City on earth, though certainly not agreeing with most of them as to the pattern of its building. He stood almost passionately for the widest possible freedom for Catholics to differ politically. "I would never excommunicate them", he said of the most extreme Catholic Leftists, "but they should not excommunicate me." Apart from myself the family were Conservatives of very varying shades. Leo was really afflicted when he found Frank and I did not subscribe to *The Times*. He paid for it for three months for us, hoping to form us in good habits. But when his subscription ended we did not renew it. Only crossword puzzles brought us back to it.

Herbert was apt to say: "You and Leo are far too inclined to think *Ecclesia est patria nostra*"—but in fact we thought it in very different ways. Leo wanted to use politics in the service of religion. Frank and I thought politics dubiously useful in any context, and in this context positively dangerous.

Once Leo's health improved, his time as a layman ended quickly. Again we were indebted to Cardinal Bourne. After a very brief period at St. Edmund's, Ware, he arranged for Leo to complete his studies privately at the Birmingham Oratory, where he had been at school. The thought of his final examination threw him into a state of nervous dread which brought back almost non-stop headaches. One day Dr. Griffin (later Cardinal Archbishop of Westminster) suggested a walk, saying, "And let's just run over the main questions you are likely to be asked." The walk was punctuated happily enough with question and answer, and as they re-entered the house Dr. Griffin said, "By the way, *that* was your examination."

I am rather rushing ahead. When Mama first thought about publishing, she talked to Mr. Thring of the Authors' Society and to all the publishers she knew. Of the skills needed none of us knew a thing; Frank always says he learnt publishing from a book, *The Truth About Publishing*, by Stanley Unwin. "Flair", said Mr. Thring, was the great thing, and Mama and I were convinced that Frank had flair. We had good friends who were authors. Gilbert Chesterton could at that moment give us only a small book of poems, because he was already under contract for thirty books with various publishers. Father Martindale gave us a manuscript for a wedding present. Hilaire Belloc urged forward our opening date that we might publish his pamphlet, *Mr Belloc Still Objects*, and his book, *A Companion to Wells' Outline of History*. There we sat in 31 Paternoster Row without telephone or electricity, distributing the pamphlets by means of Herbert's car—he incurred a fine for parking outside the office where two cars could not possibly pass one another. And every day we received from Mr. Belloc lengthy letters of advice on publishing—looking back I should say that he knew, if possible, less than we did.

9

BOOKS, A BABY AND A HOME

BELLOC, unlike the Chestertons, was much more my mother's friend than mine, but he was deeply interested in our beginnings as publishers. He wanted to be in some way associated with the firm, but what that way should be he could not determine. Many letters were exchanged; would he help in the administration? No, that would not suit him. Would he read MSS? Definitely not. Would he publish with us? He could not commit himself. Probably, like Gilbert, he was already deeply committed. But he sent us an immense document working out what each item in publishing would cost us and how long it would be before we could count on returns on our outlay; this remarkable document perished, alas, in the Blitz—I say, alas, for it was the more fascinating by proving fallacious in every particular. My husband decided to stick to Stanley Unwin.

In any case, the amount we *needed* to begin with was quite irrelevant; we had to do with what we had—which was £2600. Publishing is notoriously a gamble, but in our case it appeared likely to be even more so than for most, for three reasons. First, even in pre-Second-World-War values, our capital was small, and this at the moment when depression had hit the country. The easy money of the early twenties was no longer; and while we (apologetically) commented, "That's the spirit" when a man gave up whiskey for a month to buy one of our books, we could not hope that this would become a custom.

Secondly, there was a real question as to whether Catholic publishers could possibly live on books alone. None of them were doing so; statues, rosaries, breviaries, missals, Gardens of the Soul were the bread and butter of all the existing firms. "In answer to many enquiries," we announced in the first number of our house organ, "we do not sell crucifixes, statues, rosary beads or medals: we sell books."

The third reason that made our risks probably greater and our profits most certainly less was set out in the first statement of our policy. A Catholic publisher might merely deliver "externally unmistakable items of Catholicism" for Catholic consumption only—or "*he may make a real effort to express the whole Catholic mind*". The words in which my husband continued this article expressed something burnt into us by our years on the outdoor platform: "Such a policy excludes propaganda save only in the sense that truth is living and can propagate itself." "Propaganda" in its usual meaning implies that the truth in itself is not good enough, it must be "pressed in a little here and shaded there, and finally posed very carefully for the photographer".

The difficulty in a presentation of the full Catholic mind was twofold. First, it meant that many of our books would appeal only to people accustomed to mental effort in their reading. In an article called "Reading for Runners", Frank pointed out that all who run can *not* read this sort of book. They must be prepared to settle down to it, really to work. Reading detective stories is not really reading; unfortunately, in our language the same name is given to two quite different activities. Reading for pastime is perhaps less of an intellectual activity than playing bridge. Could we sell widely books demanding a real mental effort? And again, would Catholics accept a true picture of themselves, not tricked out for the photographer—in history, biography, lives of saints and comment on contemporary events? Would non-Catholics respond to the truth in Catholicism thus seriously and non-controversially presented ?

On the whole the answer to these last two questions was very much Yes, though we had our bad moments. Several of our books were banned in Eire, which awakened a lively interest in them on the part of intellectual Irishmen. Many years later a priest wrote protesting against one of our book-jackets as indecent; he was told it was a reproduction of a picture from the Sistine Chapel; he retorted, "If the Pope had heard as many confessions as I have, he would know better."

But it was another matter to keep one of the resolutions that made our task most uphill; we would never, we resolved, refuse a book of outstanding value because its sales could not possibly cover its expenses. These books often had a marvellous press; we were, we were told constantly, "enhancing" our reputation. But the sales were not equal to the reviews and we were inevitably desperately poor for many years. We could not manage to carry out some of the grand schemes that floated before our imaginations. But we did manage to publish a lot of good books. At the end of two years we had a hundred titles on our list and these included some of the most significant of our career. Despite his commitments Chesterton managed to give us three of his most characteristic books; one was *The Thing*, a collection of essays that, more fully than *Orthodoxy* though with less fireworks, and, of course, less novelty, expresses his deepest thoughts about the Church he had now belonged to for eight years. The others were *The Queen of Seven Swords*, a collection of his poetry on Our Lady, and that brilliant, though not very actable play, *The Judgment of Dr. Johnson*. From Fr. Hugh Pope came the immensely important *Layman's New Testament*.

Father Martindale gave us his *St. Aloysius* and, pioneering in many directions, was soon to add liturgy to his volumes of sermons and books about the Church in Australia and New Zealand. Despite his uncertainties Belloc had sent us *Survivals and New Arrivals*, soon to be followed by *Essays of a Catholic*. The Knox Library had begun with striking variety: *Essays in Satire*, *The Rich Young Man*, *Anglican Cobwebs* and *The Mystery of the Kingdom*. Two of these were only short books put into our shilling series. "Ronnie" was among the friends who most warmly supported our venture. His close friend and literary agent, W. P. Watt, became our friend too.

We were much engaged on the new kind of saint's life. St. Aloysius had been shown not as an emaciated girl carrying a lily but as—in his own words—"a twisted piece of iron" who had entered religion to be twisted straight. The Ghéon books, following one another in rapid succession, reinforced the realization that each saint is a different and a significant person, not without faults but triumphing over them. Ronnie wrote some Clerihews on the saints:

St. Cyprian of Carthage
Sat on the bath edge
Wondering if it would be a sin
If he didn't get in.

St. Francis de Sales
Said I have converted the Prince of Wales
O you 'ave, 'ave yer?
Said St. Francis Xavier.

St. Simon Stylites
Gave up the use of nighties
Hearing of which St. Chrysostom
Said it would never have suited his system.

Looking back at the beginnings of such intellectual life as I have had, I feel indebted to three men of genius: Browning, Newman, Chesterton. But in my middle age, while we owed much as publishers to many men and women, foreign and English, the most powerful influence on the thinking of both myself and my husband was certainly Christopher Dawson.

Leo had introduced me to him and to Edward Watkin, whom he had come to know at Oxford. Both were converts, Christopher having come from the same Anglican background as my paternal grandparents—at their date he would almost certainly have been, had he so desired, Master of Balliol or Dean of St. Paul's! I had never met anyone who knew so much as these two. Christopher says, "I am a Latin, he is a Greek", but, of Christopher especially, we felt the reach to be worldwide. It was not only the books, although I remember a conversation on this subject with Dame Una Pope-Hennessey, who seemed literally overawed by their weight of learning—and she was not an easy person to overawe; it was even more the information on any subject that arose in conversation. From Chinese dynasties to American Indians, from prehistory to the Oxford Movement, from Virgil to the latest novel or even "Western", Christopher can talk of anything although you can also find him plunged in an almost unbreakable silence and impervious to the people and things around.

Instances float into my memory. There was the visit when Christopher met Frank in the hall with the statement: "What remarkable similarities there are between the religion of the Hairy Ainu and the Northern Siberian Nomads—although ethnologically they are quite distinct."

This subject was his own choice. But another time, on Frank remarking what an interesting book could be written on the attractions and repulsions the Catholic Church exercised on some of Hegel's predecessors like Fichte and Schelling, Christopher monologued on the subject for the best part of an hour; the monologue could have been published just as it was. Letters to Dawson from an expert in Indian religions treat him as a fellow expert;

from an expert on the history of the Irish in the United States, as an equal in that field also.

On my publication of *The Wilfrid Wards and the Transition* I felt that the reviewer in *The Times Literary Supplement* had an almost uncanny insight into the period and the streams that had flowed into it. The next time I saw him Christopher asked, "How did you like my review?"

Although proclaiming himself a Latin, he it was who made me study St. Basil and the two Gregories and from him I caught enthusiasm for them. Of him and of Edward Watkin I ask invariably the reading of my manuscripts, which will ensure the absence of the many mistakes liable to slip in—and also, what one cannot get from even encyclopedic knowledge alone, guiding lights on what a period or person *means*.

At the date of this beginning, so momentous in our lives, Christopher Dawson was the most important influence brought to bear not only on us but on the whole ethos of our publishing. He had already published *The Age of the Gods*, brought to us later to be reissued with his other books. But the immense sensation early in our career was the appearance of *Progress and Religion*. In this book he discussed philosophically, with rich historical illustration, his key topic, on which after thirty years he is still casting fresh light: all cultures grow from the root of religion and when the root is dead the plant will die too.

The Making of Europe—depicting the culture nearest to ourselves and most easy of observation by us—I have read repeatedly, each time learning more from it. In a sense I had been more conscious of Europe than most young Englishwomen of my date, but conscious in a piecemeal and limited way. I thought of Italy or of France in isolation. I had indeed delighted to repeat after Belloc, "The Faith is Europe and Europe is the Faith"—but only till I had begun to think about it!

Even Europe meant for Belloc the Latin side alone: France first and then Spain and Italy; but even more widely conceived, Europe is still *not* the Faith. I don't think I ever heard Belloc talk of Byzantium; I have often heard him speak of the Old Testament as a collection of oriental folklore; although he loved California he despised the American contribution to culture, and he certainly did not dream of an African one.

From this provincial view of the Faith and of Europe Christopher Dawson saved us. Deeply imbued with the Classics, he is just as conscious of the other streams that flowed into Christendom, of the German, of the Arabian influences. He does not isolate the Faith from its own earliest seeds in Judaism, he remembers its first beginnings in Palestine and Greece. In his schemes for a Christian culture course in universities he can plan for a Protestant as well as a Catholic curriculum. Dr. Pusey, President of Harvard, spoke to my husband of Dawson's "exacting intellectual standards and total intellectual integrity". These things are what the Catholic body in English-speaking countries supremely needed, and we realized even in our beginnings that we were getting them in both Dawson and Watkin, who were giving to our publishing house the support of that immense knowledge without which even the utmost integrity can be unconvincing.

Frank had drawn his two principal employees from the C.E.G.; both were speakers, both were younger than he, neither had any publishing experience. Edward Connor, who was on the business end, had been in a lawyer's office, Tom Burns had attracted Frank's attention by the quality of his C.E.G. speaking; he hated the city office in which he was employed and was glad to come to us. Soon after this he started a periodical entitled *Order*. It did not run for long but the two numbers there were were brilliant, and the conception gave its name to the series Essays in Order which Christopher Dawson and Tom Burns jointly edited. This series of very short books contained some of the best work of our best authors: Dawson, Watkin, Ida Coudenhove, Maritain, Mauriac, Peter Wust. Frank's article already quoted, "Reading for Runners", pointed out that they were *not* the sort of thing that "he who runs may read". Books of real importance called for "sweat and tears", from reader as well as writer (Churchill had not yet added blood to this catalogue). These books should be read even more slowly than they were written, the reader's mind "should grow to them as the minds of their writers grew to them". Answering those who said they were too difficult for the average reader, Frank invented a slogan:

> If you cannot read Essays in Order
> You cannot read.

Going down to the country to join Christopher and Tom in a lengthy discussion of the series, he took a late train one night which became even later than the railway had foretold. Arriving in Devonshire at 3 a.m. he decided it was too late or too early to knock up his hosts, so finding a grassy spot, he lay down and slept till breakfast time. Despite the struggles inherent in our beginnings, he got a lot of fun out of publishing. Little as I was in the office I felt the sense of fellowship which was quickly caught by the young men joining our editorial group for varying periods. Among them were Bernard Wall, Alick Dru, Martin Turnell, James Pope-Hennessey, Michael Trappes-Lomax—all of whom became writers themselves—and Billy Clonmore, now of the publishing house of Clonmore and Reynolds in Dublin. I felt flattered when Dame Una Pope-Hennessey asked me if there was a place for her son in Sheed and Ward, as it made such an excellent start for a young man!

But Frank had constantly to be thinking of finance—seldom a pleasant subject of meditation. Although there had been many rumours of people who would like to put money into Sheed and Ward, they seemed in those days as unsubstantial as most rumours are when you try to get near them. And we both of us hated the idea of asking for money and felt resolved, if no one offered it, to succeed under our own steam.

Edward Connor is still with us and bore a very heavy burden during the War while Frank was "commuting" between the New York and the London offices. Tom Burns, after various experiences, including a wartime spent in Spain at the British Information Office, has returned to his ancestral firm—for his uncle was the original Burns of Burns and Oates. I wonder if he ever remembers a postcard from Ronnie arriving at Paternoster Row which amused him as much as the rest of us—and of which the author solemnly presented us with the copyright!

> Sheed and Ward
> Offer sacrifice to the Lord
> Not of the blood of bulls and goats
> But of Burns and Oates.

Our two names were so rhymable that others tried their hands. Beachcomber wrote in his *Daily Express* column:

When I am in my direst need
I seek the help of Mr. Sheed
But much prefer when I am bored
The company of Mr. Ward.

It was only gradually that Mr. Ward was realized to be Mrs. Sheed. Indeed, as Frank sometimes complained, the nearest many people got was to say, "How do you do, Mr. Sheed. And how is Mrs. Ward?" Years later, arriving in New Zealand, we heard that our host had been asked, "Are those two married?" "I hope so", he said. "I've taken a double room for them at the hotel."

Hilary Pepler, calling one day at the office after hours to find it shut, cried at the end of a poem of complaint:

Sheed cannot keep watch if he has to keep Ward.

Keeping Ward became indeed his problem at this time in quite another fashion.

It is interesting how marriage makes one desire children. I had rather hoped that at my age I should not have any; there were so many other things to do. But after a few weeks I was longing for a baby. While Rosemary was on the way I remember sitting in Battersea Park correcting Fr. Hugh Pope's proofs. What a first-rate book *The Layman's New Testament* is, but how reckless Father Hugh was about his references. The mixture of scholarship and carelessness was unique.

We had a little Scotch maid who broke most of my lovely wedding china but became quite a competent speaker for the C.E.G. Mary confirmed my suspicion that education is better in Scotland than in England; she had only had an elementary schooling. Frank's mother, who had come over from Australia and was living with us in our roomy flat, was very far from approving Mary's Guild activities and felt, quite justly, that I was not bringing her up in the way she should go as cook or housekeeper. But how could I? Mary soon married a Guildsman, and when I asked the maid who succeeded her if she knew how to buy a nice joint of meat she answered in all simplicity, "No Madam, I'm as raw as you are." I had thought of preparing for marriage at a school of domestic science but had never got around to it, and all I ever learned I learned from my mother-in-law, with emendations later from my daughter.

I had planned on handling the baby myself as soon as the monthly nurse should leave, but fate—or God—disposed otherwise. It is strange to watch a girl today preparing for a baby's birth and to remember the haphazard ways of thirty-five years ago. I was put on no diet and never told to weigh myself. I was taught no exercises. Already fat, I became enormous. I went about as usual; my mother was alarmed to see me swinging onto buses. I almost had a miscarriage, but apart from that appeared quite well. My baby was born on October 18th, St. Luke's Day, and we named her Rosemary Luke. (I should have liked to call her by both names but nobody co-operated and I gave up the idea.) I spent the—then usual—month in bed. I had some slight pains in my back and was supposed to have a touch of pleurisy; at the end of the month I got up, feeling rather cheap but supposing this to be normal. I remember going out to lunch with Mama and she, thinking me still weak, sent me home in a taxi. Getting up on a chair, I pushed the bed-pan onto a high shelf, remarking, "Thank heaven I've finished with that." As I did so I felt the strangest sensation, and jumping down, I realized that my heart was racing. I tried to take my pulse—I lost count at 140, I *must* be wrong. No, I *would* not be like Aunt Emily. I would not let the family nerves get hold of me.

Mama had insisted on paying for a specialist for my confinement but our regular doctor was a close friend, Helen McQuaid, whose brother is now Archbishop of Dublin. I rang her up, saying that I suspected myself of imagination but I did somehow feel very ill. She came at once and the next thing I remember was vaguely enquiring why a big black object was coming in through the large window of my room. It was an X-ray machine too large to be brought up the stairs, and I was soon sitting upright in bed, one arm in a sling, my legs immobilized by sand bags, two nurses with me by day and one by night. A clot of blood on my lung had burst and there were other clots in legs and arm. My temperature ran up to 103 or more each night, in the morning it was far below normal. The nurses would talk to one another, thinking me unconscious; it was too much labour to try to speak. For ten weeks I was between life and death, though Helen said later, when I reproached her for my not having had the last sacraments, "the danger was not proximate". The experience certainly taught me how foolish it would be to rely on a deathbed repentance. It would have needed a stupendous miracle to enable me to think or pray collectedly.

When the spitting from the lung diminished, Holy Communion was brought to me, but although conscious I was quite unconcentrated.

The best moment in every twenty-four hours was when in the evening they gave me morphia and I slept for a while. I would wake hoping it had been many hours but it never was. I was wringing wet by then and the nurse would call Frank to help her change me. One night he sang to me Bunyan's lines,

> He who would valiant be
> 'Gainst all disaster
> Let him with constancy
> Follow the Master.

I loved tune and words and after that he sang them often. He seemed to be always at hand; he translated a book at home—I think *St. Theresa in her Writings*—but we neither of us can remember with certainty—and went little to the office. I remember in a good evening hour his reading Dickens to me. Nurse Moylan was holding my head which *would* fall forward, and the bed shook as she laughed over her first introduction to Mrs. Gamp and Betsy Prig. Later she tied my head with a scarf to the back of the bed and this helped.

My mother, too, was perpetually with me. She had found a Nannie for Rosemary and carried them both off to her little house in Pelham Place. It was Mama, I think, who thought of ice cream when I could eat nothing, and she would constantly vary the flavours.

I had many prayers; several parish priests gave out my name at Mass and the Guild prayed intensely.

Specialists had been called in and the decision was reached that on a certain Monday an operation should be done, the technical name of which I forget. I always called it collapsing my lung. After this I should have been more or less of an invalid, the lung being artificially inflated (or whatever the word is) every six weeks.

The Guild redoubled their prayers. Near Marble Arch is Tyburn Convent, where with perpetual adoration of the Blessed Sacrament nuns pray day and night for the conversion of England. On the eve of this Monday the Guild decided to pray for me at Tyburn. Throughout the Sunday our speakers succeeded one another. Father Vincent too had specially besought prayers at Haverstock

Hill. That day heaven was besieged. After all our Lord told us to knock, told us to importune God as a woman did an unjust judge or as a man did a reluctant and somnolent friend.

Helen arrived early and gave me an injection of morphia. All was set ready for the surgeon. He came into the room, looked at me, took up my temperature chart and looked at it. It was still registering the same big rises and falls. He looked at me again, was silent a moment and then said: "I think we'll give nature one more chance." Helen and he left the room together, she looking much depressed, for she believed this operation to be my one hope. When they had gone I fell into a deep sleep. This was not surprising after the morphia, but my awakening was very surprising, for I said for the first time in two months, "I'm hungry." I accepted a boiled egg, ate it with real enjoyment and went to sleep again. My recovery had begun.

In all this there is no question of a technical miracle such as the Bureau at Lourdes chronicles; the surgeon had said he would give nature another chance—and nature had responded. Even Helen remarked how hard it was to be a Catholic doctor—after all your labours your patient attributes her cure to prayer! Well, God works through nature. He works through doctors and we may thank him for those ways of working too. But that this cure of mine was a special cure in answer to prayer I shall never for an instant doubt. Nor, I think, did Helen.

The cure went forward slowly and I was more inclined to be cross as I got stronger. The first sight of myself was a shock; I had lost most of my hair and grown quite a beard. I had also, however, lost much weight and that was a blessing.

By April I was able to be moved in an ambulance to The Nook where a kindly dragon, Sister O'Brien, superintended the completion of my cure. It is amusing today to remember how strict she was as I got better, on my giving up the cup of tea before Communion, allowed then only in illness. "You're well enough now to wait", she said firmly. And I (always bad at fasting) obeyed her meekly—being given the tea, oddly enough, immediately after receiving. I was reminded of a story told by Fr. Gavan Duffy of an African convert exhausted by an immense walk through the jungle who ate a banana before going to Communion. When told he should have waited he said: "Well, Father, I couldn't have waited much longer, and I thought it more respectful to let my Lord sit on a banana than for a banana to sit on my Lord."

Mama brought Rosemary to The Nook. It was the first time I had seen her since November and I almost cried as I said, "That's not my baby." The colour of her hair was different, the shape of her face, the whole look of her; this was surely a changeling. It took her quite a while to establish identity.

Sister O'Brien allowed me on our wedding anniversary to go out to dinner with Frank and we had a happy evening (but an execrable dinner) at the Bull and Bush. The waiter won his tip by abusing the food more heartily than we did, but it all gave Frank a chance of singing "Down at the old Bull and Bush" and indeed we were, to quote Jane Austen in "singing, dancing, exclaiming spirits".

At The Nook I finished my translation of Lagrange on Renan for the next publishing list. This was a very slight translation—it is not one of Lagrange's major works, and it was a drop in the ocean that we were now entering of important Continental literature.

Our first enormous success was Karl Adam's *Spirit of Catholicism*. I shall never forget the excitement of reading the MS of Fr. Justin McCann's admirable translation, all the more so because translators were a far greater problem for us—and remained so—than works to be translated. The Italian proverb says *traduttore—traditore* ("translator, i.e., traitor"), and this is only too often true, not owing to deliberate malice but to lack of skill. It cannot be said too often that translation is an art—perhaps as great an art as original writing.

The number of translations that have had to be remade in our office over the years make it possible to say something about this art, even though I myself do not possess it to any high degree. I can do a fairly workmanlike job, but Fr. McCann and still more Fr. O'Connor (translator of Claudel's *Satin Slipper*) really were artists. Claudel said of this translation that it was better than his own original.

Curiously enough Newman, for all the marvellous style of his original works, is not a first-class translator. Now and again, in the fragments of correspondence between St. Basil and St. Gregory Nazianzen, he reaches high art, but on the whole he was inhibited by the false ideas of his period. What these were can be seen in almost every volume of *The Church of the Fathers* which he edited.

Keble indeed did a lovely translation of St. Irenaeus—but look, for example, at the two volumes of St. Gregory the Great's works and letters. The translator was a scholar, he knew Greek and Latin—but he was supposed to be writing English. The same heresy springs up generation after generation, that a literal translation is a faithful translation; that each Greek or Latin word and sentence should be put into English even if this results in an English both ungrammatical and devoid of meaning. The two men who have written best on this subject are Hilaire Belloc and Ronald Knox. Belloc suggests that one should read a page of the original, lay the book aside and rewrite the page in English. Such a page would need far less correction than one done word by word in slavish "literalness". Indeed, the worst type of "literal" translation is irredeemable. For the meaning has been lost and the art of translation is to clothe the idea truthfully in the new garment of another language.

Maritain, Gilson, De Grandmaison, Berdyaev, Von Hildebrand, Guardini, Przywara, Ghéon, are only a few among the significant names that were now appearing on our lists.

My husband loves translating and does it at a tremendous pace. An early number of our house organ *This Publishing Business*, announcing Ghéon's *Curé d'Ars*, writes, "The translation is by F. J. Sheed. We do not know quite what to think of it." The public did, however, as the sales showed. It all meant so much more work; only a very strong man could have carried the responsibilities of a struggling firm while lecturing, translating and soon writing himself. For his first book, *Nullity of Marriage*, appeared in 1931, to be followed by *A Map of Life* in 1932.

Over-optimism has always been our weakness. And in the delight of my resurrection we felt more than ever that the world was our oyster. In this mood we did various foolish things. We bought a typewriting bureau (out of our very small private fortune); it was just another thing to manage and we lost money on it from the first. A little while later, on a visit to my cousin Walter Maxwell-Scott at Abbotsford, Frank, rummaging at our host's suggestion in a cupboard of MSS, came across an unfinished novel of Sir Walter's on the Siege of Malta by the Turks. Sir Walter's heirs had regarded it as unpublishable, but we thought something might be done with it and bought it for £2000. It was not easy to read, and not only because of the handwriting. When Sir Walter changed his mind about how a phrase or even a sentence should be written, he simply wrote a new phrase or sentence without crossing out the old. There was the framework of a plot to begin with, though his mind was not wholly on it—the heroine, for instance, was given three different names. But from a novel it soon turned into a history of the siege, the original characters forgotten. Unable to make out what Sir Walter was saying in some parts of the story, Frank consulted a French history of the siege to find out what did happen. It was by Aubert, written earlier than the novel, and very brief inspection showed that for the greater part, the MS was a straight translation of Aubert! There could be no question of publication. Walter Maxwell-Scott took back the MS and repaid the money.

My mother used to say, "Frank is convinced that he can be in two places at once if there is a night train", and she said too, "Please, please, don't imagine that because you and Frank can do anything you can do everything." These needed warnings mostly went unheeded.

The ground floor of Albany Mansions had been under water while I was lying ill on the first floor. Mama wanted us to move and we had the bright idea of offering in thanksgiving for my cure to open a public chapel somewhere in Surrey. The Southwark travelling mission had shown that whenever Mass was said in a new spot Catholics sprang up there almost overnight; on enquiry we found that there was such a spot at the little "dormitory" town of Horley, midway between Redhill and Crawley. "There is no mention of Horley in Domesday Book", we read in a local publication. There is not, indeed. Not by about eight hundred years. Down we went to investigate. The agent's map showed a house at crossroads, in a small road running beside it were some old buildings which we might, he said, be able to buy. But when we got there we found there was no need to look further for a possible chapel; there was a stable in a little yard belonging to the house itself. A good-sized lawn, a vegetable garden of half an acre with excellent fruit trees, and a patch of waste ground completed the small property. The house stood far enough back to make the traffic endurable, though it took us a little while to learn to sleep through the rumbling of lorries that seemed to run all night from London to Brighton and Brighton to London.

On the stable a passion-flower was growing, and inside we found a large family Bible, rather damp and dirty but with a torn leaf sticking out on which were the words, "His house". The diocese of Southwark gave us £200 to help in turning the stable into a chapel, and we promised we would not leave Horley unless some arrangement for carrying on the mission had first been made.

10

A CHAPEL, A GARDEN AND A MOTHER-IN-LAW

THE house was called The Chestnuts—not unsuitably, as large horse-chestnut trees grew on each side of the gate, smothered in spring with white and red blossoms and showering down in autumn a mass of conkers much sought after by the neighbouring children. Eliminating "The", we decided the name would do; better not change it perhaps, as we wanted the new chapel to be easily found.

The conveyance safely signed, the wife of the previous owner informed me that the cellar would always be flooded after rainy spells. Our surveyor had already insisted on proper pipes to carry away rainwater hitherto flowing from the roof into flowerbeds against the walls, so we hoped for the best. But the warning proved useful; we put nothing spoilable in the cellar and sure enough in mid-winter it was a foot deep in water. The house itself was perfectly dry but very cold. We ought, of course, to have lived in winter in the kitchen, large and light and fitted with an ideal boiler. A big scullery held the stove, the sink and old-fashioned laundry arrangements. But in those days all this was the domain of the two maids and the capable cleaning-woman, who scornfully told me that I ought not to employ her at all as "those idle girls" should have been doing the work delegated to her.

I remembered Blair, the magnificent black-silk-clad housekeeper at Arundel, telling my mother how she had begun her career as kitchen maid at the beck and call of the other servants. When there was a big party her nights were cut to half an hour's sleep—she never took her clothes off. But Mrs. Stevenson was a strong character and highly independent. She cleaned the chapel "for love"; her husband earned "good money"; what she earned from scrubbing our floor was merely pocket money and she did it with scornful contempt for those idle girls.

Mama had felt the pinch of poverty with a staff of five or six. I felt it with only two. I gladly left the supervision of our mostly young and mostly Irish maids to Frank's mother. She could handle anything, but there was inevitable strain in the reactions to two mistresses. It was only when the maidless era of today began that I realized in what comfort we could have lived had I myself understood how to run a house and therefore known what it was reasonable to ask of others. Like Mrs. Stevenson, my mother-in-law told me that the maids imposed on me. But I was mostly in the garden.

I had helped Mama to grow flowers; half this garden was vegetables and fruit and we went through all the joys and sorrows of a good crop of peas, of lettuces that "shot", of inadequate nets which saved only half our raspberries from the birds—but how delicious that half was—of giving away huge baskets of apples and storing enough to last us till March.

The little yard between house and chapel was brick-paved and brick-walled. It was amazing how many walls, high and low, the builder had contrived to erect on so small a property. Against the high wall beside the chapel we hung a lovely blue and white Della Robbia, digging out enough bricks from the paving to grow rock plants below it. Under the too-plentiful trees screening us from the meeting of the five roads we multiplied bulbs. In those happy days you could buy parcels of a thousand daffodils, hyacinths, snowdrops and the rest for a very few shillings. A strong back and a trowel were all you needed for a glorious springtime in any garden, and this we certainly achieved.

When neighbours gave us pots of forced hyacinths for the chapel the exhausted bulbs went back into the soil and came up next spring greatly shrunk but smelling, I fancied, sweeter than ever, to be picked and put into vases. The lawn was left clear for games, but the soil suited roses well and along the side of the grass was a rose border, while the vegetable garden, wherever the walls stopped, was hedged with the old-fashioned Dorothy Perkins. Scarlet Ramblers arched the paths and a box edging surrounded the borders. This harboured far too many snails and slugs but I could not bear to root it up.

All gardeners with an eye for beauty must suffer from a divided mind, unless, like my mother and Anatole von Hügel, they care for beauty only. Neither of the gardens I had loved best in my youth was allowed the smallest corner for a vegetable. Our garden was never beautiful like these; it followed the old-fashioned mixed pattern.

A big lime tree at the end of the lawn furnished a strong branch for a swing—now we were ready for Rosemary to grow big enough to use it; and we hoped for other children.

But I had left this business of marrying rather late, and, not helped by a tendency to miscarry, only succeeded in producing one more—Wilfrid John Joseph, born in my mother's house on the feast of St. John, 27 December 1930.

Frank still spoke in Hyde Park every Sunday, still took the class on Tuesdays and Fridays, but for the time being I was divorced from the Catholic Evidence Guild, apart from an occasional speakers' party in the garden at Chestnuts.

When Frank had first asked if I would be willing for his mother to live with us, I had viewed the idea with grave misgivings. My own mother was more than doubtful; Father Vincent McNabb remarked he had hardly ever known such an arrangement to work.

In fact this did, for two reasons; the first being Mrs. Sheed's own character. She was the most generous of women and, having accepted me as Frank's wife, she did it to the full. To my sister she once said that Frank was only half himself when away from me. She often left us to ourselves, going out among the circle of friends she had made the moment she landed in England. Indeed, she had begun to make them on the boat—I never knew a better mixer or a more accomplished traveller. She had gone from England to Australia when only thirteen. (The journey took six months and there was an outbreak of cholera.) Her last journey was made alone from Sydney to London at the age of eighty. Her love of travel and of the sisters and nieces left behind in Australia was a second reason for the success of our relationship; not too much strain was put upon it. We welcomed her joyfully each time she returned from Sydney; her family welcomed her joyfully each time she returned from England; both countries were home, but she could not have lastingly stayed put in either. She was amusingly unaware of this fact and would write on arrival after an exhausting journey, "I think I will get better when I am more settled."

Then, too, Frank and I were happy to realize that we could go away together, that Grandmother, as she soon came to be called, not by her grandchildren only, but by a vast circle of friends, would give the children the care that only love can give, combined with a complete loyalty to us.

Her deepest loyalty had been strained during Frank's early life. For his father was a Marxist and the family had to listen through every meal to the teachings of Karl Marx. Frank's grandfather, Captain Sheed, was a Presbyterian and for some strange reason the grandsons of the Presbyterian, the sons of the Marxist, were sent with the utmost regularity to a Methodist Sunday School and chapel every week. Frank's memory is as well stored with Methodist hymns as with music-hall songs! His mother's teaching was neither Marxist nor Methodist but the Catholicism of her childhood, and Frank made his First Confession and First Communion, in due course if with rather a sketchy preparation. In the Methodist chapel, he would bounce a ping-pong ball against the seat, trying to provoke the expulsion of himself and his brother Jack. They were often sent out but were never actually expelled, on account, he believes, of a genuine apostolic intent—the Methodists would not throw these boys into the hands of a Catholic mother. Yet much though they disapproved of Catholicism, they never attacked it from the pulpit. Frank was impressed with this and retained from those days the positive value of a devotion to John Wesley.

The grandparents respected their daughter-in-law but disliked and feared her religion even more deeply than their son's Communism. When Frank's brother died and his Catholic funeral was reported in the papers, the family was cut out of Captain Sheed's will; yet while they lived the old people welcomed their daughter-in-law and seemed really fond of their grandsons.

The idea is irritating that the simple Breton—or the Irish—peasant has *as such* a greater faith than the educated Catholic, but it arises from such families as hers. The Maloneys had been farmers in County Limerick, reduced to destitution by the Great Famine, losing everything else, holding on to God. Grandmother's own faith had carried her through years of difficulty and suffering, with the unshaken conviction that "He always does everything for the best."

That her education had come to an end too early was not a matter on which she wasted lament, but her mind was lively and energetic and she read enormously, mainly the English classics. When Frank was nine, she had introduced him to the novels of Dickens and Scott; we remember the excitement with which, late in life, she discovered Thomas Hardy. "I feel the need", she once wrote when away visiting, "of some intellectual reading or writing, neither of my dear hostesses want anything but talk."

Our good understanding was helped by daily lives too crowded for any time to nurse grievances. Running the house, developing the garden, caring for the chapel, helping neighbours in need, looking after first one and then two lively children, reading and writing —the days were too full for their length. And somehow the chapel developed even in me something that grandmother had always had—a habit of prayer. The amount she prayed was perhaps the thing that most impressed me. The chapel and mission became central for all of us, being at first far more our affair than is common for lay people.

The Bishop's secretary, Fr. Fennessey, had told us that the convent chaplain at Redhill, five miles away, would come over to say Mass on Sundays. But when we were ready to open he was ill. Frank telephoned in all directions and we secured a Carmelite for that Sunday. But the chaplain continued to be either ill, reluctant or both. He never materialized—I don't think I even saw him once. The parish priest, Fr. Hanlon, I saw repeatedly, and gathered that he had no great interest in a mission at Horley. Week after week we collected a Carmelite, a Franciscan or a Servite. Week after week the congregation grew bigger. An appeal to Fr. Fennessey brought a splendid solution; he himself would give his weekends to Horley, would come down on Saturdays in time for confessions and stay until Sunday, giving Benediction before he left.

And then came the need for a second mass. The chapel had held comfortably the forty or so people with whom we started. But Horley followed the usual pattern. There were Catholics there unable to manage the five miles on a Sunday morning into Redhill or Crawley—very few buses, if any, ran at that time. There were non-Catholics wanting to join the Church but not knowing how to set about it. And soon Catholic families came into the neighborhood, attracted by the possibility of a mass. With about sixty in the chapel and others standing in the yard we *must* have a second mass. Fr. Fennessey warmly approved of the idea that it should be sung; Frank, as the least unmusical, taught the congregation the *Missa de Angelis*, but I put in some remote preparation by teaching them to pronounce Latin. We invited anybody willing to sing to come of an evening and begin by reading the words. Gradually they gained confidence and Frank held a weekly practice after the second mass. Soon the vast majority were singing the Gloria, the Creed, the Sanctus and the responses. And not only singing them; in the course of our teaching we translated and explained the prayers, to adults, to children and to the Farmfield boys.

Farmfield was an institution a few miles from Horley where boys were sent who had got on the wrong side of the law, the degree of their mental responsibility being doubtful. There were about a dozen Catholics there who now came to Mass in our chapel. These sang with great gusto and could be heard, to the amazement of the staff, singing the Creed in Latin as they went about their work. Some of them learned to serve Mass and one took the collection but this, alas, had to be stopped when the source of his railway fare for an escape from Farmfield came into question! But they were nice boys and we had them to tea several times, when they appeared to enjoy themselves greatly and played pleasantly with Rosemary.

She was learning to speak in the early days at Horley and joined in the singing with strange words of her own, remarking, "I sing Mass very well." A death in the parish brought her running wide-eyed to say, "Miss Gaffney's in the chapel—in a suitcase."

I explained to the best of my ability the separation between soul and body that was death. A few (I hoped) well-chosen words on heaven and our new life to be lived there completed my brief instruction. "I don't want to take my body off", was Rosemary's firmly uttered comment. We would listen as she retailed to her dolls her version of what we had told her. The dangers of the main road were great. We put up a notice, *Please shut this gate for the sake of the child*. We tried to frighten Rosemary herself. Shortly after the "suitcase" episode I heard her telling her dolls, who played a large part in her life, a moral story. "Once there was a little girl whose Mummie told her not to go on the road. But she went out and then she was dead. But God took her up to heaven and made her new. So she came back and promised she would never go on the road again."

Rosemary gave us a fright before she was three by developing a violent pain which the doctor thought was appendicitis. He telephoned a specialist and we hired a car and drove to London, Rosemary moaning softly all the way. The trouble proved to be intussusception, but the appendix had to come out. After the operation, screaming became a serious matter. All had gone well but the surgeon warned us she must not be allowed to scream lest the wound be re-opened. In the nursing-home—it was the old familiar Nook—she looked a pathetic figure, asserting with all her old vigour, "I *will* scream; I don't *want* to be good." When we got home Frank hit on an ingenious scheme. Her favourite doll was called Jimmie. Whenever she screamed he would say, "Naughty Jimmie", and smack the doll. In vain Rosemary asserted that the screams were hers. The smacking of Jimmie continued till she would stop screaming, to save Jimmie.

After Fr. Fennessey took a parish, we had for several weeks a delightful Fr. Dockery, who became so popular in Horley that he and we alike hoped he might become permanent. Foolishly enough I visited the Vicar-General, an aged Italian, to put the point to him. As far as my imperfect Italian and his imperfect English carried the conversation, I received the impression that we were all extremely naughty to like Fr. Dockery so much, but above all that Fr. Dockery had sinned deeply by making himself so popular! A temporary priest, Mgr. Bamfi asserted, if I understood him aright, should show towards his flock all the reserve of one who knows he is only temporary.

Had there been any hope of our getting Fr. Dockery, the cold courtesy of the Vicar-General made it clear that I had destroyed it by my visit, but probably there never had been any. In a vile temper I prepared myself to receive the Bishop's new secretary, Fr. Healy. We have often laughed about it since, for Fr. Healy became one of our closest friends and I used to tell him that he was my unanswered prayer. I had never understood so clearly what is meant when we are told that no prayer is unanswered, since God gives us what we really want instead of what we think we want. God did not, says St. Augustine of his mother's prayers, give her what she asked for in one special prayer, in order that He might give her what she was always asking for.

Horley folk got what they really wanted even if they had asked for their pastor by a different name. A resident priest could not have accomplished more than Fr. Healy got through in his weekends. He started regular visits to Farmfield to give the boys instruction and hear their confessions. He managed somehow to fit in a good deal of parish visiting. He started an envelope collection for a new church building, since even with two masses the present chapel was becoming too small. He is now Bishop of Gibraltar, where he is loved as much as he was at Horley.

There was no reason, we were told, for any special apprehensions about the birth of another baby—but as the doctors had not been able to explain what had gone wrong over Rosemary's we were all, I think, a little nervous. Mama insisted on again paying a gynaecologist's fees and invited me to have the baby in her house. I came to her at the beginning of December and we expected Wilfrid about the middle of the month; but after apparently wanting to see the light on the feast of the Immaculate Conception, he decided instead to keep us waiting.

Mama had been at Crosby with my sister, and Rosemary and Nannie were staying at Pelham Place when Wilfrid first startled us. Rosemary had to be moved to make room for the nurse, sent for in a hurry, and Helen McQuaid tried vainly to convince her how reasonable all the proceedings were. *Why* must *she* (she asked) and not the nurse sleep upstairs even if Mummie is ill? Why must she go back to Horley next day? Obviously she felt we were all wanting in common sense, but she accepted the situation with dignity and on our return to Horley received her new brother graciously. Of jealousy there was never a trace.

Christmas Eve came and we were still waiting; I was able to attend Midnight Mass at St. Mary's, Cadogan St. At last, on the feast of St. John, Wilfrid was born; a nine-pound baby full of vigour and with an exceptionally powerful voice. I especially noticed this as my young and pretty nurse went (with permission it would have been hard to withhold) to a hospital ball on the following night. I got no sleep and listened in terror to the yelling baby in the next room wondering if anything was wrong, but with no faintest idea what I could do about it. Next day the nurse's face was irradiated with what I, exhausted and prejudiced, dubbed an idiotic smile. She suddenly asked me where the words came from:

> One crowded hour of glorious life
> Is worth an age without a name.

A doctor with whom she had danced had murmured the quotation in her ear: I felt it to be curiously unsuitable—unless one day Wilfrid was to supply the name. Gilbert Chesterton had promised to be his godfather, he was to be called after his grandfather Wilfrid Ward—but he needed only his father to make a wife and mother feel that our son would one day be someone considerable.

Meanwhile after four more weeks' rest and refreshment in Mama's company, I returned to the joys and labours of Horley; the house, the garden and the chapel.

Anyone with faith in God will want to pray to Him outside the hours of regular services and a church seems a natural place in which to pray. A North-of-Ireland friend once said to my mother, "My dear, you've no idea how many Protestant prayers I've prayed in your Cathedral." For the Catholic there is something far more in the presence of the Blessed Sacrament, and I think the expression "paying a visit" is a specially Catholic one. Americans have a verse about it:

> Whenever I am near a church
> I go in for a visit
> So that when I am carried in
> Our Lord won't say "Who is it?"

From our windows at Chestnuts we could see the occasional visitor—and also the occasional tramp. My one little shiver of fear when Frank was kept late in London came at the moment of locking the chapel. The Rural Dean, paying his rather different visit of inspection, had warned me to be very careful to make sure every night that it was empty—and I did *not* like looking behind the altar in the fading light.

During the daytime the tramps were nothing to fear, though as the Depression grew they became something of a burden. Our tea was always accepted gratefully and we did not find the bread and butter or occasional ham sandwich thrown over the hedge, as rumour so constantly had it. The other rumour—that tramps have a method of indicating which houses are hospitable and which are not—I came fully to believe. Money was another matter, but my husband's technique proved unfailing, of offering to send a reply-paid telegram to the firm in Glasgow or Leeds which had a job waiting if only we would lend our man the railway fare. "Come back", he would say, "in a couple of hours." He never sent the telegram and no man ever came back. Had he done so Frank would have supplied the money! But obviously, food must always be given, especially by the guardians of the local outpost of the universal Church.

11

DISCOVERING AMERICA

Between Rosemary's birth and Wilfrid's I first discovered America. Just before Frank had left England in 1924 the Paulist Father Elliot Ross had listened to him in Hyde Park and had said, "What about lecturing in the States?" Frank was just about to return to Australia, so Fr. Ross suggested that he go via America. With his mother, who had joined him in London, Frank lectured his way; first in Toronto, then New York, then Chicago, Minnesota and Oklahoma. Bishop Kelley of Oklahoma had listened in the Park also, and besides inviting him to lecture had offered to short-circuit his studies if he wished to become a priest and to ordain him for his own diocese. Learning that Frank hoped to get married, the bishop then suggested a legal career in Oklahoma. The lecture was the only thing accepted of these splendid offers. The tour had ended in San Francisco. I was delighted when Fr. Ross now suggested one for us both.

America later became so much a second home that it is a little difficult to remember how it looked on a first view; while the loss of Frank's diaries in the Blitz adds to my difficulty in sorting out the events of this and subsequent visits. We docked, I remember, on a misty morning and the New York skyline looked less like an adventure in modern architecture than an embattled medieval castle in a fairy tale, at once overpowering and insubstantial. A confused memory follows of lectures at the Blessed Sacrament Church Hall, near which we were staying, at Manhattanville College, at Overbrook and other Sacred Heart convents, above all of getting to know and love Mother Damman. In New York we found my cousin Minna Kerr (who had married an American, Francis Butler Thwing), and my father's old friend Mgr. McMahon. Prohibition was in full possession and we learnt the varieties of Catholic opinion on it, ranging from Mgr. McMahon's open defiance—expressed in the magnificent dinner at which he offered us cocktails, wine and liqueurs—to the view of Fr. Ross, who held Prohibition to be a law that the country was morally entitled to enact and that Catholics were morally bound to obey.

The curates at Our Lady of Lourdes all appeared on the best of terms with Mgr. McMahon and with one another; we were told amid much mirth (in which the victim joined) a story against one of them. When Fr. Bede Jarrett had been preaching the Lenten sermons, this priest had daily greeted him at breakfast: "Good morning, Bede." After a few days one of the others said, "Not very good manners to call a distinguished visitor by his Christian name." "Good heavens," he said, "is it a name? I thought it was a title."

Father Bede himself told us another story of this Prohibition period. He arrived at a convent of contemplative nuns in the Middle West, in freezing cold; the superior asked if he would like any refreshment and he said he would be glad of some coffee. She rang the bell and a lay sister appeared: "Coffee for the Father, Sister", she said. The sister vanished, to reappear with a bottle. "Thank you, Sister," said Father Bede, "but I really meant coffee." "The Father really meant coffee", the Superior emphasized and the coffee very shortly came.

The Wall Street crash had taken place a few months before, but there was still a good deal of money about. Mgr. McMahon told us that the average collection was a quarter a head. This, being a shilling in English money, seemed high for a not-very-wealthy area. Today most parishes expect a dollar per wage-earner, seven times as much on the English exchange but only four times in American currency.

While New York fascinated me, I have never cared for Philadelphia; yet my treasured memories of this first trip centre in the city of brotherly love. It was certainly that for us. We were invited by friends of my father's to stay first in Philadelphia itself and then in one of its suburbs, Torresdale. The Rivinus sisters belong to an old Episcopalian family and the coming of their parents into the Church had been through our mutual friend Fr. Maturin. For thirteen years he had been in Philadelphia as a Cowley Father and when he became a Catholic he brought them with him. Emilie often told me how hard she found it as a child when her aunts would say contemptuously, "Emilie can go to church with the cook." Outside the tiny circle of Fr. Maturin's converts, most of her friends knew no Catholics apart from their Irish maids.

My father's old friends were Walter George Smith, dead, alas, by the time of our visit to Torresdale, his sister Grace and his brother Kilby, who were still living there. Grace was over sixty: she lived to be ninety-three, white-haired, distinguished and beautiful. No duchess ever looked so much like a duchess as did Grace. I would point to that circle in illustration of the fact that America, despite the abolition of titles, continues to have an aristocracy. Next door to Grace lived the Darlingtons, a family with whom our relations would later be close. Bill Darlington was a naval man; during the Second World War he became a commander, but at present he was on the reserve list. His hobby was ironwork, of which he showed us the most beautiful specimens. There was a forge in the garden at Birdwood and Bill's work was commissioned by many friends for ornamental gates, railings, lamp-stands etc. Bill came of a Quaker family, of Westchester, Pennsylvania. His wife was one of the Bullitts of Philadelphia, cousin of the Ambassador to Russia at the time of World War II.

Nearby was Helen Ingleby. She had been at my Cambridge convent, had decided to become a doctor, and had shown a courage I deeply admired in carrying out her decision. Her family was old-fashioned county, and her horrified father would not contribute a penny to her training. She somehow got by with the help of an aunt; she told me that she hated the sight of brown bread, as she once lived on nothing else for a fortnight. She had come to the States as offering a better career for a woman, and was now in a high position at the Women's Medical College in Philadelphia.

Again I met the contending viewpoints of my youth. Helen was a close friend of both Smiths and Rivinuses; but they spoke with shudders of her work. "A lovely girl like Helen—to be doing autopsies!" They had all markedly the old-fashioned woman's outlook—differing in this from Jean Darlington, who, already full of social activities, would later run a milk round on Bill's farm, and end up by entering politics. For the first time we met on this visit Chesapeake Bay dogs. A Labrador swimming ashore from a wreck at Chesapeake Bay had mated with a brown retriever, and the resulting puppies created a new breed. They were splendid animals and Helen had one of the finest, called Alibi. She lived at Torresdale and drove daily to her hospital, making a principle of never refusing pedestrians a lift—a principle not without danger for a solitary and handsome woman. But Alibi's magnificent head lifted from the back of the car and his growl were all the protection needed. Helen later added the breeding of Chesapeake Bay dogs to her arduous medical labours and also became distinguished in cancer research for the Jewish Hospital, Philadelphia.

Before the aeroplane, getting around on a lecture tour presented problems—not least, in my case, from my insular inability to take in how great the distances were. I was tickled later by the conversation in *A Yank at Oxford* between the young American and the elderly Englishman:

> "Do you know, Sir, you could put the whole of Great Britain into the State of Nebraska?"
>
> "And with what object?"

Apart from the object I certainly had not grasped the fact. I blithely accepted an invitation to lecture in a remote part of Pennsylvania the day before an engagement in Philadelphia, under the impression that they must be close together; it meant a night in the train, and even so could only just be managed. That first tour still remains a misty confusion of planning, of travelling, of lecturing.

Caryll Houselander once said that the suggestion she should take a rest from her writing was like suggesting that she take a rest from breathing. "My writing", she said, "is my life and my livelihood—in that order." I could say the same of lecturing; a long space without a lecture leaves me played out. Lecturing can be tiring but not to lecture can be utterly exhausting; the details of the day pile up into a dusty heap of depression. The only alleviation is writing—or reading in preparation for a book. Writing, too, is a form of expression—but lecturing is more: it is an exchange of ideas, a meeting of minds, a friendly clash of personalities. In short, it is life.

Yet Caryll's simile would need a qualification. The listener often says, "How easily you do it", knowing nothing of the long preparation of one's subject, knowing nothing of the agony of apprehension with which each new lecture is looked forward to. Some subjects become so familiar as to lessen the strain, nothing totally removes it except to be on the platform and aware of the audience. From that moment all is easy, but that moment will not come in imagination. I, at least, always feel "Tonight I shall crash." My grandfather wrote to Newman of the joy of authorship and Newman retorted that he did not at all understand this—for him, writing meant "getting rid of pain by pain". But even for him joy must have followed—as in the hackneyed comparison of giving birth to a child. Lecturing too—serious lecturing, not lecturing from a card-index reshuffled in every city, but the attempt to express something one is longing to communicate—must have in it an element of pain. This baby does not always come to birth! Fatigue, lack of preparation, lack of vital response in an audience—all this may bring about not a birth but a miscarriage.

Indoor lecturing is not as exciting as the "soap-box". Both lecturer and audience become a trifle over-civilized; it is valuable for the lecturer to realize that his audience is not a captive one, for the listeners to feel free to walk away. Yet there are balancing advantages; a universal sympathy is more readily established and questioner and lecturer are not distracted by a dozen irrelevant questions all shouted together.

I think, of all our indoor lecturing, we both enjoy most what only began on later visits: Religion and Life Weeks, at various universities, and other interdenominational gatherings. As soon as the other participants realize that one is not out to score, that one will respect both the truth and other people's viewpoints, one discovers an extraordinary openness of mind. There was, for instance, the Lutheran pastor who insisted that my husband answer a question about Luther as he clearly knew more on the subject than himself. There were the Baptists in Chicago at whose church he spoke on the Trinity. There was the entirely Jewish audience who, after listening to a rationalist, and a fellow Jew, and my husband, on "Who was Christ?", spent the entire question period cross-questioning Frank as the one they *really* wanted to hear from. There was the college at which about half the professors asked us to take over their class the day after we had given our scheduled lectures. There is often the wonderful experience of meeting Newman Club chaplains who have won all hearts and, working almost day and night, have built upon the campus a magnificent Catholic organization commanding the respect of the entire university. When one thinks of the vast number of Catholics attending of necessity[1] State colleges, the work of these

[1] Almost every Catholic college is at present full to capacity. The total number of students is round 200,000. Catholics in non-Catholic colleges are nearly twice as many.

priests seems almost the high point of the Church's activity in the country and one can only give thanks for those bishops who manage to spare for each college one or even two of their priests to make it a full-time job.

I do not care much for radio and television, though I have done a little in England, Australia, New Zealand and the U.S.A. The time I got most fun out of radio also came later than this visit: a debate with John Mason Brown on the Town Hall Meeting of the Air. I am sorry this institution has come to an end; the large packed hall with questioners jumping eagerly up, the prolongation of the discussion after we had gone off the air, all made it so much more like life; I find it difficult to make an act of faith in the millions of alleged listeners: I would rather have five hundred the whites of whose eyes I can see, the reality of whom I can test.

We were to talk on bringing up our children and we had each prepared a script to order that kept very much to superficialities; we were agreed on the importance of reading *with* our young, of sharing their interests, of giving them the time they wanted just to talk to us. The chairman said despairingly, "You're far too unanimous. We *must* have a fight."

I suggested that I tear up my script, that Mr. Brown trail his coat and I try to tread on it. Sex education was an obvious issue—I believing in the parent and privacy, he believing in the master and the class as the best means of instruction. We got excited. We almost snatched the mike from one another. How, my opponent finally asked, could I doubt that the calm disinterested teacher would do a better job than the stammering, blushing parent. To which I answered, "Why do you have to blush?"

I think the most surprising group I was ever invited to address was some sort of fraternity of butchers. It was a dinner meeting; all had hit the bottle. Their enthusiasm was a trifle disconcerting.

On this first tour, however, almost all our audiences were Catholic. These too vary greatly. There are colleges and high schools, Communion breakfasts, annual gatherings of guilds and leagues, clubs and parish gatherings. Each kind of meeting has its own interest, and the question period is usually a prolonged one.

What use is it all? one is sometimes tempted to ask, after so many years of it. At first the excitement of the platform, the warmth of the audience and their tendency to ask, What can we *do*?, gave one an illusory feeling that great things would result from a lecture tour. Yet it would be equally a mistake to get discouraged. If even a few of the audience are moved by a lecture to read more, and more seriously, to study the Faith more deeply, this is worth all the energy in the world. And sometimes out of a lecture grows a study group, out of a study group a Catholic Evidence Guild.

I often wonder why we did not move to the States after this first tour. We had left behind us many requests for more lectures; there were enough people interested in Sheed and Ward to give a good start to a branch in New York; enough people in Philadelphia to start a C.E.G. Yet the idea never, I think, dawned on either of us. On my side the chief barrier would have been the utter impossibility of putting the Atlantic permanently between myself and my mother. Then, too, we had taken on the responsibility of the Horley Mission until it should be strong enough to support a resident priest; Sheed and Ward London still needed much hard work—when has it not?; we had a little of the British suspicion concerning American schools (I say "British" rather than "English", since Sydney High School and University were equivalent to an English public school and to Oxford in methods of teaching).

But I think it was heart rather than head that, in my case certainly, made the move unthinkable and took us back to Horley, where Rosemary welcomed us with a touch of shyness, Wilfrid shortly made his appearance and the daily life began again of reading proofs and manuscripts, cultivating the garden and looking after the chapel.

As the children grew bigger music of a sort filled our family evenings. Frank is not as good a musician as my father was, but is even better at leading a chorus and getting everyone else singing. Evenings of Gilbert and Sullivan renewed my youth, with the fresh element of music-hall songs dating from Frank's childhood. He has an incredible memory for these and has often maintained that the great defect of my own upbringing was absence of vulgarity. I agreed with him enough not to be at all disturbed when later on Rosemary and Wilfrid, at the seaside, picked up from a troupe of pierrots some even more modern specimens of what may truly be called the folk-songs of England and the States.

12

OUR FARCE OF A FARM

THE whole question of food for the country in general and our own family in particular was beginning to get on my nerves. I remember my mother predicting shortly after the First World War that we should all before long have to spend almost our whole income on food. Like everybody else, we were tremendously impressed by the Conservative campaign against the departure from the Gold Standard. It seemed inevitable to everyone who had lived through the War that our food would cost us more and that there would be less of it if the pound were devalued. Moreover, Frank had been in Germany, when the mark was crashing and people were selling their treasures for a few shillings to buy food. We had been in Paris on our honeymoon, when the franc was sliding downwards, and later at a hotel where the prices fixed in advance for our stay became so low in English money as to be absurd. For the first time in my life I would have voted in 1931, had I not neglected to register—but my vote was not needed in the landslide that followed.

The subsequent Conservative volte-face, and the arguments then put forward to show the immense advantages of devaluation, restored to us all our former political scepticism but did not reassure us about our food supplies. People were not buying books on a large scale and we wondered how long, with rising prices, we should have the money to buy food.

Ardent readers of *G.K.'s Weekly*, we were much affected by Belloc's financial articles. Week after week he hammered home the statement that our pound was now worth only thirteen and fourpence. I remember feeling a real astonishment that prices did not immediately rise exactly in the ratio indicated by him. On the contrary, they soon even fell a little, but we did not wait long enough to discover this. There were other articles in the *Weekly* and we were hearing too of a wonderful new society—the Scottish Catholic Land Association. There were, it seemed, being trained on farms boys from the slums of Glasgow and other large cities who would gladly work on the land for their keep and a little pocketmoney. With their assistance it was surely up to the Catholic body to buy farms and add to the country's food supply. Father Vincent McNabb, whom I had always deeply admired, was more and more urgently saying the same things as were Chesterton, Belloc and the new Association.

My first thought had merely been to increase our vegetable supply and keep chickens and perhaps rabbits on the waste ground at Chestnuts; but now a larger horizon seemed to open, and with our usual idiotic haste we invited an official of the Association to visit us for a few days. Knowing nothing ourselves about the mysteries of agriculture, it took us quite a while to discover that he knew nothing either. I shall never forget the solemn air with which a little later he put a spade into the earth (while the four boys he had brought from Scotland to work the farm stood round in an admiring circle), and told us that the soil was excellent on the run-down farm for which we had paid far too high a price. The man we bought it from had, we discovered, given £1500 for it. He persuaded us to pay £2300—and this I felt to be correct because it fitted exactly Belloc's estimate of the fall in the value of money!

We asked Gilbert Chesterton later why he had never mentioned wireworms. He appeared faintly embarrassed, having almost certainly never heard of them. It was indeed a profound weakness in the Distributist movement that the intrinsic difficulties were never faced while enthusiasm was whipped up among people prone to be fired by ideas and ideals. Friends of ours in the C.E.G.—far less able than we to take a financial loss—were egged on by our example. They bought a better farm than ours at a lower price, since another agent was selling it and the intelligent agent who had *sold* to us was helping them to *buy*. But they had bought on mortgage and had some trouble at the end of a couple of years in extricating themselves.

Upper Prestwood Farm was only four miles from Horley; we had intended to go on living at Chestnuts. There must have been some profound misunderstanding somewhere. We had promised if the farm should make a profit to share it with the staff—and we certainly thought we had been promised a manager competent to handle the boys and manage a small mixed farm. But it soon became obvious that boys only had been sent us by the Association, and they could not be left alone to cope. One of the four—an amiable and intelligent lad—had received *six months*' training. The others, with none at all, were not always disposed to obey him and he did not always know what orders to give. One day at the farm I saw on the table a letter from our visiting official of the Association; a sentence jumped out at me advising the boys to disregard any interference on my part.

I did not think I had yet begun to interfere but I felt it was high time to do so. Frank had learnt publishing out of a book; perhaps I could learn farming from my neighbours. But we should certainly have to be on the spot.

I began to haunt sales, buying a movable wooden bungalow to house the boys who were at present in the farmhouse (I think it cost £40, and it was perfectly adequate), buying cows which, by beginner's luck, all turned out well, a horse (winded, alas), and a farrowing sow which Frank transported with considerable difficulty. It managed to get two legs loose and hung over the cart at the front end, being occasionally kicked by the horse and drawing attention from passers-by with its squeals. My unfortunate husband had only moved even to Horley on condition that I would not ask him to garden—and here he was involved in a mysterious farm from which I proposed to wring our daily bread, as instructed by the Distributist League and the Scottish Catholic Land Association. For the main responsibility for this wild adventure was mine, although Frank did not discourage me. His attitude might be expressed in the proverb "Don't put all your eggs in one basket"—that one basket being our struggling publishing house. My proverb was quite different. We should be "Killing two birds with one stone"—an operation which has always had a fatal fascination for me. I probably should not have begun to farm solely for the sake of a Catholic Land Association or solely for our own bread and butter, but the combination of the two was overwhelming.

The term "subsistence farming" expressed my aim, and it was only gradually that I realized it had two meanings. On Father Vincent's lips it meant growing the food you would presently eat. On the lips of our farmer friends it meant making your farm pay well enough to support you. All our part of Surrey was given to dairy farming; you could walk many miles without seeing a ploughed field, and our Distributist friends, Father Vincent in particular, enjoyed a good many laughs at the expense of the farm supply shops which had to order a plough before they could sell us one. The Second World War did largely justify Father Vincent's line of thought—but for the moment I was not only attempting something in a field of which I knew nothing, but also attempting it in a way which seemed absurd to the experts. I might well have recalled a third proverb—"Let the cobbler stick to his last."

A friend of ours, Hubert French, was a successful farmer at Bletchingly, twelve miles or so from Upper Prestwood. But somehow the very depths of my ignorance raised a barrier against learning anything from him. Hubert knew his business too well to remember the first steps of many years back. I fancy he must have felt as we sometimes felt when we were asked a theological question by a heckler and longed to answer, "Yes, I can explain that *but not to you*. It would take months to bring you to that point." Hubert might not have minded saying this to us—but he was efficient rather than articulate. For him the boys from Scotland would have been a godsend, but he could only get angry—almost splutteringly angry—with the Association for sending them to people like us.

And we, still feeling that the principles of *G.K.'s Weekly* and the Association were correct principles, began to realize inch by painful inch that sound Christian principles without techniques were not enough for the running of a farm.

Readers of this record already familiar with Chesterton's and Belloc's books will remember how difficult they had found it to hit on the right title for their movement. Belloc wrote on the *Restoration of Property*, Chesterton deprecated the word "Distributist" as savouring of something startling, whereas what they were asking for was merely a return to the norm of human society. The word "return" recurred in their writings—a revolution was a return, you could and must put back the clock, as G.K. claimed, by a human finger, but one of the main Distributist feelings was, I think, the obscure expression of a fear. They hated machinery; all Distributists were opposed to mechanized farming; we were all to plough with horses. The extremists went so far as to call the plough itself a machine and demand that we use the spade only. This lunatic fringe did not represent the movement, but I rather think it represented something—their deep-seated fear that machinery was taking over from man, who had lost control to a point where he certainly could not put back the clock or stage any revolution that would be a return to saner and simpler living.

We let Chestnuts to the Sheed and Ward traveller Peter Stewart and his family, and moved in at Upper Prestwood. I like to think that one good result came of this move—for their small son Dick came under the affectionate care of Fr. Healy and is today a priest. Our tenants took care of the chapel and house and garden, though Frank still sang at the Sunday Mass. We had to go to Chestnuts or to my mother's house for a bath, as there was no bathroom at the farm. The boys went weekly to the public baths in Crawley or Redhill. We bought meat wholesale for them and for us, and Frank brought it from London on Friday evenings. Once on a hot evening he left it in a telephone box; it was recovered on Monday in a very high state and fed to the sow, who farrowed immediately after eating it.

Frank used to say, "Other people's farms are failures but ours is a farce"—and this is indeed the only word that describes it. We wired one large field against the rabbits, which abounded. But something had gone wrong with the sowing—the carefully protected crop which should have been oats came up as thistles, wireworm had got the oats. We bought expensive road metal to repair the winding track to the farm, but it was used by the boys while we were away one day to fill in a small pond. There were three ponds in the place and we were anxious about the one nearest the house because of the children. But we had, it would seem, neglected to say what material they were to use. A pair of geese dwelt near this pool, called by us the Sitwells because of their close attention to their eggs. Osbert and Edith only succeeded, however, in hatching out one gosling christened, of course, Sacheverell. The little procession of three would often pass us peacefully until Wilfrid one day chased them with a small stick. Osbert, decidedly bigger than he was, flew at him and knocked him down. He was then not quite two but he still has occasionally a nightmare of birds with huge wings rushing upon him.

We had lots of fresh milk and cream but the bill for cow-cake more than outbalanced these luxuries, the seed potatoes cost us far more than the value of the miserable crop we gathered. A delightful Scot on a neighbouring farm, Captain McCrea, gave us advice, but a mood of despair seized us when we found the boys one day distributing on the fields the basic slag he had recommended while a high wind was blowing it all away.

Then too—apart from the excellent head boy—they *could* not get up in the morning. We had a car which—commonly enough in those days—needed cranking. In the early morning, especially in cold weather, this was beyond my powers. I liked to go sometimes to a weekday mass at the Franciscan church a couple of miles away, but at a quarter to eight I often had to yell outside the bungalow, when a sleepy-eyed boy would appear and give the handle a reluctant but powerful jerk. Had they been working in a distant field I might have missed my mass but felt more hope for the crops.

A young cousin of Frank's came over from Australia and tried his hand on the farm for a while, but he was much happier passing on to a job at the office. A convert clergyman, now Mgr. Tomlinson, came to us in the summer of 1932 and did some very striking paintings for the walls of another bungalow—a really tiny one—which I hoped to make into a chapel. But none of this helped the farm on noticeably.

Things got better when we acquired two capable Irish maids—a very different proposition from anything we had had before. Maggie, the cook, was particularly good and the head boy did not hesitate to ask her advice privately. Both girls had been raised on a farm, both could milk, both were prepared to get up early.

With Maggie to take daily care and Captain McCrea to advise on grand strategy we did not hesitate to accept Mama's suggestion that our second maid Annie and the children go to her in London, and I with Frank for another U.S. visit and lecture tour in the autumn of 1932. We knew Mama was always as blissful with Rosemary as Rosemary was with her. She had bought her a miniature armchair and they would sit on either side of the fire at Pelham Place talking by the hour. Mama told me she thought it was good for Rosemary that we should go away occasionally, as she lived in a state of mental overstimulation. She thought her own conversation was more calming—I only remember one fragment, Mama asking, "What shall we play today, darling?" And Rosemary replying, "Don't let's play anything, Grannie. Let's just sit and talk one with each another about the time we were born." Mama explained to me that this meant she was to tell Rosemary for the hundredth time the story of her own birth, of my illness, of her being brought to Pelham Place where Grannie took care of her till I was well again.

The last letter I ever had from my mother was one of bitter complaint that her maids were more interested in Wilfrid—nice baby though he was—than in Rosemary. She, Mama said, was quite extraordinary, utterly unique. Not even little Thérèse of Lisieux had been more remarkable at the age of four than this her granddaughter.

Frank was lecturing in Minnesota, I was in New York staying at the Cenacle Convent, when the news reached me that Mama was ill, followed by a cable saying that an operation had been decided on. I booked back on the first fast boat. There were no planes then across the Atlantic, but Frank took a plane from Chicago for New York. Bad weather forced it down at Cleveland and he missed the boat. I was alone when I heard by radiogram that Mama was dead. I was too stunned to feel at first the heaviest grief of my life. But my thoughts ranged over the past and I resolved then and there that others should share with me the little I might find myself able to tell about her.

Mama's death changed much in our lives. My brother offered me the lease of the little house in Pelham Place; there was a great deal to be done in London and new prospects had opened on this last visit to America. The resolution taken during my lonely voyage on the *Bremen* remained unshaken—but I realized that it was about both parents that I must write.

Like most of the country, we were settling into the idea that things would go on as they were and that the food supply menaced by the War was again fairly secure. We have never much minded acknowledging our obvious failures and our farm was perhaps the worst of these. We decided to let it—and Hubert French now became cheerfully helpful in suggesting a reasonable rent and the correct kind of agreement.

But a conversation with him, and another with Father Vincent, showed at once how deeply I was committed at this time to Distributist theories and how absurd they appeared to the ordinary farmer. One of our aims having been to be sure of food for the children despite fluctuating exchanges, I said to Hubert, "I wonder if it could be arranged to let the rent of the farm be a certain number of eggs and chickens, a certain amount of milk—in fact so much food per year?" Hubert answered: "It would be much simpler for the farmer to pay you rent and for you to buy food from him."

When I told Father Vincent McNabb of this remark he just repeated again and again in tones bordering on despair, "Much simpler, much *simpler*."

It was not hard to find a tenant for a farm on the Sussex-Surrey border (half the fields were in each county) and the boys seemed pleased with the gratuity with which their services terminated. One of them married our cook Maggie; she was considerably older than he, but she remarked cheerfully, "I know I'm twice the woman that he is the man." This was undeniably true, but they seemed to be a happy couple. It was to this same boy that we owed a pleasing story. We had other neighbours besides Captain McCrea, some of whom regaled the boys with very tall stories of their farming exploits. The sky appeared to be the limit of their credulity—and we were told seriously that one of our neighbours had once ploughed with eight stallions. Frank knew nothing of farming but in Australia he had been an ardent racegoer. He mildly pointed out that the stallions would have kicked the plough to pieces and probably killed the farmer. Our boys clearly did not believe him—and the memory of this story has always given him exquisite pleasure.

Blake would hardly have ventured in his most apocalyptic moments to paint that little farmer harnessing and driving his eight stallions, but as we said goodbye to the farm I felt we had been trying to harness the winds and had been well paid for our temerity.

13

SUCCESS? ON A SHOESTRING

THE farm was let in the summer of 1933. Meanwhile that winter must be lived through somehow. Mama had died in November and after Christmas Frank went off for two months to New York. His mother was back in Australia, so I could not leave the children. Catherine suggested my bringing them to Ashburnham; I could easily run up to London from there, leaving them with Annie—nursemaid more than nurse—under the general supervision of Catherine herself and her remarkable factotum Josephine Lee.

Between Josephine, Boxall the chauffeur, and Jones the quaint old majordomo (who died a few years later leaving £20,000), Catherine kept at Ashburnham a kind of shadow of the old magnificent households of which her father's had not been one of the least splendid. Old Jones had begun as a page-boy and had spent his life at Ashburnham piling up, presumably chiefly from tips, his surprising fortune. Was he a successful gambler or just clever with his investments? This side of his life remained a mystery. We saw him as an exquisitely courteous old man pottering about the conservatory, apparently tending the very beautiful plants there, ready always to chat with ourselves or the children, with a sense certainly of possession in house and garden and the authority of a grandfather when counselling Catherine. She was life tenant of this splendid estate and so was Jones.

This was a winter visit, but Ashburnham in spring and summer had to be seen to be believed. Only in Australia did I see again such camelias growing out of doors, only at Kew some of the rare trees. Lakes artificially created lay in front of the house and the woods sloped up from them. It was wonderful landscaping and though the house was not beautiful it had all the convenience and comfort of "the spacious days" so frequently regretted by Catherine—and was so built that one was constantly aware of the surrounding beauty. There was a remarkable collection of pictures, mostly Italian primitives, the large greenhouses were radiant with orchids and other beautiful plants against a background of creepers—green always and often flowering. Nor could the coldest of winters destroy the Sussex landscape, and I often thought of Chesterton's phrase "the delicate heart of the winter woods".

It was a place with healing in it, and I badly needed healing. Mama once said the months a little while after my father's death were the worst in her life. I was feeling this now; Mama was gone, Frank away. His absence appeared endless—what, then, would hers be?

At Ashburnham, besides pictures, woods, fields and plants, there was the chapel. Catherine had put her heart into the beautifying of this: the loveliest of her pictures, great silver candlesticks on the altar, a profusion of flowers filled the large room which she had turned into a sanctuary. She too had a "weekend" priest—usually a Jesuit from their house at Hastings—and on Sundays it held a sizeable congregation. All through the week the red lamp reminded one of the divine presence, and it was there above all that comfort could be sought.

Alone at Pelham Place in my frequent visits to London, Mama's absence became an ache that would not be stilled—I remember one night reading *Tudor Sunset* and going to sleep at last with her own words for comfort, "There be many beautiful things given away in heaven besides palms."

I have always thought that in the Communion of Saints, God allows those dearest to us to help us very specially by their prayers when He has taken them to Himself. Whether from purgatory or from heaven we are aware of their loving activity. "I shall spend my heaven", Thérèse said, "doing good on earth"—and I cannot think it is only the canonized saints of whom this is true. After Boy's death we had been aware of it, after my father's, and now again.

The history of Sheed and Ward had a peculiar element in it—our financial difficulties arose chiefly from our too swift success. We were greatly undercapitalized. If we had gone slower and published fewer books it would have been easier in our first years. And when my husband thought of and carried out the idea of the first Catholic Book of the Month Club this began to show itself more plainly still. It was sound financially, with prices as they were in those days, to sell part of an edition of seven-and-sixpenny books at two and six to a sufficient number of yearly subscribers—but it was the kind of finance that needed a big capital and this we had not got. Hence the perpetual struggle, not helped by the lack of cash on all hands brought about by the Depression.

On the other hand, as our friend Fr. (now Mgr.) Hartigan constantly pointed out, ours were the best-selling in America of the more serious Catholic books, and when the Catholic Book of the Month Club started there it was largely supplied by us. Only the books were no longer ours—for, not having an American house, we were selling the American rights of our titles to various U.S. publishers. Father Hartigan urgently pressed my husband in 1932 to start in New York, and this was the principal object of his trip in 1933. Before he left New York on this visit we were established in an old brownstone house on Fifth Avenue. Our ceilings in particular were matter of admiration to some, though merely of *admiratio* to others. Frank had bought back the majority of the titles we had sold, and Sheed and Ward, New York, was on its feet.

We asked some of our best-known authors to give us a word of introduction to the American public and were touched and delighted by the enthusiasm with which they responded. Mgr. Knox found it a refreshing reversal of the usual order of things to be writing a blurb for his publisher. "I often have to write recommendations with my pen in my mouth if not actually with my tongue in my cheek, but not this one", which was really written "ex animo", for Sheed and Ward had created a school of Catholic literature, both by "decent translations" of the best Continental work and also "by digging out and hounding on English Catholics to write the sort of books they ought".

Sigrid Undset, I had only met once—we had done a book of hers on Scandinavian saints; she had terrified me by her grand and gloomy presence. But she called our work "great". She and Jacques Maritain both spoke, from the angle of those whose books we were translating, of the "fruitfulness" of our work. Lord Howard of Penrith, with his diplomat's experience of different lands, rejoiced that we had combined with "a unity of outlook which is convinced and very rare and impressive", the realization that the universality of Catholicism touches life at every point. Alfred Noyes, as an "artist as well as a convert", rejoiced over the appearance of the volumes and his pleasure in handling them. "Their contents represent", he said, "all the many-coloured stir and fragrance of the new spring which is quickening the mind of Christendom as it has not been quickened for many years."

Father Martindale had come into the Church as a schoolboy, and had gone through the long period of his Jesuit training at a time when the stresses of Modernism must have made such an experience almost harrowing. Before World War I he had had a breakdown. My brother Leo, still a schoolboy, going into a nursing home to have his appendix removed, had there met C.C.M. and struck up a warm friendship with him, shared by myself and a little later by Frank. He once said to Leo, "Please regard me as a suitable object for the blowing off of steam at"—and many people used him for this.

He figured frequently in our house organ, whether for his liturgical and theological books or the delightful accounts of his travels in New Zealand and Australia. Intensely alive to the needs and outlook of the world, especially through his experience of prewar, wartime, and postwar Oxford, he felt how difficult it was "to modernize" any department of Catholic art, literature, erudition etc., without incurring at least the chance of seeming "Modernist". We were, he said, not only "speaking to contemporary men and women, especially those of higher education . . . in a language they could understand about topics that interested them", but, better still, "causing such readers to *become* interested in what otherwise they would not so much as have looked at". Like Mgr. Knox, he saw this achievement as a double stream: discovery of and encouragement of home talent and the bringing over of Continental thought to an intelligentsia "far more insular than it imagines . . . This firm alone, as far as I know, has produced anything worth reading about the underlying philosophy of Bolshevism and Russian Communism." He felt we should both gain from American Catholics and give to them—discovering especially, as we had in England, the latent talents "that certainly exist".

This the distinguished Dominican Provincial, Fr. Bede Jarett, stressed even more strongly. He was glad for our sake—"Their faith, devotion, sacramental zeal, enthusiasm, will edify and inspire you"—glad for the sake of America "because I am sure you will help Catholics over there as you have helped them here. We owe so much to you for giving us books that deal with our real problems, difficulties, the sanctities of our time."

Actuality in a community which had for long spoken in a dated and outmoded language, vitality in a world which was curiously unvital despite the noise it managed to make—we felt that these notes were being struck, this tune played, by the very men who hailed it as ours. These priests were pouring life into a postwar world already becoming aware of foiled ambitions and disappointed hopes. Lloyd George had promised us a world fit for heroes—and the grim joke was being made that it was so because none but heroes could endure the horror of it. The war that was to end war looked as it receded as though after all it had left us only with an armistice between wars. I don't know whether Gilbert Chesterton was the first to say that. I met it first in his *Weekly*, and we published later a collection of his essays of these years under the title *The End of the Armistice*.

Gilbert Chesterton and Christopher Dawson may be considered as a writer's span is reckoned, to belong to different generations. Of all our authors, their outlook came closest to one another, although very differently formulated. Both felt overpoweringly the failure which faced the modern world unless it could return to its religious roots, both were constantly aware of Christendom, both had come to the Church from outside her, both, as laymen, looked at the irreligious and the religious world alike with a focus different from that of a priest. Dawson could tell you far more of the world's history—but with Chesterton's vivid imagination his *Everlasting Man* cast a brilliant light on Dawson's *Age of the Gods* or *Making of Europe*.

To both of them our work looked like a crusade. They had been deeply engaged already, Chesterton long before our firm came into existence—but they seemed to see us rallying new forces for that crusade, signing up more soldiers for it, organizing it in fresh ways. "It is perhaps", wrote Chesterton, "the one case in which I would speak for such a work as a cause." By our translations we were revealing "the other side of Europe" to many aware only of writers "on the cynical or destructive side in the modern moral debate. France has meant nothing but Zola and Anatole France; and it was implied that every German scholar was a Prussian professor of the precise type of Haeckel. The Sheed and Ward translations are a complete revelation of another and larger world."

Christopher Dawson added yet another to the metaphors called upon in these tributes. And if we liked Mgr. Knox's comparison with a school, we liked even better Dawson's with explorers and pioneers. We had hoped for greater things from the average Catholic than we had got through the Evidence Guild. Even in our best years we were acquiring far too few members—not for the platform alone but for that really useful programme of theology offered by our classes. These ordinary men and women Dawson saw as having really been reached, stirred and taught through books. Even if his estimate of the achievement was too high, it corresponded to our desires. Our reach was indeed always exceeding our grasp, but reading this page from the long letter he sent we could gratefully feel that we were not just grasping the empty air—and with his final words he was inviting the co-operation of all those who might, through reading and personal contact, do for the world what we were still hoping more of them would eventually do on that outdoor platform. Dawson wrote:

> The work of Messrs. Sheed and Ward has been that of explorers and pioneers: they have discovered new ports and opened up fresh territory. They have courageously refused to accept the traditional low valuation of democratic taste and of the ordinary man's power of intellectual assimilation. They have attempted to bring Catholic thought out of the cloister and the lecture-room into the world of everyday life and into contact with the ordinary man's thoughts and interests. And they have been rewarded by the discovery of a new public of which few people suspected the existence. They have discovered that it is not only professors who are interested in philosophy and that other people beside the clergy wish to read about theology.
>
> Even more important is the work that they are beginning to do as interpreters of the Catholic mind to that vast amorphous world outside, which is awakening from centuries of acquiescence and looking restlessly for new ways of life and thought. Public opinion, especially in English-speaking countries, has lost its old solidity and stolidity and has now become alarmingly fluid. It is impossible to say in which direction the tide of public opinion will flow, but when it turns it will flow strong and fast. In such a world the old traditions have lost their old sacrosanctity. Everything depends on their actuality and the way in which they are brought into relation with the living movement of opinion. There is a serious danger that Catholicism should be shoved contemptuously on one side as

irrelevant and out of date, simply because no-one takes the time or the trouble to consider it. Under such circumstances it is positively alarming to think how much the future of Catholicism is dependent on the Catholic publisher, but it should also be a stimulus to Catholics to accept the challenge and to do all in their power to support a programme of Catholic action in the world of letters.

I hardly remember now which was the stronger feeling—gratification at such tributes or terror lest the shoestring on which we were operating should break and we would next be heard of as a minor branch of a more affluent firm.

A time was beginning for us both of tremendous energies and considerable strain. Frank was now going to the United States three times a year. There was no air travel yet and the fastest boat took almost a week. He would clear his desk in London to find in New York another crowded one. Directing two offices, combined with lecturing, translating and finally writing his own books, was increasingly exhausting. I went only once a year, but soon after our New York office opened I too embarked upon a book.

Neither of us is a writer in the strict sense. We feel no *need* to write. We only write because, and when, we have something to say which we feel must be said. I felt now that the life of my parents ought to be given to the English Catholic world; that there were useful lessons to be drawn from it and that they were too significant to be allowed to sink into oblivion. My father had been writing his reminiscences just before his death (so had Chesterton—if one believes in omens it is not a happy one). I examined Papa's many drafts. "I have just finished", Stuart Collingwood had once made him say in a burlesque, "the fourteenth revision of my first paragraph." There was, however, enough of the reminiscences in a finished stage to use as the first chapters of my own book about him, and there were passages that could be introduced later. My mother's childhood emerged, I thought delightfully, from old letters and from the stories she had often told me. After their marriage the two narratives fused into one and I carried it in my first volume down to the end of the nineteenth century.

I remember at Pelham Place, where we stayed on for a while, hiding the big boxes of books under the drawing-room sofa when my morning's work was ended. Visitors belonging to my youth would not have appreciated the kind of room that was gradually becoming ours—papers and books on chairs, piano, floor. This last habit was dangerous with children, and not with children only. One office cleaner threw away a MS left by my husband on the floor. Luckily the author had a carbon. But when Aunt Gwendy Norfolk came to tea I hid the papers—and also adjured Rosemary to behave properly. She, alas, came in turning head over heels and I felt a very bad impression had been made (which she effaced the following Christmas on a brief visit to Arundel). But she was passing through a difficult stage and I hesitated when Fr. Healy suggested she should make her First Communion. She was only six, and though very intelligent, also at that time very naughty.

I started instructing her, not much helped by my own old teacher Mother Loyola, whose *First Communion* was written for eleven-year-olds. The only books I found of any use were Fr. Kelly's series *My First Communion*, *The Seven Sacraments*, and *The Mass for Children*, but most of it I had to do myself, and Rosemary was singularly unco-operative. Having learnt the art of the somersault she was eager to practise it at all times, and she appeared to be paying no attention at all to my lessons. At last one day I said in despair, "If you won't be good I don't think you can make your First Communion."

But her answer defeated me, though given upside down in a defiant voice: "I'll be a great deal gooder if you let me make it."

Fr. Healy had been right, as I might have known, and we crossed the river to St. George's Cathedral, Southwark for her first confession on the first day of July 1934. It was a great compliment, I felt, that (devoted though she was to Fr. Healy) Rosemary insisted that the confessional door be left open and that I kneel close by. The next day, the Feast of the Visitation, she made her First Communion in the chapel where Fr. Healy said Mass daily.

I had, I realized, been thinking too much in terms of my own youth which I had been reliving through the parents' biography; at eleven-plus one can be serious, but not at six. Rosemary and I went in the afternoon to the Natural History Museum in Kensington, and she played in the grounds there after she had had enough of the animals. She consented, rather reluctantly, to a brief visit to the Oratory, but I was convinced that all was very well and that she fully conformed to Pius X's views of what was needed for a young child's First Communion.

But for both children London was not, we were feeling increasingly, the right place. Even the acre at Chestnuts had given them room to play, and after visits to the wide spaces of Crosby, Ashburnham and the Isle of Wight, Pelham Place appeared restricted indeed. The house was not very small, it was bigger than Chestnuts, but it was joined to other houses on either side and the people in those houses greatly disliked noise. I at least could not keep two lively children quiet. Pelham Place shared a garden with the Crescent and we sent Rosemary and Wilfrid over there in fine weather. They had great games among the bushes, but came back in a state of unspeakable dirt. "Don't shout! Don't go on the grass! Don't damage the bushes! Don't go out alone! Don't pick the flowers!" London seemed a mass of prohibitions. And our tenants wanted to leave Chestnuts. Happily enough we decided to go back there.

"Three moves or a fire", the saying goes, and by that rule we should have no furniture left; I had actually acquired quite a lot more at this stage from my mother, and we were able to house it in the old chapel, which became a large and most welcome auxiliary living-room. For the new church was up by now, a convenient asbestos building, hidden behind the hedge at the back of the house, but not at all ugly even had it been visible. It was far bigger than we needed but filled up at the beginning of the next War.

The new large room was exceedingly useful for work. No longer need papers be hidden under the drawing-room sofa. The garden had been well cared for and life resumed its old train. The chief change was the emergence of Wilfrid as a powerful factor in daily life. I was already much given to what is now almost a vice—the reading of detective stories. Wilfrid would approach me with the remark, "Are you reading for work or for fun?" If I said, "For work" he would usually go away to find his pleasure elsewhere, but if I admitted, "For fun" he would say, "Then put the book down and play with me."

At about seven he began piano lessons. Lazy about practising, he would rush to the chapel just before his lesson to pray that he might play better than he deserved. As with Rosemary, we were trying to give him a living grasp of religious truth, occasionally testing ourselves in the matter. Wilfrid having said one day that he was going to the chapel, Frank asked, "Why go to the chapel? God's in this room, isn't He?" Wilfrid answered, "He's only everywhere here."

A friend had given us a set of bricks—hollow wood, light as a feather, but very strong—and with these the children would play by the hour, building marvellous structures and then destroying them. Often disputes arose as to how many bricks each should use, but after Frank had marked each brick R or W they became more disposed to pool them in one triumph of architecture. Rosemary had begun school and spent much of the evening imitating her teacher, with Wilfrid and the dolls for class. These were happy days, except for the constant feeling that Frank would soon be going to America and I must either stay home without him or else leave the children.

I took little active share in the publishing apart from reading MSS. On this I spent a good deal of time and we would, too, talk over in the evenings the various problems that had arisen. I am not at all a good publisher's reader—I am still certain that the MSS I approved were good, but I have never had that instinct for what the public will like which is essential for a successful reader. I did discover Fr. Leen and recognized the profound quality of his spiritual teaching despite his rather unfortunate style. But I remember three books, on Dame Lucy Knatchbull, Père Tarin and Father Pro, which I accepted and which all illustrated a fact that drove us at moments near to despair. You can quite easily sell the hundredth book on St. Thérèse, on St. Francis of Assisi, on St. Thomas More, on any already well-known saint. You cannot sell the first book on the most interesting character, if people have not already heard of him. Again, in those days especially, you could not sell "spiritual classics", however splendidly reviewed. This was illustrated for us by the *Golden Epistle of William of Thierry*, and by the *Passion of SS. Perpetua and Felicitas*.

A speaker at a C.E.G. conference, comparing our outdoor speaking with indoor convert classes, once said, "We have to work the stony ground." What she meant was that people come to a hall or to a class already interested in Catholicism, whereas the Evidence Guild is addressing crowds who are not interested in it in the least. We too, as publishers, were in those days working the stony ground, making a new beginning—and the proof that it was a successful beginning lies in the fact that we are now getting bigger sales for our reprints than we got in the thirties when we first published the books. We were, as our letters of introduction had indicated, doing both in England and America something toward creating a new class of Catholic reader. But it was uphill work and Frank was getting very tired.

The up and down to London was one element in that fatigue and we decided to try one more move. This time we found a house at Ealing, close to the Priory and with a good garden. The children could go on the Underground to the Sacred Heart Convent, Hammersmith, which took small boys as well as girls. The owner would rent it to us for a year, after which we could decide whether to buy. Chestnuts was put on the market—"For Catholics only", because of the chapel—and meanwhile we found a temporary tenant.

14

CROSBY

I have not spoken much of the visits to my sister's home, Crosby Hall, which—always so delightfully—broke the routine of our children's life. (There was not much routine in ours.) The whole family would migrate there, usually in the summer. There was cricket in the garden, there were long mornings in the woods or looking at the flowers, there was daily Mass in the little church nearby, there was even cider for Frank, who drinks nothing stronger. Above all there were the children who, apart from Nick, a few years older, were within months the same age as ours. Hester and Rosemary became in those years, and remained always, closer than many sisters. But we were amused over some of the arguments on the first long visit, when both were five years old, at the time of Mama's death. Rosemary was heard one day triumphing over Hester in that though neither had any grandfather left, she still possessed a grandmother. "Blundell", Hester said another day, "is a more famous name than Sheed." I should myself have accepted this without question, but Rosemary vehemently disputed it. She had to grow older to be told of Blundell the Cavalier, of Blundell the Elizabethan Catholic and of title-deeds going back to King Stephen! But this particular argument ended in perfect harmony with the agreement that Blundell was more famous in Little Crosby and Sheed in London.

For the most part the little girls went around inseparably and my sister and I recalled our own nursery days as they joined forces against the boys whenever such action was needed.

Francis was the perfect host. I loved to go round the home farm with him and to be taught what it might have saved us a lot to have known earlier. Indeed, our abandonment of Distributist exaggerations was signed and sealed by our publication of my brother-in-law's book, *The Agricultural Problem*, which dear Father Vincent bewailed and lamented in a review in *G.K.'s Weekly*. Francis certainly was living in the world about which he was writing. He had as a young man brought about the Federation of the Lancashire

Friendly Societies. He knew a lot about modern machinery and methods. He had the best herd of middle white pigs in the county, and as we walked through the sandhills where they were established, Francis demonstrated to me what clean animals they were if allowed to move in a wide space and not crowded in ill-tended styes. They rubbed themselves against his legs as we walked—and they were indeed shining white.

But it was not only on Francis's topics that we talked; I was surprised to find how interested he was in my writing—how excellent and helpful a critic. If I had taken his advice I should today be a biographer only—he urged me to direct my energies into this one channel. Although he was keenly political, being Conservative member for Ormskirk, and I knew nothing of politics, our minds met to a surprising degree on partly political issues. Despite what I held the near madness of his faith in Stanley Baldwin, Francis could never have been just a party man. He urged the Conservative local priest *not* to campaign for him, disliking clerical intervention in politics as much on his own side as in opposition. He flatly refused when one of our aunts wanted to bring a Conservative "great lady", whom he and my sister had never met, to stay at Crosby; this sort of approach to success would have been abhorrent to him.

The atmosphere of Little Crosby is hard to convey. Believing still in the general outline of Distributism and being thoroughly sick of the idealistic stories that abounded concerning the Good Landlord and the Grateful Tenant, I have always viewed that relationship with a high degree of scepticism. But the endless interviews between Francis and bailiff, gardener or farmer were impressive. And when a tenant told my brother-in-law that he was "one of nature's gentlemen" I, at least, did not merely enjoy a laugh over it.

Francis and the villagers felt they had lived through hard days together. The Squires of Crosby had for long paid the fines that saved their tenants from being whipped at the cart's tail for failure to attend the Protestant church. One Blundell ancestor had been born in prison. Francis had that quality of respect which St. Vincent inculcated in his Sisters; and the farmers reciprocated. They asked him for counsel—not only, as a lawyer, would he often draw up their wills, but he would be requested to decide the fair share for each child. The older men, however, offered their counsel in return.

"You're going to London, Squire," said one of them after his election to Parliament, "and London's a wicked place. Don't forget God."

God is, in a rather prosaic, matter-of-course way, the centre of that village. The farmers take their turns in giving the coal for the church; the village, when anyone dies, has its own prayers, led by the oldest farmer. When Francis himself died, everyone made a novena of masses and communions, the men getting to work an hour late and staying on an extra half hour, so that employer and employed each made half the sacrifice. Fr. Holden, announcing this, spoke as if it were an old custom. He was the third priest I had known there, and fitted by far the best. Much of his popularity came from his determination to work with the Crosby (indeed the Lancashire) slogan: "We always have done." This phrase explains much; it would be hard to get developments going at Little Crosby. "I've been static for a thousand years", my brother-in-law once said with a grin when I was urging a dynamic Catholicism, "and I intend to remain so." The villagers would have echoed him. Indeed he was probably echoing them, for there was plenty of dynamism in Francis.

Even in Lancashire there are few places where the only church is the Catholic one. "The Village", remarked a cousin of Francis, as he walked through the one street describing the points of interest, "has never had in it a post office, a public house, a Protestant or a prostitute." Shades of Mr. Belloc! A Catholic village that boasts of the absence of a public house, where men must walk a mile or so into Great Crosby if they want a drink! A village, moreover, only seven miles from Liverpool (where joining the Church is often called "getting Irished"), which has seldom had in one of its cottages any type of Catholic but an Englishman. "Ah dunno," said a villager once when asked about a visitor's religion, "he's nobbut an Irishman."

It was curiously tranquil, this little pocket of old Catholic England. I should have been bored to death had it been my fate to live there. But I loved to visit the beautifully tended rich black fields, the cows, the friendly pigs, the Harkirk, the little church and its priest, to whom we too became devoted.

I doubt if such terms as "Catholic Action" or "Apostolate of the laity" were ever heard in Little Crosby and I should sometimes have liked to stimulate these slow-moving folk. But when the harvest festival reminded me that this must once have been a Catholic custom, or when Fr. Holden told us of the spontaneous charity with which every woman in the village visited the mother of a lad accused of some crime to tell her they did not believe it, I realized how beautiful a genuine Catholicism can be, however static.

After nineteen years a villager said to my sister, "We're getting used to you, Mrs. Blundell." And on his silver jubilee, Fr. Holden remarked that he cared little for England outside Lancashire and little for Lancashire outside Little Crosby. Speaking for the visitors, I told him I did not believe it—and in any case how much we cared for him. We all knew by now that the affection was reciprocated, but the speech reminded me of the considerable odds at the beginning against a mutual understanding between old and new, South and North, Lancashire and the rest of England.

The happy times of our Crosby visits only lasted till 1936. That summer Richard, Wilfrid's contemporary, a most winning and lively child, died quite suddenly. He was only six. "Farmer Dickon", his father had called him, and he had been Francis' companion on every visit to pigs or cows, showing extraordinary interest and awareness. His parents were shattered. All that summer Francis was unwell, but the doctor said he could go to London for some engagements at the end of September. Frank and I came up for the night and dined with them at the Rembrandt Hotel. They talked cheerfully and we went back to our small private hotel feeling a little happier about them. That night neither of us could sleep. The telephone began to ring; it went on and on and I said to Frank, "Suppose it's for us?" "Out of all the people in the hotel!" he said incredulously. "Anyhow, far more likely to be for the management. Who even knows we're here?" I went downstairs all the same, but the sitting-room door was locked. Behind it the telephone rang again and then stopped.

In the morning we learned that Francis had died of a thrombosis during the night. The doctor had been trying to get me to be with my sister.

The body was taken back to Crosby. The entire village seemed to be present at the station and the procession went slowly on as far as the big stone cross where Fr. Holden was waiting with candles and acolytes. The coffin was laid at the foot of the cross, the *De*

Profundis recited. We went to the church and when he had prayed again Fr. Holden said, "Now I will leave you to say the village prayers", and the oldest farmer took his place before the altar. This must be, I fancy, a tradition from penal days when the priest could often only pause briefly at a Catholic house in mourning. Certainly this village was in mourning, and Fr. Holden in his funeral sermon expressed the reason for it, which lay in the central devotion of Francis' life. He had done well in Parliament, he had introduced and passed a Bill for the final lifting of the last Catholic disabilities, he was spoken of as a probable Conservative Minister of Agriculture, but "my highest ambition", he had told Fr. Holden, "is to keep this village for God."

Nick had been brought back from school and, like the anticlimax after our brother Boy's funeral, I remember the Crosby nannie as we returned from this one. She rushed at him in the hall and in a voice of mingled grief and pride exclaimed, "Welcome, young Squire of Crosby!" It was a strange greeting for a sensitive boy.

A great part of that autumn was spent by me at Crosby and when I came south again Tetta spent much time with us, at Chestnuts and at Ealing, and the two families became more closely united than ever.

To my surprise—and for the moment to my indignation—Wilfrid (aged six) was put in the First Communion class at the convent without reference to us. The nun in charge expressed her regret when I spoke to her; we talked it over thoroughly and Frank and I agreed that he should continue his preparation. But the incident reminded me of something that often vexes me: the Church upholds in theory the authority of parents—teachers in theory are their delegates. But how often is this remembered in practice? Our relations with our children's teachers have been excellent—but both Frank and I objected strongly to being told by the children what they had "decided" on matters where the decision should have been ours.

In Wilfrid's preparation I could not imagine a more perfect co-operation than that between the nuns and ourselves. Often he would talk in the evening of what he had been taught—I remember his asking me if I knew the story of Zaccheus and wondering what would happen if Our Lord came to our house. After various speculations—such as that I would not need to turn on the light because

He would light the room—Wilfrid concluded fervently, "*And* he would be even more amusing than Monsignor Elwes."

The art of teaching at Hammersmith was unusually good. At a prize-day exhibition the drawings done by the children of seven were shown; some of them were quite remarkable. The art teacher said that Wilfrid had great talent and the house began to be filled with large sheets of brown paper on which with bright crayons were depicted scenes chosen sometimes by his teacher but oftener by himself—a picnic, a house in the woods, a game of football, a game of cricket. Outside school hours he was drawing constantly. Children do sometimes appear to have a talent that never matures, and one wonders whether this is in the nature of things or whether their teachers are responsible for crushing it. I know little or nothing of that kind of drawing, but certainly Wilfrid's favourite scenes had the quality, unusual in so young an artist, of vitality; his footballers were kicking, his cricketers were hitting out. And then, quite suddenly, at his first boys' prep. school, he stopped drawing for pleasure altogether. The headmaster had not only set him at so-called "free-hand", which might well have trained him usefully, but had sneered openly before the other boys at Wilfrid's colourful brown-paper-and-crayon drawings.

There had been no bid for Chestnuts and the tenants were not paying their rent. Frank and I went down there one day to consider the situation. And that day was—absurdly enough—a shattering experience. We had been told that the tenant's nephew, who lived with her, was an ardent gardener. He was indeed. He had dug up all my bulbs and replanted them in perfectly straight rows, one behind another. It looked exactly like a nursery garden. With a shudder, but a smile—for I could easily put that right—I passed on to the chapel. Where my lovely rock garden had delighted the eye with its masses of white and purple there remained nothing but the brick yard of our beginnings. All my unruly plants had been torn up, all the bricks had been put back.

I thought we had now seen the worst—but no. The lawn was larger, the grass, no doubt, better, at the expense of the beloved lime tree which our tenant's nephew had cut down. All this in less than a year; it was hard to believe our eyes and even blind rage hardly prevented me from using mine to weep with.

When Frank reproached the lady and asked where she had stored the wood of our valuable tree she staged the most dramatic faint I have ever seen; the skill with which her nephew caught her and dragged her out gave some appearance of previous rehearsals. We sat in the porch; despite the devastation, and the noisy road, there was a peace about the place and it was full of memories. Suddenly we looked at one another and realized that we wanted to come back.

15

START OF THE *CATHOLIC WORKER*

THERE was a touch of irony in the fact that in all discussions about whether "social subjects" should be treated on the Guild's platforms, Frank showed himself far more at home with the topic than those who wanted them. He had really studied the papal encyclicals and knew a good deal about the social thought and history of the forty years that lay between *Rerum Novarum* and *Quadragesimo Anno*; besides having listened to his father on Communism, he had read Karl Marx and done a good deal of thinking on the subject. It would be many years yet before I should attempt what for me was the best—the historical approach, learning through the works of the Fathers the splendours of Catholic social action when the Roman Empire was crumbling and the Church creating a new people. But I was, in fact, making *an* historical approach—and not an altogether happy one—realizing in my background reading for my parents' biography against how black a mass of Catholic inertia and selfishness the great social Frenchmen of the previous generation—Lacordaire, Montalembert, Ozanam—had stood out.

Frank soon made up his mind to respond in his own way to the demand from the Westminster Guild that he—who did not want, who deeply opposed social subjects on the platform—should at least teach our speakers the foundation principles whereby to deal with the inevitable questions put by Communists and about Communism. These principles, dealing with the nature of man and the reasons why Communism could never satisfy his needs, together with some account of Marx's teaching, what Marx had got from Hegel and what modern Communism had made of it, he gave in a series of lectures to the Guild Senior Class, which became *Communism and Man*. I have always thought this one of his most important books, though it is less popular than the further development of his social thinking given some years later in *Society and Sanity*.

For actually we were not only profoundly interested in social thinking, but we felt it came close to theology as an essential in our work as writers and publishers. Christopher Dawson's books had been teaching us and our public that human culture had grown from the root of religion, that as religion dies human energies wither. He had shown in *The Making of Europe* the vast work of the Church as civiliser and creator of thought and art. He had posed *The Modern Dilemma*. But we were publishing other books also, pressing on our readers from other aspects the duty of Catholics to study the social field and their own responsibilities in it. *A Philosophy of Work* by Borne and Henry and *Catholicism, Protestantism and Capitalism* by Giovanni Fanfani (our only author to become a Prime Minister), translated respectively from French and Italian, were both important. Even more important perhaps were books which dealt with efforts being made here and now to do something about the world in which we were living, a world, that moving away from God, was losing the fundamental ideas brought by Christianity of each man's value and of human rights and liberties.

It was not only as a publisher that at this time I began to be interested in a number of social activities with which my life was never identified as with the C.E.G., yet which find a place in these memories. Most stories of lives set in the sort of framework that was mine abound in names of politicians, literary men and women, actors or others known at sight to the readers. My parents moved in this world of famous names and a good many of them appear in my biography of them, which tells also the story of my own youth. I have not in this book deliberately omitted them, yet I notice as I reread how seldom they occur. Never intentionally breaking away from my family surroundings, I seem insensibly to have shifted a little so that contacts once constant became incidental. Living in two countries and working fairly hard in both, it is not easy to keep up with all one's friends; and somehow between publishing and lecturing—especially at street corners—many new friends began to surround us whose claim to friendship was with some their need for us, with others what they had to give us, but with most was both.

The fact—which I ought to have learnt from Gilbert Chesterton but which, in fact, I learnt gradually from life—is that this was a wider world, filled with even more interesting people. My parents had chosen well with men like George Wyndham and Hugh Cecil, but in the movements I am going to talk about there were more people of high originality, of creative genius. And, too, these movements were really doing something in our sick society toward bringing healing, even if only to a few; they were making promises they looked like keeping. Among them they might spell out the changed world we were all longing for. I had always felt one very strong reason against discussing social subjects on the outdoor platform to be that we were not yet ready with any solutions other than a compromise with, or a toning down of, the theories of men far removed from Christianity. In *Témoignage chrétien* Mgr. Ancel once asked: Must Christians always be trying to ally themselves with an outworn capitalism on the one hand, or, on the other, with a Communism which they vainly hope to purge of its atheist materialism? Cannot they (he asked) create something new?

I began to discover that this was precisely what various groups were attempting; in the States, in Canada, in France. Later I came to see more and more clearly that if Christianity is to be the new form taken by the amorphous matter of the world around me, all its elements are needed in this truly creative work: liturgy and religious art, all the forms of charity, and supremely theology and the study of prayer. I came also to realize that study was needed of the elements the modern world itself had brought to its own shaping: technology of every kind, some appreciation of economics and world trade, of what machinery and the working with it meant, of the makeup of the machine-bred man in town or country as contrasted with the old-time farmer.

Each of the movements I now encountered was consciously seeking as well as in some measure achieving—and I threw myself passionately into this search. It became deeply part of my life—and I hope I can make the story of these mixed religious and social searchings, these groups in different countries, as interesting as in fact they were, above all that the people in them may come alive for others as they did for me.

George Orwell gives in *Down and Out in Paris and London* two pictures of amazing vividness: in Paris men die of hunger or are driven by starvation to murder and suicide, in London they are kept alive on tea and "bread-and-marge", walking from one casual ward to another—out into the country, miles and miles of it.

Men did not die of starvation in the England of the Depression, but their hearts died within them as they settled down to life on the dole, with no hope for the future and the ever-diminishing energy of undernourishment.

In America the picture was a different one, and I do not know how much the difference in government and social climate had to do with the fact that while a lot was being said by English Catholics all the real attempts at action, at getting to grips with a desperate world situation, began among Catholics in Canada, in the United States and in Europe.

In the States, which we came to know intimately after the establishment of our publishing house in New York, the way in which authority handled or failed to handle the Depression varied from state to state and from town to town. The country is so vast that there is never the same uniformity as in England, and unemployment was treated mainly as a local question. Some states dealt with it much better than others—but there is no doubt that, especially in winter, men did die of starvation. There was an immense call for private charity, and by and large it met with magnificent response.

Before the Depression the lack of powerful trade unions had resulted in great hardship for unskilled labour, of which immigration produced a constant supply. But wages were high in most of the skilled trades; Europeans thought of America as the workers' paradise. The enormous amount of instalment buying, out of the high wages, made the crash worse when it came, and the rate of public relief in many areas was terribly low. The scale on which unemployment had suddenly to be coped with often proved too much for harassed authority. Dorothy Day has given in a book published by us, *House of Hospitality*, pictures as vivid as any George Orwell ever painted: a man and baby—sent from one relief agency to another, kept waiting far into the night at a police station, interrogated and threatened in the hope of driving them back to their home town—were finally housed by herself and her daughter, who gave up their beds to the exhausted man and his little child and themselves slept on the floor. We seem in her pages to see the hunger marchers, seeking employment and begging the intervention of the Federal Government on their behalf, the bread lines stretching along the street of men with broken boots standing in New York's winter snow.

First-aid methods of meeting the sudden and terrible crisis of the Depression were made by religious organizations of all denominations. Bread-lines sprang up everywhere, clothing depots were started. I remember especially the Franciscans in San Francisco with their immense hall crowded morning and evening for free breakfasts and suppers. And while thousands of churches were doing this work it was made difficult by the impoverishment of many of their supporters. Frank was dining once in the rectory of a big church when one of the curates came in and asked: "Can anyone give me ten dollars?" One of the others obliged, and when he came back he told them he had wanted it for a man who had in the past given thousands to the Church, had lost his job and all his investments.

But charity, whether private or public, was after all a palliative. Could any answer be found other than that "going down to help" which had been in my own youth the attitude of the kinder among the rich towards the suffering poor?

Peter Maurin was perhaps the greatest inspiration of Catholic America in our generation. Yet having said this, I almost despair of bringing him to life in print. It was Dorothy Day far more than he who set on foot *The Catholic Worker*, both the newpaper and the Houses of Hospitality. It was she who was wanted to lecture everywhere; at first glance you would probably overlook Peter. He was a square, smallish, untidy man. To read he put on magnifying spectacles which he had bought for fifty cents and which sat crookedly on his nose. He was from southern France, of peasant stock, one of twenty-three children, some of the brothers and sisters being of his father's second marriage. He had travelled widely and worked at many jobs—in steel mills, lumber camps and railroads; as a travelling salesman, a janitor, a teacher of the French language. For having covered France in his journeyings, he came to Canada and thence to the States. All the time he was reading—and you can trace in the little he published the influence of Charles Péguy—all the time he was thinking, all the time he was writing.

Peter did not care where he lived, comfort meant nothing to him. He worked for four years in a boys' camp—at first without any pay, later at a dollar a day—which even at that time few would have thought sufficient. But Peter spent on food hardly a dollar a week, living chiefly on bread and vegetable soup. He did not care where he slept—he slept very little anyhow. Such money as he had went on books and papers. His pockets were always full of these and his mind of ideas, which he would spill out equally readily to "bums", to priests, to journalists, to philosophers. It was an unending stream.

Peter never stopped until you stopped him, but then he did so with the utmost good humour. He might exhaust his audience, but a man who could not get annoyed himself would never annoy them, and even if exhausted one was never bored by him.

Frank got to know Peter well. He would drop in at Sheed and Ward and in the bookroom would read or talk—or write those *Easy Essays*, some of which we published, and which expressed his philosophy of life and action and his judgements on the world around us. We were in the very depth of the Depression, and college graduates felt themselves lucky if they could hold down a job in a restaurant or a department store. One day Peter was in the bookroom talking to Frank when a total stranger came in. Peter suddenly swung round and addressed him in an "Easy Essay":

The Vincentians were founded to work among the poor.
But instead they run colleges,
In competition with the Jesuits.
Don't you think it would be better
If instead of competing with the Jesuits
They co-operated with them
By running Houses of Hospitality
For graduates of Jesuit colleges
Who cannot get jobs?

Our startled visitor made for the door but Peter was not disconcerted. Like ourselves on the outdoor platform, he often had the experience of losing an audience—but he also kept many. And on his arrival in New York he had gone, as if by special guidance, to the family of the second genius in the Catholic Worker movement: Dorothy Day.

Dorothy had been away, following the march to Washington of the hunger strikers: when she got home she found Peter in the kitchen lecturing to her Communist sister-in-law. This is what he was saying:

People go to Washington
Asking the Federal Government
to solve their economic problems.
But the Federal Government
was never meant
to solve men's economic problems.

Thomas Jefferson says,
"The less government there is
the better it is."
If the less government there is
the better it is,
the best kind of government
is self-government.
If the best kind of government
is self-government,
then the best kind of organization
is self-organization.
When the organizers try
to organize the unorganized,
they often do it for the benefit
of the organizers.
The organizers don't organize themselves.
And when the organizers don't organize themselves,
nobody organizes himself.
And when nobody organizes himself,
nothing is organized.

It was probably not as startling to Dorothy as to her sister-in-law. Dorothy was a convert from Communism, but she had probably not yet been cured fully of the notion of throwing responsibility on governments which were increasingly, and everywhere, at once claiming more and more of it and failing more and more miserably to make good their claims. She discovered, anyhow, right away that Peter had read some articles of hers and had come in search of her that she might help him to begin a work of social reconstruction. "If it were not for Peter," she says, "there would be no Houses of Hospitality and Farming Communes. Peter has changed the lives of thousands of people."

The leaders in the Hunger March, says Dorothy, were Communists, but 90% of the marchers were not and had only accepted this leadership because "no other leaders had presented themselves". This was part of the tragedy, which she felt more and more profoundly, which had prepared her for Peter's appeal and for the work she was to undertake. She describes her impressions during the march, her reflections upon it.

I do not blame the harried police, the firemen, the reserves, even though they cursed and bullied and taunted the marchers as though they were trying to provoke a bloody conflict. I blame the press which for a few ghastly headlines, a few gruesome pictures, was ready to precipitate useless violence towards a group of unemployed human beings who were being used as "Communist tactics", as "shock troops" in the "class struggle". I watched the ragged horde and thought to myself, "These are Christ's poor." He was one of them. He was a man like other men, and He chose his friends among the ordinary workers. These men feel they have been betrayed by Christianity. Men are not Christian today. If they were, this sight would not be possible. For dearer in the sight of God perhaps are these hungry ragged ones, than all those smug, well-fed Christians who sit in their homes, cowering in fear of the Communist menace. I felt that they were my people, that I was part of them. I had worked for them and with them in the past, and now I was a Catholic and so could not be a Communist. I could not join this united front of protest and I wanted to . . . The feast of the Immaculate Conception was the next day and I went out to the National Shrine and assisted at solemn high Mass there. And the prayer that I offered up was that some way would be shown me, some way would be opened up for me to work for the poor and the oppressed.

When I got back to New York, Peter Maurin was in the house waiting for me.[1]

Peter's programme was: A Catholic Labour paper, Houses of Hospitality to meet the immediate and continuing needs of cities, farming communes for the country. He often echoed Father Vincent: "There is no unemployment on the land." "On the land you need not lose a minute of time or a scrap of material." And, unlike his co-worker, Peter did know a good deal about the land. Dorothy was by upbringing a city woman, a journalist, had not only been a Communist but had also married one. She has one daughter and one of the difficulties she felt most keenly about the work she was about to undertake was the problem of educating Tamar in the heart of the Catholic Worker Movement.

Both Peter and Dorothy, like the Antigonish co-operators of

[1] *House of Hospitality*, pp. 15–16.

whom I must speak in a later chapter, felt that a philosophy of labour, much study and discussion, must accompany and inspire their active work. They must *learn*, through books, through discussion—and through action. Peter had read a good deal of history and was in particular keenly aware of what Dawson so much stresses—the creation by the Church of a new social order in the crumbling Empire. The word "personalism" he probably got from Emmanuel Mounier, but he often echoes the Fathers. It was St. Basil who established on the grand scale hospices and hospitals that grew into a city; it was St. John Chrysostom who begged his flock to have, each man, a guest-room not for his friends only but for the poor.

A theologian of some note declaimed in my hearing against the impertinence of the little group who brought into being the newspaper entitled *The Catholic Worker* and the movement of the same name. But the vast majority of priests and laity welcomed them enthusiastically. My own feeling was and is that the courage shamed us all which could confront so desperate a situation not with the usual "Something must be done", but with the resolve, "We must do something."

"We are liable", Dorothy wrote, "to make mistakes in the paper, not being theologians or philosophers, nor experts in the line of economics and sociology; but we can make no mistake in feeding God's hungry ones."

The paper had to be written at a kitchen table, in the back yard, waiting in the relief agency, in the momentary intervals between handling an immense breadline, sorting and distributing clothes, helping evicted families to move their goods, taking sick people to hospitals, calming drunks, very occasionally cleaning house, washing clothes, and trudging to the municipal baths to wash oneself—for the slum tenement acquired for purposes of hospitality contained no bathroom. It was always full to overflowing.

The story is told of the first years, 1933-8, in *House of Hospitality*, which I found on a rereading almost more moving than I did twenty years ago when first we published it. Dorothy Day is a poet and a seeker after perfection. Not least interesting is the record of the books she chose for spiritual reading, liberally quoted from, of the early efforts at carrying out some part of the Liturgy, of the determination to achieve daily meditation before or after the mass that was never missed. She faces all the difficulties, describes the profound despondency resulting from overwork, strain, lack of sleep and often of adequate food. She tells of the immense generosity shown by fellow Catholics. And she gives us glimpses of the sudden joy coming in prayer, in moments of quiet, in glimpses of beauty through music, people and growing things. Here is a passage that seems to me to give the atmosphere of this remarkable book and brings back the days in which Dorothy was writing:

> The sun was shining and a little girl was dead, a little girl from one of these crowded tenements hereabouts . . . where the rats, as little Felicia said, are chased by her father with a broomstick.
>
> There is sun in the street but from the cellars and area-ways a dank and musty smell redolent of death rises. There is sun and gaiety in the streets, and the little girls skip rope around the push-cart of pineapples, but one little girl was carried in a coffin down the street, while the band played its slow, mournful and yet triumphant dirge. She was through with this short and dangerous life which is yet so dear to all. There is one less to skip from beneath the wheels of trucks and gather around the crowded kitchen table in the tenement. There is one less mouth to feed, one less pair of shoes for the father (who supports eight on fifteen dollars a week) to buy.
>
> One less little girl.

I am only, in this chapter, glancing at the *Catholic Worker* during the Depression years—and at the two people who brought it into being, a movement that was certainly in these years a chief feature of New York Catholic life. I imagine St. John Chrysostom found it no easier in pleasure-loving Antioch or wealthy Constantinople to persuade people to bring the poor into their houses than did Dorothy Day in Depression-stricken New York. She records one or two instances—and I knew another a little later, of two sisters who rented a big apartment with no heating, with none of the comforts they could well have afforded for themselves. They managed with two of their friends to take care of four other girls, who were by health or circumstances unable to pay their own way. Such generosity is rare; giving money, food, clothes is commoner, and probably Chrysostom, like Peter and Dorothy, found purse-strings loosened, if only in shame by those who refused to go any further.

One thing this movement began to express I find a little hard to explain adequately. When you get back to a realization of the value of a man *as* a man, still more when you become aware of the doctrine of the Mystical Body, you can no longer think in terms of "going down to help" your fellow man. We are all part of a body that is impoverished, that is diseased. St. Basil used to tell the rich that they were the "fellow slaves" of the poor—because all alike are God's property with the duty to work in God's vineyard.

And psychologists today are becoming increasingly alive to the fact that those who have suffered from a mental or spiritual disease are often best able to help in curing it; thus Alcoholics Anonymous cure their fellow drunks, Divorcees Anonymous persuade other women against divorce, people once racked by nerve trouble lead others into calm. Those who worked in the Depression were learning to realize that the principle of "like to like" enunciated by Canon Cardijn (worker to worker; student to student) did not merely apply to fellow workers at a machine or a desk, but to the fundamental oneness of humanity. We help, if we help, from inside, not outside.

The *Catholic Worker* in America quickly realized, as had the Catholic Evidence Guild in England, that lack of education did not prevent men from studying serious books and discussing what they were reading. In *House of Hospitality*, real or imaginary dialogues present frankly both the aims of these studies and some of the current criticisms from outside and even inside on the running of the *Worker*. It is interesting to note how deeply these discouraged Dorothy, yet how well she hid it. There were soon half-a-dozen Houses in different cities, and going from one to another she had to bear to a great extent the burden of them all. "If you *are* discouraged," she writes, "others will relapse into a state of discouragement and hopeless anger at the circumstances and each other. And if you are *not* discouraged everyone tries to make you so and is angry because you are not. . . . The only thing is to be oblivious, as Peter is, and go right on."

They had a cat called Social Justice and Dorothy found one of their less intelligent guests washing him one day with *her* washcloth, drying him with her towel! Another took one of Dorothy's blankets to cover an old horse "who helps us deliver our Manhattan bundles of papers every month. He is a truly *Catholic Worker* horse, Dan says, and when they go up Fifth Avenue and pass St. Patrick's Cathedral, the horse genuflects!"

She tells these stories with perfect good humour, even if wryly—and faces the fact that with a house filled with people broken in body and soul you cannot expect very good order or even great cleanliness. Notes that she has washed A.B.'s sheets or sprayed furniture infested with bed-bugs come between resolutions against impatience and criticisms of others—and renewed assertions that all work done must be voluntary, not by rule. I cannot but feel that here, by all the rules of psychology, the founders of the movement were making a serious mistake. So many of their guests were broken in mind and body that they would not insist on work from any individual—and Dorothy tells of the grumblings and dissensions resulting between those who volunteered to work and those who idled. But I think they would have mended up these broken lives much better by a gentle discipline of work, while not putting so great a strain on those of better will and—perhaps—more capacity. Dorothy in her poetic way sometimes idealizes in her book the picture of what was being done—as, for instance, when she describes the garden at Staten Island. I remember visiting that "Garden Commune" and looking with dismay amounting to horror at the undug land positively crying out for work while four men spent a beautiful afternoon talking around the fire. Later experience at another Worker House in the Mid-West, where rules of work were made and kept, convinced me that in this view I was right.

But how those worked who did work—the chief of them being Dorothy. And I smiled as I thought of any attempt to translate what she and Peter were doing into the sort of pattern that we should have offered had we tried to give from our platforms "the social teaching of the Church". These two were not thinking in terms of the worker's rights or even "duties" in the social order. They had come to realize that in this hour of crisis only the supernatural could save the natural. Their movement was an expression of the Christian Revolution.

In two "Easy Essays" Peter put the bare bones of the changed outlook in (almost) natural terms.

> The training of social workers
> enables them to help people
> to adjust themselves
> to the existing environment.

The training of social workers
does not enable them
to help people
to change the environment.

And in the second

The Communitarian Movement
aims to create
a new society
within the shell of the old
with the philosophy of the new
which is not
a new philosophy
but a very old philosophy
a philosophy so old
that it looks like new.

The Communist party
stands for proletarian dictatorship.

The Communitarian Movement
stands for personalist leadership.

And Dorothy, pouring into the work the tiny rent from her cottage and any money she managed to make despite her energies in the House, writes, "I do feel strongly that we must put everything we have into the work in embracing voluntary poverty for ourselves. It is only when we do this that we can expect God to provide for us . . . This is one of the fundamental points of our work in stressing personal responsibility before State responsibility. It is only when we have used all our material resources . . . that in good conscience we can demand and expect help from the State."

But I should have hated to recite to an out-of-work crowd the end of Peter's "Easy Essay" on making a living:

But they say
that there is no work to do.

There is plenty of work to do
but no wages.

> But people do not need
> to work for wages.
>
> They can offer their services
> as a gift.

And Dorothy suggests:

> If each unemployed nurse went to her pastor and got a list of the sick, and gave up the idea of working for wages and gave her services to the poor of the parish, is there not security in the trust that God will provide?

And Peter again:

> There are guest rooms
> in the houses of the rich
> but they are not
> for those who need them.
>
> They are not for those who need them
> because those who need them
> are no longer considered
> as the Ambassadors of God.

And in another essay:

> We need Houses of Hospitality
> to give to the rich
> the opportunity
> to serve the poor.
>
> We need Houses of Hospitality
> to bring the scholars
> to the workers
> and the workers
> to the scholars.

This was a favourite idea of both his and Dorothy's—but she complains that part of her problem in the House is that while students are heroically working with their hands, some of the manual labourers are joyfully seizing on any sit-down clerical jobs and avoiding hard work. She calls it the difficulty of "a time of transition"—but just at moments she is as realist as Peter always is about original sin and the desire to shirk personal responsibility and, even more, hard work.

People say:

"They don't do this,
They don't do that,
they ought to do this,
they ought to do that."

Always "They"
and never "I".

Rejecting the suggestion of one of the young hotheads of a united front with the Communists in demands for social justice, Dorothy rejects it on the ground that it would result in physical violence and class war—"Hate your enemies, which is all wrong." She goes on to say, "We are not working for the dictatorship of the proletariat, so why work with the Communists? *We believe not in acquisitive classes but in functional classes.*" I italicise these words as they are so important a statement of the temporal aim of the movement. But it must never be purely temporal. Her one temptation to violence is, she admits, against the movie men and the advertisers "who have corrupted the minds and desires of the youth of the country". I have commonly given only fragments when quoting Peter's *Easy Essays* but this chapter may best be ended by his full *Credo* in one complete essay and by a brief quotation from Dorothy in *House of Hospitality*. Peter says:

The Catholic Worker believes
in the gentle personalism
of traditional Catholicism.

The Catholic Worker believes
in the personal obligation
of looking after
the needs of our brother.

The Catholic Worker believes
in the daily practice
of the Works of Mercy.

The Catholic Worker believes
in Houses of Hospitality
for the immediate relief
of those who are in need.

The Catholic Worker believes
in the establishment
of Farming Communes
where each one works
according to his capacity
and gets according to his need.

The Catholic Worker believes
in creating a new society
within the shell of the old
with the philosophy of the new.

Dorothy says:

The only remedy is a new life in the Holy Ghost, a return of all of us to the paradox of the supernatural, a determined assent to the poor, crucified Jesus. That is the road to the rebirth of the West; there is no other way.

16

SOCIAL SUBJECTS AND THE APOSTOLATE

THE Guild's spectacular advance of the early twenties was not repeated but a steady progress was maintained all over England. By the mid-thirties there were some 500 speakers in all the guilds combined. The word "ecumenical" would not be uttered in its newest meaning for many years to come, but I think I can claim that we aimed at being eirenical to a degree almost unheard of then in religious discussion. We tried to train our speakers to appreciate truth and spiritual values wherever they found them, not to defend the indefensible in Catholic behaviour past and present, and to bring light rather than heat to bear on disputed questions. Our failures were many, especially in the rather feverish conditions produced by crowd psychology, but we were aiming at a genuine meeting of minds.

The fact that many attended classes who never became speakers was not sheer loss to the main aim—a temporary experience of meeting face to face living men and their difficulties fitted all Catholics to do this work more adequately in the daily run of their lives. And there was something else: fallen-away Catholics brought back to the sacraments.

This happened frequently at our meetings; marriages were put right, children baptized. We came to feel that this, while it had not occurred to us when we began, was perhaps the most important thing of all. Badly instructed Catholics grew fervent as they learned more about their faith. Others joining the classes realized that they had been attempting to meet mature minds with only a child's knowledge.

We did not count results; it was suggested that the Guild start a magazine to record progress but this was voted down on the ground that studying and lecturing absorbed all the spare time at our disposal. As one girl put it, "I go to the class two nights a week and speak three. I must have two left to see my friends and keep my clothes tidy." One a week was almost the minimum of outdoor speaking, and speakers sticking to this and also attending classes improved at an astonishing rate.

Conversion is a fascinating phenomenon; it may mean primarily the turning of a life to God, as with St. Augustine, or the turning of an intellect more fully to the light of God's truth, as with Newman. And these two great men remind us that there are in many lives more conversions than one. Newman had as a boy a first conversion both moral and intellectual, his later approach to the Church was a slow and painful intellectual process, an opening of the eyes of the spirit. St. Augustine's moral conversion was preceded by a turning of his intellect from Manichean errors to Catholic truth. All we can know is that it is the work of God—we knew *we* could not convert anybody, yet by presenting truth clearly and winningly we might open men's minds to God's grace. It was the *teaching* of St. Ambrose that dispelled St. Augustine's misconceptions as to what the Catholic faith really meant, it was through a historical article on the Donatists that Newman first saw the Church of England as schismatical.

My husband had a letter one day from a persistent questioner: "You may be disappointed when I tell you I am not going to join your Church, but I want you to know that you have given me back my belief in God and my belief in Christ."

He was not disappointed; but this was not all. Half a dozen persistent hecklers at Tower Hill came into the Church, and two are now Cistercian monks—conversions chiefly due to one speaker whose ability and knowledge are matched by great sacrifices for the work's sake. As a young man his employer warned him to expect no promotion if he continued it. He ignored the warning and bore the penalty. This story is matched by that of the Australian Guildsman, Peter Gallagher mentioned earlier, who refused a judgeship because he would no longer be able to talk on the outdoor platform.

This book must not become the record of achievements we have always refused to keep, but one or two stories must be told. One atheist heckler in London attacked us for two years, another in Leicester for four; both became Catholics, the Londoner converted his mother and his brother and himself became a speaker. The Midlander became a priest. The Londoner married and had three children: one of them contracted a painful illness; he prayed that he might bear the pain and she either get better or die peacefully. The child did die painlessly and quite happily and he proved to have the illness. Frank visited him frequently in the hospital, deeply admiring his faith and courage; and when he died our Midland ex-atheist said a Requiem Mass for his soul.

We had one Irish speaker who made a great point of hanging around at meetings, before and after his own lectures, and getting into conversation with hecklers. Twice at least he showed extraordinary intuition, being the first to recognize as a nun the heckler spoken of earlier and discovering also an ex-priest whom he persuaded to return to the Faith. Guild speakers, I fear, invariably look at the sky and long for rain as their turn to speak approaches. But one way and another, despite periods when we felt our work to be both barren and deadly, we realized that something was being achieved. And usually at our despondent moments we were given some small uplift by hearing a chance story—meeting some Little Sisters of the Poor who told us of a dying man sending his child to call them as he had listened in Hyde Park and wanted to die a Catholic; hearing from a priest in Edinburgh of a convert from the same source, from a priest in Hampstead of husband and wife coming to him, unknown to one another, from two different pitches and asking for instruction, hearing of a questioner of forty years back who is now a monsignor.

Inside the Guild there were now no spectacular rows, but there was one question which divided us deeply: Whether Guild speakers should give on the outdoor platform the social teaching of the Church—especially the teaching concerning the relation of worker and employer and of citizen and Government. As with the whole of this unvarnished record, I can only tell it from the Sheed (and Ward) point of view, and to make that point of view clear in this particular matter I must leap back to the year of our marriage.

In 1926 occurred the railway strike, alternatively called a lockout, defeated by a voluntary mobilization of the upper and middle classes. The threat of a general strike in support of the railwaymen was denounced by, among others, Cardinal Bourne, and we returned from our honeymoon to find considerable bitterness among Guild speakers. Our theological charwoman, Miss Cozens, had been so shattered by the Cardinal's pronouncements that she had felt unable to go to the sacraments until after a long conversation with Father Vincent NcNabb. It need hardly be said that on this question Father Vincent was poles apart from the Cardinal. I knew far too little to form an opinion, but my feelings were that I would rather be wrong with Father Vincent than right with most other people; he, more than anyone I knew, was in closest touch with the people most deeply affected, he had a love of God and man which was my constant admiration. And through this very love he was able to show Miss Cozens that to bar from herself the means of grace because authority was—if it was—mistaken, would be utterly wrong. We were not bound to agree with the Cardinal's views—but obviously, as speakers of the Guild we could not publicly contradict them.

I have known so many interesting people that it is hard to choose one as the most interesting, but certainly Louisa Cozens was the most amazing. She had taught herself Latin, had studied a great deal of St. Thomas and read her way into the Church. Allergic to heresy, she would utter a shrill squeak if anyone made a serious error. I remember my brother Leo, about to be examined for his chairman's licence, saying, "Oh, Miss Cozens, I forgot to look up the definition of 'person'." She obliged instantly with the definition of Boethius, at that time quite unknown to the average layman. Thanking her warmly, he went in and passed.

Miss Cozens was our first "Devil's Advocate", the Guild name for the lay person who examines with the examining chaplains, asking the type of question put by the crowd. Later on, when she moved to Southwark, the bishop, though notoriously anti-feminist, confirmed her perpetual appointment as an examiner. Wanting to find work for her more worthy of her intellectual powers than scrubbing floors, I came to realize that she preferred to remain as she was. She was proud of her own class and had no wish to *s'embourgeoiser*. She could think as she worked and she scrubbed her floors to the rhythm of the Athanasian Creed.

While we were living in Battersea, Frank suggested that Miss Cozens should write a book on the great heresies. As she had no quiet place to write, we invited her to make use of our flat of an evening, and would creep in to avoid disturbing her—and sometimes to avoid being drawn into an exhausting theological discussion. *A Handbook of Heresies* was an astonishing achievement. Fr. Hugh Pope said it was the best short treatment he had read of the early heresies, which he had studied most closely. I recognized it as the best outline treatment of Modernism, on which I had worked a great deal; and this was the verdict of experts on many other heresies.

But our little Scotch Mary came to me after a few evenings of Miss Cozens and complained that "she chewed bits of blotting paper and spat them about the floor". Mary objected, not unreasonably, to cleaning up after her—and the great problem with Miss Cozens was that while theologically she had reached real eminence, she had never bothered to carry her self-education into any other field. Her grammar and choice of words fitted her theology—but not her accent. I shall never forget hearing her exclaim in a voice of near-ecstasy, "'Oo shall compre'end the incompre'ensible God?"

Society had treated her ill: her mother had died in a workhouse and the officials could not tell her, out of several coffins, which her mother's was. She had become embittered against what were then always called "the upper classes", and it took a long and patient wooing on my part before friendship could grow between us. I made the almost fatal mistake of trying to give her a pair of fur-lined gloves; her hands were so raw and chapped, the winter so cold. The only present she would ever accept from me was a breviary, but once we did become friends complete trust was established. An acquaintance said once, "Did Miss Cozens learn her theology from you?" And I answered truthfully, "No, I learnt mine from her."

Miss Cozens and I talked much of these industrial troubles. We did not see eye to eye on every political and social issue, but we agreed in rejoicing that Guild rules forbade discussion of them from our platforms. The whole Guild agreed that politics must be kept from our outdoor meetings, but there was a minority—at times large, though always fluctuating —which held that we should "give the crowds the social teaching of the Church". But when do politics begin in dealing with such subjects? And how far can Catholics differ on social subjects themselves? These two questions faced us every time the matter was approached. A perfect example was the General Strike.

Another good instance would be the astronomically rising death duties. The Conservative would call these "daylight robbery", the Socialist would justify them, the Distributist would feel that while, as Chesterton put it, it is as much a negation of property for one man to have all the farms in one estate as it would be the negation of marriage if he had all the wives in one harem, it is equally a negation of property for the State to seize all the estates.

Curiously enough the leaders in the desire for social subjects were two Dominicans, themselves poles apart in their outlook: Father Hugh Pope, Director of Studies of the Birmingham Guild, was an old-fashioned Conservative, Father Vincent McNabb a passionate Distributist. It was absurd to call him a Socialist, as some people did, but he was very far from being a Conservative. Any Distributist found it hard to fit into a classification—I have myself been called an anarchist, and there is no doubt that a profound scepticism about modern processes of government did possess many Distributists. Since both would have been there as teachers, the impression produced on a crowd by Father Vincent and Father Hugh answering the same social questions from the same platform would have been odd indeed.

This was an immediate objection to "giving the social teaching of the Church". Catholics disagreed profoundly and quite legitimately as to that teaching. We could all certainly lay down a few fundamental principles—but no one can run a meeting simply by laying down principles. You have to be prepared to maintain and apply those principles amid a hail of questions, perhaps for thirty to forty minutes.

In the conditions of street-corner speaking, if we refused to apply our principles to concrete situations, we should arouse the crowd's derision; if we did so apply them, speakers would differ strongly, even passionately, among themselves. My husband remembers an occasion, very early in the Guild's history, before the rules were established, when a speaker was applying his own social views at some length, while another speaker, white with anger, was waiting his turn to get up and contradict him. The two speakers were agreed on the Church's principles; and neither had any doubt that his own application of these was according to the Church's mind.

It seemed to us that if social subjects were admitted, application was unavoidable, differences among the speakers were certain. You lay down the principles of the right to strike under certain circumstances, of the right to a living wage, of the right of a grossly underpaid employee to help himself from the office cashbox, which the theologians call "occult compensation" and the law calls "stealing".[1] Are the circumstances of *this* strike, you are asked, such as to justify it? How much *is* a living wage here and now? Should a man close a factory and throw hundreds out of work if it is not doing well enough to pay a living wage? When does taking enough to make your wage a "living wage" cease to be occult compensation and become thieving?

A few years later there were speakers who believed we should campaign for Franco as a modern crusader, while others held (as Frank and I did) that, though the Communists were worse, the best to be said for Franco was that he was the lesser of two evils.

And, in these our own days, who would venture to give *as the teaching of the Church* either that to possess the Bomb as a deterrent is legitimate or that it is indefensible?

But there was a profounder reason for leaving social subjects alone. If they came in they would push the great dogmas further and further out. Upon the relations of worker and employer, of the citizen and the Government, every man has his own strong opinions: the dimension would swell and swell: the seemingly less immediate, but actually more vital, facts of revelation and their meaning would get less and less of the time. And these are not only the justification for the Guild's existence—under the open sky of England it alone utters the revelation of God day in day out; they are actually the justification of the Church's social teaching itself. Her moral teaching, of which her social teaching is a part, is rooted in her dogmatic teaching. The moral laws are what they are because God is what He is, man is what he is, man's goal is what it is. To try to teach the laws to people who do not know these greater realities is idle.

We do talk of the moral law; we give the Church's teaching on sin, which involves discussing particular sins. I recall one childless husband, now a father, after long arguments on birth control with one of our speakers! But these are not our chosen topics. They do not, as social-political topics would, tend to take up the whole time. We do not make much headway with them, precisely because the crowd lacks any view of reality as a whole. When a questioner asks about contraception we have a despairing feeling that he is wrong about God, wrong about the meaning and the goal of human life,

[1] See Henry Davis, S.J., *Moral and Pastoral Theology*, vol. 2, pp. 311–14.

wrong about sex, wrong about marriage—and we must try to put him right about birth control !

Something else, as the years went by, Frank and I felt increasingly. What the crowds were asking of Catholics in the social field was not what the proponents of social subjects fancied—they did not want to know Catholic teaching; what they were asking for was Catholic performance, Catholic social *action*. I remember some of their questions as the Depression drew on. "Why has the Bishop of So-and-So got a gold-fitted dressing-case costing £200? I know he has—I made part of it." "Why does Bishop So-and-So always appear at public gatherings with Mr. Such-and-Such, who is known as a peculiarly heartless employer?" "Why does the Pope live in a palace?" "Why does he have a golden telephone?" (This was actually a present from the Knights of Columbus.) "Why", Father Vincent was asked—and it was the only time I ever saw him embarrassed—"don't the Dominicans help the housing shortage by building houses on the priory grounds?" Father Vincent would gladly have filled the priory itself with slum-dwellers, let alone the grounds!

I remember how, on the other hand, when hecklers were arguing against convents, a man in the crowd would have none of it. "I've tramped", he said, "all over England, and no convent ever refused me food." And he concluded that nuns must be pretty good people after all.

We had many of us made one great mistake after the War. Taxes had risen immensely, the Welfare State was on the way—and we thought both that it had already come and that the problems of poverty were thereby solved. Just after the War, what with gratuities and the boom, this was perhaps true. The Depression rapidly changed the picture, but we had to learn and to act before we could teach. First the thirties and then the years after World War II showed many experiments in many lands: the *Catholic Worker*, with its Houses of Hospitality, Friendship House with its interracial work, the Young Christian Workers and Farmers, the Canadian Co-operatives, the Priest-Workmen in their early ideals and in the achievements of those who retained the ideals, the vast work of Abbé Pierre in France and its spread into other countries, the books and magazines put forth by the Éditions Ouvrières, the Éditions du Cerf and other publishers. Through all these movements and this literature Catholics were to learn, first that the whole structure of society was changing, and secondly that we must all bear our part in building that structure anew on human and on Christian lines. As Abbé Pierre insists again and again in his periodical *Faim et Soif*, we have a double social duty: attention to the shaping of society as a whole, a daily charity to our neighbour in particular. And, as Father Vincent was already saying urgently, all our social thought and action must be based on, must spring from, the Gospels.

I shall return to the subject of social action in the next chapter; here I want only to emphasize that while my husband and I realized increasingly the need to study and to act, we saw such study and action in organized form as having to be done by other societies. The work of the Catholic Evidence Guild was to teach Revelation—the *mysterium*, for the unfolding of which St. Paul had found a lifetime too short. Our speakers must be taught to teach the Trinity, the Incarnation, the Redemption, the Mystical Body, the supernatural life, and sacraments, the Mass. And on all these subjects we could—and in fact did—learn to go deeper with every year of study, learn to see the point of insertion into the mind of the crowd, learn how to interest them so as to make them desire what they so sorely needed.

I only once discussed the question of social subjects with Father Vincent. Although we did not agree, the disagreement did not go deep and he seemed willing to leave the question alone. I fancy he realized that in Westminster the opinion of the Guild as a whole was with us. Also, during Cardinal Bourne's lifetime the rule was certain to remain as it was—and it soon became evident that Cardinal Hinsley took the same view. In the provincial guilds it was different: the rule varied from guild to guild, most bishops taking the same line as Westminster, some not.

On this matter, as on many others, Father Hugh Pope was very different from Father Vincent. Year after year he insisted on a discussion of "Social Subjects on the Platform" at our annual retreat!

Although I never loved Father Hugh as I did Father Vincent, I was really fond of him. He was a delightful companion, full of amusing stories of his friends and his experiences. "Calls yerself a celybite," one heckler had said to him, "'Ow many children 'as yer?" This specially delighted Chesterton—that the fact should not be in doubt, but only the number. Father Hugh loved to talk about Mgr. Wallace of Brighton, who had been educated entirely out of England, stories about whom so much abounded that they were known as the Wallace Collection after the well-known gallery in London. Mgr. Wallace had said when Father Hugh remarked that he was not acquainted with a certain town councillor of Brighton: "But you *must* know her. She is a public woman of the town." After a quarrel with his bishop the same Monsignor, urged to reconsider his position, said, "I cannot go back. I have burnt my breeches." A high personage he described as "a little gutter-snapper".

In Father Hugh's sermons, beside his humour we felt his modesty in relation to his own learning—his Scripture studies had been profound but he hardly ever alluded to them. He gave us a lively sense of the splendour of our work and always made us feel the immensity of the feast on which the retreat centred. His sense that the Holy Ghost was really descending upon us here and now "over the bent world" with "ah, bright wings" would seize upon us the first night. He had one phrasing that made us smile, so often was it repeated: "May we say? . . . I think we may. I think we must."

His morning and evening meditations would have been pure joy could we have put away all thought of those dreadful afternoons when we should again be forced to argue against the treatment of social subjects. Those who desired this were entitled to urge it on the Guild, but we felt that a retreat was not the occasion for controversy, year after year, upon the one matter which seriously divided Guildsmen.

Gazing at this division so long after, I seem to see one difference which I did not see at the time between the holders of the two views. Both where wholly sincere. But those who wanted social subjects thought of their introduction simply as an advance in the Guild's work, not as touching its essence. They did not regard their annual defeat as utterly disastrous. But those who felt with us thought then—and Frank and I still think—that their success would have been fatal to the Guild's existence. The result was that the other side could go into the argument with a certain casualness, we could not. There was never, thank God, any bad blood; we all remained the best of friends. But we felt that we were fighting for the Guild's life; for every discussion of the topic we felt we must make rigorous preparation.

Frank did at last give utterance to the feeling that possessed us both. He said in his speech how he had hoped to be able to pray, hoped to gain much from the meditations. But he had had to stay away from the meditations and devote the morning to preparation on a matter of such importance to the Guild. He would go back to London with his "starved little soul unfed".

Father Hugh looked startled—for the first time it seemed to dawn on him that there was another element in all this. I really believe that for him these discussions had represented relaxation, fun and games, breaking the monotony of his work. But if he was watching games we were the gladiators in the arena—and the fact that our view continued to prevail (whenever a vote was taken) made it no easier to start again the following year.

PART 3

THIRD QUARTER-CENTURY

1939–1964

17

FROM "PEACE" INTO WAR

SHEED and Ward had, of course, made the same mistake in the States as in England—started with too small a capital—and it was to be some years before we overcame the resultant difficulties. The country is so vast that a large selling organization is called for. There, as in England, we had opened our book club; there, as in England, the Depression was at its worst. The welcome we received was astonishing in its warmth and generosity, but we had to work hard to keep our heads above water in the early years. Both of us, Frank especially, were in demand as lecturers, and the money made by lecturing helped to support our publishing.

I remember, after one tour, parting with all my earnings with a sensation similar, I imagine, to leaving the dentist's chair after losing all one's teeth. What a pleasant life we could have had, I often felt, if we just wrote books and lectured; whatever made us start a publishing house? It was much worse for Frank than for me because much more continuous—England to America, America to England, problems and struggles on both sides of the Atlantic.

No wonder he was exhausted—but he was no worse than exhausted, and I later told my doctor friend Helen Ingleby that she had really played a low trick on me when she persuaded me to take him to a heart specialist, and then urged the heart specialist (an old friend and admirer of hers!) to give me a thorough fright. This he certainly did, with great skill, for it was done by manner rather than by words. Our local doctor remarked later that he had rather wondered what all the fuss was about; anyhow, I spent a summer watching Frank and he spent it watching village cricket down at Horley—and growing fat for the first time in his life. Perhaps this increased his already abundant energy, for the years immediately before the War were very fruitful ones.

This Publishing Business for 1936 and 1937 gives a good cross-section of the books we were translating, urging our authors to write, writing ourselves or just finding in the day's post.

In England there were still Chesterton and Belloc, who each gave us a book in 1936—and in that year Mgr. Knox began to do things with the Bible. His translation was not to come for quite a while, but he made a shortened version of the Douai invaluable for schools or for the simpler reader making a first attempt to get his teeth into Bible reading. Halliday Sutherland's *Laws of Life* and Alfred Noyes' *Voltaire*, both published that year, were among our spectacular best sellers, while Dr. Arendzen on *The Trinity*, Father Leen on *The Holy Ghost* and Tyciak's *Life in Christ* added to the library we were building of theology for the layman.

But it is interesting today, when so many of our writers are American or English, to note the enormous proportion of translations. Europe was still producing the great writers who had begun in the early years of the century—but some of them were growing old, and no one of their stature was yet appearing among the younger men.

From Switzerland came at this time Otto Karrer's important book *Religions of Mankind*. From Germany, Guardini's *Spirit of the Liturgy* and *Sacred Signs*, which marked a big step in the return of the Liturgy; *Peace and the Clergy* (published anonymously) and Pinsk's *Christianity and Race*, which courageously face the problem, now so acute, of the right relationship between nationality and the universal Church. And writing in the same country, despite the Hitler regime, Waldemar Gurian, in *The Future of Bolshevism*, showed that "far from being a bulwark against Bolshevism, National Socialism is but another form of it". The Totalitarian State was the great enemy of both religion and culture; Germany and Russia in the form they were taking were cut out of the one cloth. And Helen Iswolsky, daughter of a one-time Premier of Russia, giving the same picture, saw hope only in the fact that a little relaxing of the anti-God front was coming about in Russia.

Communism, however, was claiming to be the one answer to nationalism, offering a vision of the lifting up of the poor in the classless society and of consequent peace among the nations. In her *Hymns to the Church* Gertrud von le Fort, who had the good fortune to find in Mrs. Winthrop Chandler a translator of genius, gave to a new generation the great vision to which men's eyes had grown dim. "You can meet a vision only with a vision."

From France came Mauriac's astonishing *God and Mammon*, in which he faced the problem of the born Catholic who will "never be able to escape from the Faith . . . never be able to leave it." Yet Mauriac was aware of an antagonism "between the disinterestedness of the artist and what I called the utility-sense of the apostle". This antagonism he had once deemed unconquerable, but had come to believe he *could* conquer. But it loomed gigantic in the modern world, and was reflected in its literary work. He lived in a world of distorted values which the Catholic artist must portray. "What stands out most vividly for me", he writes, "in the colossal and putrescent work of Proust is the image of a gaping hole, the sensation of infinite absence and it is this chasm and emptiness—the absence of God, in fact—which strikes me most about mankind according to Proust."

This vast void made the work of the Catholic writer at once difficult and urgent. We were constantly aware of it—no one could speak and write without having it forced upon him. And as publishers we felt always that our choice of books must be such as to build a deeper awareness of God among Christians and try to awaken it from the depths of those pagan minds which, after all, were God's creation.

Ghéon's lives of saints went on and were immensely practical in their vivid pictures of men to whom God was utterly living. The Franciscan, Fr. Piette, in his *Life of Wesley*, to which a Methodist minister wrote a preface, helped in this same urgent task of making men look again towards their Creator. But of all the books on our list perhaps the most tremendous in its impact was Claudel's *Satin Slipper*, of which that year we had a new edition. This haunting play contained lines that came to be quoted constantly, such as, "Sin also serves", and above all the "proverb" on the title page, "God writes straight with crooked lines." But more important than these sayings was the whole atmosphere of the play: a sort of extraordinary radiance seen somehow through black clouds, which do not so much break or dissolve as radiate light while losing nothing of their blackness. This sounds nonsense perhaps, but it seems impossible to express otherwise the effect of not only a first but every subsequent reading of this tremendous book.

In the field of philosophy another book published in 1937 made the same impact on at least one reader—Gilson's *The Philosophy of St. Bonaventure*. "For him the sole knowledge worthy of an immortal spirit is of immortal things, God and souls; and if the sciences have profited by a circulation taking the opposite direction, they have shown their incapacity to enable man to live a human life; indeed when applied to equip with tools a generation devoid of wisdom they threaten to make human life impossible." No atom or hydrogen bomb was on his horizon when Frank wrote this in 1937, but we were already living in "the mad world that had very properly followed the mad war" and was fast rushing into another.

My brother Leo came from Japan for a few weeks and I felt it pathetic to see how his intense love for the people he had made his own blinded him to the wrongs of China in their long-drawn-out struggle. He had converts among the personnel at the Japanese Embassy, including the Ambassador's wife; and Ambassador Yoshida, though himself very far from being any sort of Christian, gave a party for him at which I met some interesting Japanese Catholics. Leo had brought a young convert with him and had hoped to return with enough money to build a new church at Yokohama. I understood for the first time how a missionary tends to become identified with the country that is his field—and this is even stronger if, like Père Lebbe in China, or Leo in Japan, he wants that country to be no mere mission field but a self-governing part of the universal Church. Leo had bought—and moved—a house in Karuizawa for use as a summer residence for Japanese seminarians. He had also built a lovely little church there.

It is easy to move a Japanese house, the walls being made of paper. Leo told me of his embarrassment when, making a point in an argument, he also made with his finger a hole in a friend's wall! He had found a fruitful field, as far as his halting speech allowed, among the Japanese, many of whom were seeking a religion that would take them deeper into reality. No one has told of this search and its fulfilment better than the Chinese convert John Wu, whose book *Beyond East and West* we later published, and the presence of Bishop Yu Pin in London reminded us again of the unhappy side of nationalism, creating in the East barriers similar to those in the West. For some of our friends were telling us that Leo, with his enthusiasm for Japan, was "queering the Bishop's pitch". What with China and Japan, the Spanish Civil War and the invasion of Abyssinia, we were all during these fateful years moving uneasily under a sense of guilt, and of a great uncertainty about the answers in the human order. Bishop Yu Pin and Leo Ward would have agreed as to the long-term divine answer. But what could and should be done by this man or that, here and now? On this they would almost certainly have differed.

"I think", an American friend in London wrote during the Blitz, "I take rather the child's attitude nowadays. I have the right to. All my grown-up scruples went in Abyssinia, China, Spain—when it seemed as if we might buy peace by the sufferings of others. That was a guilty feeling if you like, but nowadays there's no time and no great reason for slashing at one's nerves."

Slashing at one's nerves was precisely what everyone was doing—and angrily at that. Read George Orwell's *Homage to Catalonia* and then try to recall the fury with which his former friends received his factual account of the realities of Communism in Spain; I think it will re-create for you in the national order the atmosphere of those years, just as *Down and Out in Paris and London* re-creates the social atmosphere of the Depression.

Among those most angry with Orwell were journalists who had been describing events from a very considerable distance. I have not the faintest doubt that a Catholic enlisting in Franco's army would also have been greatly disillusioned—and that his fellow Catholics, especially if they were journalists, would have rejected the corrections offered by first-hand experience (indeed, this precisely was the reaction of many Catholics to Bernanos' book). During this period, especially, suspicion began in the mind of the ordinary citizen that much of the news he heard, from whatever source, had been doctored. In the First World War we spoke of propaganda as meaning the spreading of the truth—but it had not confined itself to truth even in official statements. By now certainly the word had highly dubious overtones. And in World War II care was taken to speak only of Ministries of Information.

Mercifully, for Leo as for us, one obvious task stood out—if God were brought back to men's minds as a living reality whose commandments were binding on their wills, the social and national order alike would be changed. In this case what looked the longest way round was indeed the shortest way home—but even so it was a damn long way and the business was likely to remain unfinished in our lifetime. I said goodbye to Leo with no faintest conception that this would be the last goodbye—we were to come one day to

Tokyo, and he urged the advantages of the journey by rail through the Soviet Union!

There was, of course, plenty of light relief from these sombre thoughts, especially with the children, and even more after the return to Horley than in the brief periods in London and Ealing, during the second of which Leo's visit had occurred. We had for neighbours a partly French family, Nicole about Rosemary's age, Peter about Wilfrid's. I remember Chestnuts as teeming with young life, especially during visits from my sister and her children. They all loved acting, and Nicholas Blundell and Rosemary were both good at "Hits, skits and jingles"—to use the title of an Australian volume of verse. Several entertainments were put on in the large room, once chapel. The Blundells and ourselves also joined forces for the summer holidays, Normandy and Littlehampton each furnishing its own forms of entertainment.

The shock was heavy that followed Chamberlain's promise of "Peace in our time" even for those, like ourselves, who had put no great faith in him—or any other politician. And very soon the whole country was growing alarmed. The idea that we had won peace for ourselves—even at the expense of others—was heavily shaken. We all, I think, expected the worst as 1939 drew on.

I had gone into the chapel for the second mass that Sunday morning of September. Frank, who was listening to the radio, came in and whispered that war had been declared. He announced it loudly from the back of the church as the people went out. A few minutes later the sirens sounded and one or two air-raid wardens hurried out for what proved to be a false alarm. These men had been appointed and gas masks served out to every man, woman and child in anticipation of instant air-raids. But for several months the wardens had no work except chivvying us in the matter of blackouts. There were one or two air-raids indeed, but how mild they were. In one a rabbit was killed, in another the bombs fell harmlessly on Ashdown Forest. There were so many false warnings that we began to feel an ill-based sense of security. We grew to love the huge balloons shaped like vast inflated pigs, in colour a gleaming silver, which symbolized safety for London—for England.

Remembering vividly the declaration of war in 1914, I realized how different was the national feeling. There was no elation but a grim determination. Only once do I remember in the early days going with my husband into the Lyons Brasserie in Coventry Street and finding people singing. They sang "Roll out the Barrel", "Run, Rabbit, Run!", and above all, "We're Going to Hang Out Our Washing on the Siegfried Line". We have both always loved what I hate to call community singing and we enjoyed that evening—but what a strange irony we felt later about the last song, which became very popular in the Third Reich and was used by Hitler as a morale builder.

We had come up to London that Sunday to speak in Hyde Park—and it was strange enough to be holding these meetings still in the midst of the blackout. We moderns hardly knew what darkness meant. Only in a fog had we hitherto had to grope our way to the platform guided by the voice of the previous speaker. We could no longer see our hecklers and Frank one day accused a man of contradicting himself—only to be told indignantly that it wasn't the same man. In the country the blackness was blacker yet. Our chapel had been built to admit the greatest possible amount of light. It was so difficult to black out the windows that when we started daily rosaries for peace, we tried to say them before darkness fell.

We were busy with other things besides praying for peace. Very early came the evacuation of the London children. Poor little things, with their boxed gas-masks hanging round their necks, utterly lost without their mothers, innocently mischievous in their ignorance of all country lore—that gates must be shut, or that you must not roll in a field of uncut hay. On Sundays mothers and fathers would come and visit them; our chapel was filled to overflowing. And Fr. Barry, who had replaced Fr. Healy (now with the Southwark Rescue Society), had to organize instruction for the children on a new scale. Now there were several classes—of which Rosemary, aged twelve, took the youngest—and troublesome little urchins they were. She remembers a sense of total despair about teaching them anything at all. After Mass the garden was crowded with soldiers and airmen quartered in the neighbourhood, to whom we dispensed tea and beer.

Our organist had joined the forces and Fr. Barry appealed to the congregation for someone who could play. A young American who had for some time been coming to Mass offered her services. She played remarkably well, also joining in the singing. Beatrice Warde, daughter of May Lamberton Becker of the *New York Herald-Tribune*, herself a director of Lanston Monotype, was not yet a Catholic, but she was almost literally blown into the Church a little later by the Blitz.

You would think I had had enough of trying to grow food—but in fact this was my main preoccupation in the first weeks of the "phoney" war. I remembered the last war too well to be under any illusions as to the kind of rations likely to be available if this one went on and the U-boats got really busy. A garden or an allotment would make the most enormous difference to a family, but enquiry soon showed that most of the fields around Horley were in the hands of the speculative builder. I started a newspaper campaign and, when I had succeeded in getting hold of a large field, offered a money prize for the best-kept allotment. We now had chickens ourselves and I remember presenting to a poor neighbour young chicks, which he informed me he was "bringing along with a hot water bottle".

Later on all this was fully justified, but at the moment it was not taken very seriously—apart from a question from one of the town councillors which staggered me. "How", he asked solemnly, "will they find a market for their vegetables?"

After Christmas, as everything seemed so quiet, I decided I could go with Frank to the States. We had picked up out of our congregation a builder's labourer, a Scot with an Irish wife, who was under instruction with Fr. Barry. This man we were employing to build a bungalow at Upper Prestwood, which he was to rent from us when it was completed. Our tenant had agreed to let him have a sizeable piece of land for his own cultivation, and it seemed, again, an excellent way of killing several birds with one stone—housing a family, increasing food production, improving the farm. That cottage cost us only £100—it was not luxurious but adequate for a small family. Meanwhile we arranged for the couple to live at Chestnuts—Frank's mother and the children would have that perhaps overrated commodity, "a man in the house".

We travelled overland to Lisbon and there took an Italian boat, which was brightly lighted and had a vast Italian flag painted on it. In the States there was much talk of Lend-Lease and a good deal of journalistic disappointment at the dullness of this war. Otherwise the trip was normal, business and lecturing both as usual. We returned in April, by an American boat, escorting the niece of an acquaintance who was to join her own family in England, a slight example of the way we had all been lulled to sleep while Hitler perfected his plans and his army. Very soon the movement of the young would all be in the opposite direction.

On our Italian boat in February all had been friendliness and charm, but now as we landed in Naples we felt a strong wave of hostility. We had only a few hours before our train left for Rome so we foolishly accepted a guide who had amused us by presenting himself in broken English as "a Lancashire boy". Despite a very large tip, he made a scene at the station and shouted abuse after us as the train pulled out. The train was crowded with men in uniform who looked at us askance. We were glad in Rome to find our friends the Girods, both former Guild speakers, she English, he a Swiss banker working and living in Vatican City. Rome is not Naples and they were, they told us, happy enough there. Phyllis got on splendidly with the Italians, especially the shopkeepers, who would go out of their way to do her a kindness. She and Auguste still believed that Mussolini would manage to remain neutral.

But the German invasion of the Low Countries had already begun and we reached home only just in time not to be caught by it.

There followed what has been so often called the miracle of Dunkirk—when the small British army, almost encircled, was brought back by hundreds of civilians whose trade or hobby was the handling of a boat: merchant ships, pleasure steamers, sailing boats, row-boats, in the merciful stillness of a summer night, setting off across the Channel and bringing back their loads. Living close to us, Beatrice Warde was sharing our experience as we listened through that night and the day and night that followed. She wrote to her mother;

> Train after train, going fast. I lay and listened with a grateful heart. Even if many of them were, must have been, hospital trains; even if the rest were filled with men who hadn't closed their eyes for seven nights and days in Flanders: still every train-load was one more to count, of those who had somehow got out of the trap, who had got through the ports, whose transports hadn't been sunk by all those thuddings off the southeast.

Shortly before the War Belloc had queried whether our town-bred and softened civilians could take the strain if the War was really to mean what Hitler threatened. They were at least making a fine beginning. Dunkirk, as Beatrice noted, was the least exclusive episode in English history.

Horley had a very fair contingent of these men—among them our own Mr. Stevenson, whose wife reported him as "sleeping it off".

The question was pressing on us which had presented itself insistently on our journey home—what ought we to do next? Neither the London nor the New York office could be left to itself; Frank must go to and fro. Three American friends had written begging us to send the children over; on the other hand, the committee of a boys' orphanage in the East End of London were imploring us to let Chestnuts to them so that they could move their boys to safety. Our cellar, now treated with waterproof cement, would, they believed, make a good shelter, but anyhow Horley was at that time considered a safe area. The children evacuated there had mostly by now returned to London, as the parents had been too lonely without them and they without their parents.

I could not face an even worse separation from my own—but Aunt Philippa, living a few miles away, was asking me indignantly how I could reconcile it with my conscience to subject innocent children to the dangers of an Atlantic crowded with U-boats. To her the last war was more vivid than this, but even so the question was a pertinent one—as the sinking of the *City of Benares*, with its load of young life, was so soon to show. Then, too, there was Frank's mother to consider; if the bombing came she could hardly be left alone. Finally we decided that we would either all go down together if a U-boat got us or else establish Grandmother and the children in the States and ourselves go back and forth between London and New York, leaving them in safety with our many good friends.

The night before leaving England we spent in lodgings near St. Mary's, Cadogan Street. Our landlady had bidden us goodnight with the words, "At least you're safe here." So it felt. The night was very still, dark yet clear. I sat up late reading Belloc's essays. They gave me, as he always does, a sentimental feeling about the English countryside. But I would see it soon again, and I think my last thought as I fell asleep was of the gleaming balloons at Marble Arch that kept us all so safe.

We crossed on the *Volendam*, almost striking a mine as we passed out of the Channel, taking a fortnight to reach New York. It was a gay trip for many of the passengers; the children were highly excited, there was a piano in the saloon and much playing, singing and dancing. A good many refugee Jews were on board, luxuriating in their safety.

But the sailors were gloomy enough: all of them Dutch, they could get no news of their families, their own fate was to journey from London to New York, from New York to London, until a U-boat should get them. We watched their faces as they crowded round the radio. We talked to some of them. And we soon realized that quite a few were planning to lose themselves in New York when the ship docked. It was their last opportunity, for this was the last safe sailing of the *Volendam*. She was sunk at her next crossing.

We meanwhile had reached New York safely—but our journey ended rather surprisingly on Ellis Island.

18

PEACEFUL TORRESDALE AND THE BATTLE OF BRITAIN

IT was no act against the United States Government nor any suspicion of such an act that brought us to Ellis Island; all the passengers were with us (unless they were citizens, but I don't remember seeing any Americans on the ship). During our leisurely progress across the Atlantic some new regulation had been introduced so that while our visas were valid when we left England, they were not valid when we reached New York. It was a mere technicality, but we arrived late and all the senior officials had gone home. So to Ellis Island we went. Jessica Tandy, with whom we had made friends on the boat, was allowed to go away with her brother, the British Consul in New York, but the rest of us had to spend the night there. It was an amusing experience. Frank and Wilfrid slept in a dormitory for men, Frank's mother, Rosemary and I in one for women. Rosemary remembers what I had totally forgotten—a Rabbi in his robe, holding a service in one corner of our room. Everything was spotlessly clean, white tiles abounded. I had a bath in splendid hot water with plenty of soap and towels—but there were no locks or bolts in the bathroom or lavatory. We had to go to bed—or at least to our rooms—and to get up, exceedingly early. The food was good but the meals were rushed through at a pace which even I, a very fast eater, found disconcerting.

We were taken into a yard for our morning air and exercise and there was a large recreation room where one could use the telephone. My husband rang our office and they got in touch with Mr. Mulholland of the National Catholic Immigration Service, who came and collected us. Meanwhile we had been interrogated in such broken English as to suggest that the official had himself begun his career as an immigrant. Perhaps, we speculated, he came there like us and the Government thought it a good idea to make use of him. The same questions were repeated so often that we also felt he had time to kill—so it was late in the day before we were free.

We calmed our friends, who had wished to receive us in a very different fashion, and soon we were enjoying them as much as the news from home allowed. The children spent part of that summer at Rye, with the Ross Hoffmans, and part at the Darlingtons' farm in West Chester, Pennsylvania, where Wilfrid met his future wife, then aged eight. He paid scant attention to her, being chiefly occupied in learning to swim from her eldest brother Dick. "The people", Grandmother wrote ecstatically, "in every part of the country are vying with one another in showing such boundless hospitality. It shows what great souls they have and I hope God will spare their marvellous country." After a series of visits Jean and Bill Darlington offered to lend us their house at Torresdale, as they had moved to West Chester and Birdwood stood empty. With the limitless generosity which we were to experience throughout our residence in the States, a friend of theirs and Grace Smith's (Mrs. Seton Henry) whom we had not yet met sent furniture from her own (also empty) house and I got more from auction sales in Philadelphia.

The garden was lovely, full of bulbs and flowering trees; there were the most magnificent peonies I have ever seen and other delights season by season—beginning with an autumn of unimaginable colours on maple and dogwood. After our browns and russets, the trees of an American fall seem clad in something more like flowers than leaves: delicate pale primrose, glowing crimson and all shades intermediate, with the oaks turning from their earlier deep red into an entrancing dusty purple. I had glimpsed this beauty on earlier visits—but only to rush through it between city and city. Now I was living in fairyland, for the fall was followed by a winter in which ice turned the trees into glittering sprays of glass. In spring all Philadelphia seemed on Sunday to be gazing at the wisteria on Grace Smith's house, which was next to ours, and at the vast Japanese flowering cherry which in our garden followed the magnolias and forsythia and the trees whose name I have never learnt, hung with hundreds of little white bells.

The village store was rather scanty for the week's shopping, but we had engaged the former gardener of the friend who had lent us the furniture. He solved our problems by driving us to the nearest shopping centre. Out of work, owing to the Depression, he owned a car and also a cottage at Tom's River, which we rented one year in the blazing heat of August. He drove us over from

Torresdale, picking up a week's provisions and a huge block of ice for the old-fashioned icebox. The beach was a safe one; both children were in and out of the water all day. I realized anew the evils of modern industrialization: Birdwood is on the banks of the Delaware, but the water was fouled by the great factories of Trenton (slogan: "Trenton makes, the World takes"). Our neighbour, Kilby Smith, used to tell us how as a boy he swam in the river and would sit with the fishermen on its banks round a fire of driftwood and eat the fish they had caught. The only fish I ever saw were lying on the shore, killed by the factory chemicals.

But Kilby was growing old. In England I had noticed the veterans' tendency to see 1939 through the spectacles of 1914, but Kilby tended to talk in terms of the war between North and South, in which his father had been a general. There was something fascinating in the mixture of modern and traditional, American and English, in Kilby and his sister. The labour-saving devices, so much less known to us then in England, the huge glass porch taken down every summer, re-erected every winter, the three maids and the gardener, the Philadelphia clubs and Kilby's English clothes. In many ways the Smiths' outlook was that of the English country house of my youth. I have heard among their friends expressions of regret over the breach with England. The atmosphere of Torresdale was that of which Chesterton denied the existence—an American village.

We had a vast garden and I dug up grass in order to plant vegetables. Kilby helped me with the gift of a wheeled hoe and digger—expatiating on my folly in growing food that I could buy more cheaply. But after Pearl Harbour the displacement of Japanese on the west coast sent the prices soaring, and anyhow, no tomatoes or sweet potatoes ever tasted so good. Wilfrid grew expert with the hoe, and at, I think, twenty-five cents an hour, supplemented our weekly gardener. There was a forge and a tiny bungalow at the end of the garden and after Dignam (the gardener) got a full-time job we took pity on a small tramp, employed him to dig and let him live in the brokendown buildings. In Frank's absence, however, he frightened us by appearing one day roaring drunk, together with a man whom he was bringing to live with him. The energy supplied by drink appeared to have added a cubit to his stature, and the second man was twice his size. It was a bad fright—but I cannot remember how we managed to get rid of them.

A delightful Polish priest taught me bee-keeping and our abundant flowers helped to fill the hives with honey, which he, however, came over to gather—for I never became brave about stings. Father Sokol's two recreations were bee-keeping and afforestation. He had bought seventeen acres and he showed us his seedling trees, his early and later plantings, with boyish enthusiasm, inveighing against the "priest on the golf links" for wasting hours that could be employed so pleasantly and so profitably for soul and body. Through him we saw something of the considerable local Polish community, with its fine hospital and the various clubs and groups to which he invited me to lecture.

Within a short walk of Birdwood was Eden Hall, the Sacred Heart Academy which I think we would have chosen out of all the schools we knew for Rosemary's education. We were less lucky for Wilfrid; there was no alternative to the parochial school, taught by the same nuns, but deeply mortifying to his manhood by the fact that boys and girls were in class together. He had been in a boys' school for almost two years and this seemed the most retrograde step.

Wilfrid was rather lonely and temporarily anti-social. He was unwisely threatened at school with being sent back to the bombs in England, and as this was his passionate desire, the threat produced no improvement. Baseball was the one consolation. It, too, became a passion both to play and to watch. But he was not really happy till later we moved him to Delbarton, a Benedictine school in New Jersey, where he weekly-boarded, coming home from Friday to Sunday evenings.

The monthly reports from Delbarton showed high marks, especially in subjects that seemed strange to us for a boy of ten—"Public Speaking" and "Civics"—but they were high also in Latin and French, the average being pulled down by a low mark for "Etiquette", a puzzling word which, however, signified not manners but order and tidiness.

At Delbarton Wilfrid, beginning to be interested in words, discovered Byron's 'Prisoner of Chillon' and, with great excitement, the Gettysburg Address—but this was ruined for him, alas, by the strange punishment of being made to write it out ten times.

My gratitude for Torresdale became deeper as I realized that the plan Frank and I had made was impossible to carry out. He could get the permits to go back to England which had become necessary, but I could not. Grace Smith had a chapel in the house and the Christmas of 1940 she had, as usual, three masses at midnight. Wilfrid served, nearly asleep by the last, but proud of his achievement. I loved making Christmas trees and I had discovered a fine spun glass called Angels' Hair. The lights shimmered through it with an enchanting subdued radiance. Each night I sat looking at that tree for hours when the children were in bed and the house was silent. Frank's letters had begun to come from England. His ship had picked up at a Canadian port the survivors of the *Jervis Bay*, a former passenger ship, given a few guns and sent to convoy a group of thirty-eight freighters across the Atlantic. A German warship appeared; the *Jervis Bay* went for it with all her guns blazing. She was sunk, of course, but delayed the raider long enough for the convoy to scatter in all directions; only four ships were sunk. The survivors were astonishingly cheerful; one of them, aged seventy, had clung to a raft for forty-eight hours in the North Atlantic in November and was the most lighthearted man on the ship.

My letters were not from England alone. The States still neutral, I was able to correspond with my brother Leo, of whose wartime experiences in Japan I shall speak in a later chapter, and with C.C.M. (Father Martindale), who was interned in Denmark. He told us later that the Jesuit house was only a few hundred yards from the Nazi place of execution—whence every shot reached his ears. He wanted news of Leo and of his other friends, asked me if I had ever seen a frozen sea—"leprous"; told of the coffee made from barley which still comforted him by its heat, of strange cigarettes, certainly not made from tobacco, but which somehow helped by being "choke-producing".

He could not, however, ask for news of the Battle of Britain, which was at its height. On the night of 30 December 1940 came that near-annihilation of the printed word in England in which we and so many publishers were involved. That part of London which is called the City is a desert at the weekend, and Frank, among the rest, had left it. The night before he had, to save time, slept on the office table, but on Saturday afternoon he had gone to stay the weekend with Christopher Dawson at Oxford.

In his next letter he wrote:

On Monday morning I came back bright and early to the office and there wasn't any office—just a handful of bricks in a hole. The big incendiary raid of the night before had wiped out most of Paternoster Row. Of our place nothing at all survived—all our books were destroyed and all our records—we don't even know who owes us money; also we don't know to whom we owe money, but they, doubtless, will tell us.

The only member of the staff to show any signs of emotion was one of our packers, who gave one look and then brought up his breakfast. We are taking another office nearby and hope to be running more or less normally again in a month or two.

Sitting by the Christmas tree reading these letters, devouring the papers, visiting in New York May Lamberton Becker and sharing her correspondence with her daughter Beatrice, I have never before or since lived in two worlds with equal intensity. I decided quite early to shape out of these and other eye-witness accounts a small book which I entitled *This Burning Heat*—from the words of St. Peter, "Think not strange the burning heat which is to try you; as if some new thing happened to you."

Growing up in surroundings of peace and plenty, experiencing the First World War only with a similar second-hand experience, I might have been too apt to think of this burning heat vaguely, mistily, as something strange; if there had not been living in the midst of it my sister and brother, my cousins who were almost sisters, and all their families, my closest friends and, for frequent periods, Frank also. Leo in Japan would later suffer more than any of them, but as yet neither the U.S.A. nor Japan was in the war.

Wilfrid found for me a consoling phrase about his father's frequent sea and airborne journeys. "Daddy", he said firmly, "is immune." Actually he crossed the Atlantic fifteen times during the War and never saw or heard an enemy. But we were learning daily of death and disaster—and it is the weakest of understatements to say that these things mean more if you know the places and people involved. I did not want to frighten Grandmother or the children, I could not talk constantly to our friends here, dear though they were becoming. It was with a heightened imagination that I threw myself into the writing of a book in which I could, I felt, live the Battle of Britain. I write of it now, too, at second hand, but not even my own painful consciousness of safety could turn it into a fully second-hand experience.

So small a town as Horley had few casualties. Minor places on the way to London were only attacked by planes coming over or returning to Germany and dropping the occasional bomb. One of Wilfrid's schoolfellows boasted of a thousand falling on Horley in a few months—however, there had, in fact, only been one casualty. But we lost in London raids two of the priests who had served the Horley mission: Fr. Dockery, who had been with us only a couple of months, and Fr. Barry, Fr. Healy's successor.

Looking back at Horley days I see Fr. Barry, not as one of those heroes created by the War, but as having had always a hidden fund of heroism. Young and delicate, he was always working beyond his strength. He lived at Wandsworth in one of the orphanages of the Southwark Rescue Society. Thence after Mass and breakfast he would travel to the society's office in South London for a hard day's work. On Saturday afternoon he came to Horley for a crushing weekend, covering an area of many square miles on a bicycle which during the week he left in the sacristy with a standing order that it might be borrowed by any member of the congregation who needed it.

It had always been the custom for our priest to come into the house midday and eat his roast beef with us. But on very many Sundays Fr. Barry would excuse himself with a "previous engagement".

Presently we discovered that it was in the cottage of one or another of our very poorest Catholics that he was eating his Sunday dinner. I am sure they gave him something better than the potato which was all the Curé d'Ars would accept, but it was of the Curé that Fr. Barry reminded me. He had all his gentleness and patience and I have never in all my life received such exquisite gratitude for such very slight reason as from this priest of ours. It still makes me happy to think that after we left he wrote to my sister, "I miss them more than I can say."

After his death the Bishop sent a resident priest to Horley and Frank was there to serve the first Mass!

Beatrice Warde had decided to stay in England; she was able to help many through food parcels and clothes sent by her friends in the States, both she and her mother were busy over that exchange of books which should be a clasping of hands between those who believed in freedom.

"I'd like everyone", she wrote to her mother, "who sent for the *Pattern of Freedom* to know that I, standing in Bumpus's, did in fact open that book at the Gettysburg Address. I shall always feel that Abraham Lincoln made a special trip to England to let me know that *he* didn't think I was such a fool for staying on."

To a group of friends who had sent parcels she told a story of what the clasping of hands could mean. Conceive the awful solitude of a woman buried under heaps of masonry. It would take hours, carefully moving the stones, to dig her out. She was a young surgeon with trained and sensitive hands. "It was only her hand that they could reach. A soldier appeared out of nowhere: he had no first-aid training or knowledge of rescue-squad technique. He just stayed there holding on to that girl's hand. Didn't let go the whole time. When they finally got her out he disappeared again. The family is trying to trace him; they'd rather like to thank him."

We had, she felt, all worn ourselves out over our vicarious responsibility for China and Abyssinia, now we could take a *mental* rest. We were being allowed just now to give God something valuable, if only a little suffering in fortitude.

> After this phase is over, *whichever* side wins, it's bound to be a "trying" (in the literal sense) time for anyone who believes in the individual soul and its rights . . .
>
> Still that time is not yet; and meanwhile we're excused from worrying. How it turns out is God's affair. The sun shines, the honeysuckle is drenching the garden with its scent, the first roses are coming out, and there are masses of cinnamon pinks along the front path.

This was a fascinating thing in the letters from England. People elsewhere seemed only half alive and the proportions were amazing of daily human joys versus the terrors of bombing. Waking in the morning to find oneself still living, new-found beauty in flowers, "sun, moon and stars and the wind on the heath", the thrill of books, of a peach or a banana (I knew of one banana that passed from hand to hand as a precious gift, to end up, I think, with a sick child). "Good evening, Jerry", the children began to greet the at-first terrifying planes. The windows were pasted criss-cross with paper to diminish the effect of blast. "I like them like that", one child wrote. "Was that a knock at the door?" "No, I think it was a bomb", was an interchange reported by Rosemary's former teacher. "Are we supposed to go to shelter?" my husband asked on his first arrival at Liverpool; the man in front of him in the queue answered in a "reasonable" voice: "If we do we'll miss the bus." The whole queue stayed: the bus came forty minutes later, bombs falling and buildings cracking unpleasantly close.

It became difficult to persuade people to shelter. And in fact the shelters above ground were little better than the houses—they felt safer, they said, under the kitchen table. The only real security was underground, and there a shelter life came into being which future historians may fancy was an interesting tribal habit.

Through the *Grail* magazine, I had become acquainted with Caryll Houselander, before Frank went to England. Now she and I were corresponding and he had persuaded her to write *This War is the Passion*, which established her at once as a spiritual writer of power and originality.

I think of Caryll in those days as I found her at first in the magazine, wandering through the streets of London and making contact with the bombed-out people, each of whom had for her a unique personality. Those who had lost their homes could not face the fact and it was one of authority's greatest problems to persuade them to leave the ruins. They would try, too—impossibly, and at great inconvenience for other shelterers—to re-create home in some corner of a shelter. Caryll wrote:

> We saw the illuminated "S" that stands for shelter, and crawled down a spiral staircase that never seemed to end. We were in a disused underground railway station, hundreds of feet beneath the fires. It was a tunnel a mile long, and the walls were lined with rows of three-decker bunk beds. The track had been boarded up and now there were single bunks along the walls, then a gangway, then two rows pushed close together, another gangway, and another single row stretching on and on, until the eye could no longer follow them.
>
> They were putting the children to bed, undressing them and fixing them securely in the lower bunks, the very small ones being laced in, with pieces of string. In the shadows a woman, a

girl almost, had wakened her child to feed it, beside her was a wooden apple box, within it lay the baby's shawl and a blue celluloid rattle. He was half asleep and the milk trickled down his chin. She smiled faintly at us. She had been sheltering there for two months and the baby had been born there. Her husband was fetching cocoa from the canteen; he had been reading and the book lay face downwards on the bunk. It was the Penguin edition of *The Compleat Angler*. Strange shades of sunlit water, and branches bending over streams and flies and fishes in this vast subterranean dormitory a mile long!

A million people asleep in the Underground, millions in other shelters, all in the helplessness of sleep, all wanting something they do not even realize. For life in the shelters is making even the blindest see that homes and families do not last for ever, but can be snatched away in an instant. There is nothing permanent, and the sad efforts to turn a few feet of stone wall into a home are only an admission that the one thing all these people want, is something that will last for ever. These shelters are fields, ploughed by the plough of God and waiting for seed. It is the war that has performed the almost unbelievable task of opening eyes to the true values of life.

Beatrice Warde, working in London, living in the countryside I knew so well, wrote of how she was now playing the *Missa de Angelis* in our chapel, of how splendidly the people were singing the Gloria and Creed, of how she planned to train a "local lad" to take her place as soon as possible.

It was the care of the Church to safeguard and explain words that had first drawn her to it. Beatrice has always loved words; one smiles to hear her description of the Magnificat—"I'm glad the Blessed Virgin Mary knocked off such a good bit of copy while she was about it." And, "What a pleasure it is to go to church these days . . . knowing that the same actual words are being uttered at that moment in every country in the world where it's not yet noon, and that they will sweep round the globe on the wings of the morning."

Her central theme was the same as Caryll's: "You won't ever forget these are days of glory, *real* glory of which the reality consists in the reality of danger. All this crude bombing business is only an imperfect (but illuminating) *analogy* for the normal adventures of the human soul."

It seemed a fit hour for beginning again to work on my biography of Chesterton. Before leaving England I had talked to all the friends of his youth and written the earlier chapters. Now a friend lent me an almost complete collection of his books, Notre Dame University provided a file of *The Eye-Witness*, *New Witness* and *G.K.'s Weekly*. I had brought with me most of the essential papers for the chapters not yet written, but the War had brought me to a stop. I was jerked into action by the appearance of that unfortunate book *The Chestertons*, written by Cecil Chesterton's widow. Even if it should prove hard to concentrate while Frank was in danger, his visits to England would make the work possible. He could bring me from Dorothy Collins, secretary and adopted daughter of Gilbert and Frances, any further material needed. He could interview doctors and other friends about the absurd suggestion made in *The Chestertons* that Gilbert's wife had refused to have sexual intercourse, and make clearer from their memories what a distorted picture of G.K.C. himself the book had given.

The generous welcome given to my biography was a recognition by the English people that Chesterton represented the thing for which they were fighting. Especially did *The Ballad of the White Horse* appeal during the darkest days of the Battle of Britain when men indeed seemed to have

> . . . Joy without a cause
> Yea, faith without a hope.

Beatrice Warde felt Dickens coming alive once more in London's bombed streets. A man wrote to one of the papers boasting of a unique experience in being "blown off a lavatory seat while reading Jane Austen". The essentially English writers were crying out to the English, and among them Chesterton. But of them all, he had, I believed, a much wider appeal, and it was fitting I should be tracing so far away that road which is the path home for all mankind. Chesterton had taught so many of us that the most wonderful paradox of Catholic Christianity lies in its being at once universal and intensely local. In Grace's little chapel, Frank's mother and I, praying for his safety in England, could think of him serving the same Mass in Horley, or joining in it at Westminster Cathedral.

Nor could I even despair of a future unity with the Germans at whose side I had drunk the waters of Lourdes or sung the Creed in front of the Basilica.

Beatrice, as she watched the bombing of London, was reading the proofs of her mother's book on Dickens. "Remember", she wrote, "that English readers are now capable of noticing with delight that Mrs. Gamp still has a window to lean out of and that Poll Sweedlepipe's shop down below hasn't had to be weather-boarded." When I read her words about the Alert in the human soul sounded by the Church, I remembered another scene drawn by that greatest of novelists—the return of the funeral party after the burial of Mrs. Gargery, who talked as they drank their port and sherry "as if they were of quite another race from the deceased and were notoriously immortal".

Catholics are not so much safer from this delusion than all mankind; the death of friends, the lists of daily accidents, do little to dispel it. But those fires of doom in the skies (one heard the comment that hell could be no more fearful), the obvious immediacy of peril did something remarkable to Englishmen. Walter Lippmann was saying that their behaviour restored belief in human nature, Caryll that she could sleep in a shelter warmed by the feeling of the goodness of the people around. There is an immense difference between even strong faith and realization. Shane Leslie wrote, "We all appreciate and almost feel the hands of God moving around us like the old mystics." And it was a man of the world who had never spoken to her of religion who remarked one day to Beatrice Warde: "I heard them coming our way, then that extra loud whistle; I pointed out to the Almighty that I was there, and that I had no idea what arrangements had been made in that regard, but that on the whole I was willing to think that any decision would be a sound one."

19

INTO THE MARITIMES

We in Torresdale were surrounded by sympathetic friends but my first lecture tour in wartime had shown me how strong the element of suspicion was. Americans of German, Italian and Irish descent were convinced that England was trying to drag them into the War. Most of our audiences were Catholic, so most were German, Italian and Irish. But even an English Bostonian in our office noted with relief that *This Burning Heat* was "factual" and "not propaganda". Yet there was more sympathy even among American Catholics than always appeared on the surface. After one lecture Frank was invited to a party at which his host opened the conversation by an attack on England. He listened for a while and then said, "I think you can carry on this conversation more happily in my absence." But when he got up to go, he found every guest was following him to the door.

Bit by bit, with the Battle of Britain, sympathy grew greater; on a second wartime tour I felt an immense change. This time at St. Paul, Minnesota, the lecture was arranged by a mixed group of Catholics, Protestants and Jews. The audience was equally mixed. Archbishop Murray was in the chair and I had been talking of how in London a priest or minister usually visited every shelter of an evening to say at least some prayer, to bring help and strength to the spirits of all those hidden under the earth from the Blitz above them. I told of one priest who would ask all present to make an act of contrition and would pronounce the words of absolution over the vast crowd in half a dozen shelters. Much moved by this but a little vague as to its exact meaning, a member of the audience asked the archbishop for an absolution. The archbishop, after a moment's hesitation, gave them his blessing in Latin and all fell on their knees to receive it. A touch of comedy was introduced by a rather ill-instructed Catholic, who asked me afterwards whether she need now go to confession on Saturday, since she had received absolution from His Grace.

That tour took me also to Canada, and I had never before realized how keen a joy one could feel at hearing the notes of "God Save the King" at the beginning or end of a lecture. Indeed, I had never before heard the National Anthem played so often. But these wartime visits to Canada meant something else besides the sense of national brotherhood: the discovery of another fascinating movement and of the men who had created it.

I had been in Canada before, had fallen in love with Montreal and made a host of friends there. Frank and I had also, sometime in the thirties, landed in Halifax and gone from there overland to New York. But although I lectured at St. Francis Xavier University (usually spoken of as St. F.X. and pronounced "St. Avex") it was only now that I discovered the co-operative movement in the Maritimes—which means the three provinces of Nova Scotia, New Brunswick and Prince Edward Island.

The fishing, mining, wood-cutting men of Nova Scotia were hopelessly enslaved economically, especially during the years of the Depression. The names of the slave-owners varied from place to place, but the pattern was the same. They dictated the price to be paid for the catch of lobsters, smelts and swordfish, for the logs, for the work in the mines. Usually the same man or company owned all the houses and the one local store—so that besides selling to them the men had to buy from them, and at both ends they fixed the price.

Heroic efforts had been made in past years at co-operation, which had petered out, usually because they depended on a single man's energy and leadership. The great achievement of Fr. Coady and Fr. Tompkins, both from Antigonish and double first cousins, was to throw the responsibility on the group, to insist that every man understood what he was doing, and supremely to put heart into him for the doing of it.

For the men of the Maritimes had lost hope; work was scarce, starvation imminent. "I have heard men weep for joy", says Father Ward of Notre Dame University in his book *Nova Scotia*, "because now their families have three meals a day, when before the children were often sent to bed with one meal a day." Yet although mostly Scots, they were not thrifty; when there was money it often went on drink, nothing was saved.

The saga of Fr. Tompkins at Canso, his first parish, shows his highly original method. "He never showed us what to do," one man said, "he just got mad at us." And an observer said "All he does is to go around and stick pins into people; to get them to do things for themselves."

This worked so well with the men of Canso that, breaking away from their local tyrants, they shipped a catch of lobsters co-operatively to the Boston market. A cheque came back almost double the previous year's rate. But then the dealers said, "If you don't sell the big lobsters to us, we won't take the small ones for canning." Again Father Jimmy was consulted; again he raged. Nobody seems quite to know who made the suggestion that the fishermen build their own canning plant. There were logs to be had for the cutting, land was easy to get—but how to buy the machinery? Father Jimmy borrowed the $1000 which paid for it—and which they paid back within a year, besides making a profit. And it was Father Jimmy later who bought the land on which eleven families built their own houses and which they naturally called Tompkinsville.

Fr. Ward saw him as a figure recalling both St. Francis and Socrates, but the wasplike fashion in which he expresses his love for men is his own special hallmark. One coal-cutter said of him, "That man wouldn't put out the cat for you, and he'd make fun of you while you put it out." But they know what he really wants; he wants people to find out how, and then to do.

All English and most American co-operation is unfortunately almost indistinguishable from big business. It had to be rediscovered in the Maritimes. And this is especially surprising when one comes to realize that the principles to which every Maritime co-operator constantly refers, which are almost a Bible for him, are English, are Lancashire. The Rochdale Principles, largely forgotten in England, reign in Canadian co-operation wherever it is connected by origin or teaching with Antigonish. They have to be discussed and accepted by any group planning a co-operative. There are eight: (1) One man, one vote. (2) Fixed rate of interest on capital. (3) Goods to be sold for cash—no credit (in one group this needed two meetings before it was accepted). (4) Goods to be sold at a market price. (5) All profits (after a safety reserve and money for education have been put aside) to be paid in dividends to members. (6) Political and social neutrality. (7) Funds to be set aside and used for education.

Rule 6 has indeed done a wonderful thing in Canada, overcoming the national cleavage between the French who once owned Canada and the English who took it from them. Father Jimmy preaches, "Who is neighbour to the man who fell among thieves? Who is my neighbour, anyway? How do Christians, how can Christians be neighbours now, not only among Christians, but among all men, Samaritans and Jews? If indulgences were once granted to men who built bridges and went on pilgrimages, why not now to men who can fish, build houses and cut coal? Why not to men who cure cancer or T.B. or catch fish, or teach people to teach themselves? . . . All men belong to God and all are one in Christ."

Very different in personality is the university professor, Dr. Coady, never called by anything except his name and title—a name of awe in the Maritime co-operatives, the philosopher of the movement, Father Jimmy being the chief field-worker. In this man, says Fr. Ward, there is an evident power, and yet also a suggestion somehow of undiscovered, unexpressed and undeveloped power. And that is just what he says is in the people; goodness, courage, power that never quite arrives, never becomes aware of itself; it is there, and after all not there; "ever not quite". This is because, so far as the people are concerned, our education "does not face reality" and "does not afford vision". The young leaders of co-operation in Nova Scotia say, "You don't know anything about this movement till you get to hear Dr. Coady." The condition for success (he says in his book) is "first to break existing mind sets, second to help people to make up their minds anew and to rebuild both themselves and society".

He demands a serious preparation for the work. "Good will without the necessary means amounts to nothing, any more than morons with the money but without the motive." Of the people in eastern Canada, 84% were without property, without security. Yet he hated to have them ask for State aid. "I don't believe that the people who look for aid are 8% efficient." Efficiency in fishing, in farming, in women's work at home, he demands insistently. "Always," says Fr. Ward, "he begins his speech with a kind of explosion . . . a series of blasts." Like Father Jimmy, he injects his own vitality.

The ideal order in which co-operation should be established is seen in five steps: (1) The Study Clubs. (2) The Popular Library. (3) The Credit Union. (4) The Consumer's Co-operative. (5) The Producers' Co-operative.

Some groups add small-scale co-operative farming, co-operative building and even co-operative medicine and co-operative insurance. But the first principle never varies—men must begin with study, and they must study always. Before the building of Tompkinsville an architect, Mary Arnold, came from New York and the group studied with her a full year before they began to build. At Reserve Mines I found in that tiny community eleven study groups based on the library. Father Tompkins' own books are all in a common stock; his house is the library.

I say "is", but this is all a long time ago; Father Jimmy and Dr. Coady are both dead, almost twenty years have passed since Frank and I drove through the glorious countryside learning something of the transformation in the lives of its people. At Louisdale Fr. Landry said, "From 1933, through 'four, 'five, 'six, there was terrible suffering here. Out of our ninety families in the parish, sixty-five were on dole during the winter of 1934-5; and that means 72%. And the dole per family came to five dollars' worth of grocery for two weeks."

This seemed worse than anything we knew in England—and the families were large; four, eight, and in one case sixteen children. Their credit union began in 1936 with $40; two years later there was $2600—and it was usually all out, lent to members for profitable undertakings. Twenty-six years later in one year, 1962, the credit unions of Nova Scotia, out of assets of over $17,000,000, lent out *over* $11,000,000. Is there any parallel to this in making money work? For the money is lent for creative purposes. Not in Canada alone but in many other countries, not in the West alone but in Asia, and Africa, this essential basis of co-operation is spreading today. The men of Louisdale, as elsewhere in the Maritimes, learnt to make small gardens, to grow patches of grain and potatoes instead of buying them, to can strawberries and peas, to make bread, and milk a cow. It seems strange that these skills should have been so new to them—but I suppose, like Kilby Smith before the War, they had felt before the Depression, with good wages coming in, that it was cheaper and less trouble to buy vegetables, bread and milk.

As I looked at the wide sweep of the countryside I felt it must after all have been easier for these men than for the English to beat the Depression. Yet even for them it was not easy. It meant continued study leading to hard gruelling work. One wife, whose husband had been stirred by Borsodi's *Flight from the City*, had promised to read it. "Only," she said, "if it is to work that way on me, I hesitate." To eternal vigilance as the price of liberty must be added a labour that seems unending. After hewing coal and cutting wood, *must* a man dig his garden or build his house, must a woman left exhausted by her housework can peas, feed pigs, make rugs?

Yet, this movement was doing for the souls of men what Beatrice Warde rightly said a *consciousness* of the Christian view of life would achieve. Like Englishmen living through the Blitz, these co-operators had an alertness, an awareness lost by the wage-earner of today. They had been starved of beauty, starved of ownership. The companies' mining shacks are dreary unpainted places—I seldom saw a flower except among the vegetables in co-operators' gardens. "We never noticed they were dull", one man said, "until we were out of them." "The fourteen new white houses, stretching up a green hill over the ocean, looked like a flock of white birds or a handful of butterflies against the woods."[1] This was Villa Nova but Tomkinsville had been built first—during the study period. A patch of land, twenty acres or so with brush and scrubby timber on it, had been cleaned and eleven houses built. On the rocky barren soil, with its gravel and brickish clay, radishes, beans and potatoes now grew, some shabby little pens housed chickens or a pig, but what struck me most was that though designed under an architect, each man's house was built to suit his own fancy.

"Did you ever own a house before?" someone asked Joe Laben, the first leader of the group. "Never," he said; "nor a pig or a chicken. And we never hoped, any of us, to own anything, nor ever thought of it." That is the story from the outside, but there is at Tompkinsville an inner spirit, ten times as important.

"I would say", Fr. Ward puts it "that the main thing they have discovered is that man is a person. That is the fundamental change; everybody now is somebody."

Back in Halifax Frank and I were told that a Captain McCrea had been asking for us. Our old friend who had once done what he could to save our farce of a farm was now convoying merchant ships across the Atlantic. Often he did not, he told us, go to bed for two weeks at a time, but just lay down on his berth ready for immediate action.

[1] This is a quotation from Father Ward, to whose observation I owe much of my own understanding of the movement.

Twice his ship had been sunk, but, though no youngster, he had not the least intention of giving up his dangerous and exhausting job.

"Who's looking after your farm?" I asked, and in a voice of intense pride he answered, "Tammas." "Tammas" was his son, a boy of sixteen. I suspected that Mrs. McCrea too was doing her share—but in time of crisis boys fast become men, and Tammas was not doing so much more than many boys in England then, or even than some of the boys I had seen in Nova Scotia.

Beatrice Warde was writing from London of "the formula that the common people devised for their own consolation and inspiration the minute the trouble started. 'We're all in this together' . . . The civilians' own slogan shifts the emphasis from his part to the whole; and you know how excited I get at every fresh hint that *that* is what the 20th century is really doing, recovering the Sense of the Whole . . ."

"If anyone had told me", said one miner, busy building another man's house, "that I would work for the other fellow for nothing and that he'd work for me, I'd have laughed at him. I didn't believe anybody'd do anything for anybody." "Selfishness is not co-operation", said another. "This co-operation is kinda on God's side."

How wide was the gulf between these ideals and the world of the moment. Frank must soon go back to England again. It was a joke among our friends that we commuted across the Atlantic. But now it was no joking matter. Annoyed at being put off one boat because a V.I.P. had been given his berth, he learned afterwards that it had been sunk on the voyage. Once the ship he was in developed engine trouble, and, left behind by the convoy, limped slowly to the Azores, where there was nothing to do but look at the scenery, nothing to buy except watches—and no money to buy them with. Once he crossed on a bomber.

But I was left behind—to read Chesterton and dream of an England not unlike the picture of Ethandune in *The Ballad of the White Horse*:

> The fires of the Great Army
> That was made of iron men,
> Whose lights of sacrilege and scorn
> Ran around England red as morn,
> Fires over Glastonbury Thorn
> Fires out on Ely Fen.

20

MY BROTHER LEO

I LEFT Leo in an earlier chapter when he had just fought his way through to the priesthood. Now he was, and had by 1941 been for nine years, a missionary in Japan. His missionary vocation was a little unusual; it had come suddenly through two friendships made about the time of his ordination, with Violet Suzman, a Jewish convert, and her friend Fr. Totsuka—a Japanese priest and doctor, from whom he caught an intense wish to evangelize Japan. It all seemed very remote, as he would not have dreamed of leaving Mama. But after her death he went at once to consult Cardinal Bourne. Missionary work is normally carried on by missionary orders, and Leo was a secular. Each country has its own mission areas, and there were no English missionaries with whom he could work in Japan.

"I can do nothing for you," said the Cardinal, "except give you a *Celebret* [permission to say Mass] for six months, and a letter to the Archbishop of Tokyo. After that, you must just sink or swim."

It was all Leo had wanted. Father Totsuka was about to open a hospital in Yokohama where Violet was going to nurse. Fr. Totsuka wanted Leo, who spoke both French and Italian, to make contacts for him with the European colony in Yokohama and Tokyo; meanwhile he could be learning Japanese. The French Archbishop of Tokyo received him warmly.

Much had happened since; Leo had worked hard for a native clergy in Japan and it was under a Japanese archbishop that he was now established in a parish at Meguro, a suburb of Tokyo. Leo and I were able to correspond, although letters came slowly. He sent us his friend John Pilcher from the British Embassy, who gave us fairly cheerful news of him. Then, after a long gap on both sides, came a letter dated March 11th, 1941, showing that it was not only I who had been starved for news. He had not heard of the bombing of our office, was deeply relieved that there were no casualties: "To hear that you are all right, Frank home safe and well and Tetta well was *tremendous* news."

But what were (he asked) the most important, the spiritual effects of the War—anti-Catholic feeling? Many or few conversions? "Are people losing their faith or gaining a deeper hold on it?" He himself had converts both English and Japanese. Then came a P.S. "The Maryknoll and Canadian priests will stay here, even if there is a war. Please tell Cardinal Hinsley I want to do as they do (No risks)."

That spring he begged me to see the architect of his little church at Karuizawa, who with his wife lived not far from us at New Hope, Pennsylvania. Karuizawa was a summer resort for Europeans. It was here that Leo had bought a house for Japanese seminarians, and he went there whenever he could get away from his work in Tokyo. His church (or chapel) had drawn the attention both of *Architecture d'aujourd'hui* and of *Art sacré*, which hailed it as a model and inspiration for village architecture. Nothing in the church was prefabricated. It was built by Japanese workmen, under the direction of the architect, Mr. Raymond, and was of largely Japanese character. Leo had shown himself as what *Art sacré* most desiderated, a priest determined to get away from the assembly-line, and to encourage something indigenous. He and the workmen too had borne their share in inspiring Mr. Raymond and carrying out his ideas.

New Hope was a delicious spot, especially in springtime. The house had been designed by the architect himself. It was the first time I had seen a room with one whole wall of glass. From your bed only the tops of the locust trees smothered with white flowers lay between you and the wider scenery. Mr. Raymond spoke fascinatingly of his art, dwelling especially on the artist's need for humility in face of his materials: the stone, the wood, the countryside itself.

I wrote to Leo of our great pleasure in our visit to New Hope, and he answered me in a letter that began about the Raymonds and his desire that we should become friends (they were, he said, "true allies of mine at Karuizawa"), but went on:

> How strange to be preoccupied with all this when world events of unlimited magnitude are unfolding.
>
> Today is Our Lady of Mount Carmel's feast and I feel more vividly than ever that only prayer can help us.
>
> Surely if the Soviet falls it must be an immense good for the

world—by removing an immense evil—although one is naturally alarmed at the vast power opposing it.

But I try hard not to think of politics.

On the eve of another feast of Our Lady five months later, Japan attacked the States, destroying at Pearl Harbor a great part of their fleet. December 8th, Feast of the Immaculate Conception, is the patronal feast of America. It fell that year on a Sunday. We were all stunned as the news came to us bit by bit, but it was many months before I knew what had happened to Leo. I was not feeling alarmed. He had so many friends in Tokyo, the Japanese Archbishop Doi, the Apostolic Delegate, an Italian; the Jesuits at the University, almost all Germans. In a long letter the Delegate (now Cardinal Marella) gave me a picture of Leo's years in Japan. Feeling he knew me from the photo on my brother's desk, and from all he had said of his home, he wanted me in turn to know how Leo had been loved:

> Our relations were less those of priest and bishop, than of friend with friend. He was already in Japan when I arrived there in 1933, and I was told at once of his valuable influence on behalf of the Japanese Church. His fine intelligence, united with the greatest simplicity, won my admiration—and also the warmth of his heart. He was at that time working devotedly as Father Totsuka's assistant.
>
> While doing his utmost in this way for poorer people, he deliberately built up excellent relationships with Tokyo's best society, being welcomed and loved by everybody. Needless to say here too he remained supremely priest and apostle. Despite poor health and frequent painful headaches he never slackened in his various forms of activity if he saw any good to be done. His lively interest in politics sometimes raised a smile among his friends—but to him politics were only a background, against which he was always looking at the interests of the Church. Throughout the world and especially in Japan he shuddered at political trouble or international tension because of its possible repercussions on the souls of men.
>
> An education and training of high quality served him well with both great and small. But surrounded by universal esteem, he continued to have doubts of himself, and would often come to me for advice and encouragement. He fancied that his imperfect

knowledge of the language held him back from all the good he longed to achieve. I did my best to encourage him, and he always left me happy and bubbling with enthusiasm.

On returning here after a short holiday in England, he wanted, while still keeping his old job, to work also in a more central parish, chiefly to be able to do more for young students. Established later in a parish of his own, it was an immense joy to him to feel himself the father of so many souls. On the other hand he was vividly conscious of the weight of the responsibility he was assuming.

Soon after this, Japan passed through a crisis of intense xenophobia. Father Ward asked himself whether it might be better—not for him but for the Church—to bow for a while before the storm and return home till a better day dawned. On mature reflection, he made the decision to stay to the end. War broke out between Japan and Europe, and Father Ward was at once arrested and put in solitary confinement. His many friends, including the Japanese, were amazed and grieved. They all did their utmost to help him, the Archbishop of Tokyo and myself at once approaching the Government. We were told that he was suspected of espionage, but was being well treated.

He was allowed to write occasionally during his imprisonment, and I remember with emotion one card in particular, conveying to me his good wishes for Xmas and New Year. He congratulated himself on the conditions of his imprisonment and on his gaolers. His health had, he said, improved and he had never spent a Christmas more full of peace and spiritual happiness. His only worry was lest his arrest should have got his Japanese friends into trouble.

His writings had been seized and were subjected to severe scrutiny by the tribunal. And the result was the categorical statement by those very men who had arrested him as a spy: "The Reverend Father Ward is absolutely innocent of any suspicion of any activity against this country. He is moreover a convinced and true friend of Japan." No more complete acquittal could have been received and the Reverend Father Leo was shortly set at liberty and allowed to go back to his dwelling in Meguro, a suburb of Tokyo. He was allowed to receive visitors and to make visits. When I went to see him he kept repeating that he had been well treated and had no complaints of anyone. In saying this he showed great magnanimity—but it is true that he had won even the hearts of his gaolers by his dignity and good humour . . . His love for Japan was unchanged, indeed it seemed deeper than ever . . . Yet God knows what he must really have suffered under the conditions of Japanese prisons at that time. Your brother was to an extraordinary degree a model missionary. While he could have shone in the "great world" he chose freely and eagerly to bury himself here and the country won him absolutely. Other missionaries have the support, moral and physical, of a religious order or a missionary society. He was utterly solitary, but none the less went ahead with the greatest trust in God, pouring out without measure, both his money and his love. He won the respect of all—friends and enemies—if one can really speak of his enemies. It may in truth be said that his coming into our midst was a real gift from heaven for this Church. His family and his country may justly be proud of him.

After Leo's death *The Tablet* printed his own story of those four months in prison, written in a fashion so irenical that it ought not to be forgotten, although entitled by him "Before Forgetting These Things":

I was arrested on December 8th, the feast of the Immaculate Conception, on which day Japan entered the war. I had said Mass and finished breakfast when the door-bell rang, and a young Japanese friend living in the presbytery told me that the military police had come to see me. I did not know that Japan was at war, and was still hoping that peace might be preserved in the Far East. But a friend who had an acquaintance among the Military Police had warned me that their activities among foreigners were likely to be considerably increased in the near future. So I was not surprised when four entered the house, and politely asked my permission to examine all books and papers. I was somewhat alarmed when they asked me to return with them to their headquarters, and still more so when they added that I had better pack a small suitcase and bring it. Even this, however, failed to dispel my confidence of safety, which was based not only on my consciousness of innocence before the Law, but also on the fact that the Civil Police had given a very favourable report about me only a month previously when I had applied to become a teacher in the Tokyo Higher Normal School. The leader of the group was, moreover, quite friendly in manner, and assured me that he would explain my inability to attend school and a lunch engagement at the Canadian Legation that very day. Before leaving the house, however, I was told by my young Japanese friend that war had broken out. "The English and Americans have attacked our ships", was the brief account of what he had heard over the wireless.

I was now driven through Tokyo by my new acquaintance to the Headquarters of the Military Police, where, after an adequate Japanese lunch, I was interrogated by the leader of the group, whose manner rapidly changed from friendliness to extreme severity as he found fault with each of my statements, and especially blamed me for having friendly relations with members of the British and other Embassies and (more naturally) for having written letters to the newspapers on the situation of the Church in Germany (I had been warned by various friends that I ran a risk of being arrested, I suppose on account of these articles). My examiner finally told me that I was arrested on two charges: (a) that of having conducted anti-German propaganda after His Majesty the Emperor had signed the Three-Power Pact with Germany and Italy; and (b) of having given information about Japan to the British Embassy (a charge which was more or less dropped in the later stages of my examination).

I was now driven to the Great Tokyo Kochisho Prison, where I saw in the entrance hall about a dozen foreigners and many Japanese. My clothes were examined and all but the necessities were taken from me before I was conducted through long and dark passages divided by iron gates to a dimly-lighted cell, where I slept on the usual Japanese mattress on the floor. Rather better than I expected. Later I was allowed a bed and blankets.

During the first few days in prison I was given Japanese food, which was plain but wholesome, and on the third or fourth day, I began to receive European meals. Apart from the shock of surprise and the complete uncertainty of the future it was impossible, with faith and an optimistic temperament, to be unhappy. Life, however, was monotonous without books or news of any kind, and I was relieved on the fifth day when I was led upstairs to begin my examination. Incidentally, we wore the most picturesque straw hats, which covered our faces whenever we were outside our cells.

During my four months in prison I occasionally passed other European prisoners in the passages going to or returning from the examinations, but I recognized no-one, though a friend (Mr. Vere Redman) recognized me and recalled to me quite accurately what I had said and done as we passed each other.

The examinations lasted from five to seven hours daily. They were aimed at discovering whether I had abused my work as a missionary in the interests of political propaganda. They were thorough and minute to an astonishing degree, and on the whole were not unfair. I was naturally anxious to prove that as a Catholic priest I had no anti-Japanese prejudices, and had never intentionally conducted English propaganda in my parish. In proving this I felt that I was aiding other Catholic missionaries. I did not know that a French Bishop, a French priest and an Anglican Bishop had been arrested on the same day as myself . . .

My examiner was alternately kind and stern, but even when in the latter mood, he was not guilty of any worse incivilities than slaps, mild kicks and accusations of lying. My reputation for candour was, I found, called in question owing to the fact that I had never revealed my skill in sportsmanship, although four large silver cups (the chalices in the sacristy of my church) were testimony to it!

I do not think he was unjust, and I still think there was sufficient reason for examining me, though I cannot understand why it took four months to arrive at a decision in my regard.

The daily examinations ceased for a whole week at the New Year and were concluded in their first phase early in the third month. After that I was informed that my friends were being called up for examination about me, and I was left in my cell with the consoling companionship of a Breviary, a Bible and a complete one-volume Shakespeare. Books had not been allowed me during the early stages of my examination. In spite of books the weeks of solitude often seemed a strain on the nerves and during one whole week a tired head compelled me to do nothing all day but physical jerks.

When my examinations recommenced they were conducted

by a judge (by name Neda), a pupil of the famous Catholic Professor of Law, Dr. Tanaka, of the Imperial University. It was hinted to me that my case would probably not involve a formal trial, though I was alarmed once when the judge asked me how I thought my health would stand a year's imprisonment.

The judge's examination was concluded within a week, and then I waited two weeks more, wondering when I should hear my fate and what it was likely to be.

On April 7th, after a day of quite unusual depression of spirits (almost for the first time I felt unable to idealize my situation even in the light of Faith) I was sent for by the judge and told that I would be liberated that day.

That evening I was led home to my presbytery, now occupied by a Japanese priest, to be interned there as his guest for the next four months. I was immensely happy and quite proud of having grown a white beard which I was foolish enough to shave off after two days. During my internment at home, I was allowed two hours of walking on nearby roads—my chief need as we only had ten minutes daily in the yard of the prison. I was able to say Mass again, and though not allowed to visit or invite friends, I could receive a fair number of uninvited guests. My parishioners overwhelmed me with kind gifts, so my meals were abundant. I was profoundly saddened by the news that the Holy See had ordered all American and British priests to leave Japan. But for some time I hoped against hope that this order would not finally be insisted upon.

I shall never forget the kindness of my Japanese friends during these last months. The Apostolic Delegate (Mgr. Marella) was among my first visitors and before leaving I received a visit from the Japanese Archbishop, Mgr. Doi, who thanked me for my work in Japan, and assured me that I was to consider myself Parish Priest of my old Parish, 17 Nishi-Koyama, as soon as peace was restored.

I read in the *New Yorker* an account of this same prison by a journalist who was there at the same time as Leo. The picture is painted in very much darker colours. He had been badly fed and bitterly cold. He had filled the long empty hours by an attempt to remember all the States of the Union. (The man's memory must have been a poor one, especially if he had been to an American school.) Leo did tell a friend that he was fearfully cold, adding, however, that it was largely his own fault as he had broken the earthenware charcoal-burning brazier that was his only means of heat. It was never replaced. The food, he said, did grow scarce—but, he hastened to add, it was scarce for the Japanese themselves.

Mr. Redman, the friend who had recognized him in the prison, wrote:

> His relations with the prison officials were similar in character to his relations with all mankind. He seemed well-disposed, eloquent and quietly conscious of that which raises a priest above ordinary men. It was quite obvious that the humiliations, both actual and attempted, of the prison regime had made no impression whatever on his inherent dignity. He remained as a priest should, completely undefiled and undefeated by his environment.

Dignity is one thing, cheerfulness quite another, and I always feel that Leo's cheerfulness in imprisonment was a minor miracle. I met many years later a friend received by him into the Church at Yokohama who said, "I think helping me, helped him. He was very depressed at the time." And Cardinal Marella had told me of the same continuous depression in daily life that Mama and I knew so well and had been helping him to fight ever since his Jesuit noviciate. Indeed, in a letter to me, shortly before, he had written of brainfag so prostrating after the least extra fatigue as to make him fear that he was going out of his mind. A Japanese brain specialist had advised him to go, when the War should end, to a psychiatrist (European or American, also Christian) who would "make me work like anyone else by probing the root of the trouble. But it might take him a long time to do this . . . Meanwhile I wait happily, perhaps I shan't live so very long or live uncured if that is His Will. Am very well and happy, if very prudent." A later letter apologized for this "grotesquely egotistical" letter and told me how seeing Mgr. Marella had cheered and reassured him by showing him "quite accidentally how keen he is on my being here in Tokyo".

Quite apart from the results of his breakdown, Leo had from childhood always needed reassurance. His doubts of himself were deep; and the more good he did the more he seemed to doubt. Much of his work both in Yokohama and Tokyo had been with the Europeans, which made the Japanese suspicions of him understandable. But his heart was given first and foremost to Japan. He once sent us a photo of himself seated in a group of Japanese—and it would have been hard to tell which was the Englishman. Curiously enough, though his spoken Japanese remained halting, he could preach almost eloquently, and echoes have reached me of the deep affection he inspired in the parish which Archbishop Doi had literally forced on him.

With deep reluctance he left Tokyo and embarked for England. Sister Violet and many others left on the same boat. It was soon clear that she was not well enough to go on, and Leo got off at Lourenço Marques to establish her in a hospital. He came on by another boat where he found various friends. He began at once every morning to say Mass at 5 in the engine-room for the Catholic Goan sailors. He had been given a good cabin but exchanged it with a Dutch priest for one on the lowest deck of the boat, and terribly airless. Suddenly he became very ill with encephalitis. To a friend who said he would soon be home he answered that it was another home for which he was bound. He received the last sacraments and died peacefully on the feast of Saint Thérèse, patron of the missions, to whom he had always been devoted. He was buried at sea, and the sailors to whom he had ministered sang his requiem.

Frank was in England but Torresdale was still our home when Leo died. At the Sacred Heart Convent where Rosemary was at school our friend Mgr. Hawks, of the Philadelphia Catholic Evidence Guild, sang his requiem. The words of the Gospel seemed meant for me and his voice rang out with the conviction that, as Christ Our Lord promised, our sorrows shall be made joy. "Your brother shall rise again."

That promise was uttered to our dear Grace a little later when Kilby died, to all her friends when Grace left us at the age of ninety-three.

Our little Torresdale community of friends are dead or scattered, but they are not merely a tender memory. "I am the Resurrection and the Life."

Heavy as present grief was, I felt even then that Leo could not have borne to live far away from the country he had made his own. Later I realized what it would have meant to him when the atom bomb was dropped on Nagasaki—the first and abiding centre of Japanese Christianity. However great our losses in the earlier phases of the war, especially the Battle of Britain, we had all been walking in an air of glory. But now we were partaking in a deed of shame which would I think have broken my brother's spirit.

21
ON THE BORDERS OF HARLEM

FRANK had been in England when Leo died—waiting with my sister to welcome him home. When he got back we found that our pattern of living must be changed to fit the new scene of America at war. Torresdale is on a main line from New York through Philadelphia and Washington to the South. The trains began to be crowded to suffocation; chiefly with soldiers. Large camps had been opened in the South for training the new recruits—an excellent idea for climatic reasons in winter and as a means of bringing prosperity to the poorest part of the country. But Torresdale was so small a place that an obvious move for speed was to cancel it as a stopping place for expresses. There had only been two a day but those two had made a vast difference to us.

Both Frank and I began to sleep oftener in New York, and in a New York hotel I finished *Gilbert Keith Chesterton.* We corrected the proofs together—filling a large thermos with coffee overnight, and starting work at five or six in the morning. Little as Gilbert had liked the dawn it seemed to suit him, and we both felt a sense of exhilaration. There was anguish in the many cuts to be made, but economy there must be, if only because of the paper problem. Kilby Smith commented sardonically on the restrictions which followed one another in rapid succession. The Government, he said, thought it a point of honour to make their citizens as uncomfortable as the British. This was a rich country—no need to ration coffee, no need to limit paper. He viewed with sharp displeasure the growth of forms "to be filled in quintuplicate" and the increasing grip of bureaucracy.

Movements of soldiers and increase of regulations—but also the passing of the Depression. With munition factories, uniform factories and the new army, underemployment seemed to become overemployment almost overnight. Everyone had a job—often two jobs; domestic or garden help was almost impossible to find.

Memory telescopes into one picture changes which took eighteen months or so to come about and which were turning our thoughts in the direction of New York. And then two things happened. Rosemary's sight, always short, was getting worse and the oculist threatened to forbid school altogether. I had come across Aldous Huxley's *The Art of Seeing* and I wrote to ask him about the Bates method. I had met Aldous when he was at Eton. Mrs. Warre Cornish, wife of the Vice-Provost, had, I remembered, read Anatole France aloud to us and we shared a certain amusement in her efforts at skipping improper passages—and landing in the middle of them. Leo and he had been friends at Oxford. They wrote mocking verses about one another, of which I remember one:

There once was a terrible neo-
scholastical bigot called Leo,
Who set out to prove
That, though Rome doesn't move,
She develops *scherzando con brio*.

Aldous Huxley had not heard of Leo's death; he wrote warmly of him and told me more about the treatment that had for him cured near-blindness. There was no Bates practitioner at Philadelphia but a first-rate one, Mrs. Royse Conrad, in New York.

And then our hostess at Torresdale revealed that she was hoping in this hour of easy money to be able to sell Birdwood. Frank was again in England but I went up to New York and found a vast choice of apartments. A little later New York would be overcrowded, but now landladies were offering "concessions" of a summer month, or even two, rent free.

The idea of an apartment on Riverside Drive startled my Philadelphia friends—"You *cannot*", I was told, "live on the West Side." I pointed out that an apartment twice the size was approximately half the rent of one on the East River, and it was just as fresh and pleasant to live over the Hudson. But as I looked back on England I realized that it had taken me the removal to another country and a cooler observation from the outside to get snobbishness out of my system—if indeed one ever wholly loses it.

The summers that followed our move were as pleasant as I had dreamed, living in a corner apartment and looking at the river. Most New Yorkers sweltering in the city would rush off to the country and return complaining how hot they had found it; we were never without a breeze. New Jersey from our windows was not beautiful, but at night, water and lights are always beautiful. And the foreground was a daylight joy, the river itself, the swift stream of cars on the highway, the trees clinging to the sharp slope below. Double-decker buses went from apartment to office door faster than one can imagine today, with a conductor to take the money as well as a driver. The subway was even faster, but I can never reconcile myself to underground travel even on the best of systems, and New York, though the fastest, is the dirtiest and the noisiest I know.

In the opposite direction the bus ran to the Cloisters, that most wonderful of museums. Moved from Europe to New York and reconstructed, these former ruins are linked together, adorned by a gently playing fountain, a herb garden, a mass of irises, purple and white, tubs of oleanders. There is a chapter-house, a chapel and several galleries filled with changing exhibitions of medieval treasures. The dates are various but the harmony as perfect as in a cathedral built by many generations. Twice a week there is a concert of medieval music. But the best time is the quiet of the early morning when, almost alone, one can imagine Mass in the chapel and monks passing through these cloisters to the chapter room.

Besides this historical resurrection, our neighbourhood offered a valuable library. I had always had difficulty in saying the Rosary and had discovered ways of helping myself that might help others. The chief of these was theology, but I wanted too to sketch in a background of history. The Union Theological Seminary Library had all the books I needed plus a reading room and cafeteria. Caryll Houselander contributed rhythms for my book: *The Splendour of the Rosary*. It found more readers than any I had written except *Gilbert Keith Chesterton*, so I suppose it did something of what I had hoped.

I was still living two lives through Frank's visits to England, letters from my sister and cousins, from Caryll, from Molly Walsh and Dorothy Collins. Though I could not stop a single bomb, I could do something for those on whom they were falling. The British censorship hampered me by forbidding requests and cutting out from letters any direct reply to enquiries. But one question might be answered: "What was of most use in my last parcel?"

I got various replies: the sugar, the butter, the tea, the ham, the hot-water bottles, the pretty clothes so really appreciated when all in England were just drab and functional besides being strictly rationed. Some correspondents were cleverer than others at the game which developed between me and the censors. My sister was my despair, telling me only that my parcels were always a joy. Molly Walsh, carrying on her House of Hospitality, described the destination of each pound of tea, each ham, hot-water bottle or parcel of bed-linen. Caryll's letters were a poem that Cinderella might have addressed to her fairy godmother, not useful in guiding my selection—but the best of all in conveying how much the parcels meant for spirit as well as body. Choosing their contents was a major activity, but after three years of it I learnt of a firm in Canada which understood the business better than I did. Sending a list of people and parcels to them was dull but common sense.

The arrangement of the school year in the States had many advantages in our complicated lives. Frank's absences were liable to occur at any time, but we did not lecture in the long holidays—usually the first week in June until after Labour Day (the first Monday in September).

Wilfrid was still weekly-boarding at Delbarton, Rosemary going daily to the Sacred Heart Convent at 91st Street and twice a week to the Bates practitioner, Mrs. Royse Conrad. Frank, too, suffering for years from almost continuous headaches, decided to consult her. Rosemary was so shortsighted she would almost panic if she mislaid her glasses; she could not read the numbers on the buses, she could not see across the street. On our first visit Mrs. Conrad removed her glasses—and attacked me for staring; eyes should move constantly and how could I expect my daughter to use hers properly if I did not? Slightly irritated, I pointed out that my sight was excellent, though too long, Rosemary's very bad and much too short. But later both Wilfrid and I consulted her and realized that by using our eyes correctly we too could see much better than we had realized. Correct vision was a crusade for Mrs. Conrad, and before long my husband joined Aldous Huxley on her altar as a sort of demigod. Here were two immensely busy men who found time for their exercises—in her eyes the *unum necessarium*. Frank, too, was to give up at once the glasses he had worn for twenty-five years; he should never have worn them at all. What, asked Mrs. Conrad passionately, would you think of the medical profession if half the population of New York were walking about on crutches—and what are glasses but crutches for the eyes?

Oculists have tried since to argue with Frank about these quack methods. His only answer is, "Whereas I was blind, now I see." And the headaches were reduced to reasonable infrequency.

Rosemary had to spend two hours a day on her eyes, and the nuns arranged for her to palm—which meant covering the eyes with the palms of the hands—while listening to certain lessons. I helped her homework by reading aloud while again she palmed. Mrs. Conrad's further stipulation was that pleasant thoughts should accompany the palming! Fortunately Rosemary's memory is a good one. I was horrified at what she told me of her friends sitting up till twelve or one over their homework, an increasing problem in all countries. No wonder so many, after school years, never open a serious book again.

We were living close to Columbia University, to Corpus Christi Church and to New York's chief negro area: Harlem. There was to be found Friendship House, a movement which had begun in Canada during the Depression: in the States it concentrated on work for the coloured. Like Dorothy Day's Catholic Worker, it was founded by a woman and was, in the days I knew it best, a predominantly feminine movement. We published two books by its Russian foundress, Baroness Catherine de Hueck, usually called "The B".

In *Friendship House* she describes how she learned the bitter lesson that the class she belonged to had betrayed their trust before they in turn were betrayed. Fleeing before the first Russian Revolution, she came to her old home to find the tenants "bedecked in red rags and ribbons, armed with old rifles, butchers' knives, scythes, sickles . . . a ridiculous and terrible mob". Those whom she had sought as friends shut her up to starve, and during interminable nights and days she thought of past wealth and thoughtlessness. Was it, she asks, on one of those endless nights that she started on the road to Harlem?

Liberated by anti-Communist troops, she went later to Canada, determined to devote her life to giving Christ to the worker. The movement began in Toronto (1930), then in Ottowa (in 1936). Each house had its library as well as bread-line, discussion groups as well as clubs and clothing rooms. Indeed, apart from the special accent on the coloured, it was almost exactly like the Catholic Worker. The books read and reread were such as Dawson's *Religion and the Modern State*, Fanfani's *Catholicism, Protestantism and Capitalism*, and the papal encyclicals. "We Catholics", she notes, "live under the illusion that we must 'talk down' to the workers. We worry about their 'understanding' the encyclicals and decide against having them read or explained publicly—this in spite of the fact that Communists have been reading these same encyclicals to millions of workers only to criticize them."

Dorothy Day is of English stock, Catherine of Slavic. Dorothy's life has been hard—but she has not tragically lost most of her family or herself been close to a ghastly death. Catherine's cries of despair and bursts of tears punctuate on page after page the stories she tells of human waste and suffering, of spiritual desolation. Dorothy's quiet voice penetrates despite almost under-emphasis. Which will affect the reader most is a matter of temperament. But both have a terrible tale to tell, both have experienced its reality, and both want to remind us of the ghastly possibility of a return of conditions only partly remedied by the even ghastlier sufferings of a world war.

Baroness de Hueck's second book, *Dear Bishop*, relates in the person of a working girl her experience in carrying out an assignment given her by Bishop Shiel, Auxiliary of Chicago, to investigate the impact of the Church on worker and soldier, what place it held in their minds and lives. She must, she felt, become a part of the scene she was to paint; as chambermaid in a hotel, as waitress in a bar, as factory worker, she asked the Bishop's question. And her answer was: the Church holds *no* place in the workers' world in America, has *no* impact on their lives. "They don't even pay her the compliment of anger. They ignore her. She just isn't there." As Kathy the Polack, Catherine met Catholics gone Communist, others who had drifted away, an occasional fervent young Catholic trying—alas so ineffectually—to get across the idea that the Church was for the worker, had a message for him, and a hope.

A negro boy said to her: "Yesterday my father took me to a Communist meeting, and I heard them preach the Brotherhood of Man. The Catholic Church also teaches the Brotherhood of Man but under the Fatherhood of God, which is better. But the Communists practise what they preach, and the Catholics don't. Who should we go to?"

The sheltered Catholic is startled by this question. The

blood-baths of Stalin are known to him, have been openly admitted by Khrushchev. Millions of Russians died of starvation in the early thirties, because the Soviet would not import the grain that would have saved them.

The Church can point to the creation and maintenance of hospitals and asylums of all sorts, homes for orphans and the aged, hostels for pilgrims and travellers. Unfortunately Catholics, like Communists, only look in one direction. It is a sobering thought that the attacks upon the Church are often based on our reluctance to face such facts as the terrible social conditions in South America and Spain, on our failures in personal charity, our lack of zeal for social reform.

It was the high moment of Communism in the States. Russia was the ideal, re-established even in the eyes of doubters, after Germany attacked her. Catholics mentioning blood-baths and purges did so almost apologetically, in a world looking at the courage of the Russian people, not at the tyrants who ruled them. We published at this time two books on tortured Poland, but they got a poor press and few readers. No wonder the voice of Catherine de Hueck grew shrill in her effort to tell us of the sins we were committing—one of the worst being Jim-Crowism.

Other voices were raised as a result of the War. Down to the South soldiers were streaming. The tiny Catholic churches were suddenly filled to overflowing, men in uniform stood hearing Mass through windows and doors. And men from East and Mid-West were horrified when they saw German prisoners seated in the "White" waiting-rooms of Southern stations, while coloured American soldiers were segregated in the small airless rooms marked "Negro". And worse—there were churches for whites only, or else the coloured people knelt far back and received Communion only after their white brothers.

Northerners were shocked by all this—an article in the *New Yorker* focused attention on the soldiers—but the North was not spotless, nor could Catholics claim that their teaching had rent asunder the invisible veil dividing white and coloured. Even in the North, employment had to be full indeed for the negro to experience no difficulty in getting a job—he only got those unwanted by the whites. He was worse paid, worse housed, worse educated; coloured people streamed into Friendship House to get clothes for their children, assistance in winning their legal rights of sanitary housing, social security and above all, education.

The list of Catholic colleges admitting negroes was pitifully small when Friendship House opened in Harlem, and a chaplain of a college near New York urged upon me the argument that I would not want my daughter to bring home a coloured class-mate. I answered that I knew many coloured girls I would prefer to some of her white acquaintances.

I had heard a lot at Torresdale about "helping" the coloured. Mother Catherine, foundress of a religious order, and Mrs. Morrell, her sister, were close connections of Grace Smith. They had founded twelve schools in the South for coloured children, a University in New Orleans, where we lectured to the students and the students thanked us by singing lovely spirituals. Oddest of all, Mother Catherine had started another order—for coloured nuns: the word "integration" had never been uttered. With total devotion these women had worked for, but not with, negroes—lived for but not with them.

Catherine de Hueck wrote an article called "Living with Negroes"; if America, she said, was really a democracy, if Catholics were really Catholic, this article need not be written. In business, socially, in schools, everybody would be living with negroes. As it was, their bitter struggle to get a first-class education was followed by the even bitterer realization that their colour blocked them from the full results. America promised life, liberty and the pursuit of happiness, the Church proclaimed the brotherhood of men—but both Church and State broke their promises to this eager, ardent race among whom the workers of Friendship House rejoiced to live. "But they and we both live behind—THE VEIL."

The witness of Friendship House was its most important act; white girls and coloured slept in the same rooms, a mixed staff lived and ate together. And they battered at the doors of every Catholic college, asking for opportunities for the boys and girls of Harlem. At about this time I think Manhattanville College took its first coloured student, a girl with a magnificent contralto voice who became their star singer.

Staff workers gave their time totally, gave up their jobs to live in poverty, were fed on scratch meals (the staple foods being soup, salads and sandwiches), were clothed from the room of cast-offs, had no spending money except a couple of dollars a week pocket-money and took part in a scheme of regular prayer: morning Mass and meditation, evening Rosary and Compline. We of the Outer Circle helped in our spare time, with discussion meetings or the library, Scouts or clubs. From this grew one development which turned out differently to what we had anticipated and lasted ten years. But before talking about our own small part I must tell the story of what was, surprisingly, the high point of Friendship House.

The Baroness moved between the houses, and various staff members were resident heads. In Harlem, after Anne Harrigan went to Chicago, Mabel Knight and Nancy Grenell were in turn head of the house. During Nancy's term a whisper began of a romance between her and Donald Dubois, a man from the West Indies of mixed race. That a girl and a young man, both attractive, both well educated, should fall in love, would appear normal and indeed satisfactory, yet even here in Friendship House the colour-bar suddenly made its appearance. The Baroness was terribly worried: an interracial marriage within Friendship House would undo the result, slowly and carefully achieved, of breaking down barriers. She had assured parents anxious about their daughters in the heart of Harlem that no such thing was possible. Others of the staff-workers felt too that it would jeopardize the work. And by and large we of the Outer Circle shared their fears.

Nancy stood firm, but she was somewhat solitary in the weeks preceding the wedding. Her fiancé, of largely French descent and culture, did not appear unduly worried by the fuss over his negro blood. And Nancy, very much in love, was probably not as distressed as I feared. Their married life did not begin easily in New York. But both have strong characters and a steady driving purpose. Soon they were able to buy their own little farm in New Jersey—and here in a country community their children felt it a distinction to be the only coloured boys in the Catholic school. Nancy taught me how artificial is the feeling against interracial marriages. "Of course," she says, "as society now is, there are difficulties, but what human life is without its difficulties?" Three splendid boys, in a home full of love, seem worth a few difficulties however you look at it—one of them is now at Maryknoll, training for the priesthood. And the next time a friend of mine wanted to make an interracial marriage, although I felt she must face those difficulties, I had no great fear that she would be unhappy.

As for the movement, Nancy's marriage did more for it than anything else in its history, showing that an interracial marriage could be a success and that at least somebody meant what we were all saying. Logically, once you recognize the equality of the two races where are you to stop? If you really believe that two Catholics are both members of Christ's mystical body, by what right can you prevent them from becoming one flesh in the sacrament of marriage?

What we all feared in the name of expedience turned out to be supremely expedient, but how strange that those dedicated to rending the veil should not have seen their great opportunity. I have always had a weak tendency to agree with anyone who seeks my sympathy—and the Baroness wept on my shoulder while Nancy did not. But I look back on myself with bewilderment. I had, I thought, already learnt the lesson of total unity in the Mystical Body—especially through Friendship House. And the Outer Circle was already functioning in our apartment every Sunday evening. Beginning with about twenty people, coloured and white, our numbers grew to one hundred and twenty-five. I wondered one evening, as I counted them, how on earth they fitted in. Rosemary and I stepped over legs and ducked under arms as we perilously carried our coffee-pots. They were sitting on the floor, they were standing against the walls—and judging by the noise a good time was being had by all.

In the New Testament, one realizes a human factor of enormous importance. The reproach against Our Lord was that He ate with sinners. St. Peter was blamed by the Jewish Christians not for praying, but for eating, with the Gentiles. He was blamed by St. Paul not for praying apart with the Jews but for leaving the common table at which St. Paul (himself a Hebrew of the Hebrews) continued to break not supernatural but ordinary bread. It is not religion only that we must be prepared to share, but *life*.

For some unknown reason, while the numbers grew the proportion of white visitors to coloured remained so high that we might have called the experiment a failure but for the new direction in which it developed. We had rejoiced in both the Catholic Worker and Friendship House, because they were doing so richly what the world really asks of Catholics in the social field; acting, not just theorizing—and acting with immense self-sacrifice. And in both movements the leaders were well aware of the need for what Dorothy Day has called "indoctrination". Catherine de Hueck describes in *Dear Bishop* the pitiful failure of an attempt on the part of a young Catholic graduate to preach the social encyclicals. As we had learnt at the street corner there is always on this subject a brush-off with the casual, "Sure your Pope says those things but Catholics don't do them."

And anyhow, how far does social teaching get you? To a large extent today the workers have what they demanded; are they any nearer to the Kingdom of God? Crime waves instead of unemployment fill the papers, juvenile delinquency, gang warfare, sexual vice. And there is everywhere a religious hunger which men do not recognize for what it is; they have become so used to it. It was not to teach us about all men's right to "the good life", as it is so often called, that God came on earth, but to unfold the mystery that had been hidden from generations, and was now to be revealed. For this men hunger. And Catholics must, alas, be included among those who are hungry, for "man does not live by bread alone but by every word that proceeds from the mouth of God". It is not only in order to tell it to others that Catholics need theology.

We discovered in the States as we had in England that the younger generation were becoming very much aware of this hunger in themselves and were looking for help to satisfy it. Small groups would ask my husband to meet them weekly, talk to them, answer their questions, and guide their reading. We had from the first been greatly concerned as publishers with the Catholic mind, and a little before the War struck America, we had started a series of reprints there on a new plan. Eight books were chosen for a year's study: theology, history, sociology, poetry—not text books but literature which brought one into the atmosphere of the Church in its growth and development, its teaching, the effect that teaching would have on life if really believed, the *kind* of poetry that springs from the Faith, the kind of man (St. Augustine's *Confessions* was one of the books) the Faith can create. The books were, we believed, masterpieces: and as such highly readable. My husband wrote for each volume a tutorial introduction, dividing the subject into four, showing the reader how to read this particular book. They were called Tutorial Masterpieces, with the advertising slogan "A Masterpiece a Month to form a Catholic Mind."

Unhappily rising costs and Frank's overwork prevented our continuing a scheme that was certainly fruitful. Out of the first groups emerged leaders to guide other groups. Each reading period was followed by a discussion, members taking turns to lead it.

The increasing membership of the Outer Circle resulted from the same desire to get deeper knowledge, to teach the Faith to others, to live by it themselves. We did not give the Masterpieces to the Outer Circle but we chose a subject each week and picked two speakers. They talked, my husband heckled them and then talked himself on the same subject. It was an amalgam of the Tuesday and Friday classes in the Westminster Guild but of a milder vintage. We were not preparing these speakers to meet atheists on street corners, but to these meetings came several members of the New York Catholic Evidence Guild, and one of them, Alice Vislocky, who spoke several times, brought us an invitation from the Moderator to address a wider audience on the street corners of New York. We have been doing it ever since and what an audience it is—New York is the fulfilment of a Guildsman's dream. Immense crowds gather at the drop of a hat, questions are plentiful, questioners are polite and there is no interference from the police.

The shaping of lecture tours had become much easier since we were there. No need to cram all our engagements into a month or six weeks: we could concentrate on one area for a couple of weeks and rest in between: certainly my own speaking gained in vitality when I was not in a state of perpetual near-exhaustion. I remember one tour in Wisconsin when I spoke four times on one day, driving 200 miles between the lectures. Something went wrong with the heater and we wrapped our legs in newspapers to keep out the bitter cold. But I enjoyed that day—I have always enjoyed Wisconsin.

In Milwaukee I was invited to speak on the subject of the Catholic Evidence Guild in the presence of Bishop (later Cardinal) Stritch. A group of Chicagoans suggested starting a Guild but nothing came of it. Buffalo went well until the tragic death of Paul Dearing, who was working for Catholic Charities in the Empire State Building when a naval aeroplane struck it and slew so many of the staff. I shall never forget the Requiem in St. Patrick's Cathedral at which eleven widows were present. Alas, the Guild in Buffalo was not rooted deeply enough, long to survive the death of its leader. The same was true of Indianapolis, where Thomas Sheerin had initiated something new in Guild history. Not managing to gather crowds in the city itself, he started meetings in surrounding small towns and villages. These were astonishingly successful; at one time there were forty such pitches; but after the death of Mr. Sheerin these too disappeared.

The fate of guilds in the Middle West has always seemed to hinge on an individual; street-preaching by priests has been more permanent. Father (now Bishop) Leven, who got his first experience when a seminarian at Louvain on the street corners of London, started a guild in Oklahoma City. This died with his departure, but in his new, wide, country parish, he did an immense work of outdoor teaching, helped by seminarians and college girls and using his brightest high-school pupils for an occasional simple talk. His own success was phenomenal. Again, as in Indiana, it was largely among the scattered groups of farmers. One old man, he told me, requested to be allowed to feel his forehead, suspecting the presence of at least incipient horns. But in the central town of the parish he was asked by teachers in a Baptist school for outlines of Christian Doctrine, and he won the co-operation of all the local ministers for the erection of a vast outdoor crib at Christmas. When Fr. Leven left this parish, he had 500 people corresponding with him about religion. He is one of the world's great Guildsmen.

A chief joy of lecture tours is reunion with a multitude of friends, and a co-operation at least of sympathy with all their doings. I am a miserable correspondent and I remember with shame letters unanswered, visits thanked for only verbally. Yet it is far oftener personal memories that shoot into my mind than the lecturing itself: seeing the Catholic Worker in action in Detroit and being taken out by Lou Murphy to visit their farm; meeting Fr. Trese at the home for delinquent girls where he was chaplain. (Two of the girls seized the opportunity to run away during my lecture.)

With Frank's recurrent trips to England, we were trying harder than ever to minimize the time spent apart on lecture tours. We conned our schedules looking for chances to meet. (I remember one occasion when this happened at a convent near Chicago. In the midst of our swift interchange of news and gossip, my eye was caught by a framed sentence on the wall: "Cease, the heart of Jesus is here." We both got the giggles over this highly untheological remark. Seven-year-old Wilfrid had done better when, contrasting our living-room with the chapel, he had said, "God's only everywhere here!")

The worst moment of all was when Frank was starting in 1943 to lecture in Australia: this would be a long, long, parting. I managed to get to San Francisco to see him off. And four months later I arranged a tour south beginning in New Orleans, and ending with our meeting in Los Angeles. New Orleans is a special memory of enchantment. Trees hung with purple wisteria or grey moss, camelias as plentiful as weeds. On my second visit in the garden season of Louisiana even my passion for flowers was sated; the moss-hung live oaks gave relief to the glowing colours. I wished only that I could have seen more than pictures of boats pushing their slow way through bayous, sapphire blue with the lovely but destructive water hyacinth under the Spanish moss.

Moving about was fiercely difficult by now. I travelled by coach from New Orleans to San Antonio. There was no diner but halfway through the night we stopped at a station where, O Joy, I saw coffee being served, to be told, "This is for soldiers and their families only." A young woman in the queue next to me responded gallantly. "I'm a soldier's wife," she said firmly, "and this is my mother-in-law." I have seldom felt more poignant gratitude.

22

NEW YORK TO LONDON

THE summer of 1944 was a good one. Frank was back from Australia and would only be going to England in October; we had many weeks all together. Rosemary's graduation present was to be a tour in Canada where I was lecturing, finishing with a visit to a ranch in Texas.

Frank was still in New York when we left: he saw Wilfrid off to school and then started himself for London; only Grandmother remained in the apartment. At Montreal we were met by our friends the Hacketts. And then I felt ill, found my temperature was somewhere up in the hundreds—pneumonia had got me. The doctor said that with modern drugs I might pick up most of the tour, but much telephoning and rearranging had to be done. Linda and Florence Hackett were marvellous, Rosemary extremely efficient. I lay peacefully in bed reading Fustel de Coulanges' *La Cité Antique*. I have always enjoyed having pneumonia, but I felt sorry for Rosemary losing fun and shouldering responsibility. We picked up the tour at Calgary and were thrilled by the sight of the Rocky Mountains. Still more I enjoyed Vancouver, where I met Chesterton's old friend and cousin, Annie Firmin, who talked much of him as a child.

And then I was called to the telephone. It was a doctor speaking from Morristown, New Jersey, to tell me that Wilfrid (now thirteen) had polio—in his back and in both legs. My first thought was of his baseball in America, his cricket in England. He came nearer to perpetual motion than any boy I knew. I asked, "Will he ever run again?" There was a pause and then the doctor said, "You're very lucky he's still alive."

We tried to get back quickly but there was no quick movement for civilians just then. We reached Seattle by boat and there Rosemary and I both got some sort of influenza infection and had to go to bed. It seemed an eternity of waiting before I was sitting outside the window of Wilfrid's room in the isolation block of the Morristown Hospital and hearing his cheerful voice. To Frank in England he had written, "My life no longer fluctuates between Latin and baseball but between sleep and sleep." His amazing courage brought us all through the months that followed. I could not tell Frank the worst by letter and I was still hoping against hope that the worst would not prove true. I sought out the best reputed specialist in New York and he recommended a physiotherapist. We moved Wilfrid to St. Vincent's Hospital, which is a specially miserable memory. A doctor there was trying a drug which he thought might help, which made Wilfrid miserable with shuddering fits. I asked the specialist if we could take care of him at home, and Rosemary and I indulged in a rarely fervent embrace the day we moved him to Riverside Drive.

I put Wilfrid into my big bedroom and until Frank should get back slept on the sofa in the living-room. I had at first the idiotic notion that he might want me in the middle of the night. He never did. Anyhow, sleeping was a problem, but I drew much comfort from reading Gilson on St. Bonaventure. A routine was soon established: the physiotherapist came three times a week and taught Rosemary and me to do the exercises with Wilfrid on the intervening days. There was steady improvement in the back and one leg but the other leg remained dead and Wilfrid was measured for a brace.

On Frank's return we had much discussion with the specialists. The Australian Nurse Kenny came into our minds. She was now in Minneapolis and we half hoped she might be another Dr. Bates, cold-shouldered by the profession, able to work miracles of healing. But all the doctors we asked agreed that she had made valuable discoveries, all declared that her methods were now used everywhere. The public had been more astonished than the profession at her cures, not realizing that in the majority of polio cases there is no paralysis. And the doctors added a warning: Nurse Kenny, they said, was apt to push her theories too far. One had seen cases where her refusal to allow the use of a brace had resulted in twisted feet and legs. Frank knew of a patient of hers still—and apparently for keeps—in a wheel-chair, and all this put us off trying the experiment.

We were briefly beguiled by a man who had, a friend told us, marvellously cured her mother with a treatment in the use of which leeches figured; this ended with a scene in which I called him a charlatan, and he abused me in a picturesque mixture of English and German. Meanwhile the physiotherapy went on; Wilfrid began to hit paper balls about from his wheel-chair and to get out on the Drive with our neighbours, his close friends the Kennedy boys. He began to walk on crutches and then with the brace on one leg, to manage with two sticks and finally with one.

Before this end was reached we made a bid for another possibility. Like everybody else, we had heard of Warm Springs, for President Roosevelt had been treated there for polio. Swimming was a chief exercise prescribed by the doctors; Wilfrid still swam well, and in the baths to which we took him in New York I got tired at last of counting how often he could go from end to end without resting. Warm Springs, it seemed, had wonderful swimming facilities and every new appliance. It was the Mecca for polio cases. It seemed impossible to get Wilfrid in—and then we discovered that we knew somebody who knew somebody else whose influence at Warm Springs was supreme. And so, in the way that these things happen, we were shortly on a train taking Wilfrid down to Georgia.

The first thing the authorities at Warm Springs did was to throw away his New York brace with every sign of contempt and measure him for another. Theirs certainly was a beautiful brace, so light and yet so strong. But that brace was about the only good thing we got out of Warm Springs. We left Wilfrid with high hopes, but before six weeks had passed he was begging us to let him come home. Warm Springs, he said, had nothing to give that New York could not supply. The famous big pool was shut owing to wartime shortage of assistants. Everybody kept telling him that having polio would not prevent him from becoming President of the United States—but he did not want to be President, only to play baseball and football.

We could not let him travel back alone; we both went down once more to size up the situation. Certainly there seemed little point in leaving Wilfrid in such distant exile from family and friends unless some great good promised. Obviously it did not. The doctors talked of possible surgery in the future—and about this Wilfrid had already made up his own mind. Better a brace to unlock when bending his knee than a permanently stiff leg. And the staff were making a curious attempt to build the morale of this fourteen-year-old boy about the life possible for him if no complete cure could be found. It was far too soon for this. We were, and he was, utterly determined to work on for a cure. Time would not only show, but would in the showing do, by God's grace, its own work if what now seemed utterly unendurable had to be accepted.

Back we went to New York and somehow this journey was happier than the other. But I had some training of myself to work at. By the time that Wilfrid was using two sticks he felt capable of going out alone, getting on trains and buses, meeting his friends for a party or the theatre. I *knew* that I must let him, but I have always tended to be a fusser; when any of my family are late I invariably imagine some frightful accident. One night I got a lesson. Wilfrid had gone out with a friend, and at past midnight I felt I *must* check; he might be at his friend's home or both boys might still be out together, but *if* his friend had long been home? . . . What happened was that I woke up both the parents, whose reaction was anger with their son. That was the last time I did any checking.

Riverside Drive was not such a good place to live in winter as in summer, and that winter was a very bad one. The sloping roads between the Drive and Broadway were covered with ice and terribly hard to negotiate. One day coming in from Mass, a high wind blowing, I began to slide downhill and only stopped myself by clutching at the arm of a delivery man who delivered me ingloriously at the back door of our apartment house. Wilfrid took a good many falls that winter, but he took them imperturbably. We had been planning for him a few years at an English school in preparation for Oxford, but had already discovered with dismay that between sports, which alone had had his full attention, public speaking (for which he had won high marks), American history and other subjects in a crowded curriculum, his Latin had come off poorly and he had not even begun Greek. The best part of a year out of school had not helped, and during the next few years the problem of his education had to be faced besides that of his physiotherapy.

All this was one factor driving us back to England, another being the increasing need for more of Frank's time to be spent in the London office. We decided on a family return, but as it happened things did not work out as we had expected. The life began, made possible by the aeroplane, of spending about half the year in each country. The flight to England in 1946 was my first and an immensely exhilarating experience. We stopped at Gander and at Shannon and the journey took about fifteen hours, which today seems slow, but after steamer travel miraculous, especially to one who had always been sea-sick.

Bombed London looked shabby enough, though the ruins were veiled with a green that would soon be a glow of colour; flowers blossoming in every nook and cranny. But for the moment we did not live in London. We could not go to Horley, as the house was let, but we stayed as p.g.'s for several months with Dorothy Collins at Beaconsfield.

It was marvellous of Dorothy to invite us and to crowd so many into her small house—how marvellous I only fully realized after experiencing the rigours of rationing in England; about enough meat for one full meal a week, a monthly pound of jam for each person and tiny allowances of butter and sugar. Dorothy and her valiant maid did marvels with fish and with rabbits which were fattened at the far end of the garden. That half-acre produced an astonishing amount of fruit and vegetables.

The maid was called Frank—a name given to her years ago when she worked for Frances Chesterton, in order to avoid the confusion which now began when anyone shouted either for her or for my husband. My Frank was able to go up daily to his office, the young were sent out to lunch in the village while Dorothy and I lunched cosily together talking much of old times. The cottage stands on a piece of ground chopped out of Top Meadow garden, left by the Chestertons to Dorothy with money for the building. Crammed with Gilbert's books in various editions and translations, and with other books innumerable, it was an ideal spot to think and to work in. When I speak here of the young I mean not Rosemary and Wilfrid—for he was at Downside—but Rosemary and my niece Hester Blundell. Dorothy had contrived to fit her in too and she was now typing for me—catching up easily on each day's writing, for, as she joyfully noted, my huge script boiled down on the typewriter to very few pages.

I had begun the book which I believe to be my best—*Young Mr. Newman*—and this had been one element in our decision to return to England, for it required an immense amount of reading. For the moment I was occupied with the published sources: the biographies of Pusey, Keble, Whateley, Tait, Arnold, the Froudes and the rest, the background books that brought to life the Oxford of the early nineteenth century—and going further back, the books illuminating its origins; what had made Newman's Oxford precisely what it was. I tend to live in the book I am writing and I certainly lived in that book. The coming alive of the Young Newman was an exciting experience. Canon Mozley lent me many unpublished letters giving a vivid picture of family life: dear Mary and the other sisters, the two eccentric brothers, the sensitive and adoring mother whose whole life was in her children.

At the Birmingham Oratory, and reading again the wonderful collection made by Anne Mozley, I met the young men who were Newman's world in the University, that "city of young life". At Oxford itself I re-created imaginatively the setting of the story. In a sense I had grown up with it all—I was, as I had often been reminded, a grandchild of the Oxford Movement. But my father had so concentrated on Newman's Catholic life that Oxford appeared, as it was for Papa himself, chiefly a nostalgic background. Now I was seeing it as the scene of action, with its own vital responses, its own resistances. It seemed more and more strange that my father's scrupulous obedience to Newman's wish that his early life (dealt with in the *Apologia*) should not be rewritten should still have inhibited later biographers. I came to the conclusion that they had mostly written from my father's researches, not their own. Sean O'Faolain presently told me that he was adumbrating a book on the Newman family! This eventually turned into *Newman's Way*, which followed my book about a year later.

At Birmingham I was irked to find that no woman was allowed upstairs into the room that had been the Cardinal's. Fortunately Frank had come with me and he could go up and forage. He brought down mountains of files. What a contrast to the way Chesterton kept his papers! Everything was in exquisite order: the letters meticulously dated, arranged chronologically; letters from Newman's friends, his own letters or notes of his answers written on theirs; the biographical notes commented on and corrected by him at various dates. No-one can ever have been more interested in his friends, his family, or his own life than was Newman.

Frank helped me to read and copy and we carried away a rich harvest. Father Tristram made our labours easier by lending me his own copies of many unpublished letters to take home, but I felt my exclusion from Newman's room was a little cruel. Father Tristram told me a French nun had spoken indignantly of getting a higher authority to intervene, and he had replied that the Pope alone could alter the rule. I hardly hoped for intervention at this level! He told me that I was one of scores of people, chiefly from the Continent, visiting the Oratory for their work on Newman, but that I was the only person since 1885 except my father who had wanted to read these early personal letters.

Newman at first so absorbed me that I had no mental leisure for contemporary stocktaking. Besides, there were so many relatives to see, so many links to pick up. And there was the question of a home. Between bombing and demobilization it was almost impossible to find a place to live in London—and London was where we now wanted to live. The idea struck me that I might try to see a member of the Chesterton family; theirs was one of the best firms of real-estate agents in London. I told Oliver Chesterton that I was the author of his distinguished cousin's biography, and when he acclaimed it as "a jolly good book", I boldly begged his help. He at once sent me to Oakwood Court, and Frank and I together viewed the immense flat that became our home for the next eight years.

Before evening the flat was ours, and we could arrange for delivery of the immense crates coming from New York. The largest contained Wilfrid's ping-pong table, installed in what should have been the dining-room, but we had also brought a vast mass of electrical appliances: a toaster, electric blankets, a gramophone, even Christmas-tree lights, having heard there were shortages of these things. There were indeed, but despite "adaptation", most of the American gear would not work in England. The gramophone played with excruciating deliberation, the lights went plop on the tree, the toaster just conked out. We were meeting other shortages more satisfactorily. Parcels were now being sent by the New York office, and before the summer was out I had bought another farm. As usual, I wanted to kill two birds with one stone. I was using the money from G.K.'s biography and he, like me, had loved Poles. I installed a Pole as manager. Over the first year's working of the farm it is better to draw a veil! The weather was appalling, the loss £1500. But after that we met and employed another Pole, Adam Zaleski, and the worst of our troubles were at an end.

On a deeper level than shortages, what was this England like as it appeared after the long travail it had been through?

As I have said earlier, I doubt if all the sensible reasons for taking the children and their grandmother to the States would have prevailed with me had I known that I too would be immobilized there; I had seen Frank go with alarm but also with a certain envy.

Few of my friends wanted to talk of their own (often terrible) experiences, and my first impression was chiefly that everybody was very, very tired. I was painfully struck by the extent to which so many had aged. It was a country of convalescents; and although no longer firewatching half the night or kept awake by bombs, they had few of the amenities that convalescence calls for. At the end of the First World War the fighting men had felt let down, great heroism seemed to have been spent in vain. In this war the whole country had been the hero. All their letters had cried *Sursum Corda*. They had certainly still the sense of having lived through a great experience. Helen McQuaid told me one day how she and her two partners working in casualty after a raid did thirteen hours at a stretch. They did not stop for food, but the matron of the hospital fed them with egg-nog at intervals while they worked. At the end they could none of them sit, but all lay flat till their tense muscles had relaxed. And then she said, "I often feel nostalgic for those days."

It was the sense of "togetherness" stressed by Beatrice Warde that Helen missed. To some extent this was inevitable. During the War party strife had been suspended and a Government drawn from both parties. Now we were in the aftermath of an election, and this is not a moment when any country looks notably united. Churchill had been a marvellous wartime leader, his rough voice on the radio magical in its effect. But his party had been thrown out, and anyhow he too was tired, he was old, he belonged too clearly to one class and he had never taken any great interest in domestic politics. No-one had emerged remotely likely to take his place in keeping hearts up at this perhaps even more difficult moment. The spirit, I realized, still existed that had won the Battle of Britain. When the Government were projecting the request to America for a loan some people were behind me talking on a bus and I heard one of them say, "I'd work my fingers to the bone rather than take it." I believe they would have, and millions with them. The thing that hit the English people hard was that after six years in which they had fought and sacrificed, England should become a backwater, a satellite of America. There was still pride to be stirred up, but nobody was trying to stir it.

We had noted in the States the steady growth of bureaucracy. This disease of our century was even worse in England, and because the country is so much smaller the bureaucrat is more pervasive. Had people been encouraged to do things for themselves much of their weariness would have been shaken off: houses might have been built, more food grown, but the lesson of the Circumlocution Office—"How not to do it"—had been well and truly learnt. Efforts at self-help were discouraged, sometimes ruthlessly. Incidents were reported daily in the newspapers: a boy stopped from collecting swill from neighbours to feed his pigs because this needed a licence; a youth who put together scrap from old cars, collecting four wheels here, an engine there, until at last "the darn thing ran"—when he found himself charged with purchase tax of hundreds of pounds. Then there was the butcher who opened after official closing hours to distribute to his poorer neighbours soup he had made by boiling down bones. In vain did he plead that he did not sell this soup—he gave it away. He was fined for late opening and told not to do it again. *Time and Tide*, under the heading *Why?*, published each week the most startling instance sent in of bureaucratic tyranny and/or ineptitude, giving a guinea to the sender. This went on for many years—what a collection it would make.

It took months, sometimes up to two years, to get a building permit from both central and local authorities. A friend of mine, a Belgian who had helped 500 English and American soldiers to escape through Spain, had been tortured in a German prison and thanked by Churchill in person, wanting to settle in England, got what he believed to be sufficient permits and built his house. This house was pulled down by order of the local county council and the bill for demolition sent to him. At the time his wife was pregnant and the shock produced a miscarriage. Let no man think that under Conservative rule the bureaucracy is one whit less oppressive, one whit less pervasive than under Labour. This council had a Conservative majority. Later on we had the case of Crichel Down—substantially a triumph for the lesser bureaucrat, who is our real danger because there are so many of him. A Herculean struggle may displace the head of a department, but the underlings cling like parasites to the plant they are destroying. The disease they carry has one fatal symptom—an increasing inclination to dependence, a feeling that "the Government ought to do something", that the thing that pays is not work but persistent demand, relentless pressure. And anyone who saw much of the country outside what Cobbett had called the "wens" (London being the "great wen") realized that even after two wars in which we had been forced near starvation, the urban population from which most bureaucrats were drawn seemed to have grasped little of the problems of our food supply. Good agricultural land was often taken for parks and playgrounds when inferior land could well have been used. It was again assumed that we could live mainly on what we imported. The War Agricultural Committees, which went on under another name, varied from county to county. Some farmers found them helpful, others dismaying. One leading official I met had himself failed as a farmer in another part of the country, which of course equipped him marvellously to dictate to the local men.

But it was well worth having a farm if you had the energy to argue, and when necessary, fight. I got on well enough with the various officials, although I remember one comic incident. Refused a permit to erect a house for my cowman, I thought what had housed forty soldiers might do for one small family. Bringing an old army hut from Surrey was expensive, as the lorry was not allowed (heaven knows why) to go beyond the county border, and we had to transfer the hut to another lorry. My architect made plans for adaptation which were turned down; he could not make out from the form sent him what *would* be acceptable. As he lived in Surrey, first my manager and then I called on the clerk of the local council. My attitude seemed to terrify the clerk, although he did not look timid. At last he said, "You have the same mentality as your manager, you want a straight answer, yes or no." When I said that that was rather the idea, he gasped slightly and after a pause said, "Well, look here, you send your architect to see us. We shall talk the same language."

In relation to my dear Mr. Zaleski I partly understood this. The local farmers loved him, but his words and manners were certainly foreign. His idea of striking a bargain was to shrug his shoulders, spread out his hands, palms upwards, and say "Shall we partage?" His accounts showed that this partaging was seldom unfavourable to us. But I had been talking plain English, asking for a decision vital to my farm's existence, only to be answered in a sort of double talk. My architect could be supposed to talk the same language because he had grown patient through much listening to it. It took us over a year to get our permit, and then it was given for twelve months only and had to be renewed year to year. Meanwhile the Zaleskis shared the farmhouse with the cowman, and both families were decidedly cramped.

In towns even more than in the country housing was the worst shortage. In Kensington, squatters took possession of houses, left empty perhaps because they were insecure, shaken by the blitz, perhaps only in the hope of a good sale later. Gas, electricity, water, had all been turned off and you could see the squatters moving about by the light of a few candles. This movement was soon squashed; it was allegedly Communist-inspired. But it was not necessary to conjure up Communism to explain why men should try to escape from intolerable conditions, a whole family, or even more, living in a single room. Obviously no Government could allow people to seize the property of others, but Abbé Pierre's experience later showed that these squatters could have built houses for themselves; after all they were the same material out of which had been fashioned the soldiers, the munition makers and the rest, most of them were the same men and women. Why should they now be incapable, fit only to be spoon-fed by other people whose capacity for the task I took leave to doubt?

The leader of one self-build group showed me photographs of twenty-four houses built in their spare time by twenty-four men, largely white-collar workers, with one policeman and a few labourers. Spacious and well built, they had cost little more than half the normal purchase price. I asked my friend what had been his hardest task and he answered, "Keeping the group together for the two years it took us to get the permits."

With some of these stories I am getting ahead of the time of our return to England, but I did, even in the first few months, see a surprisingly representative cross-section of my fellow-countrymen. I talked to farmers in the country and, of necessity, to bureaucrats. In London, again speaking on street corners, I met a great variety of human beings, expressing themselves with great freedom. And a horrible feeling at moments assailed me—the being pushed around to which I objected was no new thing to the mass of people—only to that small and privileged class to which I chanced to belong. We had been the pushers and now we had become part of those pushed. For the others it was perhaps rather fun to watch us wriggling.

Rereading all this I meditated on a friendly criticism: "How strange that you should ignore the immense social revolution taking place in England. So much that you clearly wanted has been achieved. Why look only at the incidental blemishes, however irritating?"

My first reaction to this criticism was: This part of my memories concerns what happened to me and this *is* what happened; it is told as of how I felt and this *is* how I felt. But the question goes much deeper. In the States my more socially-minded friends were asking me excitedly for news of this revolution, which might, they felt, save the world from Bolshevism by fulfilling all the just demands of the worker. The Labour Party had ceased to compromise—nationalization was the magic word and we were being told, for instance, that the railways were now *ours*. I don't know whether anybody—especially as the years went on and fares leaped up and service deteriorated—was able to take pride in that thought. I certainly was not. I rejoiced at a fairer division of the national resources, at the higher wages in all trades—but all this had been won not by any political party but by the century-long work of the trades unions. Rationing, for instance, had come in under a Conservative Government and I remember the groans of a rich woman with no coupons for a new dress—"Fancy", she said, "being naked with a cheque book!"

With some things done by this Labour Government I was in profound agreement—above all the Health Service. Health is something like air, like water, that should be free to all. Abuses there may be in the working of it, but it is something in itself profoundly right and almost inevitable in our present society. We who are well should be only too thankful to pay for those who are sick. But even with the Health Service the flood of forms to be filled in, the proportion of organization to actual healing, is terrifying. Teachers make the same complaint, merchants make it with groans. The whole thing is top-heavy; overwhelmed by it, the organizers cease to think in terms of the little man who should be trusted. He had two needs, that little man, after the War, and he still has them. He needed a home, he needed liberty and the chance of self-development.

Suppose another kind of nationalization had been tried. Suppose the railways and the running of them had been handed over to the railway unions. Suppose heavy death duties had not meant a false income for the Government to waste but some sort of co-operative ownership of land by those working it. Suppose the miners had been told: "The mine is yours. Your lives depend on it; it is up to you to make it succeed." Then there would have been incentive, pride of possession, urge to work for a success.

How much of a revolution has it really been? Speaking of the national character during the Crimean War, which exemplified the usual pattern in English wars of deplorable official muddling repaired at great cost by individual courage and initiative, Newman wrote: "Such is England, the Government weak, the people strong." So did Dickens depict the awfulness of Nupkins in a village and the Circumlocution Office at the centre of government. English officialdom is especially alien to our character and now has become a chief feature in all our living. The wage slaves are no longer scattered among private owners, they are gathered in one vast Government compound, and while many of the overseers are kindly, an attempt to escape seems doomed to failure. But for the most part the compound appears a world of sleepwalkers dreaming to rule and crying out occasionally for more wages and shorter hours. A Conservative Government after the War might well have been worse. Who can tell? The postwar world is full of governments called by various names but they all seem built on a tyranny of paper, an ignorance of what life could and ought to become. I am as ignorant now, I feel, about the processes of national government as I was when I embarked on our first farce of a farm. But I felt and feel often a profound nostalgia for Father Vincent and the Distributists, with their respect for human dignity and personal effort; still more for the co-operatives of Nova Scotia. My excellent farm manager could barely keep his head above water what with rules and regulations, papers to fill in and inspectors to satisfy. It amazed me that he still managed to produce food. A country cannot be healthy in which personal effort is made so costly, initiative all but dead.

On the street corner the crowds were not too different from before the War, but very different from the picture I had painted out of the letters and records of the War years. They had not lost the engaging qualities I had always loved: the humour, the inconsequence, the friendliness, the immense curiosity. But I did not find the religious feeling I had heard about during the Blitz. Men were disillusioned as well as tired; in all life there is a rhythm, and strain is followed by slackening, by depression and discouragement. The Desert Fathers were beset by *accidie*; a word hard to translate, compounded of discouragement, bitterness, sloth. And if there is no great driving purpose in life, if religion has been without the bones of dogma and therefore appears ghostlike once the strong emotions are passed that made men call upon God, if they have lost the realization that life itself is good, how is this bitter sloth to be cast out? We had not heard yet of angry young men but perhaps we were meeting the weary fathers who partly explain them.

23

PRIEST-WORKMEN

ONE trouble England did not have which we read of with horror in the French newspapers—the idea that traitors were in our midst. However much Englishmen differed over what was now to be done, they had all been together in what had been accomplished.

One of the joys of a peace-time return was that the gates of the Continent were open to us again. Paris looked wonderful after battered London, but there was in the air a far profounder disillusionment than that of the exhausted and undernourished English. Reading lately Simone de Beauvoir's *The Mandarins*, I again realized that our postwar depression was infinitely less grievous. In France men were being shot daily as collaborationists, personal vendettas sheltering sometimes under a cloak of patriotism. The novel conveys too that curious atmosphere in which the decision of a young man to take or refuse the editorship of some literary magazine is supposed to be absolutely earthshaking. Partly this represented the instinctive determination still to consider France the centre of civilization, partly a salute to the dawning on the literary world of the new philosophy of existentialism and of its prophet Sartre. The book is much less interesting than the same author's *Jeune Fille rangée*, but it conveys terribly well an atmosphere that I felt but could not begin to understand.

What I did realize was a keen stirring of life in the French Church. Before long I was subscribing to eight French periodicals, of which the most interesting were *Masses ouvrières*, the chief journal of the Catholic French workers, and *Maison Dieu*, an expression of the liturgical movement. This latter had not only articles of great depth and beauty on liturgy and theology but also fascinating *reportage*, including long conversations illustrating the subject chosen for the month; each issue dealt with a single subject.

But what was urging me to France as soon as possible after our return was the fear that a very old friend known to me from childhood as Aunt Marianne might be dead if I left my visit too long.

"Aunt Marianne" was Lady Ashbourne—wife of the eccentric Irish peer who had swum in the winter sea at Eastbourne, discussed philosophy with my father at Dorking, and then turned his attention to studying Gaelic, proclaiming himself an Irish patriot, and wearing a saffron kilt because the Irish had formerly done so. After the First World War the Ashbournes had gone to live at Compiègne in a house belonging to Marianne, whose father was French, her mother German. I had stayed there before the War and been amused at the exclamation "Voilà, l'Écossais!" which greeted the kilt. The Ashbournes had suffered a great deal in the second war, first going south with the mass of refugees, then returning to their home. Ashbourne, as a citizen of Eire, had been regarded as a neutral, but when he died, Marianne refused to shelter under his name or her mother's race. "I am French," she told the Germans proudly, "French under a double title, for I come from Alsace." Interestingly enough, they treated her with considerable respect.

There was a magnificence about this old lady, as well as a great tenderness. She was still a beautiful woman, but so deaf that her solitude seemed at first almost impenetrable; she caught only a word or two of a sentence—her imagination had to do the rest. And then one realized how much the eyes were helping; what she said might not answer one's words but there was a deep communication of spirit. Of us all Leo had been closest to Marianne and she loved to talk of him. They had corresponded regularly and she had painted pictures and chosen statues for his little church. "Union de prières" was the phrase that recurred in all her letters and we realized how much this meant to her.

Marianne said once on this visit that she became aware at times of vast spiritual powers around us that we could release if we but chose. She had always worked vigorously, helping the needy, teaching catechism to the children in five villages. She had bought a little property at a central village called Chevincourt, where she grew vegetables and gave holidays to poor children from Compiègne. Her chief assistant was her maid Lucienne, far more like a daughter than a hired help, to whom she had left Chevincourt in her will—and with it all her works of mercy. They called one another "Ma Mie", and it was the greatest comfort, seeing her now so old and physically feeble, to realize that she had such a daughter to love and care for her. In so much that I was to witness of class hatreds, especially in France, I would see the utter artificiality of the divisions in terms of Marianne and Lucienne, just as I had seen interracial unity in terms of Donald and Nancy Dubois.

Rosemary's first job on leaving school had been the translation of *Priest-Workman in Germany*, by Henri Perrin, S.J. We had made friends with Père Perrin by correspondence and very soon after our return from the States we met him at the headquarters of the Vatican Mission in Paris. After a dialogue mass in the chapel we talked of Henri's plans. His book had told of his experiences when the Germans refused chaplains for Frenchmen being sent to work in Germany in 1943. Père Perrin, among others, concealing his priesthood, went as a labourer.

Like Baroness de Hueck, he found that the Church meant nothing to the workers; among his comrades were a handful of Catholics, a few who hated the Church, a majority who held it in contempt if they thought of it at all. With a young Catholic layman, Jacques, he made of his experience an opportunity of inserting Christ in their midst.

Imprisoned for his religious activities, he told in a diary written on scraps of wrapping or lavatory paper, sometimes hidden in the soles of his shoes, of his life of intense prayer and charity. The sharing of his parcels became a major sacrifice, the going up last and therefore getting least of the soup which was almost their sole food required an effort of heroism which seemed almost beyond him. He describes the rare opportunity of saying Mass in a cell where some of his companions were still sleeping, while one made use of the primitive lavatory in the cell itself close beside the improvised altar. He felt himself alone yet lifting up the whole world of men towards God in Christ's sacrifice which is also ours.

When he had finished, one of the "sleeping" prisoners said, "Your Mass is pretty terrific". Père Perrin was determined not to lose the contact with the worker that he had for the first time in his priestly life begun to make, nor yet the contact with German Catholics. The Gestapo dubbed him "an Idealist" and sent him back to France. Other priests were sent to Dachau or Buchenwald; Perrin, lucky to escape with both life and health, discovered that during his absence an important movement had begun in the French Church.

It may seem strange to compare the two efforts for Catholic revitalization—Modernism in my youth, and priest-workmen so many years later. But, in the different spheres of the scholar and the manual labourer, they had in common a desire to renew the great days of the Church's history by speaking in a language the modern world could understand, to cure men's spiritual diseases and to stir complacent Catholics from their lethargy into an awareness of the hungry multitudes around them. And in both movements large numbers of their leaders deviated from this aim, abandoning the Church's *mystique* for that of the Modernist in the one case, the Communist in the other.

The word *mystique* was not in use when Modernists were flourishing, and the sound of it recalls how much the later movement meant to me. Here in France was something that must pierce the heart of anyone who had been watching the stirrings of Catholic vitality seeking for new ways in Canada and in the States. Here in France was by far the most important of all these beginnings—for here was the vast potential of a country with a great Catholic past and with great Catholic thinking in her present. I soon learnt that what I now began to call the New French Revolution had been spoken of in a book entitled *France, pays de mission* by two young abbés, Henri Godin and Yvan Daniel. More would be needed than a straight translation to make it of value for English and American readers. I decided to embody it in an account first of Abbé Godin's life and then of various aspects—studied in a series of visits to France—of the movement which he above all had set on foot. I called the resultant book *France Pagan?*

As a chaplain of the Young Christian Workers, Abbé Godin had realized that he was not reaching at all the vast paganized world around the little islands into which Catholics had more or less contentedly settled. The blank incomprehension of the Christian concerning the surrounding world struck him even more forcibly than the world's ignorance of Christ.

How could he begin to reach it? When Cardinal Suhard called upon him and his friend Yvan Daniel to write a report on what he had discovered, he asked this question passionately. France was in many areas a mission country, in others the Church still seemed strong but the danger was of her losing, there too, the working classes. As, in China, Père Lebbe made himself Chinese (and as I read I thought of my brother Leo's determination to belong to Japan, the Church of his adoption) so must the priest who would reach the proletariat learn new modes of thinking, learn a new language. This whole proletariat was, Abbé Godin felt, amorphous, unshaped, accessible to Christian influence, but only if brought to it in its own fashion of thinking. And he multiplied stories, in support of Abbé Daniel's figures, of amazing successes the two of them had had in winning to a Christian life boys and girls who were quite unimaginable as altar-boys or Children of Mary.

The Cardinal agreed with his two abbés. The Mission de France had already been started to furnish missionary clergy to those bishops who wanted them. In the training given in its seminary was included six months' work in a factory or on a farm, so that before ordination seminarians should learn something of the world they would be evangelizing. Abbé Godin's heart was given to Paris and he wanted something at once wider and narrower than the Mission de France—narrower because devoted solely to one great city, wider because his missionaries were to be not priests only, but young men and women and above all married couples, wider again because it would include priests of deep learning like Père Chenu, O.P., and professional men like Dr. Tremolières, as well as those who were working with their hands.

To anyone working in the same field—as were we of the Catholic Evidence Guild—some of the findings outlined by Abbé Godin were deeply heartening. He saw, as we had, that the Church's evangelizing approach had long been far too negative, combative, and therefore superficial. We must not be afraid to teach the full Christian *mystique*. "In the degree to which a Christian lives his faith mystically, he must live by it intellectually also." To bear witness is not enough. A catechist had, he believed, the special graces of his state in life to *show* truths. He called this a "charism" given him for the sake of the whole community. We must try always, not so much to prove the truth, as to continue to explore it, going deeper and deeper into the Christian mystery—"You can talk to anyone," he often said, "even to the simplest, about the Trinity."

In January 1944 there was a solemn High Mass and Cardinal Suhard launched the Mission de Paris. In doing so he made two chief points: The mission was designed entirely for the conversion of the heathen, but "its indirect end is to show the Christian Community that it must take up a new attitude, a shock is needed."

Henri Godin was only thirty-seven, and his great work seemed just begun. But he said as he returned from the High Mass, "Now I can disappear." Several times he repeated something of this kind and it sounded strange to his hearers. That night the chimney of his stove got blocked and fumes pouring into the little room killed Abbé Godin in his sleep.

His last Mass had been that of Our Lady, and he left among his papers a prayer, an entreaty to her, to take in hand the task of which he was just the sheep-dog. "When he is too slow, clumsy or awkward . . . take up your crook, swift and lovely shepherdess, and fly to his help . . . and later on in heaven, a little corner near you, oh so tiny, lying in the middle of the flock, now all safely gathered in forever."

For three days Catholic Paris mourned at Henri Godin's bedside and then followed his body in a procession that amazed the city. How far the influence of this little abbé had spread became visible for the first time, Catholic Paris at least had received its shock . . . And it was with his disciples—still vibrating with memories, still working at his mission, and still full of high hopes—that I became intimate, nearly three years after Henri Godin's death.

There were humorous elements in what I like to call, "Looking for Godin". We had a friend with a job in a large Anglo-American firm, Jean Dhavernas, who had asked us to take a young cousin for a month to learn English, and Rosemary in turn had stayed with her family in Paris. I was staying with Françoise's parents when my quest began, and I experienced once again the problem of living in several very different worlds. Abbé Depierre, who had shared Abbé Godin's flat at the time of his death and was now a priest-workman, was saying Mass that evening at a house in Montreuil. My host insisted on driving me down—and I realized that what filled me with joy was creating in him a profound repulsion. Mass was said at the kitchen table, was dialogued to the fullest degree possible. The sermon was by a worker and for workers. Jean Dhavernas would have loved it, but my host was a Catholic of traditionally bourgeois vintage. It had never occurred to him to dislike the remote, rapidly murmured Mass of the ordinary church, the chink of money and the noise of chairs as the *chaisière* did her work, the heavy thump of the *suisse's* staff, or even the operatic singing at a church like the Madeleine. Here in this room was for me the realization of a beautiful dream, for him a nightmare of irreverence.

After Mass I remember we all sat down together—I think M. Lequeux must have gone home and left me, at my request, to follow in a taxi. I remember well this first contact with one of the cells of the mission, listening to their discussion about spiritual and temporal help to be brought to the little world of their friends and neighbours. But I felt a vague barrier between myself and Abbé Depierre and his friends, which totally dissolved with Abbé Daniel and the young proletarian couple Dedé and Madeleine Huot who had been probably closer to Henri Godin than any of his friends except Dr. Tremolières. With the doctor and his wife a real friendship quickly sprang up, and all this group seemed to love reliving their past memories with an admirer of their beloved Abbé. I met also several Dominicans, one of whom, Père Chenu, told me of a retreat he had given to forty-eight *leaders* of Mission de Paris groups in the district of Montreuil alone.

All over Paris the Mission was going on, and there were groups of priest-workmen in various districts getting deep into the life of the proletariat. Some Capuchins had put up a wooden shack in Abbé Michonneau's parish; they worked in a factory, and made their poor place a free lodging for any homeless person asking for a bed. Often enough this meant themselves sleeping on the floor, no light penance in this thin wooden building on a cold night and after a day's heavy work. Here too I joined their family mass and learned about their factory experience. Here too we ate together in deep fellowship, and after supper Père André got on his bicycle and set off to make some visits. These priests were immensely helped, they told me, by the support of their parish priest, Abbé Michonneau, who wrote later *Paroisse, communauté missionnaire*. He is a remarkable man, and his parish fulfils what Abbé Godin asked by its support of the pioneers. "The Advance Guard", Godin said, "is in danger if the army is not close behind it." And to the bishops: "We are ready for today, if you are ready for the day after tomorrow."

I saw Père Perrin again, now once more a workman. He had persuaded his superiors, at the end of his theology, to let him return to his worker status, which had, he felt, been so full of promise when he and Jacques had toiled together in Germany. He took me to lunch at a workers' restaurant, where I was glad to realize that food and wine were priced far below the lowest I had managed to discover even on the Left Bank. He was living now, he told me, with another Jesuit in an airless hole, with no drainage, no electricity, no running water. He had lost one job, supposedly for inefficiency, perhaps partly because the management had discovered what he was. Now he seemed established in another. I asked him what his comrades' reaction had been to the revelation that he was a priest, and he answered, "None at all." He was in high spirits, and full of hopes and plans.

One of the books that had affected him most profoundly was *France pays de mission.* Considering his intense attachment to the workers' world, and where it was later to lead him, his comment on a first reading is interesting. Why, he asked, does Godin so limit the problem to the proletarian world as to require a separate clergy for the latter? "They live on the same movies, the same newspapers, the same periodicals, they have roughly the same ambitions, the same tastes."

Almost all Abbé Godin's friends were telling me that his true successor in the apostolate to the workers was Père Loew, O.P., who had recently written a book entitled *En mission prolétarienne.* Père Loew had been ahead of Père Perrin and in some respects of Godin himself, having worked on the docks at Marseilles and lived among the dockers since 1942. Père Lebret, who from 1930 to 1939 had worked at St. Malo among the deep-sea fishermen (though not as one of them), and had done a job there very similar to Fathers Coady and Tomkins in the Maritimes, had started *Economie et humanisme* at Marseilles as a small publishing house mainly for the issue of documentaries. He had always regretted that the *Semaines sociales* were not sufficiently concrete. Père Loew's first book had been one of his "realizations"—a fascinating history of the dockers of Marseilles, once an aristocracy of labour, today what Jacques Loew dubbed a sub-proletariat. I had now his important second book, the first paragraph of which made me feel that I must not only translate it but get to know this enchanting man as soon as possible: " 'Père Loew, you will be studying fats and oils.' These words of Père Lebret, my new superior, send a faint chill through me. I have just emerged from the seminary after seven years' study and I certainly didn't become a Dominican in order to devote myself to peanuts and soap. Submissively I say to myself, 'Oh well, fats and oils it is.'"

Economie et humanisme had moved its headquarters to Paris, and there I was interviewed politely but coldly, not by Père Lebret, who was away on field work, but by a young Dominican who had no objection to our buying the translation rights, but no faintest interest in our doing so. I felt again the invisible barrier which I was beginning to fancy the smaller men of the movement conceived to be necessary between themselves—the workers—and the bourgeois world of outer darkness. Abbé Daniel had told me that most of the priests engaged on the proletarian mission were of bourgeois origin, but this made them only the more fervent in their new-found faith. With Abbé Depierre it had been worth the effort to remove the barrier—I seldom found this difficult, though it could take several meetings—but one glance at this little buttoned-up official was enough to make me realize it would probably be hopeless and certainly valueless. We quickly settled terms and parted with all the courtesies.

In Marseilles I was to see the solution to many of the problems contained in this vital movement. Chief of these from the religious side was that of the liaison between mission and parish. My Capuchin friends had a perfect relationship with Abbé Michonneau, but their experience was by no means universal. Dedé and Madeleine, for instance, found their parish most unreceptive and discouraging. As Abbé Godin had noted, the parish set-up and machinery was almost everywhere geared to a shut-in Catholic Group, chiefly bourgeois, emphatically not missionary.

Many parish priests would have been even more annoyed at being asked to father a proletarian mission than they were by having one established independently of them but within their area. But the difficulties were not the creation of one side alone. Cardinal Suhard stressed the obligation of missionaries to respect and to work with the parish clergy—but some of them made little or no effort to do so. The boy who remarked as we walked past St. Sulpice, "I don't go to that bourgeois mass, only to Abbé Depierre's", may have been put right by the Abbé, but quite possibly was not. The priest-workmen were over-conscious of the novelty of what they were doing and not particularly disposed to consider the feelings of the men they held largely responsible for the French Church's unhappy state. The petition of almost all was to be free of the parish. And in the first flush of enthusiasm for their work this was, in practice if not in theory, conceded by the Hierarchy. The team was controlled only by the remote influence of the bishop or, with religious, by the provincial. And for quite a while even that control was hardly felt. It must be borne in mind that this experiment was for some years the chief joy and pride of the French Church—a Church humiliated not only by the defeat of the country, but even more by the use to which it had been put under Pétain's regime. With this heroic venture Catholics lifted up their heads again and became full of confidence.

Père Jacques Loew was not only a dock labourer, but also a parish priest—he regarded this as essential in a working-class parish . . . I had now met teams of priests working in liaison with a parish, others working independently or in connection with lay groups. I had seen a seminarian doing his six months' factory work, a friend of Dedé and Madeleine who confessed frankly to disappointment. He had found selfishness in that world where he had expected the purest altruism, and was much shaken by the experience. I had met Abbé Hollande, who, though less dynamic than Yvan Daniel, was something of a philosopher of the movement. I had visited the publishers of the *Editions ouvrières*, I had met Abbé Michonneau—not himself a priest-worker but the curé of an intensely missionary parish. All this was in Paris. Now for the South.

There was a touch of the New York Friendship House about that Marseilles team of priests and the girls of the Residence, yet they were very French and French of the Midi at that. Père Jacques had been a lawyer, and a late vocation to the Dominican Order. The study of fats and oils he interpreted as meaning not the local manufactures but the workers and their environment. He went to live among them, and very soon became a dock labourer, in order to know their life from within and to be known by them as one of themselves. At the request of Mgr. Delay, Bishop of Marseilles, he took over with a small team of other priests the parish of La Cabucelle, a suburb of Marseilles, a couple of miles beyond the Porte d'Aix, and, like most of the town, a pagan area. The large church with schools and clubrooms was a relic of the days when Catholic employers had built and Catholic working families had used them. Now the church was nearly empty, the buildings unused.

The team of priests was a mixed one: a secular, a Jesuit, two Dominicans. While two of them in turns worked at the docks, the other two ran the parish; at weekends all four were in and around the church. The Residence, started by Père Jacques before he took the parish, was run on the same principle. Two girls went out to work, two were always at the service of the sick and the poor. I was interested to find Père Jacques had been inspired by the London settlements of my youth. But there were immense differences.

The priests, with a team of young men, had transformed the empty schools into flats for workers' families. One of them told me what tough work this had meant. And indeed I noticed with every team that the physical labour took a heavy toll of the priests' strength. One wing of the old clubhouse was kept for their own dwelling; they housed a family in the other, turned the room formerly used for keeping accounts into a dwelling for a Czech refugee, and adapted a hut in the yard for an old gypsy. The priests' kitchen-living-room was open day and night. Their lavatories were used by the families, large tubs in the yard were perfect for family laundry, the yard itself was a bowling ground.

The schoolhouse had an ample garden, a little of which the families now cultivate, but the greater part was used for gatherings, of which one was going on while I was there. It was run by and for the neighbourhood but the priests (now in worker's dress) moved to and fro helping and counselling, having intimate talks with parents and joining in the fun with the children, who were acting a play. A city award was being bestowed on the mother of the largest family in the area.

Certainly these priests were near the heart of the district, and their aim was to make the Church the heart of that heart. An uninteresting nineteenth-century building, it was rejuvenated and brightened by a glowing crimson cross, huge cartoon pictures changing with the seasons, an altar in the centre where all could see the priest's movements. No collections were taken, no fees for baptisms, weddings or funerals. This is a mission area and Père Jacques would agree with Abbé Michonneau as to the harm done by the "chink of money around the altar". A box discreetly hidden at the back enabled the Catholics present (who were very occasionally reminded of this duty in the parish bulletin) to give something for the support of the church. At this time the priests' own living expenses were supplied by the two workers among them. A balance sheet was pinned up monthly with a request for comments and criticisms. The only comment ever made was, "I could not keep my family on what you priests allow yourselves"—and people slipped into the open kitchen and left on the table eggs or cherries or a bottle of wine to help the housekeeping.

This team were the most highly developed teachers I ever met, both by word of mouth and by leaflet. After one mass an outline of the admirable sermon was handed to all at the church door. On every seat were printed copies of the Ordinary of the Mass and the hymns to be sung that Sunday. There were schemes of instruction for the children, and for young people about to be married. At a funeral, where most of the mourners were certainly pagans, Père Jacques gave to them the message of eternal life in Jesus Christ Our Lord: it was perhaps the best sermon I have ever heard.

Soon the bishop was asking Père Jacques to organize a second team, and St. Louis was added to St. Trophime as a priest-workers' parish.

How fast St. Trophime grew! Between my first two visits there had been a longish gap—perhaps three years—and I chanced each time to be there for the First Communion Sunday. The church on the first occasion had been sparsely filled by parents and children. On the second the crowd was so great that two Sundays were set aside, and adults whose children were not first communicants were asked to attend another mass. But it had come about, as it appeared to them, so gradually that they were surprised at my surprise.

On that second visit, Frank and I had come on from a brief holiday in Provence where we had seen enough to feel something of the horror our French friends were experiencing over the state of the Church. At Arles, the First Communion in a large parish mustered five children—three exquisitely dressed little girls, two smart small boys with white ribbons round their sleeves. They arrived in cars and the curé preached an incredibly unreal sermon to them and their parents from which one gathered that France, the eldest daughter of the Church, was still worthy of her name, that these children were going out into a world of faith.

At Toulouse a few days earlier we had seen a large churchful for First and "Solemn First" Communion. But the girls were quite openly giggling and whispering right up to approaching the altar; the long white dress, the tulle veil was the only sign that this event meant anything at all. This would be the last time the bigger boys would come to church, except for their own marriage perhaps, or their children's First Communion.

Here at La Cabucelle the children had been carefully prepared—no-one was admitted who had not attended the instructions. And Père Jacques' first words were the question—If you walked along the Cannebière, how many people would you find who believed in the real presence of Christ on the altar, and in your heart? You must be ready, he told them, to go out professing your faith, to be missionaries to the unbelieving world around you.

These children too were dressed in white—but it was very simple, so that no distinction should be made between richer and poorer. As with the abolition of different classes of weddings and funerals, there is, in these missionary parishes, nothing to distinguish the individual except the number of his friends—which may make quite a difference when the singing is done by the congregation.

Talks with Père Jacques were always the most important thing on these visits, and on this visit in 1952, we were saddened to discover his deep anxiety over the movement. I spoke of the magnificent directives put out by the Hierarchy and he told me they were for the most part a dead letter. Unsuitable candidates were being accepted and allowed to go their own way. In his own teams there was fierce difference of opinion; one man had left because he would not accept the combination of parish priest and dock labourer. A priest-workman, in the eyes of the extremists, must be one hundred per cent workman. There had been trouble in a factory between a splendid young militant layman and the priest working there: a little later this priest had left the Church and married. He was now secretary to the local Communist party.

Dark clouds were gathering. Père Jacques still believed with all his heart in the immense potential of the movement for good—but he was watching in agony that lack of direction and authority which presaged the final tragedy.

To understand what happened I must, still drawing on my experience, go back a few years, and look once more at the wider scene. In the social struggle of those years so much was cruelly unjust to the workers. The Industrial Revolution had come much earlier in England and the States, and the working conditions of France—hygiene above all—seemed to carry one back a hundred years. But what interested me supremely was the atmosphere of ideas in which two *mystiques* were being offered to the worker as the secret of his redemption.

24

PRIEST-WORKER TRAGEDY

"I hardly know the real proletariat", Henri Perrin had written when querying the need of a "clergé à part" for them. The noble compassion with which so many priests had chosen to share their lot was sharpened by a closer realization of it, especially on the temporal side. "Draw profit from shocks", Abbé Godin had warned his mission—and all priest-workers got plenty from the very outset of theirs.

It is difficult to compare standards of living on a superficial level. The poorest French family will have wine on their table when they can rarely afford meat. I remember, in Marseilles, buying a litre of excellent local wine for very little more than I would have paid for a cup of coffee. Wine, soup, bread are their staples—which partly explains Abbé Pierre's revelations in *Faim et soif* concerning alcoholism among children. But the life of the French workman is harder, his hours longer, his pay lower, than those of his opposite number in England or still more in the States; the conditions of work are usually much worse. Père Perrin, when working on the Isère-Arc project, describes his ten- to twelve-hours' day, usually including Sundays, in conditions where the men had no means of drying the clothes taken off wringing wet in the evening and had to put them on again still wet next morning. The labourers hired for the job were sleeping in overcrowded dormitories, their wages were grossly insufficient for the absent families that most of them had to support.

Up and down the country the situation varied. Immediately after the War there had been in France, as elsewhere, full employment. But in 1947 a nationwide strike movement began, and Cardinal Suhard was moved to say, "At a time when wages are clearly insufficient to support a family it is not surprising that the most various sections of the workers should have recourse to striking." Those employers who had hoped that the priests in the factories would be on their side were dismayed to discover them as strike leaders. This strike had wide support among the Catholic body in some areas—but the attitude of both priests and militants varied from place to place, as may be seen in a number of the Catholic periodical *Masses ouvrières*, March–April 1948, which was entirely devoted to records of the strike throughout the country. Doubtless the workers' attitude was largely determined by that of the local employers; there was no uniform pattern in this strike. Some employers, too, were having their problems. Dr. Tremolières had patients in both worlds and he told me a little sadly, "If I were a workman I should be for the strike, but if an employer against it."

The thing that was troubling him most profoundly was that which presently brought Abbé Pierre into action—the terrible housing situation. If a family is living in a furnished room without even a stove—as so many were and still are—cooked food must be bought, laundry sent out. A workman's family is very near starvation in such circumstances, and I think any of us who go to work in that field realize quickly on what a knife-edge even the more fortunate are walking, with little power to save money and the dark shadow of unemployment constantly menacing them. Of all this any priest has what Newman calls a "notional" knowledge—let him live in its midst and the knowledge becomes "real". And to many the idea was presented for the first time that no mere improvement here or there would suffice. The whole structure of this world of "wage slavery" must be changed.

I paid many visits to France, especially Paris, in the years 1946–54, but I am surprised, glancing at my book *France Pagan?*, written in 1948, to realize how many tendencies had already declared themselves, although their proportions altered in the years that followed.

An early meeting of the heads of various groups in which were priest workmen—Missions de France and de Paris, Petits Frères de Jésus, Jesuits, Dominicans, Capuchins and others—discussed the question of whether priests ought to join in the effort to change the shape of things, in the political, social, economic struggle. The decision was adverse: the priest might get involved through charity, he must keep his passion for justice, but he must never forget "the transcendent character of his priesthood", never yield to hatred or "partisan passion". "But", they concluded, "to keep this interior purity, with or without temporal entanglements, it is necessary to be strongly armed against desire for success, over-determination to be efficient. There must be a strong realization of the Cross. The priest must be willing in advance to be rejected and crucified by the secular messianism when it has finally taken its shape."

But already the "secular messianism" of the *Mouvement ouvrier* was gripping numbers of priests; they were increasingly idealizing the worker and his *mystique*.

I first met this under the aspect of slighting references to Abbé Godin's outlook; he had not understood this *mystique* of the workman, after all he had remained too much in the sacristy. "I must admit," I wrote at the time, "that some of the priests I met do talk as though the proletariat alone had not fallen in Adam . . . The workers have some general ideas of history as seen by a Marxist and it is obvious as seen by anybody that the aristocracy has failed and the bourgeoisie has failed. In a kind of Wellsian rosy glow they see a future in which the proletariat will succeed where these have failed. The wave of the future is for them the temporal triumph of the workers."

I did not believe it would happen, but I saw even then the danger: was the Catholic movement "strong enough not to be submerged in that of the workers instead of guiding it? The French Church is still suffering because elements in it allowed themselves to be used for the temporal ends, first of the *ancien régime* and lately of Pétain. It would suffer as much in future if the attraction now exercised over certain French Catholics by Communism were to become widespread."

But I did not yet clearly realize that the Wellsian rosy glow, "the only workers' party", the workers' movement, the workers' *mystique*, all added up to Moscow; even level-headed workers were proclaiming Communism as "the only workers' party".

A French workman is not obliged to join a trade union and at first the priests did not do so. Anyhow, there was a choice between the Confédération Générale du travail—C.G.T.—which was Communist, the Force ouvrière—F.O.—which was Socialist, and the recently formed Confédération française de travailleurs chrétiens—C.F.T.C.—which was Catholic. As the priest-workmen increasingly identified themselves with the workers' movement, they almost always joined the C.G.T., which they considered the most effective in its struggle for the workers' rights. The strike of 1947 was the first in which they had borne a part. "With the personal sharing of the living conditions of the workers", says their manifesto of 1954 which recounts the history of the priest-workmen, "the worker-priests took part in their battles, and became more and more class conscious".[1]

Naturally enough, with their higher level of education the priests were soon asked to become the leaders in trade-union activities. One of them was, for instance, elected whole-time secretary of the metal-workers of Paris. In the strike of 1950 they were involved as a body. Many church-door collections were taken to support this strike.

But unfortunately the support given to the C.G.T. by its priest members and officers was far from being confined to the struggle for better working conditions. They were becoming intensely political and their politics appeared always to be following the party line.

I do not mean to suggest that a priest should have no politics—he is also a man and a citizen with the same rights and duties in the temporal order as the layman. But when priests were telling their bishops they had not enough time in a worker's day to say Office or make a meditation it seemed incongruous that they should be able to find plenty of time to attend political rallies and engage in political discussion. And again, while some of the causes they espoused were worthy ones, they seemed never to be able to differ from the Communist leaders or to give a calmly reasoned basis for the line they were following. A prejudiced man has been defined as one who weighs the same acts in different scales according to who commits them. The hymn line that Père Perrin had once loved, "Catholique et français toujours" expressed a danger: Frenchmen of the Right (including priests) were too apt to defend the unjust acts of their countrymen and of their coreligionists. Yet they were surely justified in feeling angry when the killing of Algerians by French soldiers was called a massacre while the holocausts by Stalin and his henchmen were only a regrettable necessity. The priest-workmen, in their manifesto, put the words "Church of Silence" in inverted commas and explained in a footnote that the phrase "has become current in Catholic circles to denote the conditions imposed on the Church in the People's Democracies". One catches one's breath when remembering what those conditions were, but my Communist friends would all have said in those days that I was being misled by capitalist

[1] *The Worker Priests. A Collective Documentation*, trans. John Petine, London, Routledge and Kegan Paul (1956), p. 14. (First published in France in 1954.)

propaganda. And anyhow, "You can't make an omelette without breaking eggs." Many quite reasonable Frenchmen, even enthusiasts for the priest-workers, felt that they were becoming too indifferent to the broken eggs, too fond of the Soviet omelette. Unless the spirit of man be changed the making of a new society would be as great a mess as the old ones. What were these priests doing for man's spirit? Was this feverish political action really a way of bringing Christ to the workers?

This question of politics and the priests came to a head with the march of protest in May 1952 against General Ridgway's appointment as Commander of the Atlantic armies. Walls that May were adorned in vast lettering with the words "Ridgway go Home", and one incident was featured (inaccurately) in *Time* magazine. The police seemed actually to have first attacked the crowd, driving a truck into the back of a hitherto peaceful (although prohibited) procession and beating up savagely the men they seized, including two priest-workers. *Time* reported one of the priests as carrying an iron bar, but the true account seems that a man with a sandwich-board detached the bar that supported it and fought back with it against the police. A priest, asked if he approved of this, said, "I don't approve but I understand." This was changed by the Commissioner of Police, in an open letter to the Archbishop of Paris, into "I approve". Councillor Degornet of the M.R.P. confronted the Commissioner with the lie. But it still went on being repeated.

Cardinal Feltin, who had succeeded Cardinal Suhard in 1949, received the maltreated priests with deep sympathy. Yet the question could not but be asked—what was a priest's place in such a demonstration? Complaints were reaching Rome, but the priest-workers tended to retort that no-one objected to clerical politics as long as they were well to the Right.

The pressure on their time alone of political and social action, added to the unaccustomed strain of the long hours at work, was making a priest's normal religious schedule impossible; the authorities arranged everywhere for an evening mass; the De Foucauld Petits Frères were learning to meditate to the sound of a machine—but they had from the first declared their intention of only witnessing to Christ by their presence and of taking absolutely no part in political activity. Père Perrin had done the same in his German prison, where, of course, no such activity was possible.

The second time I met Henri Perrin as a worker gave me a shock as to how things were going. He had managed to buy a café which a group of his friends were running for various youth activities and he wanted my husband's help and mine in getting money to keep it going. He had, I found, refused to take part in a protest against the treatment of Cardinal Mindzenty on the grounds that the Church in Hungary had so bad a social history, and that "it was said" that the Cardinal had allowed the use of his grounds for the secret manufacture of arms by reactionaries. One knew pretty well *who* had said it, and I noticed later in the *Itinéraire de Henri Perrin* that André Gide, whom he had once admired, was cavalierly dismissed after venturing to criticize the Soviet self-picture. As Henri talked I felt rather miserably how the old enthusiasms appeared to be fading in favour of what he was accepting as a true workers' outlook. The Christian community seemed forgotten—the workers' solidarity obsessed him. A young "prolo" once asked me which I thought worse: to be a bourgeois Catholic or a Communist. Decidedly the word "bourgeois" was becoming a smutty one—interchangeable also with the word "capitalist"—yet it covered in fact many splendid Catholics giving their lives to the Church as they conceived it. Some bourgeois Catholics might be too hidebound to move on quickly to new conceptions; some, of course, were totally selfish. I have always disliked the French of the extreme Right, and indeed most over-rich Catholics everywhere, and found them limited in vision. But they would not be helped by my little friend who was now declaring that he would let the Communists have his café for a rally but not the Catholics of the Right. I stayed for Henri's evening mass but I lacked the courage to tell him when he asked me how I liked his sermon that I had found it lacking in the height, the depth and the breadth with which St. Paul begged his flock to see Christ's mystery. This man, who had seemed of old to realize so vividly the unseen world, had given us ten minutes of kindly chat—and I could only be thankful that after all we had had the mass for the good of our souls.

Frank had not been with me, and, since Henri expressed a great wish to see him, I arranged for another meeting on the following evening. I had promised to spend the day with Marianne Ashbourne at Compiègne. We had so much to tell and to hear that it was very late before I got back to Paris. I was amazed to discover that, as far as Frank could tell, Henri Perrin's wish to see him had sprung solely from a hope that he could approach—of all people—Dorothy Day to send him money for his café. His face fell when Frank told him that Dorothy was poorest of the poor and found it hard to get the money for her own breadline, and the other expenses of the Houses of Hospitality stretching across the country. His train of thought had been very simple—America is rich, any American can get money.

Frank entreated him as he went on talking—more fully than he had to me—at least to examine the bases of his political assumptions, and painted for him a little of that picture of Stalin which Khrushchev was later to give in such fearful detail. He went on to say, "I don't ask you to accept this from me—but have you done anything to prove that your view is true to facts and not a mere dream?"

His impression of Henri Perrin was of a somnambulist. We had both thought him on our earlier visits a really towering personality—the immense impression made by his book had been heightened by the man. I don't think we were prejudiced; we should, I believe, have willingly listened to any argument he wanted us to hear. But there was no argument, merely the statement, only too familiar, of the party line, flowing mechanically, if not hypnotically, from his lips.

There is no doubt that some of the priest-workers were suffering from spiritual starvation, that they were praying less themselves and not helping others to pray as they had when first they set out on their high adventure. Adversaries of the movement stressed the fact that several priest-workmen had left the Church to get married. I have never known the exact number, but I think the amount of talk about these failures was unfair to the movement. In any walk of life the occasional priest fails, and the workers had acquired some men whose bishops did not much want them and who were liable to have gone off the rails in one way or another anywhere. The handful of apostates I did know, or know about from my friends, gave up their working lives soon after—they could better support a family in white-collar jobs. When Abbé Daniel reproached one of them for the contrast with his former impassioned announcement of solidarity with the workers he replied, "My dear chap, that was literature."

But it was the impoverishment of the priestly life itself which stirred the bishops, and they put forth several admirable directives which, however, remained more or less a dead letter. There was an impression among those who had held fast to the old ideal of the priest's special task which no layman can assume, that the bishops were a little frightened of these subjects of theirs. Priest-workers made a point of seeing their bishop always as a group, never singly. And they would tell him that never having himself worked in a factory he could not possibly understand the exigencies of their task. Increasingly they were becoming workmen first—and I notice that their manifesto is called in the English translation *The Worker Priests*.

The climax was reached of the activities most disapproved by religious authority with the strike of August 1953. Frank and I were in Brittany spending a holiday week with the Dhavernas family, a week of immense inconvenience and (apparently) public feeling that the summer holidays were not the time to throw such confusion into daily life. Whether *The Worker Priests* judged correctly that the strike was provoked by the Government, or whether a widespread opinion was true that it was a Communist strike designed for their usual purpose of disintegrating society, I have not the least idea. Anyhow, the strike ended through an agreement reached by the Catholic and Socialist trades unions acting through the mediation of M.R.P. (Mouvement Républicain Populaire, translated in *The Worker Priests*' glossary as Christian Democratic Party of France) with the Government.

As so often when a strike ends without complete victory, the word "treason" was freely thrown about, especially by the priest-workmen who, rallying to the Communist Union (C.G.T.), made themselves spokesmen also of elements in other unions dissatisfied with the agreement. They put out a declaration in which they stated, "What has clearly emerged as the expression of a political enthusiasm entirely devoted to Christian democracy *and therefore to capitalist interests*, cannot also be taken as a witness of the Christian faith and of the Gospel message."[1]

In some ways this was the most surprising event in the whole story. In a matter concerning his life and his work on earth the layman can be at least as well informed as the priest, and here were a few score priests claiming to set aside as treachery the decision reached by Catholic syndicalists and Catholic laymen, many of them trained in these matters and outnumbering the priests astronomically. Nor was it a solitary instance; at Marseilles complaints reaching

[1] *The Worker Priests*, p. 32. Italics mine.

the bishop about certain of the priest-workmen came not from the bourgeoisie but from Christian militants deploring their identification with the Communist C.G.T., their disregard of lay Catholic opinion.

When launching the Young Worker movements Canon Cardijn had said of the chaplain in each group, "He must be everything—and he must be nothing." The "everything" must be the inspiration given by his faith and by his charity, the "nothing" must mean that in the practical order he must not be always interfering but must encourage even these boys to make their own decisions and carry them out. In several letters priests at the beginning of their workers' career spoke of the bad habits learnt in the seminary which they needed to unlearn. One of these was "authoritarianism"—and it would seem that whatever their attitude to Communist militants they were slow indeed to unlearn this with their fellow Catholics.

The French bishops had several times visited Rome to urge the immense importance of the penetration of the proletariat by the priesthood and the disastrous effect closing down the movement would have on the workers' attitude to the Church, but it was inevitable by now that Rome should act. The Apostolic Nuncio called a meeting of bishops and superiors in September 1953 to pass on his instructions to them. "Work is not the danger," was one of his remarks, "but this collaboration with the Communists." They must try, he added, to find something else to take the place of this experiment.

Unfortunately, as invariably happens, the news got out prematurely to the Press and a flood of articles followed. Cardinal Feltin, in a fine address to his clergy, begged the prayers of Catholics for these priests but mentioned the chief dangers of their work. The priest's mission lies in the spiritual order. He must not employ "human, material, political means". Our Lord did not overthrow Caesar. Charity is of universal application and must extend to every class and every race. The class struggle exists as a fact, but not an inevitable one. He added something about the danger of a failure in the spirit of obedience—which had, he said, been manifest during the Occupation. And indeed one feels that the whole story might have been different had the experiment started in a less confused period and been more carefully guided.

In October, about to start for Rome, Cardinal Feltin received the priest-workmen who, in the words of their own manifesto, "laid stress on the class struggle and on their inability to give up that struggle now unless they were to betray their proletarian state". "To forbid us all trade union activities would come to the same thing as suppressing us altogether."

The three French cardinals found the Pope in deep distress of mind, afraid both of a diminution of the priestly life of men plunged into industry, and of their being absorbed by Communism. When, ten days later, the cardinals made their statement, it contained five conditions for continued work: (1) The priests must be specifically selected by their bishops, (2) receive a sound doctrinal training, (3) devote only a limited time to manual work (this finally was determined at three hours a day, which made factory work impossible), (4) they must leave temporal responsibilities to laymen and (5) take part in the life of the parish church.

I think we were all startled to hear that seventy-two priests had refused to obey—there cannot have been many more than a hundred all told—and had said they would continue their work. Among them was Henri Perrin. Five more added their signatures later to a manifesto that can only be called a defiance. I did not learn the details of Henri's last years, until the book appeared *Itinéraire de Henri Perrin*. Not long after our last meeting the time had come for his tertianship (a period when a Jesuit withdraws for a while from active work for a life of prayer and silence). Would Henri gather up again the tremendous spiritual forces once so visible in him? Alas, his diary was destroyed, so one can only guess at what is not related in the letters. The friends who traced this journey felt that he had been out of luck in being left too much in solitude to do for himself what a spiritual guide of real quality would have helped him with. Anyhow, faced with the possibility of not being sent back to a worker's life, he finally decided that this meant more to him than did the Society. He asked to be secularized, was accepted by the Archbishop of Sens, and almost immediately got a job on the big construction work of the Isère-Arc tunnel. He was at once sucked into a deeply justified strike. He became the workers' secretary in a victory won chiefly through his zeal; writing to newspapers, approaching priests for collections, gathering in literally millions of francs. He was "Comrade Perrin" to the Communists, but the local priest was also his very good friend, the presbytery was thrown open to him and he said his Mass each evening in the village church. When, the following year, after one of several incidents caused by the lack of proper precautions, Henri was asked to conduct the funeral of a fellow worker, he made clear in his sermon where the blame lay. The management sought for an excuse to dismiss him and did so very shortly after. Again the workmen came out on strike—demanding his reinstatement. When they could not win it they made his work as secretary a paid job. He started proceedings against the management, who would, it seemed, be adjudged to pay him heavy damages. There is something in the whole story of youth finding an outlet—of gallantry, and of excitement in a fight.

But when the orders came from Rome Henri's spirit seemed utterly broken. He signed the manifesto but then asked his bishop for six months' leave of absence.

How it happened nobody knew. Henri was riding his motorcycle, it swerved, and he fell and was taken up dead. In his pocket was a letter written a fortnight earlier, asking for laicization. But he had not posted it and it is possible that he had finally decided otherwise.

I was in England when the news came of the decree from Rome and was utterly stunned by it. I had indeed noticed a few aberrations in the movement but my eyes had been for six years chiefly directed towards its centre of greatest light—Marseilles. "I *must* see Père Jacques", I said at once, and Frank answered "You must indeed."

Wanting to go to Paris as well as Marseilles, I could not immediately find the time. I do not know how much I wanted to comfort him, how much to be comforted by him. I certainly wanted to understand why this heavy blow had been struck against a movement in which I had seen so much promise, indeed so much splendour. Just before I got on the plane our editor handed me a book. "This has just come in", he said. "We are offered the translation rights and you'd better look at it." It was the manifesto of the seventy-two later translated under the title *The Worker Priests*.

I saw at once that it was not for us; and there was much that I began to understand for the first time. As I think over it all the lines of Browning run through my mind:

> How very hard it is to be
> A Christian: hard for you and me.

For Christianity always demands of us the primacy of the spiritual, the *memento mori*, the realization that only God can say, "Well done thou good and faithful servant."

The immediate task is so urgent, so absorbing, it tends to fill the horizon. The praise of men is so heady: even a priest who despised a book describing him as a "saint in hell" must have been affected by the outpouring of journalistic and popular enthusiasm which never ceased to attend the movement, must above all have been subtly affected by praise from his Communist comrades and the sense of power won through heroism. For there was much heroism in the movement, but by the confession of this book itself that heroism had been turned to temporal ends, the good new of the Gospel exchanged for the *mystique* of one class of men fighting with material means for a material victory.

"It's terrible for you", was all I could say when I met Père Jacques; but he answered, "It was much worse waiting for it."

His position had long entailed the same sort of suffering as my father's during the Modernist era. Men had left his team and had attacked him for trying to combine the life of parish priest with that of workman. And now his superiors seemed to distrust him for having been a workman. He and Abbé Daniel and the others whom I went on to see in Paris had been helplessly watching the wrong sort of man getting into the movement and turning it in the wrong direction. If only, they told me, the bishops had acted early on and insisted on the right attitude, only two or three priest-workers would have rebelled. Each year, like one of those sums about the nails in the horse's shoe, the numbers of temporal messianists had multiplied. That very year a group of nineteen seminarians had said they would not be ordained except under a promise that they could be priest-workmen. This, of course, the Hierarchy had refused—but it marked a high point in the fever.

Very near Marseilles are the Dominican headquarters and noviciate where Père Jacques had long been teaching. But now the Father-General had stopped his lectures, though most of his brethren on the spot still trusted him totally. Again his position reminded me of my father's. He had felt it a duty to tell the Father-General how, while wholeheartedly obeying, he felt the problem of approach could not be solved merely by negation—and his views had not been well received. A similar letter, sent to his bishop, has since been published in his *Journal d'une mission ouvrière (1941–59)*. His work continued with De Foucauld's Little Brothers and Sisters, both of whom had houses close to the monastery; no prohibition had come of their factory work and he was helping to form them spiritually and intellectually. The Sisters' tiny house, with its beauty and simplicity in poverty, was deeply impressive. Père Jacques had begun immediately in Marseilles the manufacture of bricks for the housing schemes in the parish; by this means the priests could all work the statutory three hours a day instead of two of them full time in turns at the docks. His farewell to the other dockers had been interesting. *The Worker Priests* claims that their withdrawal had caused infinite bitterness among the workers, had thrown them further away from the Church but—"Believe it or not," Père Jacques said, "every docker to whom I explained that the priests had been withdrawn because they mixed in politics said, Quite right, the priest should keep out of politics. Only (they added) priests on the capitalist side mixed in politics still."

But the manifesto of the Worker Priests asks a question on its final page which it does not attempt to answer, which it acknowledges many were asking, "What have you done for the workers that any layman could not have done equally well?"

Bishop Delay had asked Jacques to gather a group of young workmen—late vocations—to test them out and start their training for the priesthood. I dined with them all and felt how much of his spirit they were gaining. I spent a day of recollection with the girls of the Residence at which he commented most beautifully on the Epistle to the Ephesians. These girls too he was preparing for the carrying on of the apostolate. He indeed had brought into being that vibrant Christian Community of which Henri Perrin used to dream. It would carry on his work. He asked me to give the girls an account of the Catholic Evidence Guild and a crowd of them finally saw me to my bus and bade me farewell with smacking kisses.

But the great memory of that week is the corner of a little churchyard in Provence where Père Lagrange is buried. "Does it remind you at all of Palestine?" Père Jacques asked. "Père Lagrange used to say that the view over those fields brought back to him the Holy Land."

As an old man Père Lagrange had taught the young Jacques Loew. And we both remembered how that great man had been suspected, insulted, banished, during the Modernist period, but had left behind him a monument of scholarship, and become today *the* great name in Catholic Scripture studies. How he had continued his work steadily "in praise and in dispraise the same", had never opened his lips in self-pity, defence, or in anger.

A meditation at the grave of Père Lagrange was one way of approaching the problem of frustration, opposition, disappointment, which we find in lives of all the saints—which haunts all human effort here below. But in face of the problem of the hour—the priest-workers—it seemed too facile to see it *merely* as part of God's plan for the perfecting of holiness. After all, I had seen a character of, I could swear, immense worth, warped by a trial some part of which might have been spared him. In fact every man *is* his brother's keeper and all Christians bear some responsibility for each. Perhaps the failure of the advance guard resulted from the fact that the army was not close behind. There were Catholics who had actually *hoped* the experiment would fail, who had denounced it in advance, others who swung from feverish enthusiasm into hostility and suspicion. Henri Perrin's Carmelite cousin, her sisters, many other nuns, we know were praying ardently, but were the rest of us?

I discussed with my friends the elements that might have made up a different picture: Abbé Daniel thought a too early beginning of seminary life failed to prepare the future priest for the world he would be entering. Père Jacques had received in his team young priests whose theology was, he felt, insufficient. Yet all of these had had the long seminary years or the sometimes longer period of noviciate and training in a religious order. And the very same professors who appeared to have failed with the other men had taught Père Jacques and Abbé Daniel.

Defending the unhappy first letter to their bishops of the seventy-two worker priests, Père Perrin claimed that the language attacked as Communist was simply that of the workers—the priests had, he said, done what St. Thomas did when "to the great scandal" of the Catholic world he learnt to speak the language of the Arab philosophers.

St. Thomas had in fact done the exact opposite to the writers of this letter—the question was not one of language but of *ideas.* The letter accepted Communist ideas, St. Thomas translated Catholic ideas into new terms. This was what Abbé Godin had done, what

Père Jacques, Abbé Michonneau and many others are still doing. This was what the priest-workers were not doing. But I am certain they started by intending to, and hardly realized at what point their abandonment of the Christian revelation began.

And I wondered how many men there are in an average seminary who are capable, like Godin, Daniel or Loew, of getting the meaning of what they learn—often in a foreign language, always in more or less foreign terms. Teaching the late vocations confided to him by his bishop, Père Jacques begins *with them* the task of translation which they must carry on in the world they are to teach. Teaching a man to teach is half the job of a training college in secular learning. If the seminaries had included in philosophy and theology practice in teaching, of the sort that would prove whether each man understood what he had learnt, might not some of the tragedy have been averted over which we are still grieving?

The kingdoms of this world and the glory of them—even in the shape of a future workers' triumph—may constitute a severe temptation to some temperaments, but it seems incredible that so many should have fallen for it had they understood what they were abandoning. Formulas, however magnificent, are swept away by a vision; only a greater vision can prevail. Communists have a vision, but we have *the* vision.

25

LIVING ON TWO CONTINENTS

If one gets mixed up in movements worth writing about there is only one way of writing coherently—and that is chronologically, even if (in this case) this means turning back several years to rejoin the thread of our own life as parents, lecturers, writers and publishers in the postwar world of England and the States.

Like the telephone, the aeroplane, while solving many problems, brings others. We had never before lived fully, lived intensely, in two countries. Before Sheed and Ward, New York, was started, we lived in England and visited the States as we visited France or Italy. After 1932 Frank had begun a more toilsome visiting, clearing a crowded desk in London only to find an equally crowded one in New York. But it had still been visiting; there had been the respite of the ship—and New York was less full of other work, no C.E.G., fewer people asking his help and advice. But personal ties increase as life advances, and we had both acquired many friends—and god-children—on three continents!

I had lent money for building materials to families in a self-build group in upstate New York who were putting up the same sort of struggle against officialdom as their English counterparts. "How determined", I wrote at the time, "is the universal bureaucracy to prevent people doing anything for themselves." A book I edited not long after the war, *Be Not Solicitous*, was about such families, their difficult experiences, the lessons their lives brought of faith and courage. Some of the writers were already my friends, others became so. Molly Walsh told of family life lived under the difficulties of a House of Hospitality in the England of depression and of war, Nancy Dubois of an interracial marriage, Bill and Avis Walsh of bringing up twelve children on almost no money. My own contribution was "A Plea for the Family"—then, and perhaps even more today, under pressure material and spiritual.

Wilfrid was at Downside for only two terms; the specialist said that it was impossible for him to lead a school life and carry out the physiotherapy which might yet bring improvement to the dead leg.

One year he spent at Fordham University, which he enjoyed enormously; but usually he studied at home, and was lucky in the tutors who prepared him for Oxford.

Sometimes all together, sometimes scattered between America, England and Australia, we were in those years incessantly meeting one another or kissing goodbye at airports—Frank and I seldom flying together before our children were married. Flying accidents are so very final.

"I miss you and Wilfrid dreadfully," I wrote from England. "What a family we are." "We expect", runs a letter from Rosemary, "to be met by Wilfrid in the Olds. At least we say we expect it." Wilfrid had spent that summer (1949) with the Henry Luces at Ridgefield, Frank going down at weekends. Clare made Wilfrid learn to drive and then gave him an Oldsmobile. We were embarrassed at the splendour of the gift, but she explained that on her dead daughter's birthday she always gave a present: "Wilfrid is just the recipient."

Rosemary had been old enough when we left England to have already made many friends, and the Cousinhood and their cousins had received her with special warmth on our return. For we had returned to a degree that made both Rosemary and myself think of England as home. I was immediately asked to join a committee set on foot by Simon Elwes with the object of buying and restoring Fountains Abbey. The scheme, alas, fell through but Simon's enthusiasm was infectious, as he built on very slender foundations a dream-building of astonishing proportions: one almost heard the monks singing office, saw the ruins restored and reconsecrated. Bernard Norfolk's solid sense brought us back to earth. He may well inherit his father's reputation as the best chairman in England; no one was hustled or silenced, yet despite Simon's rhapsodies the business in hand was dispatched and the meeting finished in reasonable time.

Driving me back from an early committee meeting, Bernard remarked, "I see why you chose Oakwood Court: it must remind you of New York." We had been beggars rather than choosers, but oddly enough Oakwood had as many floors as our Riverside apartment house and was decidedly higher as the rooms were much more lofty.

We were always a full house. Hester Blundell was with us for months on end. She, Rosemary and Wilfrid brought their friends home, we had American visitors, Australian visitors, masses of people from the C.E.G. After one European Conference in the Midlands, when I found the delegates were not being entertained in London, I telephoned home and asked Rosemary to set a party on foot for Abbé Michonneau, Abbé Hollande and all the other priests, editors and politicians from France, Germany and Italy. American food plus the farm made all things possible. And Rosemary had become a magnificent cook and organizer. For six months we took in an Australian couple, who had been unable to find a home, Niall Brennan, who later wrote *The Making of a Moron* and *A Hoax Called Jones*, and his wonderful wife Elaine. After much searching and many refusals they did get housed before their baby was born. I had blenched slightly as I pictured the arrival of a baby in our flat. Grandmother felt that life was getting on top of us and even I, though enjoying each event singly, had to fall back at times on a favourite text—"Offering hospitality without murmuring."

I entered the drawing-room at six one morning intending to do some work on my current book and found Wilfrid asleep on the sofa. He roused himself to say "I thought you'd be less startled to find me here than Mike, so I put him in my bed." A door shut off the big front rooms, where the young were permitted late and noisy parties. We in the morning could work peacefully, while they in turn slept. But it was only too easy for a visitor from the country to miss the last train home. I almost dropped the tea tray I was carrying and, murmuring my text against murmuring, retreated to the kitchen.

The effect of the years in the States had been very different on our two children. Rosemary had made many friends there, but remained unshakably English; she intended, she said, to live in England, she could not possibly marry anyone but an Englishman. Wilfrid had begun his American life in bellicose mood; he was called "Limey" and gloried in fighting England's battles. At Downside and at Oxford he was called "Yank". A friend of his said to Rosemary, "I never believed Bill was English till I met you." He had become "Bill" as early as Torresdale, and hated his rather fancy name. But he had not really become "Yank". New York was better than London. Oxford was better than any experience of his earlier life. But not until he got to his father's country, Australia, did he feel that he fully belonged. One of the oddest things I have ever seen was this son of ours looking and talking after a few months there like a man born and bred in Sydney.

He got the job of Associate to Sir Edward MacTiernan, a Judge of the High Court of Australia, and with him travelled all over the country. But the return to Sydney from Melbourne, Brisbane or Adelaide he always called coming home. "Wilfrid", a cousin of Frank's said, "turns up suddenly and we discover him playing our piano just as if he had never been away." This was some years ahead: his chief need now was to get more classics and more history, his chief desire to see more countries and gain a wider experience. We too had reasons in plenty for going to Europe; sometimes son or daughter came with us, sometimes they went on their own. The Europe shut to us all for so many years opened upon them for the first time when they were old enough to appreciate it. These were full years and rich in experience.

We were taught at school that there are two kinds of play—tragedy ending with a death, comedy ending with a marriage—and the volumes of Shakespeare are divided accordingly. But there are, too, the historical plays and real life is more like them—shot through with grief and joy in a strong pattern of death and resurrection. Many had received husbands and sons back from the death of concentration or prisoners' camps or from a hunted life in woods and caves. The end of the War brought the feeling of a security that life cannot give. Two young deaths in our own immediate circle came in 1949 and 1950 within six months of each other; my nephew Nick Blundell and Muriel Nevile's Bernard. These things cannot be written of, but Muriel talking to me one day used unconsciously, almost, the words of Scripture when she said, "The agony passed into joy." These mothers had what Karl Stern has called that "profound inner relation with death" which belongs peculiarly to the Christian. "In one sense", my sister wrote, "the big light of my life is gone, yet it is *not* really gone." Hester had just announced her engagement and her mother could write in the same letter of plans, and rejoice in the fact that Hester "can't be otherwise than happy, which will make me increasingly so."

We shut up house that summer and while Wilfrid drove with a friend to California, Rosemary, Frank and I went to Switzerland, where he had been invited to lecture at Fribourg University. There was time, too, to explore, but often while Rosemary and Frank toured, I sat in the agreeable cafés of the town looking at mountains and finishing off *Return to Chesterton.*

In one way our work makes it easier for us to take holidays by giving us reasons: visiting authors, looking for new books, lecturing etc. But of course these are seldom complete holidays. Frank was putting more hard work into his lecture course than I into my book —but his easy delivery hides this fact from most of his listeners. He is supposed to talk with ease on the most profound and difficult subjects—God, the Soul, the Saviour—just because he chooses easy words to do it in: a choice that often means translating as well as thinking. I remember our arriving after a very tough period of work, to stay with friends in Vermont. Frank had relaxed totally and was singing gaily as we climbed the hills in their jeep. We had taken wine on board and other provisions for a party of undergraduates from Marlboro, where our host was a professor. All seemed set for a pleasant evening when our hostess suddenly said, "Of course a lot of these boys are unbelievers and we've been telling them you can answer their questions."

We hoped they might not ask them, but they did and the visit became literally a headache—and a raging one at that—for Frank. Sudden tension after relaxing is always the worst—and I noted the usual feeling among his listeners, "Oh, but you do this so easily." Delightful as our friends were, glorious as was the scenery, this was no holiday.

We had seen Grandmother off from New York and were now getting letters from Sydney. The indomitable old lady still went home in two directions and was perhaps even more at home on a train or a ship. (She never got into a plane.) Coming through the Rocky Mountains, she wrote: "As for the scenery, I am left in more wonder than ever at the goodness of God and the might of His works. He must have had this part of the world in mind particularly." And in another letter, "God knows how I love His wonderful creation."

Daily Mass at 5.30 she never missed. Nor her salt-water bath, during which the stewardess stood outside the door, afraid her elderly passenger might collapse. Crew and passengers fêted her on Mother's Day. She did not, she remarked, care for the "moneyed swells" on board, but had endless conversations with an American priest, contriving of course to lead him into a discussion of Sheed and Ward books and exchanging her small shipboard library with his.

At Melbourne the immigration authorities would not admit her until assured from Sydney of her family's support. Frank's bank account would have been equally satisfactory if only it had been in Melbourne. It meant a few hours' wait in a hotel, a few telephone calls—but in her *own* country! "Ellis Island all over again", she commented furiously.

Back in Sydney she was home indeed, but soon the longing to be with us had again set in. "I feel it is years since you said 'good-bye' to me on that train in Canada, it reminded me of my last parting with Jack [Frank's dead brother] but it won't be long now."

Installed at Oakwood, she watched with keen interest her grandchildren's social life, embarrassing them by her conviction that both were constantly pursued by unworthy members of the opposite sex. But her vigour had given the impression of greater stamina than she now possessed; after a slight illness and an insignificant operation, old age came suddenly. Her attitude changed towards Rosemary's admirers: the mid-twenties now seemed to her perilously near old-maidenhood and she would set her heart on one or another of the men who visited the flat. We could not share her concern, and indeed ours was concentrated on her. No one knew how she managed one evening to fall getting into bed, but she broke her leg and in bed she remained for many weary months.

I, meanwhile, was haunted by a longing to do something which life denied me: to write again the second half of Newman's life, using much of my father's admirable book. The London Oratorians were certain he had not seen all the rich material in their letter-books—and he could not have asked himself questions become urgent only after the passage of another half-century. I began to study more closely the state and position of Catholics at the time of the Oxford Movement: conditions in Ireland, conditions in England. I read or reread the lives of Pugin, Gavan Duffy, O'Connell, Lucas of *The Tablet*, Ambrose Phillips de Lisle, Lord Shrewsbury, Faber, W. G. Ward and my other grandfather James Robert Hope-Scott, Archbishop Ullathorne, my father's life of Wiseman and Purcell's *Manning*. What caused the change between an openness towards the Church expressed by the conversion of the entire village where Faber and his group of converts first lived, of several hundreds a year in little towns like Coventry, the steady stream from Oxford, the indications everywhere of a desire to hear the Church's case—and the ugly mood of the "Papal Aggression" outcry and the sudden arrest of what had looked like becoming a tidal wave?

To answer that and other questions surging in my mind much more reading must be done—and I could not do it. If the pressure on my time and energy had been an even one, I might have managed to come to terms with it—as today I save the weekends for writing. But a handful of old letters recalls how uneven it was. Life at Oakwood began well with first one then another delightful Irishwoman from the Labour Exchange. But after Mrs. Troy left us, a series followed—mostly incompetent and never long lasting. With the resident nurse there was only room for a daily maid. In a very few months, one letter reminds me, we had in succession three nurses and five maids.

The Labour Exchange barren, we tried an institution called the Elizabeths; these royally named girls were of amazing variety. There was an actress temporarily resting, an Australian teacher anxious to earn a little to prolong her visit to England, an elegant damsel who asked for a holiday on June 4th to visit her brother at Eton. Some of them worked well. "My rather grand char", I wrote to Frank in New York, "is operating with a legitimately fierce scorn of her predecessors. Nurse is as noisy as ever—but she is *cooking. Eureka!*"

I tried going over to the Oratory whenever I could spare an hour or two. All the letters of the period were copied into letter-books—arranged, not as correspondence, but as individual collections: I found in Vol. 9 Newman's side of an interchange with Faber, whose letters were in Vol. 1. Reading them *as* a correspondence, I could follow with all its currents the merging of Fr. Faber's group of Oxford converts with Newman's; the founding, first of the Birmingham and then of the London Oratory; the surroundings of bitter poverty in London's early stage in a parish full of Irishmen driven from their country by the famine; the increasing admiration, amounting almost to worship, felt for the oratorians by the Catholic aristocracy, who brought the Oratory from the slums to Brompton.

Time could always be made for reading books at home, and I found in parish libraries many which were of no literary value but which brought alive the horrors of poverty in London and Birmingham, the devoted labours of the Oratorians and other parish priests and the vast tragic background of Ireland. But the letters would be the chief material and I tried in vain to get permission to take them home. The journey to the Oratory, letter-books brought down for me to the parlour, the journey back, left little time there. And then there would be Birmingham with far more letters to be read.

The chief difference between my father's outlook and mine was that my interest was greater in Newman's opponents and their motives, in all the other people who affected the story. Newman was so intensely my father's hero that I felt a desire to see the whole story as Ullathorne, Faber or even Manning might have seen it. But indeed I had a fancy that I might cast some really new light on this old scene. I had been the first to picture the young Newman in his family setting and to pick up the hints unconsciously given in the biographies and memoirs of his early contemporaries. Books were coming out now that owed something to mine, just as earlier ones had owed much to my father's. I should not dream of superseding Wilfrid Ward's work. But I might in some ways supplement it.

Frank came back from New York when I had reached the sad conclusion that I must not try. His arrival was always a moment of delight, but that evening I burst into tears, saying that I had written my last book and now I should never know the things I wanted to know about Newman and Faber and the English Catholics.

That was the key phrase: one cannot read for a book without the awakening of a passionate curiosity. People are so exciting, and the imagination roves over what might have happened if they had made different choices, if the play of temperaments had been different. With every biography there is a touch of Chesterton's puppets in *The Surprise*. The main mistake in biography is that made by the Master of the puppets: *he* had decided how they would behave, but when they came to life and behaved quite differently he felt they were spoiling his play! If one reads without preconceptions, letting facts and people speak for themselves, making discoveries and testing them, the reading is certainly its own reward. And I would advise all temperamental women, especially those condemned to much separation from husband or children, to have on hand the kind of reading one does when a book is in the head. As with the web of Penelope, night may see the day's work unpicked, but it is a wonderful steadier for the imagination and prevents the emotions from taking a dangerous control over the reason.

In April 1951 Frank and I celebrated our twenty-fifth wedding anniversary. The last thing we wanted was for our friends and relatives to spend their money on silver teapots—we kept our secret so well that a single telegram was all we found on arrival at our hotel in Paris. It was from one of our hecklers in Hyde Park—the Edward Siderman who wrote so well of Father Vincent. Not seeing us there, he had prised out of Rosemary the information of where we were and why. It seemed rather happily symbolic of something or other. On this trip we did not want to see anybody. Frank's holiday slogan is, "Remember we are absolutely free"—or, as he once wrote to a member of the staff, "If anyone needs to get into touch with me, they can't." Change he feels to be the best relaxation—to dine in a different restaurant each day, to move from place to place as the fancy takes us. We had been obliged to come to Belgium on Sheed and Ward business, but now we fled into the mountains, going on to Clermont-Ferrand, Le Puy and La Chaise Dieu. That summer Frank finished *Society and Sanity*, and spoke for the first time on the sidewalks of New York.

A year later, in Paris again, we were followed by a letter from Rosemary telling us she was engaged to Neil Middleton. Like Frank and me, they had met when both were speaking for the C.E.G. We felt it was a good basis for a happy marriage. And in its own way it seemed as strange, as wonderfully predestined, as our own meeting. We had often marvelled over the thousands of miles Frank had travelled, unconscious of the fact that he was travelling towards our life together, of the multitude of happenings minor and major without which we should never have got to know one another. But mentally Neil had made a longer and more arduous journey, for he had begun life in a Communist family and been as a youth an ardent Communist himself. The discovery of how little there was in Communism by which the younger boys allotted to him for guidance could live turned him towards Christianity. In many ways I think the story of Ignace Lepp goes the nearest I know to his mental experience. Neil knows that his own father was a Communist of the idealist type, that theirs can be a noble attitude; that we Christians have in fact much to learn from them. Immense as he sees the danger of Communism to be, he feels that more harm than good is done by an indiscriminating blackening of all Communists and all their ideals.

Rosemary told us on our return that she had taken Neil in to see Grandmother—who had seemed to like him, though she was not very clear as to his identity. But she asked her granddaughter afterwards, "Do you think you could fancy him?"

She was getting confused in these last months, though serene and even happy. Sometimes she spoke of the open ground at the back of Oakwood Court as "The Paddock", fancying herself back in Australia. But at the time of the Queen's Coronation she was convinced that the procession had passed her window and she assured us that "the Queen outshone them all". Proud of her many years, she firmly believed that she was now a hundred and would assure me that Frank could prove it to me. Belief in her son's infallibility and a conviction that I shared that belief had always been a bond between us; we had lived very happily together for long periods. But the end was now near: soon after our return she had a stroke and sank rapidly. The nurse woke us in the night so that Frank and I and both grandchildren were with her. Her beauty after death was something quite extraordinary. A friend who came in and knelt with us by the bedside said, "I wonder who is praying for whom."

26

HILAIRE BELLOC

ELEANOR Jebb had been, like us, looking after an "aged parent" and in 1950 we had celebrated the eightieth birthday of Hilaire Belloc. Frank and I were among the multitude of guests at Kingsland, and we noted the letters and telegrams innumerable which Eleanor had pasted on the windows. The papers too had done him proud; Gladstone was not the only Englishman whom his countrymen have delighted to honour as a Grand Old Man. The sad thing was that in this case it seemed to have come too late. He seemed hardly aware of the great names in letters and politics signed on the telegrams, hardly even aware of the identity of many of his visitors. Yet even as late as this came flashes of the old Belloc. Grumbling to Johnnie Morton of his daughter's efforts at tidying him, he declaimed:

> Here let me live in peaceful dirt
> With nobody to ask me why
> And wear the same primeval shirt
> Until I die.

And to Frank about this time he improvised:

> Louis Quatorze
> Went on all fours
> But, to tell the truth
> Only in very early youth.

I had known Hilaire Belloc with an inherited friendship—despite or perhaps because of which I always called him, with the formality of my Victorian childhood, "Mr. Belloc." My father, while loving Gilbert Chesterton, had not taken to Belloc very much. My mother's affection for him dated back to the days when, as a schoolboy, her brother James had been his close friend and he had been deeply in love with my Aunt Minna, seven years older than himself. My mind went back that day to the story her daughter, Fearga Maxwell-Scott, told me of when Aunt Minna died. Mr. Belloc, she said, came to the door and asked to be allowed to see her. He went up to her room, stayed a long while and then, coming out, walked down the stairs and left the house without speaking a word. This was the more startling because his manners to our family were usually polite to the point of ceremony. He had perhaps learnt the hard way, for when I told my much older Great-Aunt Philippa of how he had said to Frank, when first his long illness started, that he spent his time "meditating on his own vileness", she retorted, "And so he should. He was a very bad-tempered boy."

The Chester-Belloc generation lay halfway between that of my great-aunts and my own. It was strange and interesting to know in their old age those who to the aunts were young, daring, indeed too greatly adventurous. In her own old age, my mother very much appreciated the fairly frequent visits Hilaire paid her ("Hilary" she, our family and he himself pronounced it). Not to me but to our mutual friend Charlotte Balfour he wrote movingly about her goodness and the affection he always bore for her. I, however, got to know him well not so much through Mama as through his growing intimacy with my husband. I have told of the abortive efforts to fit him into our publishing scheme, but they marked the beginning of a warm friendship. While I was always much closer to Gilbert Chesterton, Frank was closer to Belloc.

French on his father's side, English on his mother's, the question of his, so to say, spiritual and intellectual nationality has been much disputed. He was only naturalised English after doing his French military service. He said once in a long talk with Frank:

> My mother always said that there was a French element in me which would every so often stick out like a spike. I cannot see it myself. I write poetry the English like, and I could not do it unless I were English.
>
> My Mother was dead against my doing conscript service with the French army. She said it would stamp me as a foreigner for the rest of my life. She proved right. But I enjoyed it enormously for just over a year. Then I got bored with it and got out. They were an extraordinarily attractive lot of men I was with. I called on one of them afterwards at his home, attractive and very much of the bourgeoisie. I never saw him or any of them again. I wonder what would have happened had I married a Frenchwoman. There

was one, of a family rich, cosmopolitan, civilised. I should probably have been very happy.

It was not a long drive from Kingsland to Horley and visits could easily be interchanged. Two incidents stick out in my memory. Belloc arrived one day at Chestnuts bringing a tin of bully beef, a large lettuce and three bottles of the burgundy he bought in casks and bottled in the windmill at Kingsland. He would not, he said, eat our dinner as he had come uninvited but would dine on his own beef and salad. He sent for our small Irish cook and explained that she must on no account wash but "brush the lettuce. If you wash a lettuce the water will prevent the oil of the dressing from mixing with the texture of the leaf." I murmured to the girl, who was looking quite terrified, not to worry—if she could not get the earth off otherwise she must certainly wash the lettuce, and dry it as usual in a tea towel. But *I* need not have worried either. When our liver and bacon appeared, our guest decided that after all he would like to eat it. And the salad went neglected.

We drank two bottles of the wine: the third he left with us unopened; but by the next day it had, alas, gone sour. It had apparently disliked the journey, or had perhaps been defectively bottled.

Apart from the food problem I remember less of that night than I do of a New Year's visit paid by us to Kingsland. After dinner Eleanor, her husband and Frank went over to the windmill with the children, and our host excused himself for leaving me awhile, as he always did his accounts on New Year's Eve. In an incredibly short time (I would guess a quarter of an hour) he was back and began soliloquizing over his own expenditure. "It is surprising," he said, "how little one spends on luxuries—such as oysters." Equally surprising he found the large expenditure on cabs, the less than he had fancied on charity. But I could not resist the suspicion that the accounts themselves had been that night compounded of fancy; how could he in so few minutes summarize the complications of a year's book-keeping—even on the wild supposition that he kept any books? Long before today's income tax he had said "I must earn four thousand a year." When asked, "Why '*must*'?" he had replied conclusively, "Because I live at the rate of four thousand a year."

Kingsland had been the fulfilment of a dream, but the farm had never done anything but lose money for him. Now it was let, but it was only one of his many problems, and taxes and costs had risen while his earning powers had not. The huge success of his articles during the First World War had really been his undoing. He knew so well the country in which the armies were struggling, so much about the conditions of their warfare, that he reached an immense reading public and made vast sums such as he could never hope for again. So his annual accounts, however reckoned, were apt to leave him gloomy.

Back came the others and now we must go out into the road to hear the first sound of the bells which from Horsham were ringing in the New Year. Every door and window in the house must, he insisted, be thrown open, bitterly cold though the night was. He brought in a pebble from the road and solemnly threw it into the fire. But a man with black hair must be the first to enter. Frank still qualified, and was told to precede the rest of us. He asked what the pebble symbolized and was told, "I don't know. It's traditional." How seriously did Belloc—whom we were already calling "the old man"—take these superstitions? More seriously, I fancy, than most of us could believe. One of the oddest features in his character was the mixture of superstition with that profound faith which none could doubt who saw him pray next morning at the mass in his own little chapel.

"I have no piety," he once told Frank," that is, I have no attachment to the Church's practices, except sometimes Low Mass and always Benediction. But I have tremendous attachment to the Church." Yet I think the chapel was certainly the centre of his lovely, though highly inconvenient, medieval house. He had not even allowed his family to redecorate since his wife died in 1913. The lighting was still oil lamps, an open fireplace in the dining-room burnt logs, the cooking was done by coal. There was no telephone. "I made up my mind", he said once, "when I was in Parliament that if I had the telephone constituents and people would be ringing up all the time."

He had left the matter many years thereafter and I never remember a visit to Kingsland which passed without a frantic search for change that a member of the family or a guest might make some indispensable call from the public call-box nearby. But it was to the cottage next door that our Rosemary, on a visit to the Bellocs, was sent to telephone the doctor when the old man was found in the fireplace badly burnt in the July of 1953. He died a few days later.

In the Penguin collection of his essays made by J. B. Morton, in the memories of his friends, and above all in Robert Speaight's brilliant biography, Belloc still lives: all of us who knew him recognize the man we knew in the very accents of his voice, in all his strength and his weakness. Of all his works the essays are most like Belloc's conversation; and, rereading at the same time several of Chesterton's, I felt anew how mythical was that animal the Chesterbelloc.

Belloc himself did not realize it—for he sincerely thought what he once told my husband, that Chesterton had got most of his ideas from him. It may be noted that in his little book on his friend it is not his thinking but his astonishing power of analogy or "parallelism" that is warmly praised. I would myself say that Belloc did not understand the deepest—the metaphysical—side of Chesterton's mind. But even those who judge otherwise would agree that their approach was totally different; each had strength in a field where the other was weakest.

As talkers they were equally brilliant, surpassing any I have ever known—and I have listened to some of the best performers in an art that is always dying out. Even in this their style was different. Charles Somers Cocks told me that he had often met them together and that Chesterton had hardly talked at all. I think he preferred to listen if the other talker was worth listening to—which Belloc most certainly was. One could joyfully have listened for hours to the brilliant monologue: it was even better than reading *The Path to Rome* or *The Cruise of the Nona*. Belloc indeed could listen too, and the friends were linked by an immense gaiety and humour. There was, one knew, deep sadness in Belloc but it never spoilt a conversation; it was kept for those moments of intimacy to which it properly belonged.

But while Belloc usually gave others their fair share, Chesterton almost created that share. Every one of us became brilliant as he lifted our poor little thoughts into an air of glory in which they shone refulgent.

The Path to Rome and *The Cruise of the Nona* express a side of Belloc altogether outside Chesterton's powers. Belloc was a man of far wider experience than his friend. He belonged to two countries, he possessed Europe in the most significant way of a man who had covered large parts of it on foot. He had in the same way learnt to know California, which always remained for him a kind of earthly paradise. There is, I fancy, no historian who, as fully as Belloc, has mastered geography as "the eye of history". In this was the supreme excellence of that stunning book (I use the word with no slang meaning) *The Campaign of 1812*.

In *The Ballad of the White Horse* Chesterton has the right wing of one army facing the right wing of the other. His sense of time and place, his descriptions of the things around him with their violent colours and intensities, are elements in a vision, not something another man could see. Belloc too has visions, but they are set in a recognizable landscape. After reading him you could almost swear that you had *seen* the defeat of the Grand Army, the bitter retreat, the deaths in the snow. He had prepared us for Paris on our honeymoon and each little essay—"On the Inn of the Margeride", "On Trèves", even "On the Mowing of a Field", takes you right into the hills, the cathedral or the Sussex air. You are *there*, seeing more than you would see without your guide, disputing perhaps his conclusions but learning from them too. His is an objective world, almost laid out with a theodolite, illuminated but solid. Chesterton's lanes and trees, his station-lamps and peacocks on a suburban lawn, are part of fairyland; beware of wandering there too long, or like the man himself you will begin to get into the wrong trains and arrive in the wrong places—perhaps without his magic power of discovering that they are indeed the right places after all.

With people, however, the role of these two men is reversed—here Belloc sees with the imagination while Chesterton looks at what is—even should he sometimes magnify men's splendid virtues. The two men each wrote an essay showing the essence of the difference—and again it was a reflection of something I had noted in real life. Both of them, staying in country houses, had their pockets turned out, their clothes brushed, by a footman. Chesterton gives a line or two to the topic and smiles as he describes the sordid contents of his own pockets and contrasts them with the "jewelled trifles" that might have been found in the pockets of the rich. For Chesterton the experience was highly diverting. For Belloc it was humiliating. He wrote a whole essay on "The Servants of the Rich", whose pleasure it was "to forget every human bond and to cast down the nobler things in man: treating the artist as dirt and the poet as a clown"; and he depicts as writhing in the flames of hell "the men who in their mortal life opened the doors of the great Houses and drove the carriages and sneered at the unhappy guests".

I may be told that this essay is sheer irony—but there is too much emotion here for irony. And I remember my sister telling me how Belloc, staying in her house, terrified a timid footman (as he had terrified our little cook) by the vehemence of his refusal to let his clothes be brushed.

The little cook, by the way, is classed among those who, "debarred by their insolent superiors from approaching the guests... neither wound them with contemptuous looks nor follow these up by brigandish demands for money." They will never be seen in the "Pit of Fire. For them is reserved a high place in Paradise."

All this is every bit as notional as a landscape by Chesterton—and if there is irony in the matter it lies in the footman terrified by the man who assumed himself to be at the receiving end of a sneer. Chesterton was incapable of seeing a sneer at himself even had it existed; his interest in people was equal and constant; he had no distorting mirror of self-consciousness in the mind. Once in my girlhood when he was staying with us, our German cook, burning with curiosity to see him, came up to him, "with what looked like a laundry list" in her hands. She started in surprise and affected (he said) to have mistaken him for my mother. His interest lay in the cook and the comic element in their encounter, not in what the cook was thinking of him.

I suppose it is hard for people who did not know him to believe in Chesterton's total indifference about his own work or his career. He would, for example, treat his essays as ephemeral journalism to the point of putting in allusions that would amuse his readers of that day, light the next day's fire and be ash thereafter. Yet these allusions might well surround ideas that any other man would have set carefully in silver, if not in gold, for posterity. Dan Walsh, Professor of Philosophy at Manhattanville College, once asked him, "Which do you regard as your most important book?" To which he said, "I don't regard any of my books as important."

Again, I can only say that not to Dr. Walsh alone but to all who knew him these words carry the accent of a simple sincerity.

Both Belloc and Chesterton were obliged to give much (in Belloc's case most) of their attention to earning a living. Belloc often and often lamented this, talking of himself as a "hack" journalist, blaming for it that absence of references which would double the time spent on a book but win the respect of experts. He once mentioned in conversation that the Black Death had changed the language of the English upper class.

> Before that the rich had their children brought up by tutors. After it, they had to have them brought up by servants, who knew nothing but English. There are a lot of things I know of this sort, and I should like to write them down. But I am so set in the habit of writing for money that I cannot write otherwise. So these things will never be written.

One thing, however, he would never write for money, he *could* never write for money—his poetry. For Belloc was a very great poet. Had he given himself wholly to poetry he would, I believe, have ranked almost with Gerard Manley Hopkins.

Setting aside poetry and pot-boiling, this question of a career depended chiefly on what both men cared for most. And Belloc has put this for them both in one verse:

> From quiet homes and first beginning,
> Out to the undiscovered ends,
> There's nothing worth the wear of winning,
> But laughter and the love of friends.

As fate willed, Belloc's earliest friends were in a very different world from Chesterton's; so that friendship, which most certainly meant more to him than his literary career, became a kind of career in itself—a little like a brilliant debutante whose fun with the crowd turns into the chance of conquering London.

Despite butlers, gamekeepers, footmen, Belloc loved to stay in the "Great Houses" where he was, it seems, subjected to such strange misery. He has often been called a snob and he loved to talk of "The Rich". "I couldn't live without them", he often said. And at least once I have heard him add, "I should perish miserably". Yet he was certainly prepared to abuse them as a class—and did so constantly, both in poems and in conversation. Belloc was certainly no sycophant. A friend of his once told me he was an "inverted snob" because of his perpetual abuse of two things: the rich as a class, and the Howards as a clan.

There really was an ambivalence in his attitude which partly came from a literary inclination to generalize, partly from the fact that he had many friends among both the rich and the aristocracy and also certain pet hates. A cousin of mine in the First World War complained bitterly that she could never mention her mother (who had a title) without being thought a snob, while her fellow V.A.D.s talked all the time about theirs. With some of Belloc's critics this attitude must be taken into account, but even so the subject loomed overlarge in his mind and it is interesting to see if one can trace this fact in part from his experiences.

He was certainly a man who had been hurt: he was also a man so madly sensitive that the normal hurts we all meet as life goes on its way took for him gigantic proportions. And his powerful imagination would draw pictures of a life without any hurt in a non-existent and impossible land. California was the chief site of this day-dreaming. But I have known hurt feelings and unhappy lives even in California.

I have spoken of Belloc's friendship with Uncle James and his youthful romantic love for Aunt Minna. Every year at the Oratory School these two boys won all the prizes; many holidays were spent by Belloc at Heron's Ghyll, a country house near the Sussex downs whither my great-grandmother had moved with her children and her grandchildren after Uncle Henry married. James, as the only boy at home, was much considered by his sisters and was idolized by Aunt Mary. Even if Aunt Philippa disapproved, any friend of James was sure of an enthusiastic reception.

When I first read *Belinda*, I felt that with all its conscious and deliberate absurdity there was a reflection of Belloc's first romance as the two young lovers meet near the stream and become aware of feelings too profound to analyse.

Minna, however, was very unlike Belinda—there was no submissiveness in her character, she was daring and unconventional. She would—a comic instance—drive alone in a hansom cab, which no young lady at that date was supposed to do. She was also very pretty, attractive to men, intelligent, and as fashionable as the rather rigid standards of her grandmother permitted. She must have been very good fun and I (who only knew her so much later) can imagine her in that aspect more easily than as the heroine of a romance. Surely as these boys and girls made holiday in this Sussex countryside they are the group whom Belloc dreams of in "The Fire".

We rode together all in pride
They laughing in their riding gowns
We young men laughing at their side.
We charged at will across the downs

We were companions. We were young.
We were immortal—so we said . . .
For that which in the heart was sung
Could have no commerce with the Dead.

I wonder what happened next and I only wish I had wondered early enough to ask the questions which might enable me to piece together the whole story. It is my impression that only Belloc himself took this first romance of his seriously—with that tragic solemnity with which a boy does see first love. Seven years is a big gap—sixteen to twenty-three—twenty to twenty-seven. Minna had many admirers, Belloc much else to fill his mind and presently his heart. So it may well have died a natural death, even while leaving behind something that never did quite die.

James Hope went to Oxford, Belloc to California and to his military service in France; there was a gap before the established undergraduate at Christ Church met again the freshman at Balliol. The friendship continued, but was it still as close? The only part of the story I do know seems to show that it was. For after Uncle James' marriage to Mabel Riddell, Belloc one day turned up at Heron's Ghyll at the end of a walking tour, expecting but not receiving the old welcome. Gilbert Chesterton's description of Belloc's arrival on a similar occasion at Rye, where Henry James was living, probably fits this one well enough. He was with a Foreign-Office friend. Unshaven, unwashed, tired but hilarious, they seem to have startled the academic American. Belloc certainly startled the conventional Englishwoman Uncle James had married. He got a cold reception—how cold I can easily measure, for I myself did not fit well enough into the mould to be acceptable. I remember two phrases repeated back to me after my sister had become established as my aunt's favourite for parties and cricket weeks: "Maisie has chosen her own line." "She has made her own friends."

Yet I, even if untidy, had never walked in uninvited and unwashed—and I was a relative. Belloc was never again invited to

Heron's Ghyll—and quite certainly never came again without invitation. When Aunt Minna, after all her years in foreign parts (Athens, Peking, Petersburg, Constantinople), came to live in London he often saw her; and my mother remained his friend. But a sort of nervous irritation about the family seemed to take possession of him for which I cannot fully account. The Oratory was run, he told my husband, "as an appanage of the Duke of Norfolk". It was all he seemed to want to speak of about his old school! But when pressed he remembered Newman as exercising an influence on the boys' classical studies. "He knew his Plautus."

As to his school life as a whole, Belloc most certainly fell into the category of those to whom the university means far more than the school had ever meant. In this matter men are sharply divided. And if one did not know it from his talk one could learn it, like all the deepest truths about Belloc, from his verse. Writing poetry he could only tell truth, and writing poetry he was often tempted into telling more of the truth than perhaps he realized. But about Oxford he told it with all his heart—or rather about his College, for, as with most men whose fullest life is lived there, it is the College, not the collection of colleges, which wins their loyalty.

> Balliol made me, Balliol fed me
>   Whatever I had she gave me again
> And the best of Balliol loved and led me,
>   God be with you, Balliol men.

"The best of Balliol", felt Professor Barker, who was there at the time, did mean for Belloc the most aristocratic. But I think one reason, as Robert Speaight so well notes, is that at that period men of the upper class had in their youth wider opportunities of experience. If they came, as well, from intellectual families, they would have learnt to cultivate conversation and would have tended to appreciate a man so gifted in the art. On his side Belloc, overaware of what he believed to be three counts against him—religion, nationality, class—rejoiced in a group which actually liked men to be different. This is one of the greatest changes between the public-school boy and the Oxford man, and it is, I think, most prominent in this particular world.

Later Belloc would analyse, would over-emphasize. Perhaps at the time, despite all his subtleties, he was simply happy. "I understand English gentlemen," he once said to me. "I could have been one." I said, "Oh no you couldn't, you're much too French".

This analysing, which made me foolishly uncomfortable, was one of the most French elements in him—but the man who was a chief poet of Sussex and often thought of himself as a Sussex farmer was not as concerned as all that about the Frenchness. When in his old age he went over and over the same ground, chewing, as Ronnie Knox has put it, "the cud of earlier meditations", it was the word I had avoided which he emphasized. He said to Frank:

> I have lived all my life on the fringe of the upper class. But I have never belonged to it. I decided not to marry into it. There were a couple of occasions when I might have, as was bound to happen with young people who are seeing each other all the time. I should probably have been very happy. The upper classes are extraordinarily nice people.

Even at Oxford the end was anything but peace. No friend of Belloc's but has heard him tell repeatedly the story of how Balliol refused him a fellowship. "When it was decided that I should not live", was his favourite description of not getting the £200 a year which was all it meant. And for how many months would he have stood a life only delightful in youth because it is lived together by gay contemporaries?

It was during his years at Balliol that Belloc made his lifelong friendships.

> The only brothers ever I knew
> The men that laughed and quarrelled with me.

Out of all this tangle of events and personalities came the man I knew, the man whose complexities and simplicities fascinated me, the man who could write both "The Rebel" and "The Fire".

In "The Rebel," he depicts himself engaged in a fierce onslaught arising from a "great anger" against men and women living behind some evil wall. He will kill them all, batter their carven names, slit their pictures

> And melt the gold their women wore,
> And hack their horses at the knees,
> And hew to death their timber trees,

And plough their gardens deep and through—
And all these things I mean to do
For fear perhaps my little son
Should break his hands as I have done.

In a very different mood we have the nostalgia of "The Fire". Looking back on that ride he sees "extinction of the flame", whether it was of love or of friendship. He feels ghosts around him as he sits before the fire of his good oak. He sees the flower of his desire withered unfruiting. And he prays in an hour when he has glimpsed the need of another world to perfect the imperfection of earth:

Absolve me God that in the land
Which I can nor regard nor know
Nor think about nor understand,
The flower of my desire shall blow.

27

PUBLISHING AND SUCH

A BACKGROUND for some of our travelling was one of those acts of folly into which we have always been too easily betrayed: Louise Wijnhausen, now the efficient manager of our New York office, had come to us during the War, having narrowly escaped the Nazis and having previously had a small publishing house of her own in Bruges. Longing after the War to go back, she had persuaded us to open a branch of Sheed and Ward in Brussels with her as manager. A good start was made—and I found it great fun staying with her there. But the New York office needed her, and we were never happy with her successor, a Fleming whose French was not much better than ours and who would lapse into Flemish or into silence at crucial moments of our discussions. His real wish was to run a business of his own—and ultimately we let it go without reluctance. It was typical of an element in us both which I sometimes look at with cold despair. We always have too much to do, we can never refuse to do just one thing more.

It was more amazing in Frank than in me, for his job of editing was a gigantic one. Ronnie Knox said to me (of his own *Slow Motion* books), "I give Frank a mass of untidy notes. He says 'Hey Presto' over them and they turn into a best seller." These notes would be various versions of the same sermons to be conflated, the best pages of each to be used, the best illustrations from each version. (Though alas, Ronnie was adamant against the printing of some of his most exquisitely amusing passages.) But it takes more time and energy than just saying, "Hey Presto."

What with moves from house to house, the Blitz in London and a fire in our New York office, I cannot lay my hands on more than a fraction of the letters that Frank and I had from Ronnie. But there are several at the period of the *Slow Motion* books. Until they appeared his best sellers had been his novels, but with *The Mass in Slow Motion* it became literally true that a work of spirituality was selling better than fiction. In reply to the information that the book was having big sales, he sent a postcard with the words "Sauline I take it, not Davidic." And Frank replied, "Just passing from the Sauline into the Davidic" (for "Saul had slain his thousands but David his tens of thousands").

Letters are addressed, now to me, now to Frank, whose state of perpetual motion is frequently reflected. Sending on a request for translation rights, Ronnie says: "I imagine F.J.S. is on the high seas as usual; the Christmas party on the liner could hardly get on without him. If you had his ear I would be by way of acknowledging a letter from him."

"You were nearly right", Frank answered, explaining that he had in fact just arrived home. "But I have given up the high seas in favour of the still higher air."

"Gerry Ann tells me", Ronnie writes later, "you are going to live in the U.S.A. and only come to England as a visitor. You never owned up about this. But I don't really mind, because I think your visits are longer than your stays at home." Gerry Ann Cunningham (now Elwes) was a close friend of Rosemary and later her bridesmaid. To her was dedicated the third *Slow Motion* book, the first two having been dedicated to the two McCaskey sisters. These dedications were, Ronnie wrote of one of them, "Very Important".

You do meet friends oftener when visiting a country than when living in it, because you know you will only meet if you plan it, and planning in such busy lives as both Ronnie's and ours was not easy. There are postcards from him expending prodigies of skill on railway guides resulting in meetings in the unlikeliest places. One of these had been Banbury, and Ronnie writes: "When I was giving a Day of Recollection at Kensington Square a Pocket Edition of Maisie stopped me in the porch and told me you were on your way back to England. Which makes me wonder if it is not time the Council of Banbury resumed its sessions, not necessarily *in situ*."

The "Council" concerned at the moment a title for the sermons on the Creed which were to follow those on the Mass—an anguish-making question for both author and publisher. The title of a book can affect sales to a surprising extent, yet no one can lay his finger on just what it is that produces the effect. The title must be arresting but must also give some idea of what the book is about. Even this has its difficulties, as every reader's mind offers its own interpretation. Chesterton's *The Man Who Was Thursday* was ordered as *The Man Who Was Thirsty*. Frank's *Communism and Man* was seized in Japan as Communist propaganda, while his translation of St. Augustine's best-known book is occasionally ordered as Sheed's *Confessions. The Mass in Slow Motion* was now being bought by some under the impression that it was written to stir the proletariat into more rapid revolt.

Setting aside such oddities, the search for a title still tends to be a matter of trial and error if not of sheer guesswork. Ronnie called us both into council:

> About the Credo sermons—"Close ups of the Creed" would be an accurate title, but it is a little too Martindalian, don't you think? It has occurred to me that "Believing is Seeing", would make rather a good title, but perhaps not for this book? Perhaps something like "The Creed for Beginners", or "The Creed Decoded"—no. I think you'd better invent a title. Did you hear that Evelyn stigmatized "Let Dons Delight" as an obvious publisher's name? And I was so proud of it.
>
> We are reading the *Priest Worker*[1] in the refectory here. Did the Pocket Edition do it all by herself? It's such splendidly untranslationlike translation—and God knows by now, nobody is more translation conscious than I am.

A week later he wrote:

> If the M. in S.M. is going well, all the more reason for the Creed book to have a similar title. But I think that C. in S.M. is too similar. Creed in 3 Dimensions? A bit too long for a title, perhaps "The Creed in Perspective"? Or is that too dull sounding? I want to give the impression that the book is (I hope) different from the rather Euclidean apologetic on which the young are customarily fed. I wish you could think of something better. "The Creed Flood-lit"? (Or by floodlight?)—alternatively, some reference to Math xiii. 52, "The Treasure Room (I wish I dared to say the Lumber-room) explored"? Do *think* and make Maisie think.

Frank felt the similarity was a positive advantage but this title not quite apt for the Creed. "The Mass is an act, and motion goes with act. But the Creed is an affirmation and motion does not belong to the idea in the same way." But the "slow-motion" idea won the day

[1] *Priest Worker in Germany* by Henry Perrin, S. J. Rosemary was the "Pocket Edition" and this was her first translation.

on the suggestion from me that a brilliant and successful title can in effect be copyrighted by the author if he uses it again quickly enough.

Gilbert Chesterton described my father as having a mind strongly co-operative with the minds of others. This is equally true of my husband, but nothing can put so great strain on this quality as the relation between author and publisher. Fortunately, although himself imperturbable under criticism, Frank has experienced through me the sensitivity of the normal author. Co-operation must include criticism, and my tears of rage as I grudgingly agree to excisions and alterations, which are often developments and improvements, become a useful guide to the feelings of other writers. It is interesting that the most distinguished authors react in the most urbane manner. Three times Edward Watkin made warm acknowledgement in his preface to the help given him by Frank, three times Frank deleted this, saying that what he had done was the mere commonplace of a publisher's job.

Caryll Houselander accepted suggestions even with enthusiasm and she (like myself when rage gives place to sanity) always went forward to the completion of a better book. Suggestions are part of the raw material, they do not diminish but increase creative power. Frank's mind was constantly on publications, present, oncoming and possible. "I have pulled three books out of the air", says one of his letters. Spring and autumn lists must be made up, thought given to gaps, advice to the authors who ask, "What shall I write next?" Between the author and the publisher as they talk, a flame will often kindle—this is what being a good publisher means. This and caring for your author's books as much as for your own, or more. But both offices were always demanding another book from him; unlike my own ups and downs they are invariably best sellers.

Frank discovered at this time a new mode of creating a book which I watched with fascination. In *The Mary Book* and *The Book of the Saviour* great portraits emerged of Our Lord and of His Mother drawn chiefly from our own publications: theology, devotion, liturgy, poetry.

I had never seen my husband so excited, so carried out of himself. This was no mere anthology. I realized suddenly that he was truly *writing* this new book, though in a different fashion from *Theology and Sanity*; not with words but with prose passages and poems, each excellent in itself but each depending for its effect on how it was placed, what came before, what followed. With his own books he painted with a brush, these portraits were made in mosaic.

But we were both of us becoming increasingly aware of the inexorable quality of time. An entry in a short-lived journal (made at 5.30 a.m.), runs:

> It is the eve of the Assumption and our Novena begins. To know God's will and do it must be a safe prayer—and the first part should be fairly simple towards the end of life. But is God's will really to be found in the frightful frustration which seems today to preclude the use of the special talents God gave us—in the dissipation of energy that leaves one so worn out each evening? Yesterday Frank began to plan his book and went on to reading other people's with the realization that he badly needs a couple of months' solitude for his own. I did some housework, went shopping—and by the time I had dragged myself and my parcels home, was fit for no more serious mental effort than reading the Italian children's story . . . Anyhow, we worked all day at the sort of thing that makes you feel you are getting nothing done . . . if only we could get out of publishing and just write and lecture, how easy, as Frank says, our lives would be. Yet he has often said too that he would rather be conductor of an orchestra than first violin . . . So perhaps we ought not to get out of publishing!

As to the Guild, I had taken on since our return to England a training squad for young speakers. Listening to one beginner after another can be boring, but it is fascinating to watch them each gradually developing his own line, becoming himself. All needed more knowledge of Scripture and we decided to start a series of lectures on the Gospels, Acts and Epistles, work on which led me to my own next book: a popularization which might help our speakers. Two things were needed: a picture of the people and places in Our Lord's life and in the Church's beginnings; and a guide to the background of archaeology, history (especially Old-Testament), documents, and the language of the New Testament (William Barclay's *Word-Book* was a great help).

I felt deeply my own inadequacy. My equipment consisted of close textual knowledge of the Gospels and Acts, which I had learnt by heart at school, a near-verbal knowledge of the Epistles, and a pretty thorough understanding of the mind of the crowd whom we were to interest and whose questions we must needs answer. Also I was going to have an unusual amount of time, for we planned, after Rosemary's marriage, a journey to Australia. Yet I would probably have abandoned the idea but for the encouragement given me by Fr. Alexander Jones, whom I met first in New York in the autumn of 1953. He invited me to come later to Upholland, where he was Scripture Professor, giving me at the same time advice on preliminary reading.

On our journey I would reread the Old Testament and quite a few French paper-bound volumes. (We always tend to carry a library rather than much in the way of clothes.) From Australia we would go on to Palestine and the reading would help me to get the utmost out of this immense experience. Going on to Athens, we would walk, too, in the footsteps of St. Paul.

Our lives were setting towards change. Wilfrid, finishing Oxford, had asked Frank to let him have a year in Australia before deciding on his future. Rosemary would soon be married and Oakwood Court would become absurdly too large. We should leave it with regret—and our friends would regret it also. "None but a heart of stone", said Tony Coburn, an Australian and a Guildsman, "could fail to mourn the passing of Oakwood."

We went out with a bang. Rosemary and Neil wanted a quiet wedding, so we planned a series of parties on the preceding days. Big as the flat was, it could not accommodate all our friends at once. Kind neighbours allowed us to spread the many presents in the flat beneath us. Fr. Bevan married them and we got permission for a full dialogue Mass from the Cardinal. The Guild can dialogue with a will: as it was Easter Week, we had the Gloria and the Creed.

Fr. Healy led the dialogue from the sanctuary. What pleased me most was Robert Speaight's comment, "This is the most religious wedding I was ever at."

Rosemary and Neil were touring the countryside in search of a home, when one day, visiting the farm, I was driving with Mr. Zaleski past the pre-Reformation church of Runwell St. Mary's. I suddenly cried "Stop!" Next to the church was a large board, "For Sale", in a lovely garden which surrounded a solid-looking, well-built house with thatched barn, kitchen garden and meadow.

"It is too big for Mrs. Rosemary", said Mr. Zaleski, but when Frank and I started that summer for a tour centred on Australia but including Athens and the Holy Land, we left the Middletons negotiating for the purchase of Ilgaro.

28

DISCOVERING THE PACIFIC

We lectured across the States and then took a plane from Los Angeles to Honolulu, where we stayed with Jean and Zohmah Charlot. Both town and university boasted of fine murals painted by Jean, illustrating the history of Hawaii. The interracial groups to which we were introduced were enchantment: eating in a Japanese restaurant and discussing the Catholic world with Chinese, Hawaiians, French, Americans, Japanese and other Asians. In the Charlot world at least—and this was our general impression of Hawaii—the ideal was fulfilled of bypassing racial differences, or rather, of making them complementary instead of divisive. On a later visit we saw churches in the smaller island of Kauai, built by the congregation, adorned by artists of many races.

We flew on to New Zealand, only pausing for an hour or so on a small island in the Pacific (how lovely those islands were, looked down on from the plane!) and again descending to draw a very hot breath in Fiji. We arrived in a cold New Zealand winter, to be met at the airport by Fr. (now Bishop) Delargey, who devoted several days to showing us the North Island. We spent only a week there, lecturing in Auckland and Hamilton and absorbing a confused mass of impressions: that a Maori woman, rather specially gracious and well poised, took the chair at my speech to the Catholic women of Auckland; that the bubbling sulphur pools we looked at were horribly dangerous and had sucked in people walking carelessly near them; that a priest we visited had built a pool for perpetually warm water in his yard and had fixed up a hotter spring for his housekeeper to use as an auxiliary stove; that there were glorious lakes and other splendours of scenery; that our host was intensely alive to the needs and possibilities of the Church in New Zealand and elsewhere.

But Frank was longing for his own country, which he had not visited for ten years and where he would find a multitude of cousins as close to him in boyhood as sisters and brothers. So on we flew and landed amid a vast crowd of them at Sydney Airport. This was in 1954. And we did it all over again in 1958, the only difference being that it was by way of the South Island of New Zealand and the kindness of Fr. Curnow that we came to Sydney.

I am often asked whether Australians are not very like Americans. My instant reaction is a denial. Then who are they like—*surely* not English? Canadians? I find it hard to answer, find it hard even to say what my first impressions of Australia were, what my later impressions became. For I had lived with Australia already for more than a quarter of a century by living with an Australian—and one more apt than most to insist on his nationality. It is a point on which they are very unselfconscious. Only being away from his own land makes an Australian think about what he is. And only once have I been asked the question, "What do you think of our country?"

Many Australians have a nostalgia for the unknown England, Ireland or (especially) Scotland whence their parents or grandparents came, about which they have read so much, whose songs they sing. They talk of "going home"—until they get to the other side and quickly discover that home is what they left behind them. Yet there is a kinship: Australia was settled so recently that the links are not all broken. As to resemblance, an interesting view was put forward lately by an Australian speaking on the B.B.C. He described an elderly Englishman with whom he had formed a friendship: independent, self-opinionated, full of drive. "This," he said in effect, "is the sort of Englishman you used to be: today he is called an eccentric. When you come out to us now, you expect the Government to do for you what the Australian still knows he should do for himself. You have lost or are losing what once was the British character—we still have it. We are what you used to be." This could bear meditating on—but to me the Australian seems just himself, and the New Australian fast becomes part of something as much *sui generis* as any nation which kept its nineteenth centenary when Australia was celebrating her first.

Bush, sea and sky. Sydney is a large town but it is in this framework that one thinks and dreams of it. The multitude of bays, with beaches where Frank grew up surfing, were already a picture in my mind, though not one half as beautiful as the reality. How he despised the famous Waikiki Beach, how inferior he felt the surfing on boards practised there to riding the waves with nothing between you and them. An Australian boy grows up knowing about sharks in the sea and how to cope with snakes in the bush. Frank claims to have fallen off more horses than most English boys have seen. A townee by birth, an intellectual by nature and education, he had learnt as a matter of course to sling a hammock, pitch a tent, build a fire, and on it boil a billycan and cook chops and sausages.

We went out with his cousin Alan Stafford, then head of the Australian Institute of Architects, to the little farm where a few head of cattle can be safely left for days on end. The law against moving cattle except by day (passed to guard against thieving under night's cover) plus friendly neighbours made it possible for Alan and his wife Betty to handle the farm mainly at weekends, keeping their more central home in the city for business days. With them we picnicked among the gum trees and explored the wide stretches of surrounding country.

We stayed with other cousins in a country village close to their son's farm. He had built a dam harnessing the stream that ran through his fields to the purposes of irrigation and grew early vegetables for the Sydney market. Other friends flew into Sydney from their stations (ranches) of tens of thousands of sheep.

Two hours in a train took us into the Blue Mountains, where we could walk endlessly in some of the most magnificent scenery I have ever seen. The theory is that the unique blue of these mountains comes from a haze thrown off by the eucalyptus (called gum trees throughout Australia). National parks are hardly needed in this country for the benefit of the population, but are highly necessary for the wild life near the large cities. In one we saw, feeding on the leaves of the special gum tree which alone they eat, little koala bears, blinking in their usual semi-drunken way (another effect, I was told, of the eucalyptus). Their numbers are growing here once more after hunters had nearly annihilated them. Wallabies, so frequently confounded with kangaroos, were leaping about with ungainly gracefulness; the place was a zoo for the salvation of animal Australia.

All this, of course, is near the cities; we did not get far into what Australians call "the backblocks". Frank had too many relatives to see, too little time to spare. But even so the atmosphere of sea, sky, bush was amazingly pervasive. Far more than in Canada or the States, it is part of the world of every Australian. We stayed with the Brennans on a "farm" which was chiefly trees, two hours' drive from Melbourne. Their three-year-old boy was causing disquiet by his determination to get lost in the bush which covered most of their 200 or so acres. We met English settlers who were suffering agony over the danger of even an Australian suburb. They seemed curiously less conscious of the delight of picking peaches and grapes in your own small back yard, or of orchids growing like weeds, than of the drawback of snakes and ticks.

This background gives the special character so well analysed by Sir Denis Brogan in an article in *Harper's*—"Australia, the Innocent Continent". I am not sure that "innocent" is the precise word—but the picture in the article of that elusive thing, a national character, could not be bettered. He notes how the trouble-giving youth common to every country—then called in Australia "bodgies and widgies"—are not on the same scale of evil as in the older countries, how the air-minded Australian does not care a straw what old and shabby luggage he takes on his journeys, how careless of class distinctions and of fashions is the average Australian woman compared with her American and English sisters.

My own view became increasingly that the reason for all this is that a far greater proportion of Australians, even in urban areas, remain in close contact with life than do most other Western peoples. Amost all the town-dwellers known to me have relatives on stations and farms whom they visit frequently, all of them know the bush, which is so near their doors, snakes and wild animals are near also, bush fires sweeping the land are something to be reckoned with. Sir Denis warns of the danger that our more totally urbanised and parasitic life may be creeping into this land, also, but he sees it as still relatively free from our false scale of values.

I noted on my own visits how hardy even the town-dweller is against the extremes of weather. I was never colder than in the unprovided-for winter. I was not there in the summer heats but I knew how many houses lacked frigidaires, how many even on the city outskirts still depended on Elsans and a sewage cart, or on a cesspool.

"Huge flies", Wilfrid wrote from a friend's house, "are lounging across the kitchen table"—for there were no screens to the windows. He declared after a year in Australia that this, the most delightful of all the countries he had ever known, was also the most indifferent to comfort. But not to sport, to enjoyment of life. If an Australian goes on strike it will tend to be, not for more money, but for more leisure. Leisure to play cricket and tennis, to swim and surf, to shoot and fish, even to read. For Australians are great readers, as every publisher knows, and as I certainly discovered on these visits. On each of them I was doing a job of work for which I needed unusual books, and these books I could always borrow from my friends or from the library of the local seminary.

Perhaps the immense amount of meat he eats, beginning with chops or steak for breakfast, helps to produce the vitality which the Australian pours into his living—though not always into his work! On my first visit I felt that, inured though one should be by England, I had never met such awful cooking as in Australian hotels. And one was expected to have *finished* dinner by 7 p.m. In many hotels nothing was served later. But on my second visit the influence of the "New Australians" was perceptible: so many of them are Italians, and Italians have other ideas of cooking than the mere application of heat to raw material. All around Sydney had sprung up excellent little restaurants, remaining open reasonably late, serving well-chosen wines. Like California, Australia has first-class wines as well as very bad ones. New Australians know the difference better than the old ones do. And New Australians are also building their own houses, clearing large areas of bush and bringing it into cultivation. The country has made an amazingly good job of assimilating the huge numbers who have come in since World War II.

Visiting so many Catholic friends, we became specially conscious of the Italian settlers—so pleasantly sketched in a local best-seller, *They're a Weird Mob*. The title was aimed not at the Italians but at the men of Sydney—one of whom was, we learned, the pseudonymous author—into whose midst the Italians had come. Like a revue we saw in Sydney, the humour was too local to win world fame, but both were sparks of the intellectual vitality which is as obvious as the physical in the Australia of today. It is noteworthy that in one year London was hailing as the best play running *The Summer of the Seventeenth Doll*, as the best movie Darcy Niland's *Shiralee* (*Jeddah* was also receiving high praise) and as the best novel Patrick White's *Voss*. Since then Patrick White has written the much more remarkable *Riders in the Chariot*, Morris West has written *The Devil's Advocate*, and anyone following the reviews in the London papers becomes aware almost month by month of emergent Australian talent. Some of it the reviewers call raw and rough—some is obviously immensely finished and sophisticated. One may quarrel with the picture in places—I think myself Ruth Park, the brilliant New Zealander married to Darcy Niland, gives a truer idea than Patrick White of the ordinary "Aussie". There are, too, the detective stories of Arthur Upfield though he, like Ruth Park and Nevil Shute, is Australian only by adoption. *Riders in the Chariot* is a work of genius but much of it could be situated in almost any country.

And yet, I wonder: Is White perhaps reading his countrymen a valuable—it is certainly a powerful—lesson? In *A Town Like Alice* Nevile Shute idealizes the more comfortable, more "civilized" life of a town with cinemas, beauty parlours, all the things that over-much leisure has created, all the things for which a woman on a station must at times long (when she has time for longings); in *Riders in the Chariot* Patrick White depicts a terrible underlying corruption, a loss of the power in these suburbanites, especially the women, to realize greatness—whether expressed in the painting of the young aboriginal, the religion of the Jewish exile, or the grand simplicity of the two women who kneel by his bed at the end. It is interesting that, both for him in this book and for Morris West in *The Devil's Advocate*, religion becomes the supreme interest, and that on the dying Jew Patrick White sees marked the sign of the cross to which a Jew has been nailed by evil Christians.

No one looking at Australia today can fail to be astonished by all this literature—to say nothing of the art and music—coming from so small a community.

I nearly wrote "so small a country"—but of course the country is vast, and we flew from end to end of it. The Catholic proportion is large, mostly of Irish descent, about a quarter of the whole. While we were there the political-religious row was beginning that centred in Melbourne. Bob Santamaria, a leader in Catholic Action, started a movement against Communist infiltration into the Labour Party which ended by splitting the party from top to bottom. It has never fully recovered. Catholic opinion was deeply divided, the old and mighty Archbishop Mannix of Melbourne backing Santamaria to the hilt, Cardinal Gilroy of Sydney manifestly disapproving of politics being thus linked—as it definitely was—with Catholic Action. The outsider would be foolish to form a judgement on what must be a superficial knowledge, but it was fascinating to listen to the arguments going on around me. My only regret was that all this energy was not being poured into its other possible channel—few books were appearing that would do for religion what so many books were doing for human living. Archbishop Mannix was an extraordinarily impressive figure, already more than ninety, emaciated, almost ethereal, immensely dignified, hardly eating, motionless and long silent but with a dry wit occasionally flashing out. Startled one day by a rather effervescent Monsignor, he exclaimed, "If that is a domestic prelate, God preserve us from a wild one."

We were told he still heard confessions every Saturday and was much loved by his people. But while Sydney had evening masses daily this was not allowed in Melbourne: the old idea prevailed that it was better for the laity to have it tough. They should get up early to go to Mass—think of all the miles their grandfathers had walked, this was too soft a generation.

Nor did I once discover the Dialogue Mass in Australia, although I believe on my second visit the Sydney diocese was about to start it. The Catholic Evidence Guild was functioning in both Melbourne and Sydney but was not really well supported in either city. I talked in the Domain at Sydney and immensely enjoyed it. The crowd stood happily under the huge Moreton Bay fig-tree which could shelter a couple of hundred. Heckling was intelligent, rougher than London, much rougher than New York, but they were a friendly lot.

Frank was to follow me on the platform and was standing in the crowd when a woman of aggressive aspect swung round to him and said, "*Now* will you admit that women are better than men!" To which he answered, "They make better wives." Actually, this has a certain relevance for a complete picture of the country. I have read wonderful books, some of them by women, have listened to broadcasts and seen on the cinema the working of a Bush School. Women who can endure to live on a station, women who handle the essential teaching, nursing, or the linking telephone exchange which so often saves lives and even sanity in cases of fire, lost children, stolen cattle, and all the other recurring emergencies, are of higher stature than most of us. But in Australia the national character is formed by the men to a greater extent than in any other country I know. I could find Australian women who dispute this—who quarrelled with me after a lecture for believing that the role of wife and mother was more important than that of a woman in public life. But they are the minority, and if one compares Australia under this aspect with the States, the difference is almost startling.

Probably it was a man who named a perfectly lovely blue flower "Patterson's Curse", because for a farmer it is an annoying weed, and another equally lovely pale yellow one a "Sour Sop". Only a man's country could have christened a bird whose song rivals the nightingale's a "Butcher Bird". This lack of poetry is shown supremely when Sydney's equivalent of the Golden Gate Bridge at San Francisco is called "the Coat Hanger".

I missed speaking on the Yarra bank in Melbourne owing to a sore throat. But my most fascinating experience was something endemic to Australia, though very new to me: the religion of the countryside. When staying with our friends on a farm or in a village, going to Mass on Sunday meant packing the whole family into a landrover and driving perhaps forty miles one week, ten or twenty another. A central church would be supplemented by cinemas or halls in the different parts of these vast parishes, the priest would arrive very early and confessions were heard for perhaps an hour before Mass began. At one cinema the box-office became an improvised confessional. A local group set up the altar with lights and flowers. Small children were taken out during the sermon, but the priest was merciful and usually made it brief. I longed especially on these occasions for a greater lay participation, but the sense was overwhelming of unity between priest and people, of the degree to which the Mass mattered that brought them such a distance; one felt like exclaiming with Newman, "This *is* a religion."

29

OLD THINGS AND NEW

WRITING of a long and varied life, the main problem is precisely what a lot there is of it. Time is a useful sieve: the memories of childhood and youth, filtered through it, are reduced to manageable proportions. But events whirling around, people at the door and on the telephone . . . An old age would be wonderful in which to sit and knit, dream of the past, perhaps write poetry about it. Or would it?

I have nothing new to tell about the marvels of Palestine or Greece—my own feelings as I made the Way of the Cross in Jerusalem or stood upon the Areopagus would not be worth recording; any little value in them went into *They Saw His Glory*, which immediately on my return I began to write at Upholland College. I had a wonderful month there, surrounded by Fr. Jones' Scripture library, helped by long conversations with him and other professors. The London Library, the New York Theological Seminary Library, furnished me with huge quarto volumes to take home and even larger books of reference in their reading rooms.

On our world tour I had carried out my resolution of reading the Old Testament again, and also books of modern scholarship picking up the patristic tradition. What helped me most towards vision were books of vision, but from sheerly learned books one gained an increasing understanding of the various elements in this Jewish library, bound in one volume, which my French authors often called "The Bible", not as including but as distinct from the New Testament. We had perhaps in my youth been taught to think too exclusively of Jewish history, poetry and prophecy *only* under the aspect of foreshadowing. I italicize the word "only" because with all that we have gained today from a greater penetration of the Jewish mind, of their manuscripts and their history, the Church's liturgy treats this aspect as supreme. Throughout the year we are invited to ponder on the flowering of the Old Testament in the New and on its relevance to the salvation of the whole human race. Whatever the writers had in mind of local and of temporary, the Holy Ghost directed these things to be written with a profounder meaning which our *Mater et Magistra*, the Church, would always safeguard for her children. Obviously this was also central for what I was attempting. I had to look at what my husband has called "the thrust of the Old Testament into the New", but the New was what I was studying.

The Middletons moved into their curiously named house in April 1955, and Frank and I began to be much in the small flat over the office. But I spent a good deal of time at Ilgars that year, especially while Frank was away, first helping with the move in bitter spring weather, and then returning in the summer when flowers and fruit trees filled a most lovely garden, rapidly, alas, becoming a wilderness.

Rosemary's beginnings in her own home were infinitely more difficult than mine had been. It was only later that she acquired the services of a "paragon": just now, with a baby on the way and very sick most of the time, she had still to do her cooking, washing and ironing, and despite a washing-machine this added up to a heavy day's work. A few hours' housework a week was all the help she had, and they had failed to find a gardener of any kind. I did what little I could to help her. I had begun in our new flat with the assumption, brought from Kensington, that a cleaning woman for this tiny place would be no problem—but I soon discovered that all around us were offices and office cleaners, who operated (rather loudly) from 6.30 to 8 a.m. and refused to clean anything except an office. But however spasmodic my cleaning arrangements, eating was no problem in London; we were surrounded by restaurants and pubs. Essex (or at any rate, Wickford) had no such facilities; to eat, you must cook.

"The true autobiography", writes George Cloyne in *The Times* weekly book page, "ought to be discursive: it ought to embrace the lights and the darkness of real life . . . a vital part of human experience never gets recorded by the prose autobiographer . . . he cannot effect those rapid changes of feeling, like cloudshapes melting into one another, by which the intensest, and thus most poetic of human instincts are conveyed." This is essentially the art of the poet, "who is put in the unique position of justifying his own existence simply by revealing himself as perfectly as possible". Wilfrid's wife put the position a little differently when telling me of recent happenings and resultant feelings: "Dear me, what a schizophrenic life we lead."

Next to the poet for conveying atmosphere comes perhaps the day-to-day record of a journal. My own short-lived one recreates these later years in which, even more than in my youth, an incredible variety in every crowded day does indeed bring impossibly rapid changes of feeling. Does such a life, one sometimes asks, make sense? Choose, wise guides say, between this and that; only a child of four could have said "I choose everything."

Yet how little choice seems, as one looks back, involved—what was chance, what was choice, what simply inevitable? In my Victorian childhood or rather my Edwardian youth, I kept an autograph book. Sir Mark Sykes wrote in it, from the wisdom of his Arabian friends, "What man can escape his fate?" But another inscription ran: "Dans la vie tout concourt et tout sert."

But what days those were, bringing the material which must somehow serve! The recurrent immense swing from unreasonable misery to a delight equally immeasurable came with Frank's departures and returns when he went alone to New York. I wrote in my journal, "*Partir, c'est mourir un peu*, and it gets no better after twenty-nine years of it." On a lesser arc, these swings of feeling are often many to the day. Going on to dinner after an outdoor meeting, I heard in a restaurant queue two Frenchmen talking: "C'est passionnant!" one said, to which the other replied, "C'est idiot!" It was no bad motto for one's feelings. Opening each morning a vast mail from England, the States, Australia, often of thrilling interest, often intensely demanding in the response that must be expressed, not just experienced. Sometimes plain boring, but these letters also must be answered. Losing everything that can be lost, wasting hours searching, finding, and rejoicing as at the discovery of treasure. Going from a fruitful vigorous discussion at one outdoor meeting to another so scant that it can hardly be called a meeting. Putting down an absorbing manuscript to wash up the breakfast things then rush to visit my farm—and enjoy Mr. Zaleski's conversation. The large white sows are "arrogant" and "capricious". "They move inattentively and crush their young." However, he hopes to sell "ten bacons" this month. We discuss Christmas poultry, "the turkeys they are very bad this year, the hatcheries have not yet supplied me". "The ducks are the most succulent of birds except perhaps the caponized cockerel. These are luxurious food but they are very good." He was hoping shortly, he went on, to jump to his aunt in London and would afterwards jump to me.

Back now to the family at Ilgars, laden with a "caponized cockerel", fruit, eggs, and vegetables, to bask in their society, do a little weeding and listen with displeasure to the rooks in the churchyard, who will certainly eat all their vegetables. On to Southend to deliver an indoor lecture there, next day to London: an assembly of nurses, Irish faces and voices, West Indians just beginning to appear, who so soon will be a flood . . . People coming unannounced at all hours for help about their faith, about a job, about "a personal problem" which too often means a money problem. The telephone ringing—or not ringing when its sound is vital if the five outdoor meetings of my Squad are each week to be adequately staffed. And trying between it all to get my own books written. If only each day were twice as long! If only I had four times as much energy!

A great deal of both, alas, are wasted on recreations pursued with a mad enthusiasm more proper to youth than to age. There are periodicals and newspapers, English, American and French—especially book reviews, and the fascinating correspondences that go on week by week and even month by month. There are detective stories, to be devoured by preference over lunch when alone, over wine in an armchair or with a final cup of coffee (added brandy is recommended) in bed. And this only too often means that early bed is not the same as early sleep—how can anyone shut the book without knowing who did it?

My short-lived journal does not touch the long periods when I too go to the States. These periods, while holding a strain and pressure of their own, do break that of England and render it endurable. But one often asks: How did we get like this?

Going to bed exhausted, I remember the words of Genesis, "The evening and the morning were the first day", were the second, were the third. Every morning brings with it peace and joy wrought above all by the Mass, that great prayer of the Mystical Body going on day and night all over the world, of which each morning I become newly aware.

I wrote in my journal:

"Prepare your hearts" says the prophet, and the psalms seem to answer in the words "I swept my spirit". One of the wonders of the early morning is freshness of spirit. The jaded weariness of evening gives place to hope. Faith feels more alive. The world has been swept after the night, the earth and trees have a new look and my spirit has been swept too for the new problems of a new day.

Impossible to judge of one's own books: I spent eight years reading for and writing those two little popularizations, *They Saw His Glory* and *Saints Who Made History*, called in England *Early Church Portrait Gallery*. Both seemed to do what I was aiming at: help people at the level of our C.E.G. speakers, bringing to them the fruit of a reading they could scarcely have undertaken.

It seems strange, looking back, that after Frank's mother died, Rosemary married and Wilfrid was launched on his own career, I did not take up again the reading for a volume on the older Newman. But in our lives of change, it is very difficult to pursue a work that involves reading documents in some given place. Only the loan of Fr. Tristram's copies of letters, and material lent by the Mozley family, enabled me to finish *Young Mr. Newman*. I have often asked myself whether these decisions were sensible. To be primarily a lecturer can be an enormous snag.

> Words die so soon when fit but to be said,
> Words only live when worthy to be read.

A reviewer of *Early Church Portrait Gallery* said that I should stand higher in the world of letters if I had stuck to the nineteenth century—Newman, my parents, G. K. Chesterton, Modernism and the Church in France and England. Perhaps. I am, of course, inside that period more than even a lifelong student of it can be inside a period centuries away. I entered the world of the early Church as the veriest amateur and was deeply aware of my inadequacy. But whatever the usefulness to others, the value of the reading was to me immense, deepening my understanding of the Faith and bringing to bear on life insights to be gained in no other way.

Each step of each book I tested on the street corner, talking of Matthew, Mark or Luke, describing the world of Ignatius, Irenaeus, Chrysostom, inviting questions which came in plenty, especially from the lively-minded Jews whether of London, New York or Sydney. Now the Dead Sea Scrolls were being talked about on the radio and therefore also in the Park. A phrase from Dupont-Sommer stuck in my head as typical of the approach of the learned non-Christian. Christianity, he was explaining, was not really Essenism, it had its own original elements—you could call it perhaps *an* Essenism. It could be best described as a "quasi-Essene neo-formation". The large thing, Christianity, which none can help seeing, is explained by its conjectured resemblance to the small thing of which scholars are endeavouring to trace the faint outlines!

One of these scholars, by name Paul Winter, heckles us in the Park. He is a friend of Bultmann and has had articles in learned magazines in Germany and in the *Hibbert Journal.* He tells me from time to time of what he has written, and has met some Sheed and Ward authors at learned conferences. A little later his book *The Trial of Jesus* had a considerable press. With the help of concordances and dictionaries one can sometimes prove him wrong on a detail, but for the most part I would bow to his learning. In knowledge of languages and texts I am no match for him and we both know it. Yet of him the same thing is true as of Dupont-Sommer—Christianity is too big for him to see.

After an encounter one day we exchanged letters of apology—I knew I had been too sharp, because, as I complained, he had treated me "like a prisoner at the bar" or at best as a child caught with fingers in the jam. To which he answered that on the contrary he regarded me as a learned counsel for the defence. I think he takes pleasure in being on my side when his views permit it; we have had coffee together and he has told me of his immense admiration for Catholic piety and mysticism. "I saw a very plain woman once coming from the Communion rail—her face was transfigured: she looked beautiful."

This remark reinforced the idea that Fr. Bevan and I already rather specially had; next to the Gospels in bringing our crowds to Our Lord come His saints. It was a series of talks on saints which, before the summer of 1955 was out, had started me on the reading for the second book. I wrote in the journal:

> A very good afternoon in the Park: still on Saints. I talked of early martyrs and the monks who followed—especially St. Anthony. Winter asked a few questions, with the most distinguished politeness, and intervened to crush a heckler who

> wanted to know the relation between the sufferings of the martyrs and the tortures inflicted by Jesuits during the Spanish Inquisition!! Winter appeared delighted to be able to defend the pass for me; we exchanged smiles. Father Marteau was greeting hecklers by their first names and exchanging jokes. He left me with a crowd too vast for me to hold and an excellent atmosphere.

A week later:

> This week has been, like so many, full of interest. Since beginning to write this record I realize more than ever just how interesting our life is. It is just getting light and a lovely long weekend (in which I shall probably accomplish nothing!) stretches ahead.
>
> Sunday up from Ilgars only just in time for Park (horrible Sunday trains). I gave them St. Patrick and Matt Talbot as examples of two ways of conquering circumstances. Patrick broke through and transformed the frame, Matt lived within it and mastered it—both through God's strength, each in virtue of his special place in the Mystical Body. Profound attention—but all the questions were about the Church, Authority, Peter. A very attentive listener, whose questions I specially took, was a youngish American negro: Father Bevan, who followed me, asked if he wanted to continue questioning: he said that he was quite satisfied.

And a few days after this:

> Park Sunday: I did Ignatius and Polycarp and have finished a sketch of them for the book.

It was perhaps more these insights into the vast history of the Church, more the effects of what I saw and experienced, both through the writings of others and the contemporary scene, above all the pressure of what appeared unavoidable work, which kept me away from the nineteenth century or brought it before me in a form that could only drive me into social action. There was, too, my family, even more important now that it was scattered and widened than at an earlier stage.

I had always read MSS but now I was reading more than usual and they seemed quite curiously to fit the saying on which I had pondered: "Dans la vie tout concourt et tout sert." A French book which occupied many publishing hours that summer of 1955 was one of the most interesting we have ever refused. It was a Life of Lamennais which made it clear that Mama had, as she always claimed, based her novel *Out Of Due Time* on his story, drawn the figure of Paul d'Etranges from him and not, as everybody was convinced, from Von Hügel. The scenes in Rome, the attitude of the Pope, are the same. But she puts up a better case for the Church in her story than could be drawn from the Lamennais episode. Probably she had not read much about the hideous social conditions of the period—did not realise all that they, and the Church's seeming unconcern with them, had meant to Lamennais. We were curiously blind to them in our own country; why should we have known France better? But on the need for authority and the need for freedom, on the goodness yet blindness of the Pope, on the prime duty of the Church, carried out even in her darkest hours to "preach Jesus Christ and Him crucified", she makes her story as profoundly interesting as the real history of this very remarkable man. Before Comte, Lamennais reawakened the philosophy of mankind's solidarity; but he saw too with St. Paul that only in Christ could it be achieved. His final defection must surely be blamed chiefly on the pious churchmen who were denying the vital Christian teaching which he was emphasizing—in his case certainly *not* "out of due time". This the author of the French book totally failed to see.

Yet how overwhelmingly the whole story cries out man's need for the Church that Lamennais abandoned. The hopeless melancholy of his last years did not merely result from the judgement on him of the Catholic world, but rather from his own loss of the springs of vitality. The *Paroles d'un croyant* had a delirious success, he was fêted everywhere, his name was greater far than it had ever been. Lacordaire, Montalembert, who maintained a steadfast submission, had perhaps more to suffer, but they were alive. "I am come that you may have life and may have it more abundantly." "I am the life." More and more I feel this is the great attribute through which Christians will again sweep the world and rebuild a broken civilization.

But how? The Lamennais book reminded me again how much we had lost of the social outlook of a Basil or a Chrysostom—a realization driven home to me by another manuscript, one, this time, which we accepted, a Life of Mary Ward, called by Pius XII "that incomparable woman". She is indeed, and her story reaches a high point of drama. Abandoning a contemplative life for which she had no vocation and striking out on a new and most necessary line in education, she complained that women were supposed only to save their own souls—"a penuriousness which I resented". Imprisoned in England by Elizabeth I for her faith, she was imprisoned in Munich by the Inquisition for her works! Told that a condition for the last sacraments when death seemed near was the signing of an abjuration of heresies she had never held, she replied "God forbid". She had only venial sins on her soul and would not commit a mortal one by these false words.

The Inquisition had closed her schools: brought back from death's door, released from prison, she reopened the one in Rome and won from the Pope himself a declaration of her orthodoxy. But her mission for England was primary and there she returned to the danger of new imprisonment, even of death. As in Italy she had chosen Rome to flaunt her work, so in England she chose London. But it was in her native Yorkshire, with the pursuivants at the door, that she died, the words "Glory, Glory" on her lips. The darkness of a prolonged struggle, begun in girlhood, carried on to old age, had ended even in this world in a vision that upheld her hunted and tormented spiritual family, for centuries to be rejected by their country and denied by their Church the right to call her their mother.

Other books, accepted or refused, helped to complete the picture of a gradual resurrection of the Church from one of those "deaths" which Chesterton has spoken of as a recurring phenomenon of history, which Newman has described as a "Deliquium". (It is interesting that he applied this word in the fifties to the Church of England, but in the sixties to the Church Catholic and Roman.) Her Lord, says Chesterton, knew the way out of the tomb and like Him she would always rise again.

I was feeling more and more that one result of losing the sense of community had been a false spirituality found especially in post-Reformation books of piety. My journal, while full of the frustration brought by multiple activities, expresses also a realization that there is more reality in such a life than in the rather artificial atmosphere of my youth. Reading a recent American publication of ours I wrote:

How profound is Helen Day's prayer about the problems of being a negro in the deep South. "Not just a plain old wooden cross", she prays—Yes, she will carry a cross, but it must be more clearly a cross, heavier perhaps, certainly of her own choosing. "I'll send you a specification" she hears herself saying to God. Frustration, exhaustion, are a plain old wooden cross and it is curious how one fails to recognize and therefore to accept it in such material. One of the greatest mistakes in the religious education of fifty years ago was the falsity of its outlook on daily life and its duties. Rosemary says she wants to do her own housework, as otherwise she would be living in an unreal world. In that unreal world I was educated. The vitamins taken out of our daily bread, are given back to us as pills. The world of my youth took the cross out of daily work—and pious books offered it back to us as "mortifications". How much more real is even the tiny cross of coming in tired from Mass and being obliged to get breakfast ready than the old days when all was prepared, there were no beds to make, no rooms to sweep, no dishes to wash. But perhaps you gave up sugar in your coffee.

Curiously enough, just after I wrote this page Frank brought me a manuscript full of this old spirituality—even to the point of advising "detachment" in one's friendships. Here, above all, the spiritual books seem to have taken a wrong turning. You need not, they say, feel any liking at all for the people you are obliged to love. You must, they say, beware of feeling too much affection for this or that person, you must love him only in God. This is surely horribly wrong, but stems infallibly from the self-regarding attitude inspiring these books. The reader, even the author, piously occupied over his own spiritual growth, not only rides past the wounded man by the wayside, but ignores wounded hearts in his own house.

I realized more and more that God who had made the order of nature meant it not to be abolished but consecrated and widened by the order of grace. In the family there may be irritations, but we *like* as well as loving. And while it is easy to love in general terms a world remote from us, the effort to like the neighbour whom we are obliged to help is an essential element in Christian love. If vitality is to be there it must be in a framework of reality. Two more authors helped to complete my picture of an emergent vigorous

Church, struggling mostly in small groups to come to grips with this reality in a world very different from that in which so many Catholics seem to be living, or perhaps existing is a better word. One of these was George Ineson of the Taena Community, a tiny group but like the Catholic Worker Movement, like the Canadian co-operators, intensely alive, intensely real. I wrote in the journal:

> George Ineson came with his completed manuscript. The Taena Community in its growth is a fascinating thing. Beginning as pacifists, more or less anarchists, most of whom had thrown over all religion, they are now Benedictine oblates, reciting the Divine Office daily, still keeping to community of ownership, living on their farm, the making of pottery, wood-carving and painting. The story is not only the story of their gradual conversion to the Church but of the gradual growth of a living community. If, says George, such another community were to start even *within* the Church, it would also be subject to these laws of growth. He said some extraordinarily interesting things especially on the impossibility of starting a living growth by theories—"Something will grow up in practice and that will be a theory", and "Theories are rationalizations of what has happened or else attempts to avoid what seems the insecurity of putting yourself entirely in God's hands". This community found God through the sense of their own despair, then gradually through periods of individual and corporate meditation, through the recitation of psalms and through steady labour, they came into the Church. Such a community journey had been made previously by groups of Anglican monks and nuns: but of married people and their children (several of them old enough to make personal decisions), of young men and women—surely this story is unique. I have visited Taena several times and been much moved by the atmosphere of both chapel and house, much struck by the intense individuality and variety of the members who have submitted themselves to rule and found life within it. The woman who gave most of the money for the farm is a novice member. With her entered her gardener and the pattern is woven of many whose education and background are equally varied.

A few months later I wrote again:

Now they are more established in the farm they hope to follow an exceptionally extroverted and hard-working period with one of intensification of their contemplative life. "If we do not", he said, "follow the rhythm we are in danger of becoming nothing but an organization." I begged him to try to write something on the Liturgy, the Mass, the field work and the whole setting of their lives which makes them into contemplatives: so much I feel that such groups have a reality that today is often lacking in religious.

The other author was my sister, who had, after the death of her son, joined a small group of Dominican tertiaries in the same lovely countryside as Taena—the Cotswolds. Founded originally as an Anglican institution by two remarkable women, Miss Hudson and Miss Kessler, they work for a section of the community whose needs are little met by any existing large-scale work, which perhaps cannot of their nature be thus met. Many people today suffer from neurosis who do *not* need shock treatment, do not need drugs, but do need the opportunity of pouring out their troubles to guides able to direct them on the path to a cure. They need, too, a sane and regular daily life, they need above all a right direction in the life of prayer in its relation to the life of action and of human and divine charity. When I asked my sister once what her chief work was, she said, "Listening."

The increasing number of nuns sent to this quiet spot with its tiny stone church, its native Cotswold cottages grouped around in lovely confusion, with blazing flowers against the grey stones, confirmed my feeling that the religious life needs in many orders a rather thorough overhauling. Today this rest home is becoming a place for the care of nuns alone. They may, as one Reverend Mother gratefully told me, return to their communities fully restored to health, or they may be helped back to the lay vocation which should have been theirs. Or again they may remain at the rest home, becoming part of the Community. Indeed, every worker save Miss Hudson herself has passed through some nerve crisis; only people, as Père Jacques points out, themselves in the sea can rescue the drowning man. It is a principle more and more recognized today and I discovered in Australia (of all places!) a priest who had been actually certified and had after his own cure created from his experience a society called Recovery. This is made up entirely of ex-patients helping one another to a full re-integration into our very difficult world. Interdenominational, but profoundly religious, this society meets in small groups: they exchange experiences, study "Twelve Steps Towards Recovery" drawn up by Fr. Keogh, and very gradually but surely progress by those steps into steady and abiding mental health.

The book of the steps has, alas, not yet been completed, but in her *Other People* and *Each His Own Tyrant* my sister, under the name of Wingfield Hope, has shown much of the principles underlying the work done by both these small but very important movements. The Australian one is growing far faster than the other but it may well be that deeper roots are being struck into the soil of the Cotswolds.

Sitting one day in the garden at Ilgars, dreaming a little and gazing at the great trees and the grey church behind them, I saw a woman approaching me. She was to be all unwittingly a charge of dynamite in a life which I had never thought of as precisely sluggish.

The postwar housing shortage, if not as acute yet in England as in France, was still very serious. We had listened to Abbé Pierre's famous speech in the Salle Pleyel and had been deeply moved by him. I had visited one of his *Cités de secours*; architects were criticizing these buildings; they were damp, I was told, too far from Paris, the layout badly planned. But I talked to some of the people living in what was admittedly a temporary effort to meet a desperate situation, and found they hotly denied these charges. The houses were not damp, a special bus service to Paris had been arranged for workmen morning and evening; a civic life was growing up. And whence had these people come? From sleeping, eating, living seven and eight in a single room, from the arches under a bridge, from tents or huts, even from under a cart in a field.

England, as I had noted in the Depression, is always less dramatic than France! A French baby dies of cold in the street, another is born (and dies) in a wet field: a woman sharing a room with husband, mother-in-law and four children smashes with her fist the window kept shut by the mother-in-law and is taken to hospital bleeding and half mad. We are much tidier; our babies do not die in the streets and fields, they just are not born. "Our landlady wouldn't let us have a baby", I was told when I began to investigate the English situation.

I realize now how appallingly slow I was in grasping it. Frank and I had helped a few people to buy their houses. Molly Walsh had told us of tragic cases, but I had somehow thought of them only as individuals, not as symptomatic of a growing evil. After all, Abbé Pierre had pointed out that in one year in which France built 75,000 houses England had built 350,000. Whatever Government happened to be in assured us how splendidly the building programme was going—and I suppose I shrank instinctively from starting anything that might mean more work.

Oddly enough, it was not only a failure to help that drove me into action. It was a failure which no organization could have turned into a success.

The woman who had come to see me that lovely sunny day I will call Mrs. Smith. She had read *Be Not Solicitous* and hoped I might help her in a serious problem. She and her husband had come from a remote county where she had run a smallholding. If they could get one here they could move from the council house, which would soon be lost to them anyhow on the birth of their seventh child; they were already technically overcrowded. Then, too, she could, she said, make a good thing out of a few acres and some chickens and supplement Mr. Smith's insufficient salary.

I tried very hard; being prepared to sacrifice a bit of my farm land. But previous experience frightened me off the prefab which she declared they could buy and erect. What of council rules, what of drainage? I visited agents, drove round the countryside with the couple looking at holdings, and very gradually I realized how little either husband or wife really knew: who, I wondered, had run their former place (which I later discovered had in fact failed)? The garden of their present house had not been dug. The highly emotional wife alternated between declaring that they were all going to die in the street and that her husband would take a job in the mines whereby she seriously believed that he, a weedy white-collar worker, could earn £20 a week. It finally transpired that they owed their parish priest several hundreds and he expressed great relief that I had not been stung too when the family folded their tents and vanished from our neighbourhood.

But in a farewell letter of some venom "Mr. Smith" reminded me of my alleged sympathy with large families and defied me to relate in some future book how I had refused to help theirs. I knew that there would be many Smiths among those seeking help from the small society which I went on (with Molly Walsh) to found. In the interest of other families, in justice to subscribers, our money cannot be lent to the Smiths of this world. Yet this letter set me to examining my conscience. Why did I feel I had gone so horribly wrong with my particular Smiths? Because I had failed in sympathy. I had grown to dislike the Smiths, therefore I had told them without kindness that they were not capable of running a smallholding. I had given them time which had cost me enough to make me irritable. But in giving them time I had given them hope, and compassion should have been shown when that hope must be destroyed.

How to keep this compassion alive, to have patience and love for the heckler who shouts you down, for the homeless who tell you lies, for those you cannot help, for those who have muddled everything and must be helped all over again?

30

HELPING THE HOMELESS

I BROKE off this book to write the biography of Caryll Houselander. I had known her as a fascinating eccentric, caustic in speech but overwhelmingly charitable in action, doing her fire-watching in the Blitz while herself shaking with terror, calming a lunatic by her mere presence, helping many by her writings—and advised once, when seeking help in the confessional, to read one of her own books. Her early death was a personal loss to an immense circle and her correspondence revealed how wide her mission had been. I reread her books, above all *Guilt*, which deepened my impression that she had a very special message for the modern world, notably for the healing of neurotics. She insisted always that she could help them because she was herself a neurotic, but I think what I chiefly learned from her was that the difference between neurotic and normal in our shared human nature is more one of degree than of kind, that we can all learn profitably the lesson of how to deal with unhealthy moods and unreasonable fancies. Anyhow, I got more letters of gratitude than for any other of my books: Caryll was still speaking from its pages.

In December 1955, our first grandchild was born: Simon Middleton. He was a delicate baby, but at two months old he had gained strength; our anxiety over, we flew to New York, only to be followed next day by a cable to say he had died suddenly of capillary bronchitis. Frank, Wilfrid and I spent a sad evening together; the following day I flew home again to Rosemary. I had never before been at a baby's funeral. There was a great comfort and joy in Fr. Healy's sermon as he spoke of the Church rejoicing over a new saint when we lost a child, of Simon's happiness and the splendour of the divine vision. Still more did the mass itself comfort us. It seemed strange at first that the Church had chosen a mass with no reference to a child. Called *De Angelis*, it is all about the power and glory of these heavenly spirits—the glory they have from God, the power they have to help us. And I remembered a letter I had received asking why we were so anxious to keep little Simon from the Heaven where

God wanted him and whence he could do so much to guard and guide his family.

I began that day to pray to him for the brothers and sisters that I hoped might come and for the parents who had lost him. We buried the child of nine weeks beside his great-grandmother of eighty-five years. She surely was waiting to bid him welcome with my own mother and father and my two brothers, the child and the priest.

While we were at Wickford that Christmas Frank went up to London to collect the mail. He rang me up and in a voice that sounded stunned told me that Rome was making him a Doctor of Theology. He had opened the letter from Archbishop's House—hoping he was not in hot water for some rash publication—to find this amazing news: he came home very happy but with a blinding headache.

We learned later from Cardinal Griffin how he had wanted to ask for some distinction for my husband—"I knew you'd die laughing if you were made a papal knight." The Cardinal had himself read *Theology and Sanity* with enthusiasm. It had now, together with Frank's other books, been carefully examined by the Congregation of Seminaries and Universities, with this happy result. The doctorate was actually bestowed later by the University of Lille, chosen by Rome because it was the canonical successor of the old college of Douai where priests had been trained for the English Mission in persecution times. But the Christmas letter was the great moment.

In the two days in New York before the news of Simon's death, another bit of news burst on me—this time a joyful one. The previous autumn our old friend Grace Smith had celebrated her ninetieth birthday. At her party Frank and Wilfrid were present, and so was our lovely god-daughter, Missie Darlington, whom Wilfrid had not seen since they were both small children. Missie was seated next to Frank. Wilfrid, on the other side of the table, fell in love with her at sight. It cannot have looked very hopeful when he learned that she was shortly about to enter a convent—"to try her vocation" as the phrase goes. Wilfrid decided to try it first, and he proved a fast worker. When we got to New York we found them together waiting for us at our hotel. Missie came up with me to unpack and to tell me that she felt perhaps—she wanted Wilfrid to see the Mother Prioress—she hadn't made up her mind.

Aloud I said nothing very definite but I knew well that no power on earth would drag Wilfrid to that convent parlour and I said within myself, "My darling, I really think you have made up your mind—this visit won't be necessary." Wilfrid and Missie were married a year later in New York at the Church of St. Thomas More. Today we have six grandchildren besides the one in heaven.

But the year 1956 had not finished all it was to bring of good—sometimes heavily disguised. As we drew towards Christmas we were preparing for another birth at Ilgars. Frank and I were to go down the following week; we made our way on a horribly chilly Sunday to Hyde Park, where he was going to speak. There we found Erika Fallaux, who had recently joined our publishing house, besides speaking for the Guild. I was rather vexed, since she suffered from severe arthritis, to find her standing in the Park on such a night. But seeing no good in myself risking pneumonia, I went on ahead to the friend we were to dine with after Frank finished. He was late—but that was common enough—and then my friend was called to the telephone and came back to say that Frank had met with an accident and was in St. Mary's Hospital, Paddington.

We rushed over in a taxi to find that he had fallen off the stand in Hyde Park. Erika had got a priest and an ambulance; Frank had been anointed, was bleeding profusely from one ear, was shouting loudly and deliriously. He did not know me, and I was not reassured when I heard the young doctor in charge calling a senior on the telephone with the words, "We have a *fascinating* case in casualty."

It proved to be only a severe concussion, but that night nobody knew. Frank was gesturing and throwing himself about; he could not be X-rayed, the doctors were beset by "witnesses" from the Park who had seen him clutch his head (or alternatively his heart) and were certain he had fallen after some sort of seizure. Erika and I knew very well how Frank did gesture and fling himself about when speaking. Also, he often unconsciously grasped the crucifix attached to the platform—and this was found afterwards lying broken on the ground. It seemed clear, looking back later, that he had lost his balance as it broke and had fallen with it. They told us to go home. Erika came with me and spent the night in the flat; that night it was that she became our daughter.

This was one great good, handed us heavily wrapped up, but

there was, I think, another. Frank had been overworking furiously. Now he had to slow down; for long there were sleepless nights. The buzzing in his ear was never cured, but apart from that he seems stronger today than before the fall and lives at a more reasonable tempo for a man in his sixties.

The Catholic Housing Aid Society had by now come into being. I often wish we had called it Family Housing Aid—for it was in favour of *any* family that needed help. But in fact, the majority of our cases are Catholics and almost all our money comes from Catholic sources. We were aiming at ownership for people who could carry a mortgage but needed help with their down payments and legal expenses. Solicitors agreed to do one conveyance a year free, priests preached for us wherever a collection was possible. The money was lent interest free for part or the whole down payment needed for a mortgage. We asked many of the people to whom we had lent money to find room for a second family who would pay rent while saving to buy for themselves.

It was a far cry from my outsider's experience of the lumberjacks and fishermen of Nova Scotia, or the starving families of New York's Depression; here I was getting inside a situation immensely different, but with profound resemblances too. Many of our families were wasting high wages on television, football pools or gambling on the dogs because they had no incentive to save. One family was living—father, mother and three children—in one room 9 ft. by 9 (three strides from wall to wall), no bath in the house, one lavatory in the yard and one cold-water tap for five families; two stoves in the basement for their cooking. They had been there five years. The wife said, when I regretted her television bought on hire purchase, "We had to have some pleasure."

A man chain-smoking furiously told me it soothed his nerves, rasped by the night-time crying of the baby in their one small room which kept the whole family awake and sent him jaded to his day's work. A woman came for help under notice of eviction which would mean an indefinitely long splitting up of the family. She told me she was always under sedatives prescribed by her doctor to save her from total collapse.

The chain-smoker came in lately to pay back the money lent him towards down payment on a house of his own. From the moment we had told him, "Save £100 and we will lend you the rest", he had cut the smoking down and taken an evening job. He looked a different man; like the fishermen, he had pride in the house he owned, was putting by money for repairs, was planning for a future no longer bounded by the mere effort to get through another miserable day and night.

"We are making men and women", said Dorothy Day in the Depression. "Trust the little fellow", Father Jimmie used to say, and we have found it profoundly true in this work. We get, of course, an occasional defaulter. We get mistakes made through the good intentions of inexperience. There was the man who proudly brought us back part of our loan, having sold the house we had helped him to buy and found a cheaper one nearer to his work. A few months later this family was living in a caravan. He could not bear to tell us that the house he had bought was not his after all. He had thought the deposit secured the house! The contract not signed, he had no legal standing when the owner got a higher offer and returned his deposit. But the original house had been well and truly sold.

We saw gradually the need of a second approach to the problem—the constantly increasing problem—of the homeless family. We must ourselves buy houses, especially for families suddenly evicted, with no place to go. Local authorities deal with this by leaving the husband to fend for himself, putting wife and children in a hostel—not by any means "for free". The husband has now two sets of expenses to pay. He can see his family for an hour or so at a set time, no cohabitation; in other cases the wife and children go to relatives in Ireland, Scotland or elsewhere for months and even years. We housed one such divided family in which the wife accepted her husband's resultant illegitimate children, as the only way of rebuilding a home. Families in danger of separation we especially wanted to help. One couple in the first house we bought came to us with a week-old baby. The husband had been told the landlord would not take them back when his wife came out of the hospital with a screaming child. (Babies seem to be thought of only as screaming in our world of today and their screams to be considered more awful than roaring traffic or throbbing machines.) In the seventeen large houses we now have young families who, instead of paying out half their salaries in unproductive rent, are putting by several pounds every week. Some of them have been for years on the Council list; if they get a house their savings will pay for furniture and removal. More are hoping to buy—and so keen do they become that they add to the sum agreed upon further savings to hasten the day of ownership.

"Trust the little fellow", said Father Jimmie—but he also set to work to make the little fellow trustworthy. Nothing in modern life has trained men to accept the responsibilities of ownership on the scale of a heavily mortgaged house. Part of the answer is a return to neighbourhood. In my early dreams I had seen every parish with its scheme of saving for young couples, with its own house for families not yet ready to buy. Increasingly we felt that the solution must be a local one, ideally a parochial one. These dreams began to take substance, our problems to find an answer and our scheme to take a clearer shape with the opening of a branch at Slough, under the dynamic leadership of Fr. Eamonn Casey of the Irish Immigrant Mission. Every parish house, he insists, must have a committee of business men. It must not depend on the priest, who may be moved, it must never lack the information which every intelligent man can furnish from his own field—the lawyer, the architect, the borough councillor, and the marriage counsellor, the banker and the broker.

As with the fishermen of Canada, saving must have a high priority. And so successful has Slough been that the savings of the families temporarily housed or still in lodgings amounted after only six months to £8000. Banks and Building Societies are able by this scheme to test the dependability of families who one day will be asking for a loan. At Slough too, another side of this work has developed, unthinkable except in a parish where neighbourhood exists and the people know each other and their priests. Besides the business men, Fr. Casey has gathered a group of youths and boys who do all that amateurs can towards putting in order the houses bought by the Society before the first group of families move in. Between tenancies they make good the results of the wear and tear of family living.

Reading the Fathers, hearing Abbé Pierre lecture, was exciting me more and more with a vision of the Church supplying in the social field when the State was failing. All social work must be to a great extent pragmatic. Books were still (ridiculously) being written and translated, geared to the problems of a previous century, magnificently condemning conditions that no longer existed, at any rate in England or the States. And meanwhile *the* great social plague of our day had gone unremedied. It was their own conditions that Ambrose, Basil and Chrysostom met, it was the contemporary conscience that their words stung into activity. That conscience reacted —to create the building of a new town, of hospitals, hospices, asylums in Basil's city—but Chrysostom was driven into exile and death. A golden tongue can be too dangerous to the tyrant.

I had also noted the frustration felt, by converts especially, who, wanting to help in their parish today, found themselves asked only to organize football pools or Bingo. Where the Housing Association has been started, not only is hope awakened by the opportunity given to win a home, but zeal and skills are also mobilized and parishioners employed in work of permanent value. They become intimate with others with whom they would formerly have had just a nodding acquaintance. Parish life becomes more real, and where the Liturgy is also emphasized, people learn to think of themselves in St. Augustine's favourite simile as the grapes from whose cluster one wine is poured into the chalice, as grains of wheat from which is milled that bread which will become the Bread of Life.

As in the C.E.G., we learnt that the return of the lapsed Catholic was as vital as the conversion of the unbeliever, so in this work we learnt that renewal of Christian charity, remaking of Christian unity, meant even more than the building of houses. The families we help offer to help others. A parish coming alive in this work has come alive as a branch of the True Vine, as a limb of the Mystical Body.

31

TOWARDS EVENING

My father used to tell of an old and a young man talking about death. The old man was speaking of some horrible accident that had hurried into eternity a group of boys and girls. The young man retorted cheerfully, "Very sad Sir, but the young *may* die, the old must."

I often think of this today, and of the necessity as we grow old of doing all that in us lies to leave our unfinished business in such a state that others can carry it on.

If I were not already vividly aware of this inexorable fact of death reminders would press upon me as the century, eleven years younger than I, draws toward its three-quarter mark. There was the celebration of my seventieth birthday, and our Jewish heckler who said to me, "You have reached the biblical age." The same man stood below the platform on a wet evening holding an umbrella and adjuring me to leave this work to younger folk and let him take me to a pub!

And then there are the deaths not of my elders only, but of my contemporaries. Of Belloc I have already spoken, but in the decade of the fifties, besides Caryll Houselander and two of my cousins, three men died far more significant in my own life than Belloc, two much older than me but one a little younger. They were all priests: Dr. Arendzen, Father Bevan and Father Martindale.

The laity today criticize the clergy more openly but less defiantly than in my youth; more openly because so many priests encourage such criticism, less defiantly for the same reason. Those we call our fathers in God are our natural leaders and the less they grasp at authority the more we are disposed to grant it, both in a live parish and in apostolic work. The lament, indeed, is often lack of leadership; most groups are eagerly looking for one to whom they can say wholeheartedly, "Thou art the man."

Those three priests, all in different ways, were our leaders in the new approach to the world by mind and heart which Pope John of late so blessed. Of Dr. Arendzen I wrote in my chapter on the C.E.G. beginnings. He had now for some years been spiritual director at Ware (the Westminster Diocesan Seminary). Too old for frequent journeys to London, he had chosen Fr. Bevan for his successor. For many years Fr. Bevan had been speaking at Marble Arch and examining lay speakers. All our tests are oral, and it was a rare experience being tested by him; one learnt more theology than from many a lecture, and one learnt too something even more important. Dr. Arendzen had learned to speak the language of the modern. Fr. Bevan was a different kind of prefulfilment of Pope John, showing us supremely the road of the heart. Less learned than his predecessor, he was more personally linked with the hundreds he brought into the Church and the thousands he helped to live close to God. I never knew a man to whom his friends meant more, or who had more friends and spiritual children. A naval officer in the First World War, he was a chaplain in the second. He ministered to the men on two hundred small boats based on Scapa Flow, going from one to another in the fleet's official launch and welcomed by all denominations and all ranks. He had a curiously nervous manner and hesitating speech, but his mind and heart went straight to meet another's. He would have no truck with convert "classes", but spent hours daily in individual instruction and in hospital visiting, besides his weekly talk in Hyde Park. Each person helped by Fr. Bevan sent friends; he slept little, going to bed late, getting up at five.

Not a few Guildsmen went to him with their own troubles, chose him as confessor or adviser. And his was a tremendous support in that unconscious preparation for ecumenism that both the Guild and our publishing house had tried from the first to practise. Other religions were not to be attacked—although the Guild had not yet learnt to look for our own benefit, as Edward Watkin had urged in *The Catholic Centre*, at the values they were stressing.

Always a delicate man, Fr. Bevan broke down repeatedly; visiting him in hospital I begged him to relax a little when back again on the job. His answer was, "I do so want to hear, 'Well done, thou good and faithful servant.'"

A few months later came a thrombosis from which he seemed to be slowly recovering just as we were leaving London for New York. Permission was granted me for a short visit. He had, he told me, been very near death—when it seemed that God did not want him. With a sensation at once of immense physical pain and desolation of spirit, he was pushed back into time and space, deprived of the vision that had come so near.

Two months later, when we returned, we found a Christmas card written in a shaky hand—Fr. Bevan had obeyed the order to post early. But the day after that he was, I shall dare to say, in heaven. If any such guess can ever be sure I would hazard this one; a life utterly unselfish, totally devoted to God and man, great pain, total self-abandonment and above all unfailing love.

Although Dr. Arendzen had been the first to speak to us in the language of the modern Englishman, Father Martindale went a step further. A fine scholar, he yet showed in an early book *The Goddess of Ghosts* how much more he cared for people—ancients *and* moderns—than for bare ideas.

I knew C.C.M. (no one could have called him "Cyril" or even "Father Cyril") long before the other two priests, and he died several years later. It was a friendship made, like so many, chiefly through Leo and starting just after the First World War.

Jock, Jack and the Corporal, a book springing from his experience with soldiers (especially Australians), showed his love of these men no less than his understanding of the way they thought. Indeed, C.C.M. combined to an extraordinary degree the qualities of Dr. Arendzen the scholar and Fr. Bevan the saint. While Dr. Arendzen taught us to speak the modern's language, C.C.M. had explored his mind. From him we learned its shape; we were able to guess, so to speak, the next step. His keen appreciation of the Jocks and Jacks won their love as well as that of a host of friends in many worlds.

His friendship was a great possession and we felt honoured in having it. In his late seventies he was still immensely busy, though retired to the Jesuit house at Petworth. Frank and I loved to go down and meet him for lunch at the Swan at Fittleworth. He seemed to grow thinner every year and his face was like old ivory. The vitality of mind was no less than of old—he was reading, writing, thinking and making us free of his thoughts. Those days were a joy, and I remember wandering out with him into a garden nearby full of roses and feeling that his thoughts were still as fresh and dewy as the flowers. Yet, too, I felt, "ripeness is all".

In 1959 C.C.M. celebrated his eightieth birthday; his answer to my birthday letter was full of echoes.

> Indeed, I do remember being next to Leo in the Hampstead nursing home . . .
>
> Yes, there's a lot to be grateful for and perhaps it's a good thing to have no time even for keeping level, let alone for thinking backwards, else one might become nostalgic in the wasteful sense. Still, I did once write about my first visit to Australia: "Oh heart, not older grown nor grey—cherish your every yesterday!" One also may idly regret not having made more of opportunities—perhaps one couldn't; the human creature can absorb only a certain amount.
>
> I know too that I disappointed many people by not becoming an Expert in something or other of a "scholarly" sort: but really the only thing that ever "captured" me was *people*. Even while I "ground at grammar" at Oxford, I kept feeling more and more that I was meeting real persons, Greek and Roman; and when I read how the Porta Capena at Rome *leaked*, I suddenly wondered whether a drop fell on St. Paul's bald pate when he was arriving there—and this did me quite a lot of good when tackling his letters later on. He was not just a "theological source"! Then of course the first war settled matters for good and all, tho' there *are* two or three books I'd like to have written.
>
> I remember so well meeting your Mother and how stimulating her kindness was, and then yours and Frank's. Your Father I met only, I think, during the "Tyrrell" period when everyone suspected their neighbour and so many people did the right thing the wrong way. As for Scripture and history, I really do believe we have escaped into an air of sanity, freedom *and* orthodoxy!
>
> I'm glad you liked the "Goddess": some of it is jargon, but I think I can genuinely like the "Evening at Ephesus" and the "Quenching of Lamps": but then one never quite likes all of anything one's written.
>
> Now I really must turn to more "official" thank you letters!

The full greatness of C.C.M. may or may not ever be realized. He carried to a high point that struggle between other people's needs and his own personal fulfilment which so many of us experience in lesser fashion. He told Frank once of his rule—never to refuse to do anything he was asked to do, if it could be fitted into the time. He might well have been called a genius if he had not, in accepting all human demands, refused those of his own intellectual possibilities. Or was this his fulfilment—by a great if not simply spectacular life—a life which helped immensely the fulfilment of so many others?

On a pencilled card he wrote in December 1960: "Am rather minus 100% but you and F. and R. and W. must have all Christmas joys and blessings as always." His longest excursion now was, he wrote, in answer to my answer, "down for a humble plate of soup for dinner and a no less modest egg for supper if manageable". He was praying to say Mass on Christmas Day, but had lately only been able to "sit through it very lumpishly".

Lumpish I don't think he could ever have been—it was rather the fading from polished ivory into transparency, the body less and less able to co-operate with the spirit which will one day totally illuminate and transform it.

I must quote one more letter, dictated just before his death after a broadcast Frank and I had given in the series "Way of Life":

> How much have our vocations differed. I don't like crowds, i.e., more than two or three! As for hecklers, I'd feel either they were quite unanswerable, or, so idiotic as again to be unanswerable. I hope I am not a fideist; but I can't think anything if I'm to exclude God.
>
> I don't know if the *Month* has published my review of Caryll H. I want to write a short article on her three "great experiences" but I think it unlikely that I shall write any more. I've been in bed since before Christmas and should have been since November. For over a year, I seem unable to stand up without falling flat over, then can't pick myself up. In fact, I'm very weak and what I write is kindly taken down by dictation.

Immediately after the broadcast we flew to New York and there we heard of our great loss; on my return I read the review, which showed, I thought an echo of his own life in what he had to say of Caryll's—especially perhaps in two sentences: "Her entire spiritual life consisted in, first, a determination to see Christ in everyone, though chiefly in the most apparently degraded; and secondly, a determination to sacrifice self to the uttermost in the service of Christ in those others . . . I feel that a meticulous 'study' of this (to me) unique personality is needed, not that anyone who wants the 'conventional' will get it, or who is alarmed by intensity of spiritual or psychological life would be pacified. But he might find a lot of fun in Caryll's experiences, as she did."

Marrying late, we count ourselves lucky to have lived to enjoy grandchildren in both England and the States, to have heard our son called a distinguished novelist. He has also begun to take his part in the work of Sheed and Ward, New York, while the English house is in the capable hands of Neil Middleton. Rosemary, like myself, despite a far busier domestic life, reads manuscripts and is our ablest French translator. All this means a degree of handing over which we hope may yet increase despite the devastating habit of all work to grow and proliferate, and in so doing suck back anyone within its reach. This is my problem with the two activities looming largest in my own life: Housing and the Catholic Evidence Guild.

One of the best Latin lines is "Tempora mutantur, nos et mutamur in illis": but it had better be altered from "We change" into the pious hope, "Let us change", or "Could we but change". For six years we had done the housing work with no paid assistance—our expenses ran from £4 7. 6. in our first year to about £30 in our seventh, the number of families helped rose from 20 in the first year to almost 120 in the seventh. But Molly Walsh had had a severe breakdown, our secretary Ted Wade, our treasurer Lance Thwaytes and I were all overworked. Fr. Donald Proudman was preaching appeal sermons that charmed money out of every pocket and the work still grew. Now, with one admirable salaried secretary, it has become more possible to diminish the time spent on some sides of the central organization while the parish branches are increasingly taking care of individual cases, all of which we at the centre would formerly have dealt with. The future is not yet clear, but I think the society is increasingly prepared to meet it and adapt to it, without thereby losing the personal contacts so vital to its success as a human entity and not a mere organization.

It is far harder to see the future of the Catholic Evidence Guild, far harder to withdraw the energies which it demands almost in excess of one's strength. Why does not the Guild grow to the full potential that forty-five years ago it seemed to hold? We old fogies, weary as we are, have still to speak, still to train, still to organize, for there is no one to take our place. Partly this is because the Guild has fed so many of its members into the priesthood: there are four Cistercians, one Carthusian, Jesuits and seculars. One must not become so parochial either as to grudge the loss for Westminster of the present Master of the Melbourne Guild, of two of the best speakers in New York, of others in the English Midlands and elsewhere. Westminster, happily, is not the whole of England, still less the whole C.E.G. Marriage carries off some speakers; they go to live in the country; the responsibilities of their lives increase at the very period when they would become our natural leaders. The men often go on speaking, but cannot take office or run squads: the women may return when their children are of school age. But I know well from experience how hard it is to take up this work again after a long break; only habit makes it endurable—and the realization of it as a primary duty. "Go ye and teach", Our Lord said, and where else but on a street corner can we find the folk that most need teaching?

Our classes are full but out of their numbers not many will emerge as speakers; unfortunately, it is often those least fit who most eagerly spring forward to practise—the most capable of doing the work best realize its difficulties.

The only possible answer is more priests on the outdoor platform. For the most part the few we have are not those who train or test, the one exception having been Fr. Donald Proudman, who has been snatched away from us and been sent as Prior to Barbados. Why do we not get more? Some seem even more scared than the laymen at the idea, especially of the question period that *must* follow every lecture. They have learned their theology (sometimes, one fancies, by memory only) in Latin or Latinized English. They cannot translate. Again, most curiously, another element keeps away somc priests as well as many laymen. They are bored with theology.

Laymen from a Catholic school have been bored through perhaps twelve years of catechism (often writing their letters in the religion period or reading a concealed detective story). And priests have been bored in their seminaries, learning the great dogmas not as truths rich in themselves with which they could one day enrich others, but only as a set of obstacles they must hurdle on the way to the saying of Mass and the giving of the sacraments.

There are other priests who seem to feel that the crowd gathered at Speakers' Corner are not worth talking to. Actually there are educated people among them, but this is really irrelevant; I have often found high intelligence among the illiterate. If the most learned of the clergy, the most up-to-date in all the new developments of theology, would but test their findings on an outdoor platform, they would be surprised at the quality of the response. Any priest has of course an immense advantage: the sacrament of order has given him a charism that the greatest earnestness, enthusiasm, power of utterance cannot supply. He can, as Fr. Bevan often did, hear the confession of a lapsed Catholic then and there, walk across the Park with an enquirer, heal the wounds of a doubter or one near despair.

After each death one feels how irreplaceable is the man we have lost—and in all the infinite variety of human beings no one ever does exactly take another's place. But how great the richness in the variety, how each brings something which the other did not have; which perhaps he himself could not have had earlier. Father Martindale changed the climate for us all. Dr. Arendzen directed especially several generations of clergy.

The fourth priest to unlock doors for the Guild is still with us—Fr. Charles Davis. While Dr. Arendzen spoke the language of the modern man and C.C.M. entered into his mind, I think we can say that Fr. Davis has illuminated for us the mind of the Church and given us lessons of enormous value on how to make it a little more credible to our world. That he is Professor of Dogma at Ware, with countless other commitments as writer, lecturer, editor of the *Clergy Review*, unhappily prevents him from speaking out of doors. But he comes to us for a senior class whenever possible. And he also runs a small parish near the college, which means to the lay observer that real life saves him from the blight of the over-academic. And no-one can read his books or talk to his students without a certainty that a new era is opening in the dialogue between clergy and laity, between Catholics and their separated brethren.

I would be interested to meet a group of laymen discussing a sermon on the Trinity (I have never heard that sermon) as Guildsmen discuss my husband's lectures on that central Christian mystery. Most laymen are "witless of the Trinity"—but they are as likely as not on Trinity Sunday to get a sermon about teaching all nations the faith which has never been adequately taught to themselves.

We can hope now for more sermons on theology that will take us beyond the catechism of our childhood—I am daring to hope for more priests at Marble Arch, Tower Hill and all the other pitches.

Of all Unfinished Business in the Universal Church, affecting also my own life, the Second Vatican Council looms largest—too large and too close to be written of here. This book, overlong already, reached its end at a first writing with the accession of Pope John XXIII. Since his coming breathtaking events have been crowding upon us. One small life must look minute indeed to eyes fixed on Rome today—or on Jerusalem as Pope greets Patriarch in love and brotherhood after centuries of barren and bitter separation.

Sheed and Ward has chanced to be drawn very close to the Council through our publication of Hans Küng's books. Most of the other important theologians are appearing on our lists: Durrwell, Balthasar, Rahner, Schillebeeckx and the rest. And while one can hear today from many who seize upon the title "Progressive" statements as wild as those of earlier Modernists and from those who sturdily style themselves "Conservatives" statements as sterilizing as those of the anti-Modernists, the really great theologians add up to a marvellously balanced statement of the doctrines they are studying and developing.

Balance is often the hardly-reached climax of argument; but Piers Plowman complained that the clerks of his day were too much occupied in arguing with one another to remember the needs of the starving multitudes. While all my readers will grant the importance of our theological publications, some, many perhaps, will think I have made far too important the efforts of small groups of street speakers to feed the hungry sheep who are not being fed by books they most certainly are not reading.

Who knows?

Suppose the books and the meetings they help to foster between theologians—Catholic, Anglican, Protestant, Orthodox—brought about Christian reunion, there would still remain untouched the vast multitudes of a non-Christian East and a post-Christian West.

If big things loom too large for focusing, small things sometimes prove more important than they appear. A friend of mine, a missionary in Tokyo, told me recently that street speaking looked to him the one possible means still untried there, and it has, after all, a respectable precedent, since the founder of Christianity Himself made use of it.

The hidden work of the Carmelite at prayer and the blundering efforts of the speaker on the platform are alike building upon "the foundation of the apostles and the prophets, Jesus Christ himself being the chief corner stone, in whom the whole building, being framed together, groweth up into a holy temple in the Lord."

It is a terrible thing to let a book lie about too long. Chesterton felt that nothing would induce him to read any book he had written; as I correct my proofs, I sympathize with all my heart.

Anyhow, now for a holiday. Western Australia and the flowers of its glorious spring (which is our autumn) the Great Barrier Reef, Alice Springs, lie before me and there, please God, I shall happily be when this book reaches what has so far been a kindly public.

A rest seemed indicated from lecturing, social service, formal theology—and I have already taken refuge in the Browning love letters (read for at least the fourth time), in the poetry I have lived with for sixty years and over. More than ever these days Browning is my poet:

> Earth breaks up, time drops away,
> In flows heaven, with its new day
> Of endless life . . .

Yet

> What is he buzzing in my ears?
> Now that I come to die,
> "Do I view the world as a vale of tears?"
> Ah, reverend sir, not I!

This is the Christian humanism to which I most fully subscribe—not to decry the riches of this world because we believe in another, not to reject the temporal for fear of losing life eternal.

Christ is the light of every man, so that I hope, as Dante did not, to find Virgil in heaven, to meet many who, as St. Augustine said, were inside the City of God unrecognized, to find, too, this world transformed into a new heaven and a new earth—but still this world in its innermost values.

The Christian humanist believes as fully as the ascetic that the vision of God is the bliss of heaven, but he is more aware that in God he will find the "friends and relations" for whom he prayed as a child, better known and better loved in the light of vision, will find every human value not lost but multiplied, as the bread grew in the hands of the Apostles and fed the multitude after the Lord had given thanks. We need not lose the natural to gain the supernatural. "The poet says, Dear City of Cecrops, and will you not say: Dear City of God?"

Yet I should like to stay a little longer in the dear City of Cecrops, this world that I enjoy so much.

INDEX

(*M.W. denotes Maisie Ward throughout*)